THE
LAST
GOODNIGHT

Also by Howard Blum

NONFICTION

Dark Invasion

The Floor of Heaven

American Lightning

The Eve of Destruction

The Brigade

The Gold of Exodus

Gangland

Out There

I Pledge Allegiance: The True Story of the Walkers, an American Spy Family

Wanted! The Search for Nazis in America

FICTION

Wishful Thinking

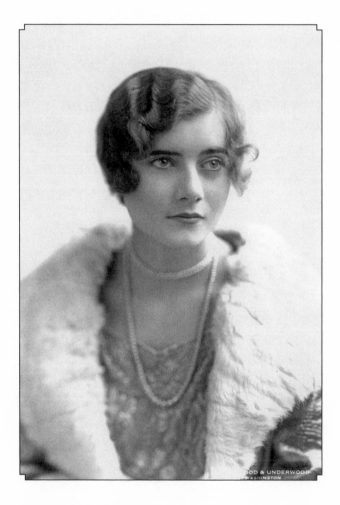

"Army Offers Its Fairest Daughter to Society: Miss Betty Thorpe, beautiful daughter of Colonel and Mrs. George Thorpe, who will be the loveliest of the army set to be presented to Washington society this season." (August 29, 1928)

THE
LAST
GOODNIGHT

A World War II Story of Espionage,
Adventure, and Betrayal

HOWARD BLUM

HARPER

An Imprint of HarperCollinsPublishers

HarperCollins books may be purchased for educational, business, or sales promotional use. For information, please e-mail the Special Markets Department at SPsales@harpercollins.com.

FIRST EDITION

Designed by William Ruoto

Library of Congress Cataloging-in-Publication Data has been applied for.

ISBN: 978-0-06-230767-5

16 17 18 19 20 ov/rrd 10 9 8 7 6 5 4 3 2 1

For Lynn Nesbit and Bob Bookman

*Friends, wise counselors, and magicians who never failed
to pull rabbits out of the hat*

The last person to whom you say goodnight

is the most dangerous.

—WARNING PASSED ON TO CIA TRAINEES ABOUT
THE PERILS LURKING IN THE BEDROOM

Using the boudoir as Ian Fleming's hero uses a Beretta, she was described by her wartime boss as "the greatest unsung heroine of the war."

—"A BLONDE BOND," *Time Magazine*'s OBITUARY FOR BETTY PACK

Contents

A Note to the Reader · *xv*

Part I · STORMING THE CASTLE · *1*

Part II · "A TERRIBLE RESTLESSNESS" · *29*

Part III · "HIDDEN IN MY YESTERDAYS" · *87*

Part IV · ENIGMA · *193*

Part V · THE LONG WAY HOME · *237*

Part VI · WASHINGTON · *279*

Part VII · BIG BILL AND LITTLE BILL · *329*

Epilogue · *457*

A Note on Sources · *469*

Acknowledgments · *487*

Bibliography · *489*

Credits · *497*

Index · *501*

A Note to the Reader

IN THE MAIN BUILDING OF the CIA's sprawling Virginia campus, past the security guards and the detection machines, up a staircase and at the end of a winding corridor that doglegs to the left, is a windowless conference room. There is no name or number on the door. Inside, it has the feel of a space that might be used for a graduate seminar; there's a whiteboard on one wall and a table long enough to sit a dozen or so intelligence analysts. But there were only two other people seated at the table on the June day when I was there—a distinguished agency historian and a press officer to watch over both of us. I had come with the hope of picking the scholar's brain about Betty Pack, the British and American secret agent who had done so much to help the Allies win World War II.

It was, for me at least, a tense conversation. The CIA official knew, I suspected, a lot more than he was revealing, and I had the difficult task of trying to pull the information out of him. But he was a shrewd man who had spent a lifetime guarding secrets; he was not about to make an indiscreet revelation to me. Nevertheless, we both seemed to be enjoying the game until he took offense at something I had said.

I had announced that the book I intended to write would be a true story.

He laughed dismissively, and then launched into a lecture on the epistemology of espionage. Even nonfiction spy stories, to his way of thinking, were a search for ultimately elusive truths. The best that can be hoped for is a reliable hypothesis. No spy tale is ever the whole story; there are always too many unknowns, too many lies being passed off as facts, too many deliberate miscues by one participant or another.

I listened; argued meekly and defensively; and then did my best to move the conversation along to another hopefully more fruitful topic.

And now, having finished writing the nonfiction book that had prompted my visit to the CIA, I want to reiterate to its readers that this is a true story.

I have been able to draw on a treasure trove of information to tell Betty Pack's story: her memoirs, tape-recorded reminiscences, childhood diaries, and a lifetime of letters; the Office of Strategic Services Papers at the National Archives; Federal Bureau of Investigation files; State Department records; the British Security Coordination official history; Foreign Office archives at the Public Record Office; and interviews with members of both the British and American intelligence services.

And yet I am also forced to acknowledge that there is a cautionary kernel of truth in the CIA scholar's warning. There are, among the official sources, contradictory versions of events. And another caveat—governments, even more than half a century later, hold on to their secrets. Betty's sixty-five-page FBI file is heavily redacted; tantalizing files at the National Archives are marked "Security Classified information, withdrawn at the request of a foreign government"; and the files assembled by H. Montgomery Hyde, Betty's wartime colleague in the British secret service and her first biographer, which were bequeathed to Churchill College, Cambridge, have been edited. Parts of this collection are "closed indefinitely"; individual documents have been removed by intelligence service "weeders"; and some papers have been officially "closed until the year 2041."

Nevertheless, I reiterate: this is a true story. The narrative, a spy tale and a psychological detective story as well, is shaped by the facts I discovered. When there were two (or more) versions of an incident, I stuck with the one that made the most sense. When dialogue is in quotation marks, it has been directly quoted from a firsthand source. And when I share characters' internal thoughts—what they're thinking or feeling—these insights are culled from their memoirs, diaries, or letters. A chapter-by-chapter sourcing follows at the end of this book.

H.B.

Part I

Storming the Castle

Chapter 1

◆

BETTY PACK HAD PLANNED HER escape from the castle with great care. Too often impulsive—her greatest fault, she would frequently concede—she had deliberately plotted this operation with the long-dormant discipline acquired during her dangerous time decades ago in the field. Yet on the blustery morning of March 1, 1963, Betty, otherwise known in the tiny village in the French Pyrenees that lay just beyond the stone walls of the ancient castle as Mme Brousse, the American-born chatelaine of Castelnou, and who in a previous life had been known to an even smaller circle as the agent code-named Cynthia, was having doubts.

Betty had spent diligent months baiting the hook, then repeatedly recasting until it was firmly lodged, but now, just as the time had come to reel in her prey, she was suddenly anxious. She stood at the edge of the castle's battlement as if on guard, a solitary figure, her gaze absently fixed on the pine forest in the distance, the raw wind charging in from the northwest with the savage shriek of an invading army. But Betty ignored the elements. The mighty wind—the tramontane, as the awed locals called it—was nothing compared to the turmoil that must have been going through her mind.

She was out of practice. She had lost her charm. At fifty-three, she was too old. Worse, she looked too old. It was a delusion, a pathetic, self-indulgent foolishness, to believe that a middle-aged woman could cast the same captivating spell that she had at twenty-nine. Her self-incriminating list went on and on, every charge in its way a pained reiteration of the same fundamental and unimpeachable truism: life, real life, always yields to age.

Then, all at once, Betty found the will. Was it simply a sharp burst of her old courage? A renewed realization that, as she had once written, "happiness never comes from frustration"? Or perhaps she told herself that too much had already been set in motion. There was no turning back.

Betty, Charles, and their driver without their beloved Rolls.

Whatever the reason—or, just as likely, reasons—Betty, as she recalled the energized moment, was suddenly on the move. Without hesitation she made her way down the well-worn stone steps, strode in her long-legged, athletic way across the terrace, where the almond trees were already starting to bloom, and continued through the cobblestone courtyard to the waiting Rolls-Royce. The chauffeur was at the wheel. Her husband, Charles, was already in the back seat, his presence an inspired bit of cover, giving a pretense of legitimacy to the rendezvous that, if all went as she had so painstakingly designed, would soon happen.

Once she'd taken her place on the soft maroon leather back seat next to Charles, the huge old car—it too a well-polished relic of another era—moved slowly forward. The Rolls threaded its way through a narrow stone archway built centuries ago and then headed downhill, away from Castelnou.

Picking up speed, the heavy car bounced along a winding dirt road where back in 1289 the troops of His Majesty James II of Majorca had charged in their bold assault on the seemingly impregnable fortress. Despite the apparent futility of their quest, Betty had heard time after time in the reverential account of the ferocious battle her husband was so fond of telling, the invaders had stormed the castle and won the day.

And now on this windswept morning, as she traveled on the same road as that undaunted medieval army, any lingering anxieties, any troubling uncertainties, any precombat jitters, turned to sand. It was once again wartime, and Betty, the veteran field agent, knew from experience that doubt was one more enemy that must be beaten back. Her confidence returned. Her spirits soared; it was as if she could already see herself rising from the depths and being lifted high above the confining castle walls. Her great escape. Another old spy would come out of his retirement to save her.

WHY WAS THIS OPERATION SO vital? Why was her determination so fierce, her decision to flee so entrenched? Why, in fact, did she want to run? It was a mission with many objectives, some of which Betty could articulate, while others remained beyond her grasp, part of a murky and instinctive logic. Although she could, if pressed, point to key events as catalysts, in truth the impulse had been brewing for a while; and no doubt it had been quietly taking shape for even longer than Betty realized.

Part of what was pushing her was quite simple: she had grown tired of her small, stagnant life. At first the move to the fairy-tale castle sitting so majestically on its lofty perch in the French Pyrenees had loomed as a new adventure. No less appealing to someone so deeply susceptible, it had offered a future sweet with the intoxicating thrill of romance. Charles, suave, gallant, mature, and so very French in his devotion to his passions, had swooped her up after the war and led her out of a staid America.

The castle, she discovered with a childlike delight, was a honeycomb of large, lofty rooms softly lit by candles and warmed by tree-size logs burning nearly year-round in hearths as dark and deep as caves. The adjacent village, a quaint cluster of red-roofed houses, contained a church built when the Holy Roman Empire ruled, presided over by a rotund priest who seemed old enough to have laid the cornerstone, and the obligatory café served up carafes of a cheap, deliciously sweet red that was smuggled in oak barrels across the border from nearby Spain. It would be, Betty told herself, all the community she'd ever require.

After her "vagabond years," as she called them, and her busy, tense war, she'd persuaded herself, she confided in breezy letters home, that the time had come to slow down and at last settle in. And after a loveless marriage to a dour, thin stick of a man constrained by his rigid British soul and his diplomat's sense of propriety, life with Charles would, in its unique way, be lush and brimming. Betty had moved into Castelnou with a newlywed's optimistic excitement.

Yet after having lived day after long day for nearly two decades as mistress of this isolated, anachronistic domain, she had come to see things from a different, troubling perspective. The castle had become a prison of cold, unyielding stone. "I would give anything to leave this castle and go to a small, manageable flat. Fifteen years ago it was a joy, but today it is a great burden," she wrote to her former sister-in-law.

Château de Castelnou, perched in the French Pyrenees.

The village too had lost its charm. Now it was simply narrow and provincial. And with the passing of the years, Charles had moved on from an appealing maturity to a burdensome old age.

Charles was almost twenty years Betty's senior by the calendar, and several lifetimes older in his stoic acceptance that the only course left to him was to putter along until the inevitable end of his journey. "We are always here, and never in London or Paris as Charles, now seventy-one, dislikes postwar life in cities," she moaned in another of the aching, frustrated letters she sent during her captivity.

Their love, too, had evolved with the passing years. Betty's marriage, as guests to the chateau observed, was comfortable and familiar, an alliance warmed by a cozy and attentive devotion; she'd prop a pillow behind Charles's back if he was reading on the sunny terrace, or tenderly arrange a shawl across his lap as he sat before the cavernous living room hearth as the night wind blew down the mountains from Spain. It was friendship, and it was companionship. But at the same complicated time, Betty couldn't help feeling it was no longer enough.

She missed the giddy, electric, all-consuming joy of high passion. Its absence gnawed away, constant and relentless, keeping her on edge, intruding into and disrupting her world. Unsatisfied, she began to think her fairy tale needed a new ending. She prayed for a handsome prince to storm the castle and rescue her.

AND THIS WAS NOT ALL. Her roiling emotions had been further unsettled by two deaths. Each at its time had been unexpected, and each in its tumultuous way had churned up memories and sensations that left her nearly shaking. Betty thought she had successfully suppressed her past, but in the mournful aftermath of these two losses she came to realize that this was one more bit of wishful thinking. Her history, her choices—they were, she understood for the first time, her lingering mysteries.

One death was her mother's. It was one thing, Betty painfully learned, to understand that your elderly mother will someday die; it was something else entirely to experience her death.

It wasn't that she had loved her mother, or, for that matter, even liked or respected her. In fact, the lessons Mrs. Cora Thorpe, a shrewd, calculating, rosy-cheeked Washington socialite, had taught Betty were all negatively prescriptive. Betty had lived in a constant state of rebellion against her mother's ambitious social agenda and prissy maxims about how women of a certain class and born with certain advantages should behave.

Cora Wells Thorpe, Betty's mother, just before her death.

Initially Betty had felt liberated by Cora's death, at last free of the pull of her manipulative grasp. With glib detachment, she attempted to consign their combative relationship to the annals of ancient history. "She disapproved of me, and I disapproved of her," she confided to a wartime colleague with a seemingly resigned candor. "You might say that she was a Persian cat and I was a Siamese."

But no sooner had she decided she had come to terms with her mother's death than it overwhelmed her. Scenes from Betty's childhood, a glossy world of boarding schools, debutante parties, country clubs, and grand European tours swirled through her mind. In their wake, old wounds were once again raw. From the grave, Cora was still battling with her daughter, and at the end of each round Betty was at a loss. For the first time in their long-running war, Betty felt pangs of regret.

It was her son's death, though, that pushed Betty to despair. Three months after having won the Military Cross for conspicuous gallantry while leading an assault on a starless night against an enemy position deep in the Korean hill country, Lieutenant Tony Pack had been cut down as he commanded his platoon in another bold charge. He died almost instantly, a twenty-two-year-old hero.

Betty, though, could find little solace in her son's brave death. Her boy, as handsome in her eyes as a "young Rupert Brooke," was suddenly gone forever. And with his death, it was as if the carefully constructed walls that had been holding back her maternal guilt for so long came tumbling down too. She could no longer repress, no longer rationalize, what she had done.

The truths were searing: just weeks after Tony's birth, she and her husband had cavalierly left Tony with a foster family. In all the years that followed, as she flitted to adventures all across the globe, she had made time to visit her son on only three occasions; she had written him only a handful of letters. Now that it was too late, she mourned as though stricken by an immense and powerful remorse.

Why had she behaved that way? How could she be so passionate in her feelings about so many things, and at the same time so heartless? How could she betray all that she should have cared about so easily? Why were her allegiances—to Tony, to her first husband, to Charles, to her mother, to the life she had made at Castelnou— all so fugitive, so ephemeral? The answers to this sudden storm of questions hovered beyond her grasp.

Betty decided she needed clarity. The time, she felt, had come for her to find the reasons for the life she had led, the things she had done, the choices she had made. For her own peace of mind, she needed to discover why she had so routinely let down those she had loved, while serving her spymasters with such loyalty and devotion. She wanted to understand why she had been such a flawed wife, daughter, and mother—and yet such a perfect spy.

The knowledge was out there, she felt. But first she would have to escape from the confines of the life she was living. She just needed her chance.

Chapter 2

◆

HER OPPORTUNITY APPEARED WITHOUT WARNING, and Betty, now that her mind was firmly set, did not hesitate. At the same time she also realized that she could not rush things; she would need to play the operation long. And here her tradecraft was impeccable. Betty, always so artful when it came to seduction, kept things casual, offhanded—until the moment came to pounce.

In the fall of 1962 the daughter of a wartime colleague had sent her a clipping from the London Sunday *Times*. It was an extract from a just-published biography of her cunning old boss, Sir William Stephenson, the director of Britain's then largely unheralded intelligence activities in America during the tense years leading up to the attack on Pearl Harbor, as well as after. And tucked prominently into this news-making exposé was a glimpse into the derring-do exploits of a tenacious female agent, a woman who in the name of king, country, and the Allied cause had nearly single-handedly won the war in one bedroom after another. The agent was primly identified by only her code name—"Cynthia."

The author was Harford Montgomery Hyde, and Betty knew him too. On a sticky August afternoon in 1941 she had arrived to meet one of her handlers for her weekly debriefing in a bleak midtown Manhattan hotel room, and Hyde, another British agent, had appeared as an observer. He didn't talk much; this was the handler's show to run. But despite his silence he made an impression: a tall, confident man in a captain's uniform with piercing dark eyes, a ready smile, and an Irish lilt to his voice that he seemed intent on disguising.

After the meet, her handler remained behind, and Betty and Hyde had walked together up Madison Avenue. Hyde was staying at the Ritz-Carlton before he shipped off on a new mission that, constrained by a veteran fieldman's sense of operational security, he avoided mentioning. As for Betty, she had a flight to Washington to catch; she too had her own covert assignment. When they parted at the hotel entrance, he said, "I expect we shall see each other again soon."

They never did; wartime had its own unpredictable demands. But she had never forgotten the young intelligence officer, or the almost dizzying pull he had exerted on her in that single encounter.

And now, a lifetime later, he was writing about her. She was astonished.

With a shock of recognition, Betty read on. There were, she'd marvel, "direct quotes from some of my reports." Hyde, she realized, "must have had direct access to my dossiers." It seemed impossible to her that "official secrets" could be so wantonly shared with the public. But then again, she asked herself, was it any less improbable that a corner of her secret life would become so very public just as she was struggling to understand it?

By the time she had finished reading the excerpt in the *Times*, the course of the entire operation she would launch had sprung fully blown into her mind. She hunted for the address of the book's London publisher and went to work. Her initial pass at her target was a brief, seemingly innocuous letter.

15th November 1962

Dear Mr. Montgomery,
I have received from a friend a clipping about your book

. . . I am already filled with nostalgia for the happiest days
of my life. . . .
As for our meeting that August afternoon in 1941, I recall
it well. . . . It would be a great pleasure to see you again.
You belong to that happy period that even in wartime
exists for those who have a common cause. . . .
Yours ever, most sincerely
"Cynthia"

(Mme Charles Brousse)

When a surprisingly quick reply came in the post, Betty's confidence undoubtedly soared: the operation was moving forward.
The one obstacle to her plan was Hyde's suggestion that she and
her husband might meet him on their next trip to London or Paris.
It was an inflexible precept of fieldwork that the agent running the
show set the terms of the meet, and Betty was determined not to
lose control. She promptly laid down the law, but at the same time
also shrewdly ratcheted up the promise of what she had to offer.

December 12, 1962

Dear Mr. Montgomery,
As it is a long time ago, I may perhaps be allowed to make a
confession now. After our meeting, I wanted very much to see
you again. . . . I have thought of you many times since. . . .
Can you imagine, therefore, how happy I am to be in touch
with you again? And how happy I should be to *see* you again?
For the most part we are always here, and never in London
or Paris. . . . The only hope I have of seeing you rests with

you. If you should come to the Pyrenees, we would give
you a happy time and would take you to S'Agaro (Costa
Brava) for a day of pure paradise.
I cannot tell you how much I would like you to come, because
I want to be with you, listen to you, absorb your presence.
Always yours,

"*Cynthia*"

Three long, anxious weeks passed before she received his reply,
and when it came it offered the heady possibility that Hyde would
not only meet on her turf but also work with her on "a series of
articles that might later be expanded into a book." But there was
a warning, too, and it carried with it the hint that Betty might've
overplayed her hand: Hyde sternly reminded Betty that he was married, and her letters must not give his wife any reason for concern.

Every operation has its moment when the agent alone in the field
realizes that everything hangs in the balance: it could go one way,
or more perilously, another. Betty had reached this juncture: her
approach had been too direct, clearly. Clearly, she was rusty; she had
been out of the game too long. Still, she did not panic but set out to
make things right. And she took some comfort from the realization
that Hyde's admonishment had been very specific: it was her *letters*
that must not cause his wife to worry.

January 28, 1963

Dear "you"
(Mr. Montgomery puts me off by its formality!)
I had worried about your silence thinking that my

outspokenness in my last letter . . . has annoyed you. . . . I
may have overstepped myself with you in recent letters and
. . . should have kept my thoughts . . . and feelings within
bounds. Please, please do not worry for I will *not* let you
down or add to your worries. . . .
As ever your

"Cynthia"

It was a struggle, but Betty did not mention either their possible
collaboration or, more tellingly, his visit. She had learned her lesson. Though she was undoubtedly longing to coax him forward,
to shove him into action, she remained aloof. If the operation was
to succeed, she knew the target couldn't feel he was being coerced;
he had to believe it was entirely his own decision to take the next
fateful step.

Her strategy worked. There were no complaints in Hyde's next
letter. Instead, rather plaintively, he wondered if she had given any
thought to his idea about a series of articles. If she were interested,
"I would gladly make the journey to the Pyrenees and discuss it."

The next day by return post, she assured him that his suggestion
was "100% acceptable"; "I will tell you and *only you* anything and
everything."

After a confirming phone call from Hyde in London, the meet
was set. She would be waiting at the small train station in nearby
Perpignan when the express from Paris arrived on the morning of
March 1. From there, she promised, it was only a couple of hours'
drive to the warming sun and the lulling blue Mediterranean waters of S'Agaro; they should arrive at the Hotel Gavina in time
for broiled lobsters and a chilled bottle of Sancerre on the hotel
terrace.

In a follow-up letter Betty made it clear that she would be ready to get down to work. "I am taking my NY briefcase with the following items: 4 big blocks of paper, several pencils, a package of carbon paper." But still calculatingly flirtatious, Betty gushed, "What heaven to be with someone like you . . . I can't wait." Her training taking hold, she concluded by sharing the recognition signals: she would be wearing a blue headscarf and a fur coat.

IN HER TIME BETTY HAD orchestrated enough meets to know that the agent in the field must always be prepared for something to go wrong. And in the days leading to her rendezvous with Hyde, she'd recall anticipating a hundred disasters. He would catch the grippe and stayed in London. He would miss the train in Paris. The French rail system would choose that day for one of their spontaneous work stoppages. Calamities loomed with increasing certainty as the day of the meet drew closer.

But on the morning of March 1, as the Rolls pulled up to the train station and the chauffeur hurried to open her door, Betty was suddenly struck by a new, nearly paralyzing fear: *He won't recognize me. I've changed too much. I've grown too old.*

As IT HAPPENED, HYDE WAS at that precise moment having very similar thoughts. When he first met Cynthia twenty-two years earlier, he had been captivated. He'd come to the hotel room ripe with expectations; Cynthia's exploits, her success in charming secrets out of men who should have known better, were already legendary in the clubby covert world he inhabited. In his feverish imagination, he would write, he'd conjured up a seductress with a pinup girl's sultry curves and a tantalizing come-hither stare. The woman he met was an entirely different sort.

Cynthia was tall, slim, and patrician. With her sensible amber-blond hair swept back off her broad forehead and a single strand of pearls around her graceful neck, she would have looked at home on a country club terrace or hosting a dinner with a banker husband holding court at the other end of the table. Her green eyes sparkled, and she flashed a wide, enthusiastic smile. But Hyde felt a small pang of disappointment; there was nothing that suggested anything more than an attractive "wholesome All-American" young woman.

But once Betty started talking, her voice soft as a whisper yet authoritative, her laugh uninhibited, even naughty, her eyes fixed on him like a marksman's, all his oversimplifications, all his stereotypes, were quickly undone. "She had a force, or magnetism to a terrifying degree," he discovered. "What," he wondered, "is this pacing tiger doing . . . in this conventional disguise?"

He had spent little more than an hour with her, but that was enough. It was engraved in his memory. She locked on to him with her radiant smile and her shining emerald eyes, determined, it seemed, to bore into his very being, and he was hooked. "The trick of making a man feel he is her entire universe," he knew only too well, "is an old feminine wile, but Cynthia had it to the *nth* degree. . . . I felt the impact at once," he wrote.

Yet as he stood with his valise in his hand in the train station waiting room, Hyde could not help soberly thinking how long ago that had been. And he knew that those first impressions were undoubtedly heightened by the romantic veneer of wartime, of intense days spent in life-or-death struggles. Besides, he had certainly changed over the past two decades.

He was fifty-six now, and the image reflected back at him in the waiting room window was that of a moon-faced middle-aged man with the beginnings of a paunch pressing against his tweed waistcoat. And while he took a disproportionate pride in the fact that the brilliantined hair brushed straight back on his head was still reassuringly thick and dark, there was no denying the gray at his temples. No, he told himself with a measure of philosophical resignation, decades had passed since anyone who recognized the rep tie of the distinguished Oxford college he was wearing could mistake him for an undergraduate. Why should he expect that Betty would have escaped unscathed by time's mischief? He could not help hoping, though, that the damage inflicted had not been too cruel.

And then he saw her. She was bounding through the waiting room door, wrapped in her fur coat, blue scarf tied over her champagne-colored hair, tall, puckish, and extraordinarily alluring. "The electric force," he realized at once, "was undiminished."

Betty approached with long, brisk strides until she came to an abrupt stop directly in front of him. Neither moved. Only a foot or so apart, the two stared at one another, appraising. Hyde finally broke the silence.

"You haven't changed," he said.

Betty had been schooled in the university of espionage. She knew a spy's words were often hollow, and the larger the deceit, the greater the apparent sincerity. But this time, how could she not believe him?

Chapter 3

◆

THE HOTEL GAVINA RESTED ON a long, rocky peninsula that stretched out into the Mediterranean. It was a stately Spanish resort, with heavy silver on the dining room tables and well-starched sheets with impressive thread counts on the roomy double beds. But the old dowager also had a temptress's soul.

By day a placid Mediterranean lapped rhythmically against the shoreline, a bright sun warmed the terrace as generous carafes of a surprisingly potent sangria were served, and the incredibly blue pool shimmered like a crystal in the sunlight. At night, the mood was the same, only more so. Candles flickered on tables, aromatic logs burned in hearths, a flamenco guitarist strummed soft melodies, stars sparkled on the calm, dark sea, and the moon lit a wide path to the sandy beach.

Betty was in her element. Like a general going into battle confident that the terrain was all to his advantage, Betty set off on the next stage of her mission.

Her "New York briefcase" was just another bit of cover, and a flimsy one at that, but during their first day together she was all business. She acted as if she was totally absorbed in their proposed literary collaboration as she let the sun and stars and sangria work their silent, lulling magic.

On their second day together they became lovers. Who reached out first to touch the other's hand? Who planted the first coaxing kiss? The answers to these questions have remained part of the forever-classified history of this operation. But in truth the specifics were largely irrelevant. The seeds of their affair had been planted on a sultry August afternoon back in 1941. Their correspondence had been their courtship. And once Betty took control, the outcome was inevitable.

They spent two more precious days at the hotel, making love in Hyde's room with a businesslike punctuality at 10:00 a.m. and 3:00 p.m. daily. Bursting with a satyr's pride, Hyde described their couplings to a friend as "torrid." Betty, the happy seductress, would later send Hyde a newspaper clipping reporting a messy divorce case that had for no particular reason caught her eye, adding her own coy handwritten note in the margin, her code to stir his memory: "S'Agaro . . . 10 am and 3 pm."

And where was Betty's husband while their passion ran its hot course? He could not have been very far away; the hotel was a small enclave. Didn't Charles suspect anything? Or was he simply complacent enough to accept things with a stoic passivity? Perhaps he had decided it was a small price to pay for the larger joy of knowing that Betty would return to *their* room and share *their* bed each night.

Neither Betty nor Hyde apparently suffered any regrets for their duplicity. There was certainly no hesitation, no misgivings about the vows they were breaking or the heartbreak they might inflict on their spouses. Their moments together had their own logic, their own morality. Both had lived the spy's life for so long that lies and betrayals came easily.

THE DIE HAD BEEN CAST. Betty could proceed to the next stage of her mission. But even as she made her move, it undoubtedly never occurred to her that she too was being played.

It is a universal conceit of players in the Great Game that every spy believes he's the one doing the manipulating. It is the rare agent who considers that his target might have his own covert agenda. Or that the victim might purposefully let the noose drop over his head. Despite all her cunning, Betty must never have suspected how deeply the old spy needed her—and what she was offering.

Money had been Betty's initial lure, a golden carrot she had enticingly dangled. She'd hoped this would get his attention. Who, after all, she'd told herself, doesn't like the prospect of a bit of extra cash? But she had not imagined the desperate straits Hyde was navigating. If not broke, he was certainly in over his financial head. Each fretful month, more bills came in than his diligent earnings could cover.

After the war, Hyde had left MI6 and embarked on an eclectic and impressively accomplished professional life. He had in rapid succession been a barrister; the private secretary to the seventh Marquess of Londonderry; an Ulster Unionist member of Parliament representing his native Belfast until he was deselected by his party after his outspoken campaign for the decriminalization of the draconian laws against homosexuality; a prolific author whose titles included three books on Oscar Wilde (whose wood-paneled rooms at Magdalen College had been Hyde's Oxford digs several generations later); and a professor of history and political science at the University of the Punjab in Lahore, Pakistan. Hyde left Lahore at the urging of spymaster Sir William Stephenson, who agreed to pay Hyde a stipend while he researched and wrote Stephenson's biography. It had been a varied and accomplished life, but the one common thread was a persistent shortage of cash.

As an Irishman making his way in London society, Hyde was a bit insecure about his humble roots. He thought a bit of flash—bespoke clothes, a flat in tony Knightsbridge, membership in a rarefied London club, and, after his first wife ran off with a dashing brother MI6 officer at the tail end of the war, a well-bred second wife with expensive tastes—would provide the cover to help him pass as a British gentleman of the military class. The letterhead of his parliamentary stationery proudly proclaimed "Lt. Col. H. Montgomery Hyde, ret." But the image he strived to maintain came at an onerous price. Hyde was perpetually scrambling to pay his bills.

His biography of Stephenson, published as *The Quiet Canadian*, met with a reception as tepid as its title; sales were quiet at best. And another worry: he'd rashly abandoned his sinecure at the University in Lahore to write the book. He was now unemployed. The prospect of telling Cynthia's tale of sex, danger, and important wartime missions offered a way to cut a rapidly growing pile of past-due bills down to a manageable size.

The more Hyde thought about it, the more convinced he was that his financial salvation lay before him. He'd gloss up Betty's exploits into a series of bodice-ripping yarns that could be peddled profitably to the tabloid press and then, with not much more work, turned into a book. A boozy lunch with his literary agent, Iain Thompson, bolstered Hyde's enthusiasm; the commercial prospects for such a tale, Thompson agreed, were good. At loose ends, Hyde was raring to get started.

Hand in hand with this motive came another, no less fundamental—he wanted to get Betty into bed. She had consciously exploited this desire, yet here, too, Betty had no idea of the susceptibility of her prey. She had no inkling of how frequently she'd stalked his imagination over the years since their first encounter.

Betty had become an obsession. As her contribution to the honorable Allied crusade against evil, Betty had famously seduced and manipulated a long list of important men. She had persuaded them to abandon prudence and good judgment. Now he wanted the adventure of experiencing her power. He wanted to see what all the fuss was about. If Betty had not sent such clear signals about her availability, he still would have jumped at the slightest chance.

But there was also more at work than either money or sex in

the decision that had brought Hyde to this warm and comfortable resort on the Costa Brava. In the months prior to his arrival, his mood had been increasingly despondent. He had come to feel, he'd write, that all his youthful promise had been squandered, and that the many paths he'd taken—eclectic careers, unsatisfying marriages—had all led to dead ends. Like Betty, he was plagued by regrets. Despondent, he too had felt the need to hunt for painful answers.

Betty's letter was an unexpected gift, bringing with it the prospect of exploring their shared past. Instinctively Hyde suspected that his only path toward a meaningful future lay in reconnecting to the high purpose of his wartime years. And in telling Betty's story, he would again be able to identify what he had lost, and what he had once so very much valued.

Chapter 4

◆

BETTY HAD PROMISED HYDE THAT S'Agaro would be "a paradise," and she kept her word. The four days flew by. There was one small annoyance; Betty complained mildly about a toothache, and Hyde, with the attentiveness of a trained watcher, noticed that she was careful to eat only soft foods. But the pain, he was glad to note, didn't seem to interfere with either her lively mood or the intensity of her passion.

On the fifth day, as Hyde prepared to head back to London, she insisted on first taking him to Castelnou.

Harford Montgomery Hyde, photographed at Castelnou.

She showed off her storybook castle. She playfully posed for photographs with her husband, Charles in a jaunty beret and Betty lithe and long-legged in sleek black trousers, her two large hunting dogs running in and out of the shots. And she waited for the propitious moment.

Betty posing at Castelnou ("with one of her 'dawgs'," as noted on the bottom of the original photograph).

There was none because what she intended to propose was at best outrageous. But finally she couldn't keep it bottled up inside her any longer, and simply blurted it out. It was the final part of her escape plan: she wanted Hyde to accompany her to Ireland.

Ireland had always exerted an almost mythological pull on Betty's imagination. She had been born in Minneapolis, Minnesota, but without too much proof she'd convinced herself that her father's Scandinavian grandparents also had some Londonderry ties. Her impetuosity, her unbridled sense of fun, even her eyes, as green as a county Clare meadow in springtime—all were traits, Betty was certain, inherited from her Irish forebears. Her logic was as intuitive as it was unshakeable; Ireland—a country she had never visited—was, she felt, her "spiritual home."

As her plan formed in her mind, Ireland had always been the final destination. It was the one place, she believed with a typically heartfelt ardor, where she could find the serenity and the inspiration to confront the troubling questions she needed to ask herself.

With her husband standing by mutely, Betty asked her new lover if he would swoop her off to Ireland. For propriety's sake, she unconvincingly assured Charles that the trip would give her a chance to work with Hyde on their book without any distractions.

Hyde agreed at once—with one caveat. He needed to go to New York first; his American publisher wanted him to do some publicity when their edition of the Stephenson book was launched in the States in April.

Their itinerary was set with equal speed. During the first week of May, Betty would fly to London, and Hyde would be waiting at the gate in Heathrow. The next morning they would fly to Dublin. And, Betty told herself with a professional's pride, she would have finally escaped from the castle—just as she'd planned.

Charles walked Hyde to the car waiting to take the visitor to the train station. He shook his guest's hand and politely wished him a safe trip. Then he walked back up the wide, well-worn stone steps to the castle's thickly timbered front door. Even if he did not acknowledge it, in the course of a few days, his world had been entirely transformed.

ON A BRIGHT MORNING IN the first week of May, Charles accompanied Betty on the long drive to the Barcelona airport. He led her to the gate where the flight to London was boarding, kissed her good-bye, and then returned to his lonely castle.

Only when the plane was high in the clouds did Betty doubtless allow herself a few moments of triumph. She had escaped from her ancient, high-walled prison. She was confident that in the course of the adventure she was setting out on, she would find the answers she needed. In Ireland, she would discover the reasons for the complicated life she had led.

But her joy was short-lived. No sooner had she celebrated the launch of her operation than she was forced to acknowledge why it was so vital. There was one more secret she had kept from Charles and from Hyde. More than anything else, it had prodded her to act.

The pain in her tooth was much worse than she had admitted. And it had spread maliciously to her lower jaw. After the oral surgeon recommended by her local dentist examined her, he had sat her down and explained with grim certitude that a biopsy would be just a formality. She had cancer. It would keep attacking until, before long, it killed her.

This would be, Betty knew, her final mission.

Part II

"A Terrible Restlessness"

Chapter 5

◆

DUBLIN HAD ALWAYS BEEN A good city in which to settle
in with a pint and share a bit of *craic*, as the hard-drinking
locals call the tall tales and brash gossip that buzz about a
convivial Irish barroom. And in this hospitable city that was home
to so many lively watering holes, a favorite destination, at least
among a crowd of politicians, journalists, actors, musicians, and
others cut from a similarly raffish cloth, was the dark recesses of the
Horseshoe Bar in the venerable Shelbourne Hotel.

For over a century the Horseshoe's walls had been painted a
deep bloodred, the distinctive tarry smell of burning peat had min-
gled with clouds of tobacco smoke, and the expert barmen could
pull a Guinness from the tap with—presto!—a shamrock magi-
cally sculpted in the creamy foam. And, oh, the stories that had
been told! The secrets those bold red walls had heard! So it seemed
fitting, if not inevitable, that it was here, seated shoulder to shoulder with Betty on a black leather banquette, that Hyde decided to
begin his interrogation.

They had arrived from London that May morning and, more
like giddy lovers on a honeymoon than two spies embarking on
their own secret missions, settled into the hotel. Cocktail time,
though, brought them out of their room, and against all odds they
managed to find an unoccupied banquette. Then once the drinks
were brought—Hyde, more Anglo than Irish, was a single-malt
man; Betty, more cosmopolitan, believed a glass of champers was
an auspicious start to any evening—without much preamble Hyde
pounced.

Suddenly officious, shifting abruptly into the role of the in-quisitive writer diligently gathering the research he needed for his book, he pulled a small notebook out of a tweed pocket and placed it on the table. And then a pen appeared in his hand, Betty must have felt it as menacing as a cocked revolver.

Perhaps it was because he wasn't sure where to begin that he decided the best possible course would be to start in at every spy's Rubicon, the crossing point between what came before and all that would ever after follow. It was the defining moment, the irrevo-cable bite of the apple, he knew from hard experience, that set in motion an agent's operational life.

"Tell me about your recruitment," he coaxed Betty. "How ex-actly did you become a spy?" She snuffed out the remains of one dark Capstan cigarette, only to quickly light another. "When and where did it all begin?" Then, having thrown out the questions as a challenge, he sat back, sipped his drink, and no doubt hoped that Betty would reach deep into her Irish soul and share some good *craic.*

Chapter 6

◆

P OLAND," BETTY WROTE IN A letter home about the country where she found herself living in the tense years before
Hitler's troops began their fateful blitzkrieg across Europe,
"is a sad, gray place." And to understand the excitement Betty was
seeking on that eventful March afternoon in 1938 when, on a golf
course outside Warsaw, she offered her services to His Majesty's
Secret Service, or what empty spaces she was trying to fill, it would
first be necessary, she told Hyde, to understand the bleakness, the
thick monotonous gloom, that had wrapped around her life. She
was suffocating.

She had arrived in Warsaw a year earlier, the twenty-six-year-
old-wife of a minor functionary of the British diplomatic caste. Arthur Pack was the British embassy's new commercial secretary, a man
twenty years older than his American bride—though some cruel observers smirked that the age difference might just as well have been
twice, or even treble, that. He was a stuffy, haughty, forever-striving
relic of a bowler-hatted England whose days of ruling the world
were rapidly dwindling, if not already a memory. Deeply insecure,
he did not dare yield to the changing times; an outsider like Arthur
Pack—no family connections, no Oxbridge degree—had to observe
a rigid formality if he were to make his way in the Foreign Office.
As a further complication for his young, fun-loving wife, Arthur was
sickly to boot; the last war had permanently strained his heart and
constitution. Betty had married Arthur out of desperation; in fact,
she had engineered the entire courtship. But now she was beginning
to realize she'd made a colossal mistake.

Arthur Pack in uniform, c. 1930.

Prior to the couple's posting to Poland, they had been in Spain. Betty, forever passionate, a woman who only either loved or detested, had adored the country. From the start, she had been swept up in the hot-blooded Latin land and its gay fiesta spirit.

But Poland, she quickly learned, was an entirely different place, and a dispirited one. Surrounded by enemies, a razor-sharp sword of Damocles hanging threateningly over the nation. The anxious Poles lived in brooding fear of the day when the blade would inevitably come swooping down, at the same time wondering whether it would be wielded by the Germans or the Russians or, no less inconceivable, both invading armies. Geography was fate, and with Hitler and Stalin as neighbors, today was tense and tomorrow uncertain.

In this problematic time, as darkening war clouds filled the sky, the British diplomatic corps, out of desperation as much as necessity, bonded together. Theirs was a very narrow social world, and yet nearly from the day of Betty's arrival, it was clear that she wasn't welcome. Perhaps tales of her free-spirited escapades in Spain had made their way from one embassy to another. Or maybe it was simply Betty's very presence—so shiny, so glamorous, so ripe, so eager—that raised the eyebrows of graying senior staff in disapproval and provoked catty envy in their dowdy wives. Whatever the cause, it was quickly made clear to Betty that she was not appreciated. She was not welcomed into the cozy circle of embassy wives. They did not invite her over for tea or ring her up to join committees. Yet she was a fighter; once pushed into a corner, she didn't try to accommodate. She snarled back.

Betty dismissed the ambassador, Sir Howard Kennard, as "a real sourpuss who disapproved of any kind of gaiety." She had also swiftly locked horns with snotty Peta Norton, the embassy counselor's wife and the reigning hostess in this clique of stolid British diplomats. "Mrs. Norton took a strong dislike to me, and I must say that the feeling was reciprocated on my side," she'd write with no attempt at apology in her memoirs. Still, the ostracism stung. Despite her bounding, vivacious energy, Betty was alone in a foreign and somber land.

Then on New Year's Eve, as she and her husband waited with the other revelers at the French embassy for the clock to strike midnight, Arthur collapsed. He was carried home unconscious. The doctor's diagnosis was discouraging: Arthur had suffered a serious, possibly permanently debilitating stroke.

At last Betty had found her mission: she would direct all her pent-up spirit to the task of getting Arthur well.

Warsaw

January 24, 1938
Dearest Family,
Please do not worry. ARTHUR IS GOING TO GET WELL. I am a demon of determination. I've never yet failed in something I really wanted and I'm so determined about him. I'm giving him everything I have in me. . . .
Your loving daughter,

Betty

A month later, still happily playing the dutiful nurse, still convinced she had at last found the role she was meant to play in this previously empty marriage, Betty brought Arthur back to England. She settled him into a rehabilitation facility on the Isle of Wight; did her best to squeeze some of the dread out of his fatalistic mood; and then, after only two weeks in England, returned to Warsaw. It was Arthur who insisted that she leave; despite his fragile condition, he hoped to convince the embassy staff that his stroke was trivial, that he was already on the mend, and it wouldn't be long before he'd be returning to his wife and his job.

Obedient, still trying on for size the new, soberly responsible character she'd chosen to play, Betty agreed to be Arthur's accomplice in this disinformation operation. After all the deception ploys she had run against him over the years, she could hardly protest.

BETTY RETURNED ALONE TO AN icy Warsaw, the city frozen solid with a wintry gloom. She bravely tried to make light of her predicament, joking that she was now "a grass widow." But while life with Arthur had been lonely, this new situation had her completely cut off, as if marooned on some distant island.

Once she was on her own, the logic that had convinced Betty just a month earlier to take on the unfamiliar role of the loyal wife was doomed. Not only did she not want the part, she also realized; she wasn't cut out for it. It wasn't in her nature.

After she'd unfastened the tight restraints that had been holding her back, life at once looked different. She was free. There was no stodgy husband around to rein in her spirits. She no longer had to kowtow to a frumpy British embassy crowd who'd apparently decreed that any giddy high jinks, or even a telltale smile, would be an embarrassment to His Majesty's government. She could let loose and follow her own bold and restless heart.

Betty soon began to spend her evenings with a fast and lively crowd of young Polish intellectuals—artists, writers, diplomats, men and women deeply caught up in the building drama of the tense times in which they were living.

Always a quick study, Betty became one of them. Their passions became hers. These long, loud nights fueled by vodka and tobacco, as opinions and theories were aggressively hurled about the room like spears tossed by opposing armies, became her university, her political education.

And toward the end of one of these nights, Betty found a lover. It was a decision she made without thinking much about it, with neither guilt nor regret. Edward Kulikowski was a soulful young romantic who, as Europe was careening toward war, had remained focused on trying to mend his own broken heart. While serving at the Polish embassy in Washington, he'd fallen in love with a well-connected American woman. But after she gave birth to his child, she not only broke off the relationship but also denied that he was the father. Now he worked in the Polish foreign office, holding a senior position on the America desk. His job, however, held little interest for him; it was an almost irrelevant corner of his mournful, self-involved life.

In one another, Betty and Edward sought a way out of their predicaments. "I was never in love with him," Betty would say to Hyde. "I like to think he felt the same about me." They were both adrift, and together they helped one another make their way.

Their evenings together in his apartment, conveniently across the street from Betty's, were a shared comfort. Lying on the tiger-skin rug, with caviar and vodka to help the mood along, Betty would listen with her eyes tightly closed as Edward played Chopin with the grace and authority of a virtuoso on the grand piano. He'd hit the final ardent chord, and with the nocturne still echoing in her mind, he'd take her hand, lift her to her feet, and lead her effortlessly to a low, wide blue divan across the room.

It was on one of those evenings, as they lay satisfied, still entwined in one another's arms, the room illuminated only by the bright flames rising up in the fireplace, that their talk turned to politics. It was as inevitable, as natural, as their making love. Just days earlier Germany had marched into and occupied Austria, and Betty asked if Poland's turn would come soon.

Soothing and considerate, Edward quickly allayed her fears. Czechoslovakia, he assured her, would be Hitler's next target. The deal had already been made. A secret agreement had been signed. He had seen the papers in the embassy. "What's more," he added offhandedly, "Poland intends to take a bite of the cherry."

Betty's mind snapped to attention. She might not have even realized that she had been searching, but she had at last found precisely what she was looking for. It wasn't companionship. It wasn't love. It was something her wayward soul could believe in. This nugget that Edward had so casually offered was the gold that would give her a purpose—perhaps even buy her redemption.

THE PASSPORT CONTROL OFFICER AT any British embassy, as Betty and nearly everyone else in the diplomatic community knew, was the thin bit of cover assigned to the local fieldman representing His Majesty's Secret Intelligence Service. In Warsaw, he was Lieutenant-Colonel John Shelley, and as luck would have it, this tall, charming Irishman from Cork was Betty's only friend at the embassy.

Or maybe it wasn't luck at all. During her time in Spain, Betty, who was a natural watcher, had now and then passed on bits of information, interesting things she had seen and heard in the course of her travels around the country with her well-connected friends. The impressed local MI6 station head had sent many of these tidbits on to London, and in return, word had come back to Madrid that he should encourage her efforts. In that way she became what those in the trade call a semiconscious asset: she was playing the game, but not officially part of the team.

When Betty's husband was posted to Warsaw, Jack Shelley had received word to keep an eye on her; here was a woman perhaps worth cultivating. For her part, Betty, as manipulative as any spymaster, went out of her way to ingratiate herself with Shelley, making him the target of her considerable charm. She suspected it was a friendship that would come in handy.

First thing on the morning after Edward unwittingly divulged his valuable secret, Betty rang up Shelley. Feel like a round of golf?

she asked. It was a blustery March day, the Nazi army was mobilizing, and golf was undoubtedly the last thing on his or anyone's mind. But the MI6 man knew a cover story when he heard one; and at the same time he must have silently congratulated Betty for coming up with a pretext that would allow them to talk without worrying about being overheard.

Brilliant, he told her. Wasn't looking forward to being cooped up in the office today.

The golf course was just outside the city. The fairways unkempt, and a bleak, wintry brown. But they gamely played a few holes to keep up appearances before Betty told the spy what she had learned. She had a strong memory, and she did not embroider. She simply repeated what she'd been told, word for word. In the same straightforward way, she related the circumstances that had led to this disclosure.

Shelley was immediately excited. "Go right back and get any more stuff that you can," he ordered. "It is going straight to British intelligence."

Betty grasped the opportunity without hesitation. The ambiguity of what she was being asked to do—the tacit instructions to continue to betray her husband and their marriage by sleeping with her source—did not concern her controller. Nor did it bother Betty. She had already decided she would do whatever she had to do, take whatever risks were required. At last she'd found the purpose and excitement she needed to save her own floundering life.

That winter the long, low divan in Kulikowski's apartment became Betty's operational headquarters. In the spring, her mission took her to the grassy banks of the river Vistula. As a bottle of vodka chilled in the lazy water, the couple would make love on a blanket spread across the new fresh grass. And Betty, the resourceful secret agent, would keep her unsuspecting source talking.

"Our meetings were very fruitful," Betty said with a perfunctory candor to Hyde. "I let him make love to me as often as he wanted, since this guaranteed the smooth flow of the political information I needed."

After each of these liaisons, Betty, following the rudimentary tradecraft Shelley had taught her, typed up her conversations with Kulikowski. Then Shelley would rush them off in the diplomatic pouch to London, where they were avidly read.

It was not long before Shelley's impressed superiors sent word that Betty should be officially recruited as an agent. She was not to return to England to join her recuperating husband. Rather, she would stay in Poland, ostensibly waiting for him.

Her new assignment: Betty was ordered to spread her wings, to fly higher in Polish diplomatic and political circles. Kulikowski's usefulness was played out. She was instructed to find new and more important men to captivate. Get them to share their secrets—and, in the name of king and country, do whatever was necessary to win their devotion and their trust.

Betty was also told that she had to keep her job with the intelligence service a secret. Even her husband, an accredited diplomat at the Warsaw embassy, could not be informed. To ensure that she would not have to pester him for spending money as she made her calculating way through the upper reaches of Polish society, London gave her a monthly allowance of twenty pounds; Jack Shelley would be her paymaster.

Without any fuss, she broke off with Kulikowski as instructed. Their affair had been, she would say with cool detachment, "simply a job I had to do."

"My big Polish romance came afterwards," she explained to Hyde. It would be the first of many romances. And of many missions.

Betty was now a spy.

Chapter 7

◆

Y ET EVEN AS BETTY SHARED the circumstances of her recruitment, she knew that this was only part of the story of how she'd found her way into the dangerous business of intelligence. And a small part at that.

Hyde was an authority on Oscar Wilde, and in preparation for their trip Betty had, with a professional's pre-mission diligence, done some homework. That was how she had come across Wilde's complaint that "people have a careless way of talking about a 'born liar,' just as they talk about a born poet." This was utter foolishness, Wilde insisted. "Lying and poetry are arts . . . and they require the most careful study." Betty, who knew a bit at least about lying, agreed. She was also convinced that espionage was no less of an art, and one that had its own long and demanding tutelage.

If she was to understand what had led the burgeoning spy to that weather-beaten golf course in the Warsaw suburbs, she would need to dig deep and recall her own years of "careful study." She would need to call up memories of times and places she had tried long ago to bury. After a lifetime of dissembling, of putting on so many masks, it was as if she was determined to strip away all the inessential versions of her biography and get to the core. She would look at her life for the first time and put the record right at last.

In the meantime, though, Betty had no illusions about the urgency of the task she'd set for herself. Her time was running out. The pain medicine she'd brought from France was no longer sufficient, so she'd asked the front desk at the Shelbourne if they could recommend a dentist. A bothersome toothache, she had casually explained. But the dentist across from Grafton Square had taken one look inside her mouth and, clearly shaken, gravely recommended that she return home without delay. She replied with one of her high-spirited laughs. "Of course I have no intention of doing that," she told him. "At least until I've seen a bit of old Ireland." She might just as well have added, *And completed the mission that brought me here in the first place.*

Her mind was set. She'd churn up the past in her search for clues, and see where it took her. She'd let Hyde, the conscientious researcher, lead her down one trail, while her memories led her down another, more hidden path. To understand the woman she'd grown up to be, she'd first have to reestablish connection with her childhood self, the girl Betty Thorpe had been.

THERE SHE WAS, AT THE tender age of ten, already a covert watcher. It was April 1921, a great occasion in the Thorpe household, a day when no less of a personage than Calvin Coolidge, the vice president of the United States, was coming to dinner, along with his wife.

Hiding on the bedroom landing, flat on her stomach, her head wedged between two of the staircase spindles that ran along the upstairs balcony, she had a perfect view across the entry hall at all the activity fluttering about the dining room. A glistening white cloth from the Canary Islands had been spread across the long table; one maid was fitting jade-green candles into the two ornate candelabrums that rose like sentinels on either end, another was laying the freshly polished silver, and a houseman had come in from the greenhouse with a basket of fresh-cut red and yellow tulips that he would arrange in a forest of crystal vases. And there was her mother, already dressed in a black lace gown, pacing about like a stern commander, shouting out one terse order after another, observing every detail with her penetrating gaze, making sure everything was just so.

Since the family arrived two years earlier from Cuba, where Colonel George Thorpe had been chief of staff of the Second Marine Brigade, and settled into the comfortable house on Woodley Road in the nation's capital, the Thorpes had hosted many lavish dinners, garden parties, and dances. Each night, or so it might have seemed to the neighbors, a procession of cars pulled up to the front door, and the lights inside the big house burned brightly.

The 1920s had just come roaring in, but Cora Thorpe was not another hostess caught up in the high jinks; her bluestocking soul was firmly intact. Hers was a pragmatic agenda, one sparked by pure ambition. Entertaining, Betty's mother believed, was essential if the Thorpes, newcomers to Washington, were to meet the right families, be admitted into the best clubs and schools, and find themselves welcomed into the upper echelons of what passed for society in this very hierarchical and strait-laced southern city. Beside, she had the money.

CORA'S FATHER HAD LIVED A real-life Horatio Alger tale. He had arrived penniless from Canada to take a clerk's job in Minnesota; married the boss's daughter; and then shrewdly parlayed that connection into a small empire of lucrative businesses, a bank presidency, and ultimately his election as a state senator.

As his fortune grew and grew, his beloved only daughter developed into a blunt, formidable, and already matronly young woman. Her looks were the sort that family friends would politely call handsome. But there was no embarrassed hemming and hawing over her intelligence. It was universally agreed that Cora was her father's astute daughter; "That girl has a good head on her shoulders," people around town had a habit of observing. In an era when many young midwestern women from good families would aspire to a husband rather than a college degree, Cora not only earned her BA from the University of Michigan but went on to do graduate work, taking courses in literature at Columbia, the Sorbonne, and the University of Munich.

The local Minneapolis boys, though, seemed intimidated by this brainy, apparently mirthless heiress. As she approached thirty, Cora was resigned to her spinsterhood. Then she met a gung-ho young marine lieutenant, a poor farmer's son but also both a hero and a scholar.

Betty's father, George Cyrus Thorpe, photographed c. 1914 as a major in the United States Marine Corps.

George Thorpe had served in the Spanish-American War, soldiered with the American expedition in Syria, fought in the Philippines, commanded a marine expedition to Abyssinia, suffered battle wounds on two occasions—and, not slowing down during extended leaves from active duty, had earned both bachelor and law degrees from New York University and a master's from Brown. After a whirlwind courtship, George and Cora married in 1908. Betty—christened Amy Elizabeth, but neither of those names stuck—was born two years later.

Not long after Betty's birth, George was appointed commander of the naval prison at Portsmouth, Maine. Six all-too-quiet years in the pine woods and deep snows followed. Cora, itching for something more consequential, grumbled that it was like being stuck again in Minneapolis, only smaller. But she persevered and, as she told friends, found a measure of contentment in being a wife and running a home. And young Betty soon had company, a sister, Jane, and a brother, George Junior.

Then in 1917 George was summoned to lead the Second Marine Brigade as they chased bandits through the Cuban countryside. It was combat duty, but Cora couldn't wait to get out of the Maine woods and head to sunny and exotic Cuba to join her husband. She set up house with the three kids on the Guantanamo Bay Naval Base, and stayed there even after George was transferred to South America.

Finally in 1919, to Cora's delight, George was posted to the General Staff College in Washington. And Cora's time had come at last to build the sort of busy, gregarious social life she'd always coveted. One of the first things she did when she settled into the house on Woodley Road was to order a copy of the *Social Register*. "The Good Book," many impious Washington matrons called it, and Cora with no less deference placed the black-covered volume by the hall phone. Inside, she solemnly confided to Betty, were the names, addresses, and phone numbers of all the people she'd ever need to know. In the days that followed, a curious young Betty would thumb through the book, trying to make sense of all the puzzling abbreviations for schools, colleges, and clubs in the alphabetized listing for each family's name. It was her first attempt at cracking an operational code.

And soon a flurry of parties began to brighten the house. Her husband's fellow officers at the Staff College could not have mapped out a more careful campaign. Each fête lifted Cora another rung higher up the Washington social ladder. When her "red dinner"— red roses, red candles, even a fiery red tablecloth—for Maud Howe Elliot, the Newport grande dame who had won a Pulitzer for her biography of Julia Ward Howe, brought three princesses to the house and, no less a tangible sign of success, was reported with a deferential awe in the Washington papers, Cora was beside herself with delight. She thought she'd reached the summit of all her aspirations. But this was before the vice president and his wife accepted the invitation to dinner.

The Harding administration had taken over the reins of government just two months earlier, and the evening with the new vice president at her table, Cora must have hoped, would be her inauguration too. She'd be anointed the town's ruling hostess—if it all went well.

She devoted weeks to planning the evening. Everything from the menu to the wines to the flowers was mulled, debated, and then reconsidered once again before the final instructions were given to the household staff. The days leading up to the great event were a time of high anxiety for the Thorpe family.

THEN THE AUSPICIOUS EVENING ARRIVED. There was Colonel Thorpe in his freshly pressed dress uniform, the creases in his trousers as sharp as the saber that hung by his side, medals and ribbons decorating his chest, standing in the entry hall at martial attention. He usually wasn't too enthusiastic about Cora's soirées or her feverish social ambitions, but that night was different: the vice president was coming to *his* home. Yet his sense of the occasion was nothing compared to his wife's. Although she wore black lace, Cora stood ramrod-straight too; she too might have been an anxious soldier waiting for the bugler to blow "charge."

Once the Coolidges arrived and the initial greetings were exchanged with all the necessary formality, the Thorpes began to relax—at least a bit.

The dinner proceeded without a hitch. The food was delicious, the wines were memorable, and the conversation around the table kept moving happily along. By the time dessert was served, Cora was convinced that she'd pulled it off. The evening had been a great success.

Carried along by her triumphant mood, when the festivities moved from the dining room to the front parlor, she suddenly decided that her oldest child should be brought downstairs to shake hands with the vice president. It would be an event Betty would surely remember all her life, something she could tell her children.

A maid fetched Betty. The ten-year-old, with her blond curls and those burning green eyes, looked adorable in the party dress the family dressmaker had sewn for special occasions. With her voice raised to a fawning pitch that must have struck even a ten-year-old as absurdly obsequious, Cora introduced the honored guests.

Betty found herself staring into the black eyes of Mrs. Coolidge.

For some reason as yet unknown to her, her thoughts still inchoate, she hesitated. Her mother prompted, "Come now, Betty." At last Betty executed a much-practiced perfect curtsy.

The young girl turned to the vice president. As if soliciting her vote, the vice president stuck out his hand. Betty stared at the short man with the bright red hair, and then at his beefy, outstretched hand. Once again she hesitated. And again Cora coaxed, "Please, dear."

Betty tried. But this time she couldn't do it. She just couldn't find the will. In a gesture that was more instinct than a reasoned decision, she turned her back on the vice president, on her mother, on the entire evening and all the other deliberately orchestrated evenings that had led inexorably up to this moment. And she ran from the room.

Four years older and many more years wiser, she gave a hint about the early lesson learned on that rebellious night, and which she had incorporated into all her rebellious nights ever after. She described in her diary—the incipient secret agent using flawless French as a rudimentary code—a mind-set that would have become a deeply ingrained article of her operational faith. With a raw contempt, the nearly fourteen-year-old Betty observed, "Life is a game where one plays one's role—where one always hides the true emotions."

Only she didn't want any part of that kind of life at all. She wasn't willing to shake the hand of anyone—even the vice president of the United States—unless he caught her fancy.

So Betty had kept running—literally. She was by nature a restless and solitary girl. And now when she looked back at the history of her formative years, she understood that the cultivation of those traits was her next complicated lesson in preparation for the secret life.

Most children find a best friend, even if it has to be an imaginary one. Betty had neither the instincts nor the desire for any sort of companionship, real or invented. There was no pal, no playmate, no girlie confidante. Instead, Betty enjoyed her aloneness. She was content living in her own mind, making her own way. Now, many years later, searching for answers, she saw with a newfound insightfulness that many of her earliest memories were "built around aloneness."

After all, didn't the family often tell the story about how even as a four-year-old in Maine, she would escape to the deep pine forest that rose beyond their house? And how the local policeman, a man who knew those woods, would need to be summoned time after time to hunt through the forest to find her? There she'd be taking refuge—her first safe house—in the nook of a tree, hiding, contentedly listening to the wind and the bird sounds.

An eleven-year-old Betty would confess to her diary: "I am wondering what it would be like to live alone, alone in a beautiful place, only to be free! How wicked it must seem to talk in this fashion. I suppose some might think me a very unappreciative, disagreeable little girl. But I love to wonder and have my 'queer feelings' and 'lonely, deserted emotions.' . . . I love the queer sensation loneliness brings me."

And when she wasn't going off alone, she was running. And as her moods fluctuated, each competed for the hegemony of her heart. Either Betty had to lay low and take refuge from the world, or she had to run from it. Unchained, she'd rush pell-mell toward anything new, to whatever seemed to be rich with promise.

"Always in me, even when I was a child," she told Hyde as she silently filed away another clue, "were two great passions: one to be alone, the other for excitement. . . . Any kind of excitement— even fear. . . . Anything to assuage my terrible restlessness and the excruciating sense of pressure . . . that was only released in action, in doing, in exhaustion."

Betty's vast, insatiable restlessness was not just a metaphor. It was real. She had no control: when a notion struck, she charged ahead. It had always been that tumultuous, often perilous way.

Betty, age twelve.

"When we were very young and running races," she told Hyde, remembering with equal measures of amusement and bewilderment the many contests that took place between the siblings, "I always ran past the finish line and ran and ran until I dropped half strangled when my endurance finally gave out. I just couldn't stop before that. There was no point in running unless I ran practically to death. My brother George used to go mad. 'You're crazy, you're crazy!' he'd shout as I raced by. 'Why don't you *stop!*' "

Betty never answered George back then. But now, if he asked, she could tell him it was all part of her training. She was the novice field agent learning her first hard lessons about living life on her own, discovering how to survive behind the lines, deep in enemy territory.

Chapter 8

◆

A NEW BRIGHT DAY IN DUBLIN, and what better way to welcome it than with a full Irish breakfast? That was Hyde's way of thinking. After the long night that had begun downstairs in the Horseshoe Bar and ended in the soft double bed next to Betty, he'd awoken with a roaring appetite. He was on the house phone to room service first thing.

Once the food arrived, enough bangers, bacon, beans, and fried eggs to feed a regiment, Hyde dug right in. Betty, without explanation, stuck to coffee and lit the first of her Capstans. She kept a guarded silence as she watched him feast.

If Hyde noticed her tension, if he felt the air in the room growing tighter and tighter, he chose to ignore it. Today's plan, he explained instead between mouthfuls, was to check out of the Shelbourne and head off on the road. He'd reserved a rental car and planned an itinerary. He would drive and ask questions. She would look out the window at the green hills and answer. "That suit you?" he asked Betty. "I drive, and ask the questions. You look out the window at the green hills, and answer."

At once Betty rallied. Whether her earlier stony mood had been due to the constant pain coursing through her jaw or the reminiscences Hyde's barroom interrogation had provoked was now irrelevant; besides, she was always mercurial. Suddenly she was elated. The prospect of at last seeing the countryside that she had so vividly toured in her imagination was the elixir she needed. Once again reconciled to her mission, she apparently decided this would be as good a time as any to present the gift she'd brought from Castelnou.

She retrieved the book from her valise, considered for a moment, then wrote an inscription on the inside cover: "It is now more than ever important that we understand each other always and about everything." She signed C, and with a quick flourish underlined the letter.

Betty handed Hyde the book without a word, but he suspected it was something precious.

Yet he was puzzled. He could not gauge its significance. The title—*Fioretta: A Tale of Italy*—left him stumped. It sounded operatic, but why would Betty—or he, for that matter—be interested in some melodramatic Italian folktale? The cover art—a primitive, rather childlike drawing of a young dark-haired woman in peasant dress—offered no further clue.

Then he saw it, at the bottom of the cover in small block letters: "By Betty Thorpe."

With genuine surprise, he asked if she was the author.

Betty's response was embarrassed, effusive and self-deprecating at the same time. "Remember that restlessness I was telling you about?" she began. "The same drive impelled me to write a novel when I was not yet eleven. It was set in Naples, where I'd never been of course. It's madly romantic and the plot was hideously clichéd—but for a girl still eleven . . ." She trailed off. "I doubt if I could do as well now."

He wondered where she got the idea, how she found the discipline.

Betty's explanation was brisk, as if an eleven-year-old girl writing a book and getting it published was the most natural thing in the world. The peripatetic Thorpe family had moved to Hawaii; her father had assumed command of the Pearl Harbor marine detachment. She had a puppy and a pony to ride, and there were lots of sunny days spent splashing through the surf at Waikiki. But her father would come home from the base and spend evenings at his desk writing on maritime legal issues, and her mother was publishing nostalgic accounts of her European travels before her marriage in the local papers. If her parents could be writers, Betty, always competitive, decided she would be one too.

The cover of Fioretta: A Tale of Italy, *which Betty wrote at age eleven.*

As for the story in *Fioretta*, it just popped into her imagination. Ideas, she explained with a brusqueness that was almost an apology, were always floating through her head. Friendless, she had found a companionship of sorts by embroidering these fantasies.

Once the story about a young girl in Naples began to take shape in her mind, she wasn't deterred because she'd never visited the city, or even been to Italy. At eleven, she was already resourceful. The library at the Pearl Harbor base had a shelf full of guidebooks on Italy. She spent several days reading, getting a sense—an admittedly broad one, she conceded—of the country until finally, driven by blind faith, she sat down to write.

Hyde had more questions, but Betty brushed them off. We need to pack, she ordered. Which was true, but she was also done talking about the book. One clue, and one clue only, is all you get.

The inscription was signed with her work name. Could she have been more direct? Besides, it was scrawled across the inside cover, impossible to miss, shouting out to him like one of the flash messages they'd get from headquarters during the war: Urgent! Unbutton Immediately! Could she have been more beseeching? How could a fellow professional read this handwritten note and not understand that the thin volume she'd given him was what was known in the jargon of their past life as an "analogue"? She was handing him the key that would unravel all the previously encoded intelligence.

Here was where everything began.

BACK AT CASTELNOU, AS BETTY prepared for this final mission, she had absently picked up the book. She had not looked at it for years, decades in fact. But once she started to read *Fioretta*, she could not put it down. Now, trying to get some understanding of the life she had lived, Betty to her amazement found that this little volume was prescient, a guidebook filled with clues written by an eleven-year-old about the woman she would grow up to be. When she read it this way, it was a revelation.

She might as well, she told herself, have assembled all the evidence lurking in *Fioretta* into a dossier like the kind the Service's vetters compiled and handed it to Hyde. You want to tell the story of my life? Well, consider—

"Little Fioretta"—as the eleven-year-old wrote in her opening sentence, trading in one reality for something that felt even realer—"sat at the large painted window waiting for her father.

"Here she lived with him, knowing no other love than his and no other parent. Even though her father's love was not tenderly expressed at times, it meant a great deal for Fioretta."

That's me, all right, Betty now understood, and clearly hoped Hyde would grasp it too. I'm the girl who had only one parent. Cora had been dead to her for decades and decades. And there had been no period of bereavement. Instead, Betty had flamboyantly danced on her mother's grave, turned her back on all the pretense and snooty conventionality that reigned over her mother's world. Free of guilt, or so she'd thought at the time and would continue to believe for years to come, a reborn Betty had entered the world.

This motherless child couldn't rest until she'd gone off and had her mad loves and her earnest, passionate affairs. Unencumbered, she charged into reckless adventures and signed on for vital, daring missions. It was as if she was led by a guiding maxim: if Cora would've thought it wrong, then it had to be right. And its corollary: love is action, not thought. A life lived by those precepts had given Betty a lot of moral leeway.

And who had taken her mother's place in her heart? It had been clear to the young author, and now the old spy finally got the message too—her adored dad. Like Fioretta at the window, Betty had measured out her days searching for the comforting warmth of paternal affection. It was no accident that the parade of men who had marched through Betty's real-life tale were routinely old enough to be her father. Take, for example, the Italian admiral she'd targeted. Or the diplomat in Valencia she'd run off with. Or the dashing patron in Chile. Or her first husband, Arthur Pack. Or, for that matter, her present husband, Charles Brousse.

Then—exhibit 2 in her dossier—there was the improbable quest that little Fioretta had embarked on. The girl's beloved father was blind and penniless, so Fioretta, barely a teenager, decided to find a way to make the money that would save him. The family's predicament, by any rational calculation, was impossible. "But," as the young Betty confidently wrote, "Fioretta had a nimble brain, and it did not take her long to find a way." Against all odds, Fioretta saved the day!

Now the adult Betty, looking back at this scenario, surely saw that it had anticipated the operational pattern for her professional life. Hadn't there always been some beloved silver-haired father figure—be it Sir William Stephenson, the head of the British spy network in the western hemisphere, or Colonel Ellery Huntington of the OSS, the American wartime intelligence unit—constantly in a jam, challenging her with impossible missions? And didn't Betty, another operative with "a nimble brain," somehow find a way time after time to pull off unlikely successes?

Fioretta had set out to earn money by singing in the streets. She had "a voice like a nightingale's," and her songs never failed to enchant the audiences that gathered around. But it was apparent to even the young Betty that Fioretta's voice was only a part of the strategy, and that the girl's other natural attributes were also put into play. "More than one pair of admiring eyes," the eleven-year-old admitted to her readers, "turned in her direction." There was "a beautiful, wistful charm about her."

Although she didn't sing, Betty too had never hesitated to

employ her fair share of "wistful charm" as she tackled her missions. "I was able to make certain men fall in love with me," she recalled matter-of-factly to Hyde. "Or think they had at any rate, and in exchange for my 'love' they gave me information." It had always struck Betty as the most natural of strategies, just one more way, as she put it, "to win the war." Now she realized that her cavalier attitude toward sleeping with the enemy had deep roots: little Fioretta had helped set the stage for these clandestine encounters.

And Hyde should take a close look at Signor Scarlatti, Betty told herself as she checked off another exhibit lifted from the pages of the book. A renowned impresario and teacher, Scarlatti had taken Fioretta under his wing and, after a demanding tutelage, transformed her into a celebrated soprano. This too was a harbinger of things to come. How could anyone not notice that he was the model for all the handlers who would supervise her in the field, the precursor to all the forbearing, rueful, demanding controllers who would guide her missions?

But if anyone doubted the book's uncanny predictive power, how it had unconsciously helped to shape the course of her life, Betty was convinced they only needed to read the description of Fioretta's home.

"It was queer, with high walls, covered with ivy on top of which the road wound, towering in many curves. The walls were moulding and crumbling to pieces, while clinging vines tangled themselves with the damp moss growing in the crevasses . . . which made the place look very old and romantic."

The eleven-year-old author had imagined a crumbling castle just like the one the adult Betty had moved into, and then set about renovating with a painstaking devotion.

Hyde, Betty might have challenged as she closed the dossier she'd assembled in her mind, you want to tell my story? You want to understand how it all came to be? Well, a lot of the answers are in this slim book.

After rereading it, Betty no doubt felt like shouting, Here's what I've come to learn: the poet had it right! The child was indeed father to the man. Only this precocious child fathered a spy.

AND NO SOONER HAD THE book, which, thanks to her dutiful father's generosity, been privately printed with colorful illustrations by Don Blanding, than Betty's tutelage took a new turn. Colonel Thorpe, after twenty-four years as a marine, resigned his commission and, their year in Hawaii at an end, led his family off on a grand tour of Europe. Paris, Nice, Monte Carlo, Rome, and— Betty's fondest wish come true—days in the much-imagined Naples. Next, while the rest of the family settled in Paris, Betty was sent off to perfect her French and her manners in a school for girls housed in a grand chateau perched over Lake Geneva.

All the exotic travel, which Betty dutifully recorded in her diary, helped to sharpen her watcher's eye. And no less practical a talent for the would-be agent, she was soon speaking French like a native, or at least one who lived in the tony sixteenth arrondissement.

But when the year abroad was over and the family returned to Washington, the burgeoning spy's most valuable, perhaps even her defining, quality started to beckon her attention. Betty was fourteen, and with a deliberate if not unseemly haste, she was ready to put her childhood behind her and become a woman.

Chapter 9

◆

WITH THE COOL OBJECTIVITY OF a scientist watching a strange new culture gradually take shape in a petri dish, young Betty noted the signs in her diary. Slowly they grew stronger and stronger, each another intimation of the woman she was becoming. At first the adolescent was uncertain where her new thoughts, her new feelings, were leading. In time, though, Betty had no choice but to recognize the power that was now shaping and defining her. And when the teenage girl finally knew, she relished it.

A lifetime later, it was with the hope of dusting off some more clues for Hyde that the older Betty had picked up this childhood diary. She read it with the fascination of an archaeologist poring over some ancient text. Now, so experienced, she must have had no trouble seeing the hints, the telltale trail starting to take shape. Still, it had begun innocently enough; she clearly wanted Hyde to understand that, and not judge too harshly the young girl she had been.

A DANCE CLASS IN WASHINGTON. Reading the diary entry, Betty no doubt could once again visualize the boys in their blazers and rep ties, all awkward, pimply, and nervous. And the girls in their party dresses and crinolines, white gloves on their dainty hands, giggling to one another as they eyed their prospective partners.

"Today I went to dancing school. I said to the boy I was dancing with, 'Je vous aime beaucoup.' I did not know he understood French."

Her first approach, and her first embarrassment. And a crucial lesson for the incipient spy: never assume your code can't be cracked. But she was undeterred, and her next encounter was more important by far than her own preadolescent stirrings.

There was Betty, a pretty ten-year-old aboard the steamship taking the Thorpe family across a calm, sun-kissed Pacific to Hawaii.

"A Mr. Wei from Boston," she wrote in her diary, "was extremely courteous. . . . He was educated in America and was a lieutenant in the Chinese army.

" 'Why do you wear blue socks, Mr. Wei?'

" 'Because I am blue,' was the answer.

" 'I don't think you are blue. You seem rather lively,' I quietly put in.

" 'Ah, that's because you're with me,' he laughed."

And Betty, although at ten she didn't quite know what to make of it, couldn't help noticing that the army lieutenant, always courteous, always attentive, doggedly trailed her throughout the weeklong voyage.

Then, after the Thorpes' time in Hawaii and their year in Europe was over, the family returned to the States, and Betty was packed off to boarding school in Wellesley, Massachusetts. Here she found further proof of the strong spell she cast over older men. Betty was a fourteen-year-old at Dana Hall School, and yet for reasons that left her rather puzzled, a fortyish naval officer assigned to the Italian embassy in Washington would regularly fly to Boston and then drive miles north to see her.

He first met Betty at a reception the Italian ambassador gave to honor the prodigy who had written *Fioretta*, and was charmed. After that delightful encounter, it seemed quite reasonable to the commander to travel frequently to Wellesley, as the adolescent without a trace of guile told her diary, "for tea and conversation."

"It was always," Betty would remember as she tried to fit this piece into the complicated puzzle of her life, "three orders of cinnamon toast for me, and our conversation was very very profound: love, philosophy, destiny. You know, all very juvenile. He took a rather sweet, paternal interest in me."

Or at least, that was what the young girl had thought at the time. But looking back on it now, Betty couldn't help but acknowledge what, however unarticulated, was also clearly going on. More amused than critical, she conceded to Hyde, "I think his interest had a sentimental side to it as well. He was very taken with my blonde curls and used to call me his Golden Girl."

It wasn't long, though, before her own heart was taking the initiative, racing with its own stirrings. Betty would always remember, she now shared with Hyde, one wonderfully wishful moment. It was her first conscious seduction, and even if it was unconsummated, at least in any orthodox way, it was her initiation into a previously unfamiliar joy.

It was the last day of Easter vacation. Thirteen-year-old Betty, already dreading the return trip to Dana Hall, was morosely spending it at the Chevy Chase country club outside Washington. Leaving her family in the dining room, she wandered aimlessly about. For no particular reason, a tennis match caught her eye. It was a fast match, well played, and a boisterous group of young diplomats—Spaniards, she judged—were cheering the players on.

The ball flew back and forth over the net, but she had abandoned any pretense of following the volleys. From her first look, she was transfixed by one of the players. He was tall and dark, and when he swung his racket a lock of jet-black hair fell over his forehead and the hard muscles in his arms, chest, and legs coiled. Betty stared at him openly, willing him to notice her. It never occurred to her to be discreet.

When the match ended, the players gathered their rackets and walked off the court toward their scrum of friends. Betty remained standing outside the fence, still silently begging him to notice her, still fixing him with a look, an intensity, she had not known she possessed. Only it went unacknowledged.

Or so she had thought. For just as he was about to head off to the clubhouse, he turned directly toward Betty, locked eyes with her, and flashed a dazzling smile. Then in a gesture that would be forever stored in her romantic heart, he offered a deep, gallant bow. A moment later he was gone, walking off with his crowd of boisterous friends.

He never said a word, but none was necessary. Betty no longer had any doubts about her power—or what she could do with it.

"MY LOOKS ARE BETTER THAN I hoped," Betty, not boasting, simply giving testimony as she might in a court, told her diary. "God was kind in that at least."

With similar objectivity, the teenager had already worked out a careful, self-aware strategy for dealing with the opposite sex, one that was as practical as it was shamelessly manipulative.

"I have strong emotions. I have too much love. I love and love with all my heart, only I have to *appear* cool. The men are the ones who change. . . . I know that if I love too much I risk losing their respect and admiration for they only seek the joy of telling of a conquest."

Having figured this all out, fourteen-year-old Betty decided she was ready to take her first lover. That summer the family had settled into an oceanfront cottage in Newport, and she might have lost her virginity to any of several boys hanging around the yacht club. But trying to wish herself in love, she had chosen, she confided to Hyde, "an old gentleman of twenty-one, who belonged to a well-known family whose names often appear in the *Social*

Register. . . . He was unashamedly poetic and passionate—which was a great change from the St. Paul's and St. George's boys. We were both lonely and we met only twice before the 'love affair' was over."

Although brief, the liaison was empowering. The Betty who returned to boarding school that fall was more confident, more self-assured. She had tapped into a new realm of experience, the "Grand Passion," she called it, and it had offered a way to assuage all her "terrible restlessness." Now desire drove her. And restraint seemed pointless.

"So many things have happened to me," Betty, now fifteen, confessed to her diary after eight months of silence. "So many affairs of the heart, so many thoughts, ideas and changes in me that I have sometimes thought I was a different person and have not always been in charge of my emotions. I have not written every day because I know I can never relive the feelings and experiences."

And what were these unexplainable feelings, these indescribable experiences?

"The greatest joy," she would later explain, taking a stab at putting her turbulent emotions into words, "is a man and a woman together. Making love allows a discharge of all those private innermost thoughts that have accumulated. In this flood, everything is released."

In her heart a woman, Betty was still required to wear her boarding-school jumper. But she didn't mind. She always liked a disguise.

"THE BUDS" WAS HOW THE Washington society writers referred to the city's annual crop of debutantes. It was a reporter's shorthand that, while a bit snarky, also acknowledged something more respectful: these well-bred young ladies were poised to open up to the full bloom of their womanhood. And when they blossomed, they would go off and marry no less well-bred husbands and assume their preordained places in the carefully manicured garden that was Washington society.

Just days before she turned nineteen, in November 1929, Betty had her debut with a bouquet of other young "buds" at a *thé dansant* orchestrated by Cora at the grand house on Woodley Road. The Great Depression was tightly squeezing most of the country, but the Thorpes and their jolly circle of well-heeled friends were largely unaffected. The next day the *Washington Post* oohed and aahed at all the pretty dresses and dutifully listed the names of the distinguished families in attendance. With this send-off, Betty, golden hair and luminous green eyes, so poised, so intelligent, the offspring of such solid, respectable stock, had her social future assured.

Betty, aged 18, 1929.

To Cora's great delight, the parlor mantel was soon crowded with a row of invitations inviting Miss Elizabeth Amy Thorpe to a whirlwind of dinners, dances, and teas. Betty would go, and she inevitably received a good deal of attention from the intrigued young men. But it soon became apparent that she was not another of the tentative and precious "buds."

"I'd come to dinner," recalled one would-be suitor, still a bit baffled after all these years by the complex spell Betty cast, "and inevitably I'd find her surrounded by a complete circle of boys. Certainly she was a beautiful girl, but the fact is she was far more reserved than most of them. She had dignity. . . . You always felt that coming-out parties and hen-lunches weren't really her cup of tea. She was fully grown up at nineteen, far more adult than we were."

Another man, one of the young diplomats who had spent some time making the rounds on the Washington social circuit with this same glittering crowd, was also struck by how different Betty was from the other girls. He was certain he had her pegged:

"There was always about her that look of challenge, something that seemed to be permanently daring one to do something with her—whether it was to play polo, go on a midnight picnic, or just leap into bed with her."

In the course of her debutante year, many young men accepted her tacit challenge. There was a sort of mayhem in Betty's restlessness. She didn't have affairs; she had encounters. And now, looking back at that uncentered time, her memory grew selective; she had forgotten more boys than she remembered. Nevertheless, she conceded to Hyde, the young diplomat didn't have her wrong. She had leaped into any number of beds.

But somewhere in the rush of Christmas parties, she met a man and, to her own surprise, gave him her heart too. Bursting with this new, all-consuming passion, she wrote in her diary,

I think I cannot quite understand
The depths of wanting unfulfilled desire,
And hating you to touch my hand
When embers die where there once was fire.

It was the sort of ardent, romantic musings many a young woman would scrawl late at night in her diary. Yet for Betty it was a lot more. The words were heartfelt. They commandeered her world: she refused to let any desire go unfulfilled.

Soon, however, Betty discovered that there could be consequences for such lack of restraint. And in the aftermath of this unsettling realization, she swiftly made the decision to launch her first fully conscious clandestine mission. Intuitively, she understood that it would by necessity need to be what those in her future profession called a "false flag" operation: her target could never know the truth, or he would certainly never cooperate.

The tactical problem: Betty was pregnant, and she was not sure who was the child's father.

Chapter 10

◆

G RAVELY, BETTY UNDRESSED AND CLIMBED naked into the bed. She pulled the duvet up to her neck, only to decide it might be more effective to lower it a bit. Her skin was soft and smooth, and she could see no reason to hide it. Then, as she related to Hyde, she "lay back and waited."

It was, she went on, the second night of a weekend house party deep in the Virginia hunt country, a green and horsey bit of aristocratic paradise an hour or so drive beyond the Washington city limits. The house, as she remembered it, was columned and big, and an allée of ancient oaks lined the approach. A patchwork of open fields stretched in all directions. And it was here that Betty, after much thought, had chosen to launch her operation.

In any mission, timing is all. Even as a novice Betty apparently understood this, and from the day she realized she was pregnant, she'd been searching for her moment. But the days anxiously flew past, and still no opportunity seemed to offer itself. Worse, the longer she waited, the more she began to doubt herself. Was she hesitating because she didn't have the nerve?

Perhaps she tried telling herself that she was being prudent, that she was merely trying to identify the course that held the greatest promise of success. But when she looked in the mirror after climbing out of the bath, she had to know it would not be too long before she was not the only one to notice how her figure was ripening. And then all would be lost. It would be too late.

It was in the midst of this troubled interlude that Betty heard about the weekend one of the girls was planning at her family's stately place in Middleburg, Virginia. After she received her invitation, without trying too hard she discovered that he had been invited too. At once all her vacillation ended, and in its place a sudden excitement kindled. The decision to move forward had been made at last.

On the chosen weekend, she proceeded carefully; her tradecraft was very deliberate. The first day she was flirtatious, but not ostentatiously so. She wanted him to get comfortable with the idea of her. When she brushed carelessly against him, she hoped it would send his thoughts racing. But she did not want him to grow too confident.

On the second day, she spent a good deal of time over pre-dinner cocktails talking intently to another boy, laughing loudly at his jokes. At dinner, as luck had it, he was on the opposite side of the table; it would have been easy to shoot him an occasional glance. But she refused to bestow that blessing. Instead Betty talked with great animation to the man on her right; and then with even greater liveliness to the man on her left. Betty never looked at her target, but all the time she hoped he was watching her, and growing envious as she seemed more and more remote. She wanted him to tingle with disappointment.

After dinner, while the others played bridge or sat with their brandies in front of the fire, Betty excused herself. She said she was exhausted and wanted to lie down.

That morning she had risen at first light, hours before breakfast, and begun her surveillance. Her observation post was the doorway of her room; from this vantage, she could survey the entire corridor. If another early riser emerged from one of the bedrooms, she had her cover story ready: Oh, I just forgot my comb. You go ahead. I'll be down in a minute. Then she'd hurry back into her room until the houseguest made his way down the stairs to the dining room. When she was certain he was out of sight, she resumed her post.

Still, there were several close calls; at one point—the awkward moment still vivid in her mind—two very confident young men spotted Betty and pestered her to join them for breakfast. It took all her tact to turn them down without causing a scene. Then finally she saw him leave his room.

His gait as he headed downstairs was brisk, as usual; he was a man who seemed perpetually to be hurrying off on some important affair of state. Betty now had the crucial intelligence: she knew which of the many doors that lined the corridor was his.

By the time dinner was over that evening, it had been a long day's patient wait. She'd done what was necessary to coax her plan along. Now she launched her mission.

She headed directly to his room and put her hand on the door-knob, only to be seized by what must have been a moment's panic. What if it was locked? That possibility hadn't occurred to her, and the would-be secret agent filed away another early lesson: all contingencies must be considered before the plunge is taken.

But this evening luck was once more with her, and the door opened easily to her touch. Her clothes flew off, and she hopped into his bed. Alone with her thoughts in the big bed, she willed him to come soon.

There is no record of what Arthur Pack said when he entered his room. Or, for that matter, what explanation Betty offered. But of course none was necessary. All that Arthur needed to know was that the naked woman in his bed was determined to give him a night to remember.

Two weeks later, while they were riding on horseback through the woods of Washington's Rock Creek Park, Arthur proposed to Betty. She had enough ingenuity to act surprised, but she was also shrewd enough not to hesitate. She accepted immediately.

"Suddenly I was engaged," Betty would tell Hyde, as if still finding it hard to believe. "I don't think for a minute he was in love with me. I know I wasn't in love with him. It was as if it was all happening and I had nothing to do with it. I went along with the events like a sleepwalker."

Arthur, too, would look back on their courtship with bewilderment.

"There she was in my bed," he told his sister. "What could I do?"

INTERNATIONAL ENGAGEMENT

MISS BETTY THORPE.
Daughter of Col. and Mrs. George C. Thorpe, who today announce her engagement to Mr. Arthur Pack, commercial secretary of the British embassy, the wedding to take place in the Spring.
—Underwood Pho

Betty and Arthur's official engagement announcement

THE DISMAL TRUTH, THOUGH, WAS that Betty was not the only one running a deception. And not for the last time, she'd been fooled too.

Whether consciously or not, she had selected Arthur Pack because, in broad but still resonating ways, he reminded Betty of her adored father. Age was one factor; Arthur was more than twice as

old as the nineteen-year-old girl. And the nearly twenty years between them might as well have been several lifetimes; Arthur had
come of age being gassed on the frontlines of a war.

Still, the chasm of years between them was probably only a
small factor in Betty's mental equation. What she saw in Arthur, as
she would explain in the letters she wrote after their marriage, was
the sort of substantial fellow who, with his rock-hard jaw, military
mustache, and rigid backbone, belonged, at least in her mind, to an
idealized class of men of means and breeding who chose a career
in public service. This was how she saw her father, the brave gentleman soldier. She was convinced that Arthur Pack, former army
officer now serving with His Majesty's Foreign Office, was another
hero cut from the same bolt of pin-striped cloth.

But Arthur was not who he appeared to be. Scratch the diligently polished brass surface, and the core was solid lead. Each day
he put on his artful disguise and hoped no one would see through it.

His people, as he referred to them, were not nearly as grand
as he worked so hard to convey. He had grown up in a council
flat outside London, the son of working-class folk. His education
stopped at grammar school. Yet he had found the confidence to
take the civil service exam and, no less of an accomplishment, had
the intellect to pass the demanding test. His reward—an appointment as a clerk in the General Post Office.

His future prospects were limited. In the British civil service,
grammar-school lads were routinely dismissed with a sneer; the
path to success was paved with family connections and the im-
primatur of an Oxbridge degree. After a year of striving, Arthur
became an officer of His Majesty's Custom and Excise. It was a
promotion that was as menial as it was dull.

The war gave Arthur another chance, but he paid a high price
for his new opportunities. He joined the Civil Service Rifles
and was sent straight off to France. After a rough year in the

trenches, he'd earned an officer's commission and been gassed more times than he could remember. His lungs finally collapsed. Diagnosed with double pneumonia, he was dispatched home on medical leave.

Arthur had suffered permanent damage, but he was rewarded with a promotion to captain. Then, despite a fitful recovery, he was shipped off to the States as a machine gun instructor to help prepare the newly mobilized US army for the war in Europe. When his regiment went to France, Captain Pack traveled with them, serving once again on the frontlines.

Arthur Pack during his stint as a United States
Infantry machine gun instructor, 1917.

At the end of the war, Arthur presented this new version of himself to the Foreign Service examiners, and now, as an officer and a gentleman, he was accepted into their rarefied ranks. But he quickly found out that in the class-conscious corridors of diplomatic power, his chances for advancement were still meager. He complained bitterly to his sister that grammar-school boys, no matter how hard they tried, had as much chance of working their way up in the Foreign Office as the proverbial camel's being squeezed through the needle's eye.

Then in 1925 he received a posting as acting commercial secretary to the embassy in Washington, DC. It was a junior post, and a lowly one for someone whose service file was filled with five years of enthusiastic evaluations, but Arthur was elated. Like so many Englishmen who come to America, he was convinced that an ocean away from his humble origins, he could reinvent himself in the image to which he had always aspired.

And he pulled it off. He was Capt. Arthur Pack, ret., with both a staunch military bearing and an impressive war record to reinforce his rank. His position in the embassy was vague enough to sound, to the uninitiated at least, like something of consequence. He had worked hard on his accent, and to American ears it sounded sufficiently plummy; no one would ever have guessed that he'd grown up in a council flat. And he spent every penny of his thousand-pound salary, and then borrowed more, to convince people he was a proper Savile Row English gentleman.

The American hostesses loved him. Whenever a spare man was needed, Arthur Pack, the very eligible British bachelor, was invited. This was the prize catch Betty thought she was seducing.

And Arthur, what did he see in Betty beyond her good looks and sexual energy? Of course either might have been reason enough for many men to propose marriage. Arthur, however, was a practical, very disciplined individual, and passionate excesses were not part of his nature.

But he was ambitious. In return for his proposal, he would be entering a union with a woman who would bestow on him all that he had so long coveted—wealth, a good family name, and an easy social grace. A marriage to Betty Thorpe would allow him to leave his past irrevocably behind.

As things worked out, neither of them got what they had expected.

"WASHINGTON DEBUTANTE TO WED BRITISH DIPLOMAT," read the prominent headline in the *Washington Post* society page. The wedding, the article reported, would be held that summer.

But it was only two hasty months later, on April 29, 1930, for reasons that the society pages never thought to probe, that Betty Thorpe and Arthur Pack were married in the Church of the Epiphany in downtown Washington. "The first International Wedding of the year" was how one paper described the event. The church was elaborately decorated with palms and lilies, and both the American and British flags were draped from the church's stone arches. In attendance were ambassadors from fifteen countries, senior State Department officials, six senators, and the sister of the vice president, as well as most of Washington society.

Cora was delighted. She had been increasingly despairing as, perhaps inevitably, stories of Betty's wild ways made their malicious way back to her. Yet now she couldn't help but utter an audible sigh of social satisfaction at the prospect of her daughter marrying a British diplomat. None of Arthur's family could attend; regrettably, they were too occupied with important work in England, he had explained. In truth, he had not invited them.

Betty was a lovely bride. A circlet of orange blossoms, the society page gushed, held her rose-point veil in place, and she wore a high-waisted gown with a flowing train of ivory silk taffeta. Not reported by the press, though, was that on the morning of the wedding a seamstress had to loosen the gown's waist to disguise the bride's growing belly. Or that just days before the ceremony the bride had no choice but to reveal to both her mother and her fiancé that she was carrying his child. And once she'd made that confession, Betty did her best to convince herself it was true.

"MR. PACK AND HIS BRIDE will spend their honeymoon in Europe," the *Washington Post* informed readers of the society page. "They will be abroad for about five months, returning to Washington in October, after making visits to England, Scotland and on the continent."

But the paper had it wrong. It was not a honeymoon. It was an escape.

Betty on April 29th, 1930—her wedding day.

Chapter 11

◆

MANY BRIDES OF BETTY'S ERA and upbringing were unprepared for the lush pleasures they might experience on their honeymoon. But for Betty, who could be quite philosophical about anything that transpired in the bedroom, the shock was of another kind entirely. On their first night aboard the liner to England, she realized that she detested the man she had married.

Alone at last, no more lingering guests to amuse, no more sentimental dockside good-byes to exchange, the exhausted newlyweds took refuge in the tight confines of their absurdly small stateroom. After all the demands of the wedding, after having for one last docile time done her best to be her mother's proper daughter and not give in to any sudden irrational whim and sneak off with the best man, Betty hoped to grab a few blessed moments' rest before it was time to dress and join the captain's table for dinner. But Arthur had other plans.

The idea had been brewing ever since he'd learned that Betty was pregnant; nevertheless, with typical prudence, he'd decided not to say anything until after the marriage vows. If he shared his plan before the wedding, his willful fiancée might call the whole thing off, and that would have been an appalling embarrassment. But both the ceremony and the reception had run their course with a restraint and dignity that had lived up to all his socially ambitious dreams. The radiant young debutante, the object of fascination to so many men, was now officially Mrs. Arthur Pack. There was no longer any reason, he felt, to restrain himself. So without warning, Arthur made his speech.

Betty's memory of *precisely* what Arthur said that evening had been dimmed by the passing years. But still, when she brought the chilling moments up once more in her mind to share with Hyde, his words, or at least the gist of them, grew clearer. And she had no trouble recalling his steely voice as it filled the tiny stateroom, his pitch alternatingly fierce, then ruminative, then indignant.

Life is responsibility, he began as soberly as if on a pulpit rather than standing by the opened Murphy bed. He had responsibility to his position, and, for that matter, to his king and his country. He refused to walk away from those duties. He refused to have all that he had worked for destroyed. He refused to lose everything because his new bride was pregnant.

Betty was confused; she didn't comprehend what Arthur was trying to say. Or perhaps, she later would realize, she did not want to. If she put her mind to it, the implications would be too horrifying.

Arthur was relentless. Now that he had started in, he had no intention of being vague. With an interrogator's shrill precision, he hammered away: Once the baby is born, how long will it be before people do the math and realize that we'd been having an affair prior to our marriage? How long before people deduce that you were already pregnant when you stood in your white wedding dress in the church in front of God and all of Washington? How long before Sir Esme Howard—the Roman Catholic moralist who as ambassador sat in stern judgment over the embassy's staff—calls me in and announces that my behavior was inappropriate for a representative of the crown, and I should consider myself sacked forthwith? Even if he somehow escaped such an ignominious end to his career, Arthur ranted, there'd be an indelible black mark on his record. Any chance of his moving up in the Foreign Service hierarchy would be gone.

Staggered, Betty tried to argue that his logic was "far-fetched." It seemed "improbable"—no, "ridiculous," she swiftly corrected—that anyone, let alone the British ambassador to America, would bother themselves with ascertaining the date of their child's conception.

But by now Arthur seemed to be in a full panic. His voice rode over her words. I did the right thing by marrying you, he said with a pride that even decades later still struck Betty as both self-righteous and self-serving. I accepted your declaration that I was the father of the child, he went on pointedly, for the first time implying that there was a scent of doubt. Now, he insisted, you must do the right thing. "You must get rid of the baby."

"Get rid of the baby?" Betty finally repeated. At that moment, it must have seemed easier to be bewildered, to pretend not to comprehend.

An abortion, Arthur explained, fierce and succinct.

Betty, no doubt, could have had the fetus aborted when she'd first learned she was pregnant. For reasons she never articulated—fear? a belief in the sanctity of life? a wishful vision of motherhood?—she'd decided not to go down that path. Instead, she had devised another strategy. Only now her carefully executed plan was falling apart.

But it was not too late. A woman with a fighter's temperament, Betty could have refused her new husband's demand. Or she could have argued. Even pleaded. Yet she chose not to respond; in truth, perhaps she was too stunned. All she could do, she would recall, was fix her new husband with a deep and accusatory stare.

Finally, she said it was getting late. They should start dressing for dinner. The captain was expecting them.

Why did Betty surrender? Was she afraid of Arthur? Intimidated by the hulking ex-soldier looming over her and shouting in his parade-ground voice? Or was she feeling guilty? That she had trapped Arthur into this marriage? That she had lied to him about his being the father of the child? Or possibly she simply didn't want the child. To this day, Betty conceded to Hyde, she remained uncertain of her motives. All she knew—and four decades had done nothing to dull the sharp edge of her anger—was that from that moment on, she despised the man she had married.

THE NEWLYWEDS HID OUT IN a rented cottage in Bignor, a tranquil storybook village in Sussex with winding country lanes, giant yew trees that had been standing since the time of William the Conqueror, and a constant background melody of chirping birdsong. Arthur found the house after a succession of London doctors refused to perform an abortion. It would be too dangerous, the obstetricians all agreed; the pregnancy was too far along.

In time, Betty would learn that all safe houses were alike, and this one was no exception—the isolation, the well-stocked fridge and bar, and the waiting, the endless, empty waiting.

Dear parents, Betty wrote in a succession of bravely cheery letters. We take long walks on Bignor Hill. We sit in the ancient churchyard and find comfort in the peace and quiet. Today as we strolled across the South Downs we could smell fresh sea air rising up in the distance from the Channel.

To Hyde, though, Betty told a less fanciful story. Arthur had insisted that Betty go riding with him every day. "But not at a normal gait," Betty remembered bitterly, "not galloping or anything like that. . . . He made me ride out of tune with the horse to joggle me up. He also made me skip rope, jump off walls, in fact, anything to bring about an abortion."

At night, Arthur drew steamy hot baths for his new bride; his wishful theory was that Betty's immersion in the nearly scalding water would cause her to lose the baby. After one of these painful sessions, a woozy Betty managed to climb out of the tub, but fainted as she tried to steady herself.

She quickly regained consciousness, but decided she'd had

enough. Betty was scared; she had begun to worry that she might not survive the ordeal. She demanded that Arthur take her back to London to see a doctor. If he didn't accompany her, she would go alone.

At the end of the examination, the concerned obstetrician sternly confirmed Betty's own diagnosis. If she didn't immediately confine herself to bed, her own health, possibly her life, could be in jeopardy.

The next day Betty checked into the Wellbeck Street Clinic, a private nursing home. She would rest, and await the birth of her child.

ARTHUR, HOWEVER, REMAINED UNDETERRED. WHILE Betty was confined to her bed, he came up with another plan. In the personal columns of several national dailies, he placed the identical terse notice: Foster mother required for newborn whose parents have been posted abroad.

He received a stack of replies, and with a well-practiced bureaucrat's gimlet focus scrutinized each of the candidates who hoped to take on the care and raising of his child. In the end, he settled on a couple who lived in the Shropshire village of Dorrington. The husband was a country doctor, and that conjured up an agreeable image of a well-educated, decent man of modest yet sufficient means. And the letter written by his wife had a polite, very English formality that he had to have found appealing; it was easy to imagine her as a cozy housewife who put the kettle on at four and tended her garden. But no doubt best of all, a doctor and his wife in distant Dorrington would have absolutely no ties to the Foreign Office. His secret would be safe.

He wrote back to the Cassells asking a few humdrum questions, more for propriety's sake than out of any real interest, and suggested, apparently without any embarrassment, that he pay a monthly support fee for the child that amounted to little more than pin money for the couple. When the doctor's wife swiftly replied to his questions with a thoughtful punctiliousness and, no less pleasing, also agreed to his financial terms, his mind was set. Without even consulting his wife, he sent off the letter agreeing to hand over their child to the Cassells.

In the early hours of October 2, 1930, Betty gave birth to a boy, Anthony George. No announcements were made, and the information Arthur reluctantly provided for the statutory birth registration was deliberately vague. He listed his occupation as "Economist." His address was simply "Westminster."

Ten days after the boy's birth, Mrs. Cassell took the train into London and retrieved the infant from Betty, who had brought it back to the Wellbeck Clinic. On the morning of the exchange, Betty thought the hardest thing she would ever have to do in her life would be to give her son to another woman. But returning empty-handed that afternoon to the rented flat in Queen Anne's Gate, the bedroom still sweet with the baby's fresh new smell, proved even more difficult.

She told herself—relying on the same convenient logic she used in a belated letter to her mother, announcing the birth—that she was not surrendering her son forever. She tried to convince herself that once Arthur's career was on track, once they were settled in a home, she'd reclaim her son. But looking back at her decision, she knew these were rationalizations, and facile ones at best. Betty could no longer delude herself. The larger truth was now undeniable: she did not want to have to pretend each day that Tony was Arthur's son.

THE NEWLYWEDS STAYED IN ENGLAND for a few more weeks, and now, unencumbered, they had time for socializing. Arthur invited Eleanor, an old girlfriend, to tea. He had been quite serious about her, and had proposed marriage while she was up at Oxford. After giving the matter some thought, Eleanor had rejected his offer. "My main concern," she would say, "was that he was so much older than me."

Another possible ancillary concern was that Eleanor, who came from landed people in Cheshire, was more discerning than the easily bamboozled Americans; despite the diplomat's mufti, she might have suspected Arthur to be not quite a gentleman. But nevertheless she was curious to meet his American wife, a woman who, Arthur had snidely boasted, was even younger than Eleanor.

"She was a ravishingly lovely creature," Eleanor, now Lady Campbell-Orde, recalled. "Very tall and slim and fair. I could easily see why he fell for her. Her coloring was superb and she was quite extraordinarily pretty."

As Arthur, teacup in hand, sat and listened, the two women had a long chat. Eleanor found she was taken by Betty's "great charm and poise." And she expressed polite concern when Betty, rather offhandedly, revealed that she had recently been in the hospital.

At that moment a gale-force storm of anxiety must have swept through Arthur's entire being. But clearly Betty was only playing with him. She offered no further explanation of why she'd been hospitalized, and Eleanor was too English to ask. To what was no doubt Arthur's colossal relief, his secret remained buried. There was no mention of the son they'd just abandoned.

A few days later, as their honeymoon was about to end and the return voyage to Washington loomed, Arthur decided that he should not leave England without seeing his family. At his sister's small house in Forest Gate, Betty was introduced to his mother, his sister Rosie—now Mrs. Rivett—her husband, and their teenage daughter.

Over tea, Arthur told stories about the important work he was doing at the embassy in Washington. Betty answered all their openly fascinated questions about life in America. It was a pleasant afternoon, and it went quickly. It was over before the newlyweds ever got around to mentioning the boy—the grandson, the nephew, the cousin—now living with strangers not much more than an hour's drive away.

Looking back on the visit, Arthur's niece would remember the occasion as a glamorous, even exciting interlude: "We were all bowled over by Betty, her exquisite beauty and great elegance."

But Rosie, Arthur's usually doting sister, had misgivings. Betty was "so lively and passionate, yet married to Arthur who found it difficult to show emotion." In truth, she "felt sorry for Betty."

But her concern was nothing compared to how sorry Betty felt for herself. After meeting his family, she realized that Arthur was an actor, too. He had clothed himself in artifice and invention. And he had played her as deliberately as she had deceived him.

No sooner had the couple returned to Washington than Arthur was posted to New York. He wasn't there long, however, before he received news of his next appointment. It was the sort of promotion for which he'd long been hoping. The Foreign Office was sending him to Santiago, Chile, to head the embassy's commercial office. And for further heady proof that his star was at last rising, there was Arthur, his face grimly set in a pose apparently meant to suggest the unwavering imperial authority that resided in the members of His Majesty's diplomatic corps, in a photograph on the front page of the London *Times*'s foreign supplement.

Arthur could not believe his good fortune. After all his diligence, he told Betty, he was finally getting his just rewards. He also, no doubt, congratulated himself on the social efficacy of his well-made marriage. It must have, he could easily have believed after all the fuss the Washington papers had made of his wedding, impressed his stuffy ruling-class bosses. They now had reason to view him with a newfound respect and, if their admiring glances at Betty were any indication, even pangs of envy.

He had triumphed, and perhaps this victory was sufficient. Perhaps it allowed him to be at peace with the trade-off he had made. If he had to give up his son in exchange for these blessings—as well as the richer ones that might come his way in the future—well, who could now blame him for feeling it had been a necessary sacrifice? Perhaps he even believed that his success proved that he had made the right choice.

THE COUPLE SAILED FROM NEW York for Valparaíso, Chile, in September 1930. Betty, just twenty years old, did not share her husband's excitement. On the long ocean voyage, she told Hyde, she kept wanting to grab Arthur by his lapels and demand, How could you? But then she knew she would have to ask herself the same anguished question, and she just couldn't find the nerve.

Instead, she kept all her guilt and disappointment locked deep inside her. It ate away, destroying, ravaging, until she had no choice but to acknowledge her own complicity in the unforgivable decision that had changed her life. She stood alone night after night on deck, her body pressed against the rail and her eyes fixed on some distant point on the horizon. Now she was capable of anything.

Part III

"Hidden in My Yesterdays"

Chapter 12

◆

I T WAS THEIR THIRD FULL day in Ireland. Betty and Hyde
had driven out of Dublin the previous morning and spent a
night in the high-spirited company of some of Hyde's literary
friends. Still a bit thickheaded from the evening's festivities, they
were now standing high above Dublin Bay, hoping the fresh, cool
sea breezes would be the elixir they needed.

Their perch was on top of one of the fifty or so Martello towers,
built a century ago as fortifications to protect the Irish coast from
an invasion by Napoleon's army. But this stone tower near San-
dycone had its own much celebrated significance. It was here that
James Joyce had set the opening chapter of *Ulysses*.

The novel began with two friends walking up the tower's "dark,
winding stairs" to the rooftop gun platform, the very climb Betty and
Hyde made. Joyce's characters, too, had also stood at the edge of the
parapet and looked out at the bay; the "snot-green sea," Joyce, with
a cruel humor, had called it. And the similarities, life broadly—*very*
broadly, he acknowledged—imitating art, had emboldened Hyde.

In the days that followed their arrival in Dublin, Hyde had been
waiting for Betty to plunge back into her story. He'd offered hints,
had tried subtly coaxing her, but she had simply refused to bite.
During his former life in the covert world, he'd learned a few
tricks. Don't push, says the handbook. Plant the seeds, and eventually the target will get around to talking. But Hyde apparently
was beginning to have his doubts about these facile operational
wisdoms. Betty, he perhaps suspected, was too shrewd—and too
willful—to be nudged into anything not of her own volition.

He understood her reluctance; "History is a nightmare," Joyce had wisely remarked in *Ulysses*, the line suddenly popping up in Hyde's memory now that the book was in the center of his thoughts. He could imagine Betty's regrets, and the anguish of re-living them. But if she didn't pick up her tale soon, then all would be lost. So much for his ever writing this book, let alone making the windfall he so desperately needed.

Betty and Hyde visited the Martello Tower in Dun Laoghaire, which is the location of the first scene in James Joyce's Ulysses.

Hyde could not let that happen.

Now, standing on the parapet, he recalled how on that very spot Joyce's Buck Mulligan had badgered a reluctant Stephen Dedalus to talk. "What is it?" Mulligan had demanded when his friend hes-itated. "Cough it up." And now, with no other options apparent, and doing his best to keep his frustration in check, Hyde too chose this moment to be ruthless. He no longer cared what old ghosts haunted Betty; she too would have to "cough it up." He resumed his interrogation.

AT THE SAME TIME BETTY'S own sharp questions were piercing her mind, giving her pause. Why had she taken a lover? Was it simply vengeful, a spiteful act meant to hurt Arthur in Chile? Perhaps it was being twenty-one years old and still needing to feel the hot-blooded excitement that comes with an animating passion. Or maybe, as she liked to tell herself at the time, she was in love. But then again, she could just as well have been searching for something that remained unclear to her, even as she doggedly chased after it.

As she silently reviewed the possibilities, she would explain in her memoirs, she knew that any of them could have been her motivation. Or, no less probable, at the crucial moment they could all have come together, a conspiracy of logic pushing her, a young bride in a foreign land, toward that act of betrayal. But she was unwilling—and unprepared, she also realized—to share these thoughts with Hyde.

Nevertheless, she must have realized that she had to answer his questions; if she refused, the rest of their trip would be a disaster. And she had so much riding on it.

She finally picked up her story just where she had left off: the zealous newly appointed commercial secretary and his elegant young wife, a mountain of their luggage stacked in the baggage car, making their way by slow train through the mauve-brown foothills of the looming Andes until they arrived at last in Santiago.

And, no doubt relieved, Hyde was now as mute as any case officer listening behind a two-way mirror. He just let her talk.

Chapter 13

◆

FOR ANYONE WHO LIVED IN Santiago—anyone of the diplomatic class, that is, Betty quickly amended as she resumed
her story—life in the city in the early 1930s was "gay and
vivacious." It was a good time and a good place to enjoy many
pleasures. And after the dowager gentility of Washington, Santiago was an exotic adventure. There were leafy, tree-lined boulevards, lush gardens, open-air markets where dark-skinned Indians
sold strange delicacies, smoky clubs where young couples danced,
waving their handkerchiefs in the air to mimic lustful roosters approaching eager hens, and everywhere one looked, nestled edge-
to-edge like a chain of dominoes around the city, rose the tall
peaks of the Andes. To this day, after a night of drinking, Betty
couldn't help wishing she could restore herself with a hot bowl of
caldillo de congrio, the joltingly spicy fish stew that had never failed
to cure even her worst hangovers.

The Packs quickly settled into their new life. The British pound
went far; their apartment was spacious, and opened onto a brightly
planted terrace where they could sit with a glass of wine and watch
a blazing sun set over the Andes. Another domestic blessing: a platoon of obliging servants was quickly recruited for an absurdly low
fee to do the housework. It was all very comfortable.

As a child in Cuba, Betty had learned a smattering of Spanish, and the language came back to her like a cherished memory.
Building on this foundation, it wasn't long before she was speaking
in a fluent and, even more impressive, accentless Spanish. Arthur
had a gift for languages too. With his customary diligence, he ap-

plied himself, and within months he was effectively cozying up to the local tycoons in their native tongue.

"The Commercial Secretary to the British Embassy, Mr. Arthur Pack," the London *Times* noted in one dispatch, "gave a luncheon today to a large number of local businessmen and representatives of the press and made a speech pointing out the necessity of confidence in the future and drawing attention to the fact that the services of the Commercial Secretariat at the Embassy were at the disposal of those in any way concerned in commerce with Great Britain."

And of course there were parties. Lots of parties. Not long after the couple had moved into their new home, Arthur, surely proud to show off his young bride, hosted a twenty-first-birthday party for Betty. The city's entire diplomatic corps was invited. The champagne flowed, a band played, and Betty looked gorgeous in the Latin moonlight. It did not take long for the new arrivals to be asked everywhere. Or for Betty, who flittered about like a preening cat waiting for the touch of a warm hand, to attract ardent glances wherever she went.

Each day Arthur would go dutifully off to the embassy, making it a point to arrive by nine sharp. Wrapped up in his new responsibilities, he would not return till after dark. Betty's calendar was marked up with luncheons and teas with the embassy wives, but this routine swiftly grew tedious. Most of the women were as old as her mother, and more discouraging, as proxy representatives of the crown they went about with a prissy, too often tyrannical watchfulness that also reminded her of Cora. She desperately needed something to fill the long days before the sun set, the parties began, and the champagne corks popped.

For a while, riding helped settle her building uneasiness. "I had always been passionately fond of horses and riding," Betty told Hyde, "and rarely a day passed in Chile when I was not in the saddle. Sometimes I rode almost from morning to night."

Then she discovered polo. "It was considered rather daring and even eccentric for a woman in those days," she explained, and that, of course, made it even more fun. "Chilean women, at least those who were married, seldom went out on horseback. Indeed, they were discouraged from doing so by their husbands, as riding was supposed to prevent them from having children.

"I was not a particularly good polo player," she acknowledged. "But at least I was up to match play." And galloping across the field in her tight white jodhpurs, Betty was the center of attention at every club chukka.

BUT EVEN ALL THIS ENERGETIC activity was insufficient to soothe Betty's vast restlessness. So when the opportunity presented itself at the polo club, she decided she might as well take up another bit of sport.

"It was during this period," Betty related matter-of-factly to the man who planned to write her story, "that I had the first love affair in my married life. . . . He was a rich Chilean called Alfredo, the head of a big nitrate company. He was also an experienced lover, very gentle and kind."

Looking back at the relationship, its long-extinguished heat and intensity suddenly once again almost palpable, Betty tried to justify her actions; she spoke to Hyde, but she was also trying to come to an understanding in her own mind. "I think I poured out on him all my love for my father, for my son, the love I had hoped to find with Arthur." And if that easy logic was not totally convincing, she came up with another convenient rationale, one that would serve her well through the years: "I was madly in love with him."

For nearly a year Betty, with never the slightest pang of guilt or so much as a hint to an oblivious Arthur, transferred her loyalty to her lover. As covertly as any spy going off on a secret mission, she snuck off for her rendezvouses. Then, without warning, something happened that brought Betty to her senses. And at the same enlightening time she picked up still another piece of intelligence that she'd rely on in the field: the pattern of deceit is a circular one.

"One day," she told Hyde, "I happened to see Alfredo with a well-known Chilean woman." Betty, who was well versed in body language, knew at once that this woman was also Alfredo's mistress.

Betty was filled with rage. Nevertheless, she hid her fury under a cloak of good manners. She spoke reasonably and sensibly, the very model of a woman of her class and breeding. Yet even as Betty, full of an icy reserve, challenged Alfredo, asking to know the truth, it never occurred to her that poor Arthur might very well have put the same anguished questions to her.

"He swore that he did not love her and that he loved only me," Betty continued. But his assurances were irrelevant. Her anger had solidified into cool resignation. "I did not want him anymore after that and told him so. That was the end of the affair."

In its place, despair filled her like a terrible sickness. "I was totally disillusioned. My son Tony had been taken from me and my first genuine love affair was smashed. I didn't have a very sanguine view of life."

BUT BETTY WAS RESILIENT. SHE was her marine father's daughter, and she would soldier tenaciously on. She would not surrender, she chided herself. And just like that, she explained to Hyde, she woke up one morning and decided her period of mourning for the lover she had lost and the son she had abandoned had gone on long enough.

At the same time, Betty intuitively understood that to put the past behind her, reinvent herself and move forward, she would need to don a new disguise. So not for the last time, she tried on a pose she'd thought she'd abandoned for good—the dutiful wife.

She would, she recounted to Hyde, stand by Arthur's side. She would make the Foreign Office take notice of her husband's steadfast service. Hand in hand, a couple, they would serve king and country. She'd find consolation, as well as a sense of purpose, in the unambiguous rightness of her marital commitment.

To Betty's credit, no actress ever threw herself with more vigor into such a demanding and unnatural role. Tall, regal, and beguiling, she stood with her husband at every diplomatic reception. She laughed appreciatively at the stiff jokes of Sir Harry Chilton the dry-as-dust British ambassador. She pretended it was all good facetious fun when a diplomat in his cups or a confident polo player moved in close to her and suggested in a breathy, ardent whisper that they meet the next day for a drink. And now that she was once again sharing only her husband's bed, she told herself it would be pointless not to enjoy his caresses or reciprocate.

And oh, the rewards of a life lived by marching in step with the crowd! Could it have been, she remembered asking herself with genuine astonishment, that her mother had been right all along? Perhaps it was not too late for her to start over. For within a year she received tangible proof that her performance had been a rousing success. Arthur's name appeared on the New Year's Honors: he was to be given the Order of the British Empire.

As a child she had written a fanciful description of the glittering ball her father had attended in Buckingham Palace in 1903. "Days Bygone," the ten-year-old had called her story. Now those days were no longer bygone, and the present offered the sort of storybook sparkle the young girl had imagined. For there was Betty, a tiara balanced on her blond head, wearing a long, flowing pale dress that made her look like a Hellenic deity descended from the heavens for the occasion, curtsying low to King George V as Arthur received his OBE at Buckingham Palace.

Twenty-three-year-old Betty, presented at court. This portrait would later hang in the Wardman Park Hotel, in Washington, DC.

In one more earnest attempt to flesh out her new identity, Betty, while in England and with her husband at her side, went to see her son in Dorrington. It had been two and a half years since she had held Tony in her arms, and the young boy greeted the strangers with bewilderment and apprehension. He had been raised by the Cassells, and in his child's mind it probably was incomprehensible that anyone other than the kindly doctor and his doting wife were his parents. Betty's optimistic plan was that she and Arthur would take their son out for a drive, and in the process begin to repair all the damage that had been done. But the outing quickly shattered into irreparable pieces.

"He was terrified and immediately started screaming and

screaming," the Cassells' daughter remembered. "It took ages to calm him down. After that he developed a stammer which I always thought stemmed from that incident."

The Packs would remain in England for another three months, but Betty, even as she tried to live up to the demands of her newfound domesticity, could not find the will to visit her son again. Instead, she did her best to persuade herself that Tony was happy with his foster parents. Her presence would only be disruptive.

And whatever small pangs of maternal disappointment that had stubbornly lingered were soon assuaged. Just months after the couple returned to Chile, a delighted Betty received further confirmation of the rightness of the new life she was living: she was pregnant. Her belly grew large, and this time she rejoiced as she felt the life growing inside her. This pregnancy was not her secret. It was her pride.

A daughter, Denise Beresford Pack, was born on New Year's Eve, 1934.

Denise, Betty vowed, would be her second chance. She would be the child Betty would never abandon.

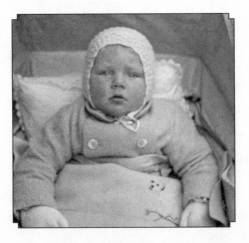

Betty's infant daughter Denise Beresford Pack, born in 1934.

◆ ◆ ◆

THEN JUST AS SUDDENLY AND impetuously as it had begun, it all fell apart. It was as if, Betty told Hyde, she woke up one morning, looked in the mirror, and saw a face branded by her own deceptions. How could she have believed there was any honor in a life built on lies, with a husband she didn't love? Her duty was to herself. Her allegiance was to her own anarchic nature.

As Hyde listened intently, Betty explained that she'd taken inventory of the many charades she had acted out in her attempt to recast her life, and each had offered only evidence of her colossal foolishness. She renounced them all.

She put an end to all the artifice, all the interior restrictions. She was done wearing the painted smile of a diplomatic geisha. She'd no longer deny that she was attractive, or run from the gifts this blessing offered. There would be no restraints on her high-flying spirit. She would soar. And she would never, never, never again share a bed with a man who repulsed her and not scream that it was a sentence in hell.

Morose, she recalled the events of the past year, and under the weight of her heavy scrutiny, they all collapsed. Even her day at the palace, she complained to Hyde, had been tainted by the tacky faux diamond bracelet Arthur bought her and insisted she wear on her wrist to meet the king. And as for the baby, well, the girl was better off with her nurse. If she had to listen to any more of the child's incessant screeching, she was afraid she might send Denise off to the Cassells too.

Yet just as Betty began to descend deeper into this low, increasingly dangerous mood, Arthur received word that he was to be transferred to the British embassy in Madrid. It was a senior appointment, and he swelled with pride.

For Betty, the news was her salvation. As she told Hyde: "It was a big thrill. . . . I felt prepared for the realization of a long-held dream."

Chapter 14

◆

WAS IT FATE? BETTY HAD always dismissed that notion as too narrow, even a little silly. Her worldview, a product of her practical Minnesota roots, was active and spontaneous: you seize the moment; you make things happen. But after the shock of her encounter in Madrid, all her steady, self-sufficient philosophy fell apart. For Betty, once more deeply in love, was certain that it had been meant to be; forces beyond any logic or reason had long been at work to make it happen. Although still baffled by it all, Betty nevertheless insisted to Hyde that "the guiding hand of Destiny" must have been shoving her along.

Up to that transforming moment, her days in Spain had been filled with a willed brightness. Stung by her disappointments in Chile, she was determined—once again!—to put her life back in order. Her first self-appointed task was to make a new home.

Within days of their arrival in Madrid in the spring of 1935, Betty found an airy, high-ceilinged apartment a short stroll from the Prado. With an intentional symbolism she did the place all up in white—white walls, white carpet, and plush white upholstery. It would be the blank canvas upon which she would create their new domestic life. Betty, who lived a roller-coaster life measured out in dramatic endings followed by even more dramatic new beginnings, told herself that in this new home she would enter into a truce with Arthur, and as husband and wife they would work together to raise their daughter. And as with all of Betty's pledges, she meant it—at least at that moment.

During those first months in Madrid, her resolve held. She

was the charming embassy wife at the afternoon bridge tables, the golf outings, the staff picnics in the green meadows of the Sierra de Guadarrama, the late-night diplomatic dinners. But even as she slipped into a sedate, accommodating version of herself, she couldn't help feeling that Spain, tempestuous, romantic, full of a fiery Latin excitement, was beckoning, urging her to join the merry fiesta celebrated beyond the embassy gates. So perhaps it had always been only a matter of time before Betty, so susceptible to passion, was diverted. But what was surprising, Betty related to Hyde, was how she found her way into the Spain she had always imagined.

It happened—as would another significant event years later in Warsaw—on the manicured grounds of a country club. This first encounter was at the Club Puerta de Hierro, a lush green oasis of privilege a short drive from downtown Madrid. The helpful wife, Betty had driven to the club to pick up Arthur. He'd have finished his round of golf with, as he'd told her that morning, a Spanish diplomat he'd originally met in Washington, and by now he'd be sipping his first martini.

Betty was scanning the tables on the clubhouse terrace for her husband when her search stopped abruptly. Standing with his back toward her was a man with broad shoulders that tapered down to a bullfighter's narrow waist and long, athletic legs. It was an incredibly evocative pose; he was as motionless as a statue, yet at the same time his presence was charged, rippling with a graceful power.

But even more arresting, in just that moment's glance Betty was certain there was something familiar in his stance. She knew she had seen him somewhere before. And that once before she had experienced an identical rush of emotions. Somehow, she understood in a startling flash she recalled to Hyde, this man was "hidden in my yesterdays."

Then he turned around. In that instant she was once again a teenager home from boarding school silently pledging her heart to the handsome Spaniard with the bright smile on the tennis court, the gallant Adonis who had bowed low in homage to her. Here he was again. Destiny, she'd always believe, was giving her its blessings, coaxing her on.

In the next moment, further proof that this totally improbable reunion was meant to be, Arthur, as if on cue, appeared. And he was introducing the living, breathing embodiment of all her worshipful teenage daydreams.

"Betty, this is Señor Carlos Sartorius," Arthur announced. "He was one of the young lads at the Spanish embassy when you were in the schoolroom."

At last armed with a name, and no longer a demure schoolgirl, Betty studied Carlos openly. The years had added distinction and assurance to the jauntiness of youth. But the wavy hair, the twinkling dark eyes, and the incredibly white, cheerful smile were as wonderful as ever.

"Well," she said playfully, "I wasn't in the schoolroom *all* the time." She was too proud to admit that a decade later she still remembered him. Yet at the same time, she was hoping to trigger Carlos's memory.

She needn't have worried; her magic was as strong and as persistent as his. He too vividly remembered their moment at the Washington tennis court. And as Arthur listened, mute, helpless, and very much the odd man out, Carlos offered up a confession: he had gone back the next day to look for her. "And before I could find you, I was called back to Spain and I have been here ever since."

Betty cherished his words.

Still, all her seductress's instincts seemed to be telling her not to pounce. She hid behind coyness. "And thinking only of me all those years, I hope," she said breezily.

But Carlos refused to banter about important things; an aristocrat and a gentleman, he knew when to be sincere. His words were spoken with an utter seriousness, and they left Betty thrilled. "Some first impressions stay new and freshen one's whole life."

For a long, deep moment the two of them looked at each other in silence. It was as if they were both lost in their memories, both wondering what this reunion meant.

Then Carlos, no doubt suddenly remembering that Betty was a married woman and that, even more sobering, her husband was there too, regained his equilibrium. He now spoke with the easy fluency of a diplomat.

"Señora," he said with a gay charm, "you take ten years to get here and then you bring your husband who is a warm friend to my family. What, in honor, can I say? What to do? Well, I shall fetch my wife Carmencita and we will drink champagne to the old days and to the new ones too. And then you will both join us for dinner."

And so there was champagne, and then more champagne, and then dinner, and then of course more champagne.

"We must begin your Spanish education somewhere," Carlos said as the four of them sat at the dinner table. "You will find Spain a very good schoolroom, I think. And perhaps with your husband's permission, I could fulfill the requirements as a teacher?"

Betty liked the idea. "My knowledge is very superficial— all on the surface. Perhaps you will teach me about Spain and the Spaniards? I don't want to live here on the surface," she said truthfully.

Carlos quickly agreed. "You will find it difficult, I think, to live on the surface in the company of Spaniards. We do not understand this way of existing. That is why we're the despair of the Anglo-Saxons. What you call dramatics, we call the very truth!"

Carlos went on talking all through dinner about the Spain, the "real Spain," he called it, that he would show the Packs. He seemed determined to cool the mood that had spontaneously ignited when they were introduced.

Betty, who knew a bit about keeping important secrets buried, went along with this operational maneuver. This was tradecraft she had perfected over the years. But it didn't matter how the conversation meandered, or where it aimlessly flowed. It was too late. The damage had already been done.

THERE WAS NEVER A BETTER, more informative guide. Good to his promise, Carlos introduced the Packs to Spain. With his wife along to complete the foursome, they went about like old friends. He took them to bullfights, shooting weekends at country haciendas, and endless rounds of sparkling parties where you could count on mingling with a fun-loving crowd of Spanish nobles. Night after night, their long evenings on the town ended at Jimmy's Place, the jaunty Scotsman at the piano playing soft love songs as the couples danced cheek-to-cheek, a river of champagne flowed, and the dawn lit up the dusty streets of Madrid.

All the time, as the four friends went about together, as they played their roles in this happiest of friendships, Betty recounted to Hyde, both Carlos and she knew what was really happening. They could feel the tension between them twisting tighter, building and building until it was near to bursting. He would look for Betty across the crowded room at a party, and she would know in an instant, her green eyes drawn to him like a powerful magnet. When the couples exchanged partners on the small, smoky dance floor at Jimmy's, Carlos held Betty tight in his strong arms. Yet at the same time, they pretended to themselves, to their spouses, that it wasn't happening. That it wasn't inevitable. This was, Carlos no doubt felt, the only reasonable way to behave; and Betty, who knew how to run an operation, let him go on for as long as he could.

When they finally became lovers, they discovered that the waiting, the weeks of torturous restraint, had made the release of all their pent-up emotion a wild blessing. Their passion was dizzying. In all her life, Betty had never known such an overwhelming love.

Madrid, especially Carlos's Madrid, was a small city, and discretion was difficult. People would see them together, see how they looked at one another, how they slyly let their fingers linger when Carlos lit Betty's cigarette, and the talk started.

Betty, always reckless, was beyond caring. But Carlos had a senior position in the Spanish Air Ministry. He worried about his career. And he was convinced his wife and Arthur did not know about the affair. He hoped to keep things that way.

Carlos rented a small penthouse apartment on the northern fringes of the city, in a neighborhood where they wouldn't be recognized, where they wouldn't need to pretend. It was a place to live their secret lives.

They would pass their mornings waiting impatiently for the afternoons. Then they would make their separate furtive ways to the apartment. The bedroom opened onto a narrow terrace. As they lay in bed together, wrapped in one another's arms, the sun setting in the distance over the purple Guadarrama mountains beyond the open terrace doors, Betty felt that life was at last sublime. Of all the safe houses she would know, this would always be the sweetest.

Yet they both understood from the start that their relationship was doomed. This was Spain, a country whose ebullience existed side by side with strict ritual. Carlos, the head of a distinguished and wealthy family of Roman Catholic aristocrats, could never get a divorce. He could never turn his back on his heritage or his family.

The knowledge that a future was impossible served to intensify every moment in the present. They relished their hours together in the bedroom of the small penthouse. If they could not have more time together, they would have it all now.

IN THAT WAY, HER DAYS made large by passion and subterfuge, by love and deceit, Betty lived an exciting year. Then, in January 1936, Betty took ill. Or at least that was how she explained it to Arthur. She said she had a gynecological problem and needed to see an obstetrician in London.

Arthur did not press for details, and neither did Betty's circle of sophisticated Spanish friends when she announced her trip. They were convinced they already knew why she was running off to an Anglo-Saxon doctor: she was pregnant, and wanted an abortion. If this were true, as it very well might have been, it was one more secret that would be forever locked away in the classified operational history of her life.

What is known, and what she very willingly told Hyde, was that despite her impending obstetric procedure, she had a very jolly trip to London. She made the journey with a group from the embassy returning to England for home leave, and accompanying this party—the life of it, Betty would affirm—was Lord Castlerosse.

Valentine Castlerosse, to his self-proclaimed delight, was a rarity: by birth a haughty aristocrat with an inherited title and a stately home, he was by profession an ink-stained Fleet Street journalist. His "Londoner's Log" column in the Sunday *Express* was required reading for England's smart set and anyone else who enjoyed eavesdropping on the wanton exploits of those in society. Another seeming contradiction: he was a gluttonous Tweedledum of a man, built like a 265-pound sand castle. Yet he was also an inveterate womanizer, waddling famously across London from one bedroom to another.

Valentine Castlerosse, journalist by trade and aristocrat by birth,
who befriended Betty and introduced her to Lord Beaverbrook.

What also distinguished him—and this was undoubtedly the secret of Castlerosse's success—was his quick wit and brash, mischievous charm. A society doyenne out to get revenge for some slight approached him at a party, tapped his massive waist-coated belly with a catty finger, and snarled, "If this stomach were on a woman, I would think she was pregnant." Without missing a beat, his lordship drawled back, "Madame, a half-hour ago it was on a woman and by now she very well might be pregnant."

When Betty was introduced to Lord Castlerosse in the dining car aboard the train taking the group through Spain and then into France, he consumed two liters of whisky in the course of the dinner and seemed none the worse for the experience. That intrigued her. And when the cool beauty across the table—who, naturally, had his attention from the moment she'd boarded the train—tried unsuccessfully to light her cigarette with a box of Spanish matches and in her frustration quipped, "This is the only thing in Spain that doesn't strike," a friendship was born.

"I'm going to use that in my column," he promised. And true to his word, he did.

They grew very close on that trip, enjoying each other's company immensely. Then, as Betty recovered from her medical problems, they spent a lot of time together in London. He would escort her to Quaglino's, where they dined on mountains of oysters and drank magnums of Dom Perignon. He confessed that his wife, infuriated by his latest indiscretion, had locked him out of his home and consulted her solicitors. In turn, Betty confided a bit about her own tumultuous life, her perpetual restlessness, the agony of being locked in a loveless marriage to a staid, pin-striped Foreign Service functionary. In that way, through mutual revelations fueled by wine, circumstance, and a shared waspish candor, they got to know a good deal about one another.

It was on one of their last evenings together, when Betty was wrapping up things in London before going back to her complicated life in Madrid, to the unsteady world she shared with her husband and her lover, that Lord Castlerosse arrived for cocktails at her hotel. Tonight, he announced mysteriously, they would be dining with a friend.

The cab took them to 13 Cleveland Row in Mayfair, a big white brick pile known as Stornoway House. Who lives here? Betty asked, intrigued by the size of the mansion. "My boss," said the lord. "The Beaver."

Lord Beaverbrook, the self-made Canadian millionaire who owned the *Express* and had served as Britain's minister of information in the last war, had a small group at his table that night. He seemed, though, to focus all his attention on Betty. Not that she was particularly surprised; Betty had long ago grown accustomed to that sort of scrutiny from men.

Still, she did find some of his questions, as well as his persistence, a bit odd. He went on about her people, her father's military service, her husband's work at the embassy, how she passed her days in Spain, her affection for the country she had acquired through marriage to a British citizen. That's what journalists do, Betty reminded herself. They ask questions. And Betty being Betty, she found no reason to dodge her host's assault. She replied with candor, as well as her usual easy, self-deprecating charm.

When they were leaving, Lord Beaverbrook escorted them to the door. "Everything you said she'd be," he told his columnist and good friend. "Only more beautiful."

Lord Beaverbrook, the British newspaper tycoon who recommended Betty to Britain's Secret Intelligence Service.

It was not long after that fateful evening that the Beaver had a word with one of his many friends who worked at 54 Broadway, just off Victoria Street in London, the operational headquarters of the Secret Intelligence Service. Whether his approach was over an intimate lunch at his club or through a carefully worded handwritten note has long been forgotten. But, as was duly recorded in the files of MI6, Lord Beaverbrook had done a round of talent-spotting over dinner.

He saw in Betty Pack a young woman from good stock with beauty, intelligence, daring, and, as Castlerosse had made clear, a shaky moral compass. No less appealing, her husband's job was tailor-made to offer the best sort of cover; her diplomat's wife passport was the real thing.

All the unsettled young woman needed, he suggested knowingly to this senior member of the Service, was a great and noble cause to which she could pledge her talent and her allegiance.

Chapter 15

◆

ONCE BACK IN MADRID, BETTY, as if obeying Lord Beaverbrook's suggestion, found a shining cause to latch on
to. But always unpredictable, she pledged her allegiance
to an organization that, despite its own strong tradition of power,
mystery, and authority, the Beaver would never have anticipated.
She embraced the Roman Catholic Church.

The ostensible reason for her conversion, at least as she explained things at the time and reiterated to Hyde decades later,
had some admirably pious logic. Days before her wedding, in a
moment that was as rash as it was hopeful, she had promised Arthur
that she would accept his Roman Catholic faith. She had never
gotten around to fulfilling that pledge, and considering the bumpy
course of their marriage, she might have easily reneged on that
wedding vow too.

But after five years of living in Chile and Spain, both countries
whose rich Catholicism she had inhaled with every breath of the
Latin air, Betty had begun to feel the lure of the church, as well
as, she insisted, the stirrings of belief. And not least, practical Betty
also reasoned that if everyone else—Arthur, Carlos, her crowd of
Spanish friends—was convinced the Roman Church offered the
path to heaven, she didn't want to be the one unbeliever left alone
on the side of the road come Judgment Day.

Yet with the advantage of hindsight, Betty, as she explained
to Hyde, could see a little more clearly what had driven her to
the church. Her sudden devotion was just one further search for
clarity, any clarity at all, to satisfy her yearnings and bring some

measure of peace. If all this new Betty, a cleansed Catholic Betty, had to do to quell the storm raging in her soul was anoint God in His Heaven as her Controller, then she was ready to sign on. And if in the process she could expiate her past sins by owning up to them, she was prepared to take on that difficult mission too. At the time the catechism seemed like the operational handbook that offered the salvation she'd always been craving.

Sharing all this with Hyde, she also reluctantly acknowledged the large inconsistencies that coexisted with her newfound religiosity. The gospel according to Betty preached a creed that any good Catholic of a pure and humble mind would have rejected. For even as she pledged her loyalty to the tenets of her adopted church, she shared a marital bed with Arthur while staying faithful to her afternoons with Carlos. Rather than trouble herself over the ethics of her own particular piety, Betty confessed that she simply chose to ignore the paradox. Besides, as she told Hyde, she'd always felt that you couldn't beat a little sex for getting closer to God.

For Arthur, her decision was an answered prayer. In his own burst of faith, he told himself that Betty was maturing, that she was ready to move on from what he, full of his usual fire and brimstone, condemned as her "American morality." Before his wife had time to reconsider, he arranged for George Ogilvie-Forbes, the embassy counselor and a renowned lay leader of the Catholic Church in Britain, to prepare Betty for her baptism.

Yet even Betty, so worldly and tolerant, was ambushed by the course her religious instruction took. Looking back, though, she must have smiled, now wise enough to be amused by its inevitability.

With good and solemn intentions, Ogilvie-Forbes announced to Betty that he had found a priest who would "keep the flame burning" in her newly christened Catholic heart.

At first the sessions of religious instruction were merely a welcome interlude in Betty's empty mornings. The priest would appear at her apartment and for the next hour or so would talk with fervor about what God expected from His beloved subjects. The catechism he preached was built on lofty ideals, and Betty, she told Hyde, chimed in approvingly.

But clearly she never gave much thought to going as far as to live by such restrictive precepts. Nevertheless, she began to look forward to their time together. The priest had a soft, thoughtful way of talking that made her lean in close to listen to his every reverent word. Another blessing: the priest was young and handsome, his faced etched with a precocious mature dignity that she attributed to the many demands of his heavenly responsibilities. During their moments of silent prayer, their heads humbly bowed in unison, Betty felt the power of a shared intimacy.

One week when the priest sent word that their next session would be at an address on the other side of the city. Betty did not give the news a second thought. Years later, and serving in another church, she'd learn one of the strict rules of tradecraft: when a contact suddenly changes his handwriting, alarm bells should go off in your head. But Betty was a novice back then, and she went unsuspectingly to the new address.

There was Madrid, the bright Madrid where she lived, shopped, and socialized, and there was the other Madrid, a tangled network of dingy streets where people like her never ventured. She made her way through the garbage-strewn streets of an industrialized slum to the drab concrete apartment building at the address the priest had given. And now, as she looked about, she realized she'd heard her friends whispering about this neighborhood: "It was where wealthy Spaniards were in the habit of taking their girlfriends for an hour or two of love-making in the afternoon." Still, she did not read anything into this small piece of recalled intelligence.

When the priest opened the apartment door, he was not wearing his cassock but dressed in a brown suit. He looked awkward, a slighter man, in the banal outfit. Yet this disguise, too, did not provoke any suspicions.

And when he reached out and put his arms around her, Betty still did not understand. For a frightful moment she thought that he was going to shake her silly and announce that in light of all her sins he had no choice but to excommunicate her. It was only when he kissed her awkwardly on the lips that she began to follow what was happening.

"I love you," he announced with a pious sincerity. A torrent of promises followed. He would forsake the church. He would devote himself instead to her. He would marry her. Hand in hand, they would leave Spain and make a new life.

It was a proposal Betty didn't seriously consider, but she was flattered. She also was quite fond of the handsome priest. She quickly began to imagine a reality where their roles could be reversed, where she could be the teacher and he the acolyte. Thinking the unthinkable was exciting. And besides, there seemed to be no polite way to free herself from the situation. She kissed him back.

That afternoon they became lovers.

"There followed," Betty told Hyde, "a series of secret meetings once or twice a week at the apartment." "As he was poor and the costs of the rooms high, I . . . helped him out with the bill." It was a tithe she paid gladly.

Betty's already knotty life had become even more complicated. She had converted to Catholicism with the hope that religion would help wrestle her demons into submission. Instead, each night she shared her marital bed with her husband. In the afternoons, she sneaked off to a penthouse hideaway to meet with his friend. And in between, she made time for clandestine rendezvous with the priest who was supposed to instill in her the saintly principles of her new faith.

How did Betty manage to live on several conflicting planes at once? The trick, as every spy had to learn, was to pledge loyalty to the one you were with, and to mean it with all your heart at the time.

AND IF BETTY'S UNRULY CHOICES weren't already sufficient cause for concern, converting to Catholicism in Spain in the tense spring of 1936 was a dangerous political decision too. A practicing Catholic could just as likely lose his life as save his soul.

Spain was a smoking political volcano, a country poised to erupt in civil war. The battle lines were already being passionately drawn, the competing wall posters shouting on every street corner.

On one side, grouped in a makeshift coalition dedicated to the defense of the Old Order, was a chorus of strident right-wing voices—the monarchists, the aristocracy, the wealthy, the Fascists, and the Roman Catholic Church. The uncompromising leader of these Nationalists was the former chief of the General Staff, General Francisco Franco.

Opposed to the forces of conservatism and fascism was a broad alliance of impassioned representatives from the left. The Popular Front, as it was called, was a pragmatic—and often querulous— marriage of liberal reformers, labor unions, socialists, and members of the Communist Party.

When Betty first arrived in Spain, the beleaguered country was already seething. Franco's well-armed troops had charged into battle with a ruthless urgency, offering little mercy to the rebel forces. A right-wing Catholic government was installed. But their victory so costly, so bloody, was short-lived.

In the tempestuous 1936 election, the political seesaw lifted the left into office. A new pro-Communist government was elected. But ballots could not heal deep and festering wounds, and it quickly became grimly clear that this new democratic Spanish Republic lacked the authority to govern. A chaos of assassinations—over two hundred political murders in just two months—and workers' strikes rattled the country.

It was an ominous, uneasy time. Few doubted that a bloody civil war loomed on the not too distant horizon. For the left, a world historical moment seemed to have arrived: the time had come for the Spanish masses to rise up and cast off their chains. At the same time, Betty's privileged circle was convinced that the cherished soul of the glorious Spain they had inherited from their fathers—conservative, landed, and Catholic—was at stake. The upper class feared, and not without harrowing reason, that the Popular Front was determined to sweep their inegalitarian Spain into the dustbin of history.

Continually stirring this rapidly boiling conflict were Spain's powerful Catholic clergy—a holy legion of defenders of the Old Order that included 30,000 priests, 20,000 monks, and 60,000 nuns. Every Sunday pious churchmen preached that any parishioner who supported the liberal cause was committing a mortal sin.

When the archbishop of Toledo vilified the newly elected government of the Republic in a widely circulated pastoral letter, the left decided it was the sign they'd been praying for. They took to the streets in rage. Priests were rounded up and thrown into jail. Churches were burned to the ground.

"It was a frightful spectacle," Betty told Hyde, the memory still disturbing after all the years. "The sky was crimson as far as you could see. Burning churches spread across night skies. But things could not go on, and everyone knew that this was the beginning of the end of the Republican regime."

As the anticlerical fury spread through Madrid, Betty's priest was arrested and locked in a prison. It seemed very likely that he was destined to join the sainted ranks of Catholic martyrs.

Fire engulfs a cathedral during the Spanish Civil War. Betty would later recall "[b]urning churches spread across night skies," as she told Hyde about her time in Madrid.

WHEN BETTY HEARD THE NEWS of his arrest, she did not hesitate. At once, she decided to rescue her lover.

It would be a freelance operation. She alone had cut the orders for this mission. The only master she was serving was her own unfettered heart.

With an intuitive tradecraft, Betty did not rush into her operation. Rather than going off pell-mell, knocking insistently on one jailhouse door after another with the improbable hope of finding the priest, Betty surveyed the various prisons throughout the city with calm concentration. Some hint to his whereabouts, she hoped, would be revealed. Reconnaissance, she understood, was never time wasted. Yet when this failed to produce a clue, Betty did not surrender. With an impressive adaptability, she quickly hatched a new plan.

She went to Ogilvie-Forbes, the embassy's counselor, and, using all her well-practiced charm, asked for his help. If the embassy made an official request, the Republican government would certainly reveal where the priest was incarcerated, she pleaded.

Let me see what I can do, Ogilvie-Forbes finally conceded with a diplomat's noncommittal caution. A career Foreign Office official who not only played by the rules but also believed in them, he dutifully checked with Whitehall. How should I handle this? he cabled.

Quickly, his query made its way across London to 54 Broadway, the offices of the Secret Intelligence Service. This was not an accident. Ever since Lord Beaverbrook brought Betty to the attention of Britain's spy establishment, they had made it known to the Foreign Office that they were keeping a watchful eye on Mrs. Pack.

Betty intrigued the talent spotters at MI6. A woman with her gifts could be very valuable in Spain, and, for that matter, in the coming battles that many in the Service believed would inevitably rock Europe. They were curious to see how she would do. A rescue mission in a war-torn city would be a good test of any potential agent's skill and cunning. The instructions were sent to help Mrs. Pack along. Just be circumspect, make sure to keep the embassy's involvement at arm's length.

Soon Betty had the name of the prison holding her priest. But short of marching up to the door, fluttering her eyelashes, flashing her luscious smile, and then asking ever so nicely that they please release her priest, she still had no plan. Once again, though, the ever-obliging Ogilvie-Forbes proved invaluable. Perhaps the papal nuncio could be helpful, he suggested.

Betty, who already had had made one priest fall in love with her, went off to meet the papal nuncio, convinced that only a small dose of her potent charm would bend another holy man to her will. And she was right. There was some initial hesitation; the nuncio argued that if he intervened for one priest, he'd need to speak out in hundreds of other equally desperate cases. But in the end, Betty's powers of persuasion overwhelmed his logic. Impressed by the authority of the Vatican's representative, the Republican government released the priest.

Once the priest was free, with a meticulousness that was cheered by the spies working at 54 Broadway, Betty saw her mission through to its operational end. She arranged for the priest to escape to northeast Spain, where the Nationalist forces were massing in an underground movement. He'd be free once again to practice his vocation. Unless, she conceded, he was still pining for her.

George Arthur Ogilvie-Forbes (right), counselor at the British embassy in Madrid in the days before the Spanish Civil War, meets members of a Republican militia group in 1936.

♦   ♦   ♦

BETTY'S NEXT MISSION WAS ANOTHER exfiltration—her own.

During the perilous first weeks of July 1936, the question being asked throughout Madrid was not whether a civil war would break out; it was, rather, whether the hostilities would commence the next day. The British ambassador and most of his staff had already scurried out of the city to the safety of the summer embassy in the seaside resort of San Sebastian, up in the calmer north of Spain, reassuringly close to the French border. Betty, however, had convinced her husband that they should linger. After all, there was a lover she still looked forward to meeting in the sticky summer afternoons.

But by July 13, as volleys of gunshots rang out across Madrid, even Betty realized it would be imprudent to stay in the city. At least for their daughter's sake, she agreed, they should leave. It was decided that they would drive north and cross the border into France. In Biarritz, they could rent a villa.

She spent the night before her departure with Carlos. Wrapped in each other's arms, they exchanged thin assurances that this was just a brief, temporary farewell. Carlos promised that he would fly to Biarritz, that they would somehow manage to spend time together. They both knew, though, that history was on the march. Unpredictable events would cavalierly shape their lives.

Early the next morning Betty and her husband, along with Denise and her nanny, left the city. "There was nothing to suggest the beginning of fratricide along the peaceful highway or in the sleepy villages that laced the way to the French frontier on our drive north," she recalled nostalgically to Hyde.

"I remember the intense colors of the new day, and also the stillness. The sky was a Murillo blue and cloudless; its only inhabitants seemed to be the magpies that harvested here and there in scattered groups within the fields. And the fields themselves spread endlessly beneath the gold of their grain with great crimson splashes of red poppies."

It would not be long before Betty, off on her next mission, returned to Spain; and by then the fields were red not with flowers but with blood.

Chapter 16

◆

THREE DAYS AFTER BETTY'S ESCAPE, the Spanish civil war began. The army rebelled, the Republican government armed civilians to fight the insurrection, and the country unraveled. Violence ruled. Both sides, furious, determined, and savage, rushed into battle. Honor justified every vengeful deed. The country bled with atrocities.

In the north, the Republican city of San Sebastian fell under siege. "We must extend the terror," thundered General Emilio Mola, who commanded the swarm of Nationalist forces gathering to take the town. "We must eliminate without scruples everyone who does not think as we do," the *New York Times* reported the general telling his troops.

From offshore Fascist gunboats anchored in the Bay of Biscay, cannons pounded away at the city, a terrifying, nearly constant barrage. From hidden nests dug out of the high ground, machine gunners indiscriminately riddled homes, stores, and anyone reckless enough to move about the boulevards. While in the foothills, the Nationalist army waited, eager for the command that would turn them loose to charge with a single blood-curdling scream into the streets of San Sebastian.

At the same time, the makeshift soldiers of the Republic, workers and peasants armed with weapons stolen from gun shops and police stations, prepared to defend their homes. Formidable barricades encircled the city, every roadway guarded by exhausted, frightened men, fingers curled tight around the triggers of their rifles as they aggressively challenged anyone coming or going. In the neighborhoods, *casas del pueblos*, as the proletariat headquarters were christened, sprung up, chaotic battle stations manned by untrained troops resigned to fight to the death against the onslaught they knew would come soon.

The British embassy and its staff, along with other foreign diplomatic legations, had moved for safety into the Continental Hotel. Civil guards were posted at the entrance, as much to keep guests in as to keep San Sebastian's populace out; the dining room windows had already been boarded up so that hungry outsiders wouldn't see the privileged lodgers eating as if there wasn't a war going on.

Inside the Continental, another sort of madness reigned. Day and night the lobby was crowded with a rambunctious assortment of exotic types: dark-suited diplomats, foraging journalists, wheelers and dealers from a half dozen or so countries, self-appointed Republican staff officers in their new brown uniforms, stern Comintern agents, and always a gaggle of brightly painted whores with eager smiles. The bar served drinks and rumors around the clock, and the communal fear was that the liquor would run out before the stories.

Sir Henry Chilton, the imperious British ambassador who blatantly sided with the Nationalists, was quite annoyed by the inconveniences he and his staff had to endure. He sent dispatches to the Foreign Office grumbling about the bullets "potting" at the hotel windows, about the "men, unshaven and short of sleep, but fired with enthusiasm for their cause, issuing orders," about "loud voiced individuals all armed with revolver, shot gun or rifle."

Then abruptly his dispatches stopped. The phone and telegraph lines to the Continental Hotel were down. There was no way to get a message in or out of the city. San Sebastian was cut off from the outside world.

◆ ◆ ◆

NOT QUITE THIRTY MILES AWAY, in Biarritz, France, Betty had settled into what might as well have been not just another country but another world. Sunbathers lolled on the warm sands of the Grand Plage. Diners in straw hats, blazers, and white pants sat on the Palace Hotel terrace picking at icy towers of *fruits de mer* and sipping flutes of chilled champagne as they gazed at a tranquil bright blue sea. When the sun set, men in evening clothes accompanied by bejeweled ladies in long gowns, many of them wealthy Nationalists who had shrewdly managed to get out of Spain, gathered round the roulette tables at the casino. The wheel spun round and round, and night after night the gamblers placed their bets, took their risks.

This was Betty's life too. And she was miserable. Two placid weeks, and she was ready to explode. The days were too easy, too straightforward. She needed something larger; she needed the liberation that came from inhabiting several lives at the same chaotic time.

Like the patrons of the casino, Betty was also a gambler. The games of chance offered in Biarritz, however, were too tame for her. A war raged across the border, and every wild voice inside her head was shouting that she had to be a part of it. She had to chuck away this comfort, this phony freedom. She needed authentic thrills, important risks. She resolved to go back to Spain, place her bet, and let the wheel spin.

But before she could leave, Arthur beat her to it. A cable from the Foreign Office arrived at their rented seaside villa. By Whitehall's customary understated standards, it was a full-blown distress signal.

The ambassador and all his staff, for all practical purposes, had vanished. No one in London knew if they were alive or dead. Pack was to go at once to war-torn San Sebastian and find out.

◆ ◆ ◆

I WILL BE BACK THIS evening, Arthur promised Betty. It shouldn't be more than a four-hour trip; San Sebastian was on the other side of the Bidasoa River, a short drive over the Santiago Bridge. He'd pay his respects to Sir Henry, then turn around and head back. A quick cable to soothe the Foreign Office, and then they could go off to dinner.

When Arthur didn't return by midnight, Betty began to worry. When he still hadn't appeared by the next afternoon, she made a plan. The idea, or at least some version of it, had been building inside her even before Arthur vanished, and now she had the excuse she needed. She had rescued a lover. The least she could do, she decided, was save her husband too.

At dawn the next morning, Betty woke the nanny and told her to watch Denise until she returned. Then with Eusabio, the young chauffeur, she launched her mission. As they headed out of town, the last of the night's revelers making their woozy way home and the sea sparkling in the first light, Betty suddenly ordered, "Stop the car." Without a word of explanation, she jumped out and strode purposefully to the tall flagpole in front of a grand seaside hotel. She studied it intently, then hurried up the hotel's broad front steps.

Moments later she returned to the flagpole with a frock-coated deskman and a bellboy in a reddish uniform and a cap that resembled an upside down teacup. Eusabio watched as Betty handed the man in the silly coat a handful of francs, and the boy in the silly hat lowered the Union Jack. It cost Betty some more francs, but the bellboy, with some difficulty, managed to fix the flag to the car's bonnet. The Union Jack's resplendent authority would make the rebels pause before they opened fire on the car, Betty told herself. Unless, she realized in the next uneasy moment, it just gave their marksmen a better target.

They had not driven much farther before Betty once again

ordered Eusabio to halt. She had made another operational decision: two flags were better than one.

She went into the first hotel that caught her eye, this time
emerging with several red cloth napkins. Quickly she attached a
red flag of sorts, a banner she hoped would be viewed with sympathy by the Marxist factions in the Republican forces, to the vehicle's antenna. With two flags flying—symbols in their way of
the bifurcated allegiances that warred continually in Betty's soul—
they headed to the border.

They approached the Santiago Bridge, their trepidation mounting. The murky waters of the Bidasoa River seemed a harbinger of
the tumult that lay ahead. On high alert, they crossed into Spain.

They hadn't gotten far before they were stopped. The Republican militiamen guards at the border town of Irun were not impressed by either of the flags.

*Rebel Fascists firing across the Bidasoa River, at people retreating
from occupied Irun to seek sanctuary in France, in 1936.*

With deadpan calm, Betty explained that she was on her way to San Sebastian. The disclosure only added to the guards' uneasiness. It seemed strange that anyone would want to go to a city about to be overrun by Nationalist troops.

"Get out of the car," one of the soldiers ordered. He pointed his shotgun at her chest to make sure she obeyed. "You must go to the *commandancia*."

"What about my car?" Betty demanded, hoping she sounded confident, all haughty and indignant.

"Requisitioned," he replied tersely.

Two scruffy men carrying submachine guns positioned themselves like bookends on either side of her. Betty smiled at one, and then the other, flashing her hundred-watt charm. Neither of the soldiers noticed; their eyes looked straight ahead, flat and vacant.

"They will take you," the man with the shotgun said.

"What about my driver?" Betty tried. "I won't go without him."

"Don't worry about your driver."

One of the soldiers nudged her in the ribs with the barrel of his machine gun, and she started walking.

"Your papers," the commandant demanded.

His hair was greasy and uncombed. He had not shaved for days. A bandolier loaded with bullets stretched across his dirty shirt.

Betty gave him her passport and the identity card the Spanish government issued to all accredited diplomats and their families.

He glanced at each of the documents quickly, as if they were irrelevant. Contemptuously, he tossed them onto the wooden table in front of him.

Strutting across the room, a king in his tiny kingdom, he found an opened bottle of brandy. He lifted it to his lips, and took a long swig. When he was done, he wiped his mouth with the back of his hand.

He looked closely at Betty, inspecting her, focusing on every curve. She had endured that sort of scrutiny from men before. Sometimes she didn't mind. Now it frightened her.

The commandant took another long swallow of brandy. Suddenly he slammed the bottle down hard on the table. In the small, windowless room the noise sounded like a gunshot.

"These papers are forged!" the commandant shouted. "You are a Fascist spy. Franco is your boss."

He called for a militiaman.

"*Abajo!* Take her downstairs."

Chapter 17

◆

THE SMELL IN THE BASEMENT was overpowering, a fetid, nearly suffocating mix of cigarette smoke, sweat, and fear. Soldiers filled the room, many drunk, many half naked because of the heat. Captured in yesterday's fighting, they expected to be executed soon; they would have done the same if they had been the victors.

Suddenly alert, the prisoners watched as a tall blond Anglo in a tight-fitting dress was led down to join them. They were living out their last moments, and now they had company.

Betty took a seat at the very edge of a long bench. Three men were seated at the other end. She slouched, but even as she did, she knew it was futile: it was impossible to hide. The three prisoners started inching up the bench.

"Guard!" she called. "I must speak to the commandant. This is a mistake. I'm the wife of a British diplomat."

The guard ignored her.

Betty could feel the bench shaking as the men slid toward her. From the opposite side of the airless room, a cluster of prisoners began shuffling forward. They were furtive, taking their time, waiting to see if the guard would stop them.

"Guard!" Betty yelled again. She tried not to sound desperate, but she knew she was not fooling anyone.

As she looked up, she saw that the guard was speaking to someone. At first she thought he was a prisoner; his clothes were grimy and disheveled. But she realized that he could not be: the guard listened with respectful concentration. Betty decided she must catch this man's attention.

She fixed her green eyes on him, and at the same time she silently prayed to any saint whose name she could remember. Give me this one gift and I'll never ask for anything again, she remembered promising.

A moment later he was sitting next to her.

"Señora?" he asked helpfully. Betty noticed that the three men had quickly returned to the far end of the bench. The other prisoners had also retreated.

"How kind. I knew you would come and help me," Betty began, and then paused to offer him a smile shining with the full force of her gratitude. It was a wonderful performance, the culmination of years of practice, and she let it linger.

At last she continued. "You know, you can see, it is all a mistake that I am here. I came over from France, not Spain, and my baby is there. You must get us back to her.

"You *will*," she insisted, as if her wish was as good as a command.

The man stared at Betty, both puzzled and entranced. Who was this woman? he seemed to be wondering. What was she doing here? And why did she think she could give him orders?

Yet in the next moment, he must have decided that the answers did not matter. And that he had never seen anyone so dazzling.

"But of course, señora. It is all a mistake."

Saying that he would go speak with the commandant, he rose, offered a small bow, and went off.

Betty waited. Minutes passed like years.

And then she was back in her car, Eusabio was at the wheel, and her savior was waving good-bye. "Buen vijae, señora!" he yelled.

Eusabio put his foot down hard on the accelerator. "Faster!" Betty ordered. At any moment the commandant's mind could change, and the bullets could start flying.

In half an hour she was back in Biarritz. One stiff drink later she was on the phone to the Foreign Office. Get me the duty officer, she demanded, as confidently as if she'd been a fieldman filing flash messages to London Station all her operational life.

A Mr. Greene listened without comment to her report: Spain had dissolved into total anarchy. No British citizen, whether diplomat or traveler, was safe. The navy had to send warships to San Sebastian to evacuate the embassy staff at once. Any delay could prove disastrous. Lives were at risk.

When she had finished, Mr. Greene politely thanked her for the information and promised he would pass it along to the proper authorities.

"Tonight!" Betty insisted vehemently.

Mr. Green broke the connection without saying another word.

That night the Admiralty dispatched the HMS *Verity* and *Veteran*. The ships' orders were to proceed to the port of San Sebastian with all deliberate speed and welcome all British citizens on board. Still, it could be as long as four days, possibly even five if there was rough weather, before the vessels arrived.

EARLY THE NEXT MORNING BETTY returned to Spain. A shaky but loyal Eusabio was at the wheel as the car crossed the Santiago Bridge, flying the same two flags. As an added precaution, he had loaded the trunk with a half dozen cans of petrol; the Republican government had requisitioned all the country's fuel supplies, and he wanted to make sure that if they were lucky enough to survive, they'd have enough gas to get back to the safety of France.

Why had Betty, the previous day's harrowing adventure still fresh in her mind, decided to return? No one forced her. No one had even asked her. She had made a promise to rescue her husband, but it was only to herself. And it was a little too late in their marriage, or her life for that matter, to pontificate about the sanctity of her word. Why put herself at risk—she'd been fortunate she hadn't been shot or raped or both in Irun—when there was no compelling reason to return? Why venture once again into an out-of-control situation where she'd be at the mercy of a bunch of unruly, heavily armed thugs?

Looking back, with the enlightenment culled from a wartime packed with daring missions, Betty decided the answer was quite simple: she wanted to. She wanted to because in that one perilous day she'd been more alive than ever before in her complicated life. After making her telephone report to the disembodied Mr. Greene, Betty had felt the gratifying glow of accomplishment, of a job well done. When she drove back into Spain, it wasn't as if she had a choice. She wasn't doing it for Arthur. Or England. Or love. It was, she explained to Hyde, because at last she knew how she wanted to live.

But this knowledge came to her only decades later. That morning Betty had other burning concerns: her car was once again stopped at the Irun crossing.

The same ragtag clique of guards stood at the gate, but this time they greeted Betty like an old and slightly crazy friend, the Anglo who insisted on driving toward the fighting. Betty laughed along with them; her itinerary *was* irrational. When their leader, abruptly grave and officious, announced she must once again see the *commandancia*, she stopped laughing.

As Betty walked slowly to the headquarters building, she had a vision of the leering commander swigging his brandy, and then in the next instant she could see herself in "that awful hole" filled with desperate men. When she made up her mind to return, she had persuaded herself that this trip wouldn't be like the previous one. Now she prepared herself for the likelihood that it would be much worse. Her uncertain courage would be tested, and she made a silent vow to keep her mounting fear locked inside. She would not succumb until the pain and humiliation were beyond her endurance.

Her stomach dropped with a sudden, sickening rapidity when she was led into the familiar tight, dark office. She expected to see her tormentor standing behind the wooden table, welcoming her with his malicious sneer.

But another officer was seated at the table, and when Betty entered, he stood politely. His hair was combed, his uniform clean. There were no threats, no insinuations. Instead, he spoke with genuine solicitude.

"Turn back," he pleaded. "There is heavy fighting all along the road to San Sebastian. You could get caught in the crossfire. Perhaps ambushed. The soldiers on both sides are not too particular about who they slaughter."

Betty thanked him for his concern, but she had not come this far to retreat. She was determined to reach the city, to find her husband.

The commander considered. Finally he threw up his hands in exasperation. "If your mind is made up, I will not stop you," he said.

With mournful resignation, he wrote a *salvo-conducto* for Betty and Eusabio. "You get stopped, a safe conduct pass might help. Or it might not. But don't expect a piece of paper to deflect any bullets," he warned. As a further and more practical precaution, he assigned two armed militiamen to accompany them on the journey.

Minutes later, Betty was back on the road to San Sebastian.

WHAT WAS THE MOST TERRIFYING part of the trip? Driving full-speed, Eusabio's foot flat on the accelerator, Betty hunched low in the front seat, as the car raced through a whistling volley of bullets? The sudden artillery fire, shells exploding, the road in an instant pockmarked with craters, the car shaking from the impact of each barrage? Hiding behind a rock, clinging to it, the ground trembling beneath her, waiting for the shelling to stop? Realizing that the trunk was loaded with cans of gasoline, and one stray bullet could ignite an inferno? Perhaps it was not knowing what waited around the next curve, wondering what was coming, and always expecting the worst.

The twenty-two mile drive to San Sebastian stretched on forever.

At last the car stopped in front of the Hotel Continental. Betty tried to compose herself; there had been moments on the road when she'd been convinced she was staring death—cruel, impassive, and inevitable—in its grim face. She was still shaking, and telling herself she'd been very lucky was only a small comfort.

She sat silently, hoping her nerves would settle. Finally she gave Eusabio a handful of bills. "Get yourself a stiff whisky. The militiamen, too. You earned it."

But Betty had to complete her mission.

The lobby was crowded, a nearly solid wall of apprehensive, loudly jabbering people. Betty pushed her way forward. When she reached the center of the lobby, she saw Arthur.

I did it! she silently shouted, tingling with excitement, proud of what she had done.

"What are you doing here?" Arthur demanded. There was no greeting, no acknowledgment of the risks she had taken to find him. "I thought you were with Denise. Taking care of her."

If that was the way he wanted to be, Betty decided she would pay him no attention. "I need to see the ambassador," she announced. Her tone was dismissive and peremptory. She waited in silence until at last he led the way.

Her report to Sir Henry was precise and professional. She described the dangerous conditions all along the road from the French border and then informed him of her call to the Foreign Office.

"Do you think they should send a destroyer?" Betty asked dis-
ingenuously. She was well-practiced in tiptoeing through risky
ground.

"Yes, indeed. Tell them to send one most urgently." He tapped
the table in front of him as if to underline the sentiment.

Betty relaxed, and revealed that she had already made the request.

"Well done!" he exploded. "Well done!"

Then he gave her instructions. She was to return to France at
once. There were several messages he needed to convey to the
Foreign Office. He dictated them, and then listened as Betty read
them back. "Excellent," he said. "You must call the Foreign Office
as soon as you're in Biarritz. Tell them what I said. Word for word.
I'm counting on you."

"As soon as I'm home," Betty agreed.

Arthur glowered.

He waited till they were in the lobby to attack. "How could you
risk your life? How could you leave our daughter?"

Betty knew he wouldn't understand; she didn't even try to explain. "Sir Henry is counting on me," she said, full of her newfound authority. Without another word, she walked off.

Arthur followed, reluctant to make a scene; unseemly public
displays were anathema to him, the sin of sins for a diplomat. And
he knew Betty relished a good battle, any time or any place. Sty-
mied, he seethed with a quiet, building anger.

As Betty crossed the lobby—a sulky Arthur trailing a few feet
behind—a group of five young soldiers approached. A tall, thin
boy with haunted eyes and hollow cheeks, their leader, apparently,
did all the talking.

"We are Franco supporters," he explained. "If the Republicans
discover us, we will be executed. You have a car; we saw it out
front. Can you take us to Fuenterrabía, up by the border? We can
make our way to safety from there."

Fuenterrabía was in the mountains, a long way from the Santiago bridge that led to Biarritz. It was impossible to know what obstacles lay along that route, but they were easy to imagine.

Immediately Arthur intervened. All his indignation now boiled over. He began to shout, and for once he did not seem to care if anyone noticed.

"You can't do it," he ordered. "It's too dangerous. It's not your concern. Tell me you agree," he demanded.

"Yes," Betty lied.

Three hours later she left the five grateful soldiers at the side of a dark, winding road in Fuenterrabía. And two hours later she was back in her villa in Biarritz.

She called the Foreign Office. When the duty officer answered, she repeated the ambassador's messages word for word. Then she made him read it back. She did not hang up until she was certain he had it all.

That night, she'd still remember a lifetime later, she enjoyed the soundest sleep of her young and just-burgeoning life.

Yet in the morning all her newfound joy was shattered. A cable arrived from her mother: her father had died at the Washington Naval Hospital of lung cancer. Betty knew that he'd been ill, but she was still stunned by his death. She had not realized how quickly his condition could deteriorate. And now it was too late. She would never see him again. She never even had a chance to say good-bye.

Her only solace, she tried to convince herself, was that her father, a battle-tested marine, would have been proud of how his daughter had performed on her mission to San Sebastian.

IN THOSE TWO DANGEROUS DAYS, and in recognition of the valuable reports she had made to the Foreign Office, Betty had become what her new masters in London called "a symbolized agent." She wasn't a full-fledged spy, on neither the Firm's books nor its payroll. But they had thrown their yoke around her neck; she was one of theirs. No longer were the MI6 wise men in their wood-paneled offices on Broadway in London simply keeping a sharp eye on her. She had become an "asset," part of a small private army the Service could call on in a pinch. If the situation demanded, she would be their woman in Spain. They knew they could count on her.

And no less, Betty, she divulged to Hyde, counted on the Service and all it had to offer. Her sense of desperateness, her anguish on losing the single person to whom she had felt bound by an unqualified love had threatened to push her out of control. But in the Service she hoped to find a worthy substitute for the love she had lavished on her father. It was the springboard she'd use to jump forward, and a way to placate her unsatisfied emotions. She still mourned—but, she wanted Hyde to understand, in her heart her duties and allegiances had never been clearer.

Chapter 18

◆

FROM THE HILLTOP BETTY WATCHED plumes of dark smoke rising in the distance. Across the river in Spain, Irun was burning. Rather than allow Franco's advancing troops to capture the city, the Republicans had set it ablaze. Betty was twenty miles away in Hendaye, France, and as the thick gray smoke floated toward her across the starlit night sky, she could feel the war's danger and intrigue prickle her skin, urging her into action.

Her last mission had been a revelation; she was still giddy over its success, empowered by what she'd accomplished. Just days after her call to the Foreign Office, the Royal Navy had steamed into the port of San Sebastian. Protected by a gauntlet of His Majesty's marines, the ambassador and his staff made their furtive escape from the hotel and then scrambled up the gangplanks of the two battle-ready destroyers. The following afternoon, their heads once again held high, the diplomats disembarked at the picturesque French fishing village of Saint-Jean-de-Luz.

Much to his embarrassment, Sir Henry grudgingly set up a makeshift embassy over a grocer's shop a few miles away, in Hendaye; it was the closest town on French soil to Spain, just a stone's throw from the border bridge spanning the Bidasoa River. Arthur and Betty, along with many of the embassy personnel, abandoned the gaudy comfort of Biarritz to find housing in nearby Saint-Jean-de-Luz, a cluster of modest, starkly white seventeenth- and eighteenth-century buildings that looked straight out on the Atlantic. Their new flat was a low-ceilinged maze of tiny rooms that smelled strongly of fish.

Betty (#3), Ambassador Sir Henry Chilton (#1), and
Arthur Pack (#2) in Saint-Jean-de-Luz, France.

"We do not know how much longer we will be here," a gloomy Betty wrote in a letter to Arthur's sister Rosie. "What a dreadfully heart-breaking and tragic three months this has been. My beloved Spain being so ruthlessly tortured . . ."

Although she was safe in France, the war's horrors still weighed heavily on her mind. "Some of their atrocities are beyond the bounds of imagination," Betty wrote in another dispirited letter from Saint-Jean-de-Luz. "In Barcelona they split open the abdomens of pregnant women and put these women in shop windows saying 'these women are nuns.' In one province little children were hung by feet downwards and left to die of hunger and thirst. And there are many other such crimes to their infamy. It is a *nightmare.*

"Worse," she complained, focusing now on her own predicament, "the life to which we settled down was one of waiting."

What was Betty waiting for? As she passed her empty days in a quiet French fishing village, as nearly the entire northwest Spain fell into Nationalist hands, as Madrid and large tracts of the south remained under Republican control, what was she hoping for? Like any agent who had tasted the thrill of the secret life, Betty was looking forward to the summons to her next mission.

When the call finally came, two separate operations were thrown at her. They presented themselves without warning, and each was seemingly unconnected with the other. Yet both, as if by design, played out in tandem. And while one was a mission of mercy, the other was more personal, launched in the name of a deep and abiding love.

AUGUSTIN, VISCOUNT OF ALTAMIRA, OFFERED the initial opportunity for Betty's return to the field. A descendant of an ancient and fabled Spanish noble family—Goya had immortalized one young and haughty ancestor as his "boy in red"—Altamira was passing through France on his way back to Spain to join up with Franco's soldiers and, with nothing else to do on a quiet night in Saint-Jean-de-Luz, had invited Betty to dinner.

She had first met Altamira, a suave charmer who had inherited his family's crisp, angular good looks as well as their well-bred manners, during her time in Madrid. He was another of the handsome faces that appeared at the same parties as she did, a traveler in the carefree set who, happily tipsy, would greet the dawn on the crowded dance floor at Jimmy's. From her memories of those now too ancient days, she recalled a slightly bemused vagueness, a man who seemed only to lift himself from the depths of his perpetual weariness to light the cigarette of an attractive woman.

But the war had energized the viscount. The man Betty now encountered was determined to fight to preserve the title and traditions that were, he emphatically affirmed, his birthright. It was 170 miles from the border to the medieval cathedral city of Burgos where the Nationalist forces were massing, and Altamira had made up his mind to get there.

The journey promised to be a tense one: well-outfitted Republican troops still held many of the roadways. Altamira's plan, as he explained it with undaunted confidence over their long seaside dinner, was to stay off the main routes, and instead drive through the perilous backcountry mountain roads. If the car didn't skid off a rock-strewn curve and fall hundreds of feet into an abyss, it was also possible, he acknowledged with an indifferent shrug, that Republican gunners would spot the vehicle and use it for artillery practice. Yet no sooner had he finished laying out the obstacles he'd be facing than he offered Betty the chance to come along too.

If the danger wasn't inducement enough, Altamira, without even realizing it, had conveniently already suggested another rationale on which Betty could hang her decision. Earlier in the course of dinner, the viscount had talked about the primitive conditions in the field hospitals. Scores of people died unnecessarily. With the proper medical supplies—antibiotics, surgical equipment, anesthesia—lives could be saved, he reported gravely. Betty had listened with horrified attention.

When Altamira threw out his invitation, Betty in an instant cut the orders for her next mission: she would tour the hospitals surrounding Burgos; find out what they needed; and then, expense and logistics be damned, somehow obtain the supplies and get them to the war zone field stations.

"I'd love to accompany you," she told the viscount as he walked her home that night along the beach, the waves lapping against the sand, the autumn moon lighting the way.

Neither Arthur's predictable objections nor her responsibilities to her young daughter gave Betty any pause. All the reasonable,

cautionary arguments against returning to a barbarous, unpredictable Spain, she promptly decided, were not worth a moment's
thought. This unexpected opportunity was precisely what she'd
been waiting for, and that was all that mattered.

Then, as Betty was enjoying the prospect of this new chance for
adventure, the operational gods, with a sudden generosity, dumped
another mission into her lap.

There was a knock on the front door of the house in Saint-Jean-
de-Luz, and Betty opened it to find Carlos's wife, Carmencita. But
she too had become a different person. Carmencita's flight from Madrid and her long journey to France had been an ordeal. The woman
Betty quickly welcomed into her home, once so gay, so chic, had
become another of the war's victims—ragged, penniless, and bereft.

After Carmencita had bathed, changed into one of Betty's
dresses, and sat down at a table swiftly covered with plates loaded
with an assortment of cheeses and cold meats, she shared her sad
story. Between ravenous mouthfuls and long swallows of wine,
Carmencita reported that Carlos, along with his brother officers
in the Spanish Air Ministry, had been "taken away in the night."
She had tried to discover what had become of him, but it was impossible. No one would tell her anything. For all she knew, Carlos
could still be suffering in a Republican prison, or he might have
been put up against a wall and shot. Either fate was very possible,
she conceded tearfully. When she finally accepted that there was
nothing she could do, and that the Republican avengers would
probably come for her next, she ran.

Betty listened, and tried to steady herself. Even as Carmencita
spoke, Betty's mind flashed on images from her intense, sultry afternoons with Carlos in their penthouse hideaway. They had been
in love, or at least that was what she'd told herself at the time, and
now the possibility that he might be wasting away in a dank Republican jail left her shaken. Who would help him?

There was no one else; she would go search for him.

Even as she made the decision, she realized that she had no clues, no starting point for her investigation. The possibility that Carlos was dead was too sad to contemplate, and so she dismissed it. No, she told herself firmly, he was alive. In the course of her mission with Altamira, she would start asking questions, making inquiries. She would somehow find him, just as she had found her priest and then her husband.

There was, however, one immediate problem: Arthur forbade her to go with Altamira. Not only, he insisted with good reason, was it too dangerous, but as a British diplomat's wife, Betty could not be seen to support the Nationalist faction. Although the sympathies of many in the embassy, including the ambassador, were with the conservative and royalist forces, His Majesty's government had endorsed the democratically elected Republican regime. The Foreign Office would be enraged, Arthur sternly lectured, if they learned that his wife was assisting Nationalist field hospitals. His career would be destroyed.

Betty didn't argue. There was no point; her mind was set. She was quite prepared to tell him anything he wanted to hear and then slip away in the night. But as she began plotting her escape, Arthur was summoned to London. Whitehall had scheduled a two-week conference to discuss commercial issues, and his presence was essential.

So early one morning Betty accompanied Arthur to the train station; kissed him good-bye; promised that she would take good care of Denise; and then hurried home to scribble a quick note informing him of her departure. Leaving it on the dining room table, she drove off minutes later with Altamira.

"Come with me, señora, and you can see for yourself what we need."

It was Betty's second day in Burgos. The three-day trip through the mountains had been blessedly uneventful. They had not encountered a single Republican patrol. No whistling bullets. No pounding cannons. Even the dirt roads twisting through the peaks had proved surprisingly manageable. And now Altamira, proudly outfitted in a well-tailored colonel's uniform, had escorted Betty to the headquarters of the Red Cross. As promised, he introduced her to his old friend Dr. Luis Valero, the head of the Spanish branch of the international medical organization.

The doctor was a tall, painfully thin man with a bushy mustache that spread across his face like the wings of a bird in flight. Betty quickly explained why she had come; her plan was to learn what the hospitals needed, purchase the items with money she would raise from her well-heeled friends in Biarritz, and then return to Burgos with the supplies. She spoke with certainty and conviction, as if it would all be as simple as that.

Dr. Valero could not dare to doubt her; he was desperate. His response, heartfelt and immediate, was an invitation to accompany him, "to see for yourself."

"What I saw was heartbreaking, even for a field hospital," Betty would decades later tell Hyde. "In makeshift conditions, wounded and dying in every stage of suffering lay on the floor, their bandages improvised from any kind of paper at hand."

Afterward the doctor gave her a long list of what was required—drugs, antiseptics, cotton wool, gauze, surgical instruments. He spoke with the wishful optimism of a timid child asking for Christmas presents, doubting that his grandiose request could be fulfilled, yet at the same time fervently hoping. When Betty promised that she would return shortly with all the supplies, she suspected that he was trying very hard to believe her.

Only on the trip back to France did Betty begin to wonder how she might accomplish all that she'd promised. It would be very expensive, far beyond her own resources. Yet there were many wealthy Spaniards sitting out the war in Biarritz. How could any of them refuse to assist soldiers wounded while fighting on their behalf? And how could any of these hot-blooded Latin aristos turn down an attractive woman's ardent plea?

She traveled straight to Biarritz and, unannounced, appeared at the grand villa of an immensely wealthy Spanish refugee. An element of surprise, she had decided, would work in her favor.

The man was old enough to be her father, but he had flirted energetically with Betty for years. On the dance floor at Jimmy's he had held her very close, and from time to time his heavy hands would carelessly wander. Betty had responded to these advances with an indulgent smile; she'd long ago come to the conclusion that men were silly, helpless creatures, and that old men were the worst. But now the time had come to collect on the many petty indignities she'd endured with such playful good nature.

It was all surprisingly easy. As with many habitual flirts, especially those of a certain age and a dubious virility, the Spaniard's lustful attentions had, Betty suspected, little to do with genuine desire. In fact, Betty would say, he seemed astonished that she had come to him, that his persistence had actually succeeded.

He was content to share a glass of wine, sit next to her on the sofa, and no doubt silently congratulate himself that his playboy charm had not faded with the passing years. Besides, he was a married man, and his life was already sufficiently complicated by one demanding mistress.

They sat close to one another and chatted. When in the meandering course of their flirtatious banter, Betty revealed that she'd come to ask a favor, he was prepared to listen. "Anything, my dear," he agreed with a reflexive charm.

They need medical supplies in Burgos, she said. I have a long list.

"Done!" he said at once. And no doubt he considered himself lucky; jewels were, he knew too well, much more expensive.

Betty moved closer to him on the sofa and clutched his liver-spotted hand. "I'll need everything tomorrow," she purred.

"Of course, my dear," he agreed. Then, satisfied with the way things had gone, he rose and politely walked her to the door.

But now she had to deal with Arthur. On the way to the flat in Saint-Jean-de-Luz, she contemplated the uproar that would break out upon her arrival. An indignant Arthur would castigate her for breaking her promise, abandoning their daughter, and going off to Spain—to help the Nationalists, no less! That, she knew, would be bad enough. But when he learned that she'd be returning to-morrow to Burgos, the full self-righteous force of his anger would erupt. It would be an all-out battle that few marriages could survive. So be it! she decided. Damn the consequences! Nothing was more important than this mission.

But once again, her operational luck held. Arthur had returned from London, only to be sent off to inspect the Republican-held territory in the south. He'd be gone for days.

The next afternoon, her car tightly packed with the medical supplies Dr. Valero had requested, she returned to Burgos.

Three days later she was standing in the garden behind the Red Cross building. Dr. Valero had assembled the staff, and there were tears of gratitude in his eyes. He presented Betty first with a home-made armband with a red cross on a white background, and then with a bouquet of roses picked from a garden that had somehow survived the war.

With great dignity, he delivered a short, earnest speech of thanks. The staff applauded, and Betty, deeply moved, tried not to cry. She held herself tall and erect as she imagined her father had done when he had received his medals.

When the ceremony was over, the doctor unashamedly handed

Betty a new and longer list of much needed supplies. He was now a man who believed in miracles.

"I will do my best," Betty vowed.

She was returning to her car, ready to set off on the long trip back to France, when a military officer approached. "You will be good enough, please, señora, to accompany me," he said. The words were spoken with an impeccable politeness, but it was clear they were an order. "Your presence is required at the Foreign Ministry."

"At whose request?" Betty challenged. In wartime there were many grounds for a summons to a government office, and all were cause for concern.

"Señor Don José de Yanguas Messia, Viscount of Santa Clara de Avedillo," he answered firmly, "would be honored if the señora would graciously permit him a few minutes' conversation."

Avedillo was Franco's foreign minister. If he wanted to speak with her, whether she graciously permitted it or not, Betty knew it would happen.

"Of course," she said. There was no way out, nowhere to run. She let the officer lead the way, and tried not to think what might be in store for her.

For any agent, one of the cardinal operational rules is not to exceed your brief. Betty's mission was already twofold: she would deliver medical supplies and at the same time make discreet inquiries about Carlos. That was what she'd set out to do, and it was challenge enough. There was no reason to take on anything else, and put those two formidable missions. But in Betty's meeting with the foreign minister, common sense deserted her.

Perhaps she felt invincible after her successful delivery of the medical supplies. And Avedillo's approach was artful. He offered a glimmer of hope just when Betty desperately needed it.

It had come to his attention, the minister began as they sat across from one another in his huge office, that Betty had been making inquires regarding Señor Carlos Sartorius. Possibly he could be of assistance. He'd be glad to have his ministry use its resources, if Señora Pack so desired.

On both her trips into Spain, Betty had asked all those she met if they had any idea of what had happened to Carlos. Despite her persistence, the results had been dismal: no one had heard even a rumor. A well-connected and powerful minister, though, would have more sources. He might get an answer. "I'd be most grateful," Betty said at once.

"Good," agreed the minister. "I will see what I can do."

Now that he had dangled the carrot, Avedillo deftly moved on to explain why he had summoned Betty. He had a sealed envelope he wanted Señora Pack to deliver to Sir Henry Chilton, the British ambassador. With a nonchalance that was either feigned or betrayed a colossal naïveté, he disclosed its contents: it was a request that the ambassador formally recognize the Franco government.

Betty's first response was disbelief. If she delivered the letter, she'd be assisting a representative of the rebel regime. The Crown recognized only one government in Spain—the Republic. For the wife of a member of the embassy staff, and a lowly one at that, to take delicate foreign policy matters into her own hands—acting on her own initiative to convey an approach from an insurgent government—would create a full-blown scandal. It was wrong in so many ways that even Betty, a master of convenient rationalizations, could find no justification. It was the sort of ill-considered escapade that would leave a permanent blemish on Arthur's career.

And yet, she reminded herself in the next instant, the minister had offered to help find Carlos. However faint that hope might be, it was enough to overpower all her reservations. Not only would she save Carlos, she exulted, as paradoxical as ever, but Sir Henry would congratulate her as enthusiastically as he had when she'd turned up without warning in San Sebastian. It would become true, simply because she wanted it to be.

Betty took the envelope from the foreign minister.

"I left Burgos," she told Hyde, "and drove to Hendaye. It was evening when I arrived and the lights were still on so I went in. Someone on the staff told me my husband had returned from his trip and was very angry about my absence. But I did not want to be scolded then as I first had to see the Ambassador and give him the envelope. . . .

"As it happened when the Ambassador had finished with me, nothing my husband had added subsequently mattered. I went back to Biarritz, delivered Dr. Valero's second list, and lay down on my bed and cried."

YET BETTY WAS RESILIENT. THE ambassador's words—she vividly remembered their harsh, imperious tone, but little else from his tirade—had stung. But now she pushed them aside. Betty reminded herself, as she would at countless low moments in her turbulent life, that she was not her mother: She would not be swayed by what other people thought. Only one voice mattered in the unruly chorus singing in her head—her own.

Everything that she believed in was telling her that she must go back to Burgos, deliver the next batch of medical supplies, and find Carlos. That was her mission; as long as it was still possible, she would not abandon it.

Two days later, her car packed with the fresh supplies her benefactor had obediently purchased, she headed across the bridge into Spain. This time the guards ordered her to stop. She must report to the *comandancia*, they told her firmly.

It was only a short walk to the concrete building, but in those few yards a dozen contradictory possibilities stormed through

Betty's mind. She did not want to end up again in the hole. She saw herself abandoned in a cell crammed with desperate prisoners. Anything but that, she prayed.

Yet in all her imagined scenarios, she had never anticipated that a familiar figure in a Nationalist colonel's uniform would be in the commandant's office, standing at attention to greet her.

"You must go back to France. You must go back!" the Viscount of Altamira ordered as soon as she walked in. He was excited, and his usual elaborate courtesy had disappeared.

As she tried to make sense of what was happening, he continued in a grave but forceful voice. If she refused, he said, he had orders to arrest her.

"On what charge?" Betty finally managed to ask.

"Espionage."

Betty was stunned. Either her actions in San Sebastian had caught up with her, or, just as likely, the authorities were simply guessing. But she did not delude herself. In wartime, facts were unimportant; only the charges were relevant. And the penalty for spying was death.

Still, there were medical supplies to deliver.

"It just can't be true," she said. "Someone has made a mistake.

"I don't think there is any mistake, Betty," her old friend said emphatically.

But Betty refused to panic. She pushed away thoughts of a premature death and coolly offered up a compromise. "The only possible thing to do is to telephone military headquarters in Burgos and ask them to check. Tell them I am here with you and have got to get on to Burgos to make my delivery to Dr. Valero. If they want to arrest me there, they can."

Dutifully, the viscount made the call. He listened, and Betty watched as his face tightened. When he put down the phone, his tone was flat, the resigned voice of a man who has no choice but to follow orders.

"It is as I thought," he said. "Someone has denounced you." The military authorities had been informed that the wife of the British commercial counselor was using the pretext of working for the Red Cross to enter Nationalist territory. The real purpose of her trips, according to the charges that had been filed, was to gather intelligence for the Republicans.

"Who could have made such an unfounded charge?" Betty asked, genuinely mystified. "Why?"

"I think I know who it is, and you do too," Altamira said. He pointed to France and, raising his voice in frustration, shouted, "It's that woman."

He spoke a name. As soon as he said it, all the pieces in the puzzle fell into place. It was the wife of the man who had paid for the medical supplies. "She has a cause to be jealous of me," Betty had to concede. The charm that had made her mission possible, she realized, had become her undoing.

"I have been ordered to escort you back across the border," Altamira said without ceremony. "If you refuse, I will have no choice but to arrest you."

Betty understood she would have to obey. But she made one request of her old friend. She asked if he'd take the medical supplies from her car and make sure they were delivered to Dr. Valero.

"Certainly," he agreed.

IT WAS ONLY AS BETTY and the colonel were driving back across the bridge toward France that he disclosed that the foreign minister had asked him to pass on some news.

There was an unconfirmed report that a group of air force fliers, including Carlos, had been incarcerated in a Republican prison. It was old intelligence, the minister stressed. He had no recent information; there was no way of knowing with any certainty whether

Carlos was still alive or had been executed. But since Carlos had been a serving officer, it was very possible, the minister believed, that he'd have been treated as a prisoner of war. He'd be kept alive, a captive in a military jail.

Where? Betty asked, all the day's disappointments suddenly fading. What prison?

The minister did not know. He had heard it was in Madrid. More than that, he didn't know. "But you understand, Betty," Altamira lectured with concern, "you cannot go to Madrid. Now that you've been accused of being a spy, you won't be safe anywhere in Spain."

Betty was no longer listening. She was planning how she would make her way to Madrid.

Chapter 19

♦

MADRID WAS A CITY UNDER siege. In the bloody summer of 1937, Franco's troops had advanced from the south while Mola's army marched down from the north. The plan was to squeeze this Republican-held stronghold until it surrendered.

The Nationalist planes dropped heavy bomb loads on residential neighborhoods. Their artillery shot off barrage after barrage. Their tanks lumbered forward toward the heart of the city, bulldozing whatever lay in their paths. "I will destroy Madrid rather than leave it to the Marxists," Franco promised.

The Republican militia built fortifications along the banks of the swift-flowing Manzanares River and prepared to defend their homes. Waving their revolvers high in the air, commanders urged their men to die in the trenches rather than flee like cowards. "*No pasaran!*"—They shall not pass!—became the rallying cry.

Still, it was with a renewed sense of joy, more foolhardy than brave, that Betty planned her circuitous route to this battleground. That she would need to cross through the Nationalist lines and then enter enemy Republican territory did not dissuade her. That the Nationalists considered her a spy and had issued orders to arrest her on sight was not an obstacle. Nor was she deterred by reports that no neighborhood in the city was safe; any block might suddenly be leveled, a sniper could be hiding anywhere, looking down his sights, preparing to pull the trigger. And she certainly was not put off when Arthur boomed, "I forbid you to go." This was a mission she wanted to save herself as much as to save Carlos. She could not endure another vacant day in the claustrophobic low-ceilinged flat with Arthur, the baby, and the sickening smell of fish.

Although too often rash, in the field Betty turned cool and deliberate. She proceeded with careful tradecraft. First she wrote to the Republican embassy in Paris and requested a visa. This was duly granted—Betty was the wife of a diplomat whose government recognized the Republic—but she needed to drive north to the Spanish consulate in Bayonne to fetch it. Document in hand, she purchased a ticket on the daily early-morning flight from Toulouse, France, to the Mediterranean coast city of Valencia, Spain. The street fighting, for the time being at least, was a long way off, and the Republic had prudently moved its seat of government to Valencia; Great Britain, in a show of support, had set up a chancery in the medieval city. Betty hoped that in Valencia she'd be able to convince a British diplomat to help. Or if for once her charm failed, she'd be close enough—only two hundred treacherous miles or so away—to improvise another way of making the journey to Madrid.

Her timing was shrewd. She waited for a morning when she knew Arthur would be sleeping late; there had been a bachelor party the previous night for a member of the embassy staff. She handed a note announcing her departure to the maid and told her to take it up with her husband's breakfast; she informed the nanny that she should consider herself in complete charge of the infant until her return; and then she moved quickly. A friend's car and chauffeur were waiting as instructed down the street, the motor running, and she hopped in. The Toulouse airport was about forty minutes away. "Hurry," she told the driver.

Betty was soon flying through the clouds to Valencia. Nevertheless, she imagined she could hear Arthur's wail of rage and frustration as he read her note.

◆ ◆ ◆

"You will take the first plane out of here. I'll have nothing to do with you," John Leche, the British chargé d'affaires in Valencia, admonished Betty.

Leche was a career diplomat, a tall, stylishly tweedy man who served the crown with a ruling-class sense of duty to the empire and, no less deeply ingrained, a wry undergraduate irreverence. Just days after his arrival from Buenos Aires, he'd sent a dispatch describing the conditions in Valencia that caused a stir among some of the more fussy umbrella-and-bowler sorts in Whitehall: "I have not yet got over the idea that I have landed in a lunatic asylum. . . . Every crank and busybody in the world, amongst them I regret to say, a great many British, seem to be gathered together. . . . Every kind of fisher in troubled waters of both sexes seems to be collected." But his supporters—and there were many in the Foreign Office—read the cable as typical Leche: smart, observant, and refreshingly impertinent.

This June afternoon, however, Leche's cavalier manner had given way to something hotter. That the embassy in Hendaye had sent this woman to ask for his help in getting to Madrid astonished him. Didn't they know there was a war on? Why, he'd spent the past two days moving heaven and earth to get two British women *out* of Spain. And now this silly creature wanted help in getting right into the thick of it! "Hendaye has let you come here on a fool's errand, without consulting me first," he barked.

He reinforced his words with the well-practiced stare he used on particularly dim underlings. But if he thought the attractive woman in his office would be intimidated, Leche swiftly realized he'd underestimated Mrs. Pack.

"Hendaye has nothing to do with it," Betty said matter-of-factly. "I ran away to go to Madrid, *and I am going to Madrid.*" She let that sink in, and then added with a small, bemused shrug, "No doubt Hendaye is even more furious with me than you."

Leche was inclined to disagree; no one could be more furious than he was at the moment. But instead, Betty recalled to Hyde, he just plowed on gruffly. "You have placed me in an intolerable position. Madrid is being bombed and shelled day and night. There is no one at the embassy there. If you go and are killed, I shall be responsible and there will be one bloody row. No! Back you go to where you came from!"

But Betty's mind was set. No one was going to change it. Besides, strident diplomats did not scare her; she charmed them for sport. Without another word, she picked up her small suitcase. Head held regally high, she walked slowly out of the room.

"Just a minute. Where are you going now?"

"Oh, only to have a look around. And then find a place to sleep. I have had no sleep for the past two nights."

Leche studied her for a long, pensive moment. She really was a splendid-looking woman. Pigheaded. Foolish. But splendid.

"While you are looking around, you had better get yourself a bathing suit."

His tone remained abrupt and peremptory.

But Betty knew the signs: he was softening.

"A swimsuit?" she shot back with a soft laugh. "Do you think it is necessary for me to swim the river Manzanares in order to enter Madrid?"

Leche refused to play along. At sundown the bombs begin falling on Valencia, he explained tersely. "The chancery staff takes refuge outside the city in Las Palmeras. There's a nice bit of beach. You can go for a swim and I'll make sure there's a room for you. You can catch up on your lost sleep there."

"It sounds ideal," said Betty.

*Sir John Leche, whom Betty first met when he was the British
chargé d'affaires in Valencia during the Spanish Civil War.*

IN HER NEWLY PURCHASED SWIMSUIT, Betty swam in the warm
Mediterranean waters and then lay on a superb sandy beach. Restored, she put on a low-cut cocktail dress. She made sure her hair
was perfect. Satisfied, she joined the others for dinner.

Leche, in open-necked shirt, tan trousers, and espadrilles, looking more like a man on holiday than His Majesty's chief diplomat
in a war-torn country, set the evening's breezy tone. With great
ceremony he placed Betty on his right, unseating the stunning
secretary who usually had that honor, and who spent the rest of
the meal alternately shooting daggers at Betty and looking with
aggrieved longing at her boss. Leche paid no attention; sardonic

one moment, scowling the next, and constantly keeping up a droll, flirtatious banter, he focused on Betty.

With the wine flowing and the starlight dancing on the placid sea, Betty was at ease and in control. She could play along and at the same time never lose operational focus. She waited, and when the time was right, she abruptly shut down her charm.

"You have been very kind in having me looked after in Valencia and inviting me here, Mr. Leche," said Betty. "But that is as far as my gratitude goes. Not so very far, is it?" she challenged.

"Would you be good enough to tell me what the devil it is you want?"

A radiant smile was her customary preamble. Then: "I want some form of authorization from the Spanish authorities permitting me to go to Madrid by whatever means I can get there. Otherwise"— she now shot a warning glance at the secretary whose place at the table, and apparently in the minister's heart, she'd taken—"I am likely to be your guest here for the rest of the war."

Then with great dignity she rose and followed the moonlit path to her room.

The next morning Betty left before breakfast. An early-rising member of the clerical staff was happy to give her a ride back into the city.

She spent a long, tiring day making her way through the offices of countless Republican officials. She brazenly asked each for his help in locating Carlos. Some were polite, others rudely dismissive. But none of them would offer even a tiny clue. Dejected, she took a lonely, aimless walk around the city.

Late that afternoon she returned to the chancery. She had no plan, but she also had nowhere else to go. As soon as she entered the building, Betty was told the minister wanted to see her.

Leche was stern. He was imperious. He made it clear that Mrs. Pack's behavior was totally unacceptable. He had had enough.

"I want you to know that I am not deliberately being a nuisance," said Betty with, at last, a measure of apology. "I had been obliged to make a secret get-away from Hendaye. Now I am going to do the same thing from Valencia," she said, trying to be brave even in defeat.

"Oh no you're not."

His words rankled. A moment earlier Betty could easily have broken down in tears. But not now. She had had a difficult day, but that was all. She would not give up. She would not return to France. If the minister thought he could force her, he was in for a battle.

"My secretary went out early and got this for you."

He handed Betty a thin piece of paper, the seal of the Ministry of Defense of the Spanish Republic emblazoned at the top. She read the short paragraph that followed with astonishment: all soldiers and officials of the Republic were to grant Mrs. Pack and her chauffeur "free transit and every assistance and protection."

"Be downstairs at eight o'clock this evening," Leche continued even as she read and, still not quite believing, reread the document. "A car will be waiting. You're on your own now. Good-bye."

Once again Betty had half a mind to weep. But she managed to hold off until she left Leche's office. When she finally did, she cried tears of gratitude.

Chapter 20

◆

BOMBS POURED DOWN FROM THE night sky as they rode
through the night.

Along with the Spanish driver, Leche had provided a
Captain Lance—his name was an alias, his rank an invention, and
his ostensible role at the chancery further cover; he was the resident
spook—to accompany her for the two-hundred-mile journey. But
when the droning buzz of a swarm of Nationalist bombers filled
the darkness, there was little an MI6 agent, however skilled and
resourceful, could do. All he could offer Betty was a hard shoulder
to lean on as they huddled together in the back seat. A nearby blast
rocked the vehicle, and in silent unison they prayed the next explo-
sion would not be the last sound they ever heard.

From time to time they managed to stop the car before the planes
got too close, then scramble to a roadside ditch or take shelter behind a
rock outcropping. When the convoy of bombers passed and the earth
stopped trembling, they would get back in the vehicle and continue
their uneasy, perilous journey. Headlights off so as not to signal their
presence on the road, they drove on slowly. But then there would be
the awful sound of the next wave of planes coming their way, and again
they would dart from the car in helpless panic.

The irony of this journey, Betty knew, was that these were
Nationalist planes, bombs dropped from the night sky by pilots
whose cause she supported. And why were her sympathies with the
Fascists? Her allegiances, she explained to Hyde, were, as always,
personal. The Nationalists were the party of the church, of her
lover, of her wealthy and aristocratic friends. To have chosen the

Republican side, even though they were the legitimately elected government, would have been, she said, a betrayal of all the people she loved. But that night, with the bombs raining down, she had no politics. She just wanted to survive.

She arrived in the first light of dawn in Madrid. Captain Lance offered a small salute, and, his mission accomplished, left Betty alone in front of the abandoned British embassy.

Almost at once the bombing started. Betty pounded on the embassy door, and after what seemed like a lifetime, the surprised caretaker appeared and let her in. The grand rooms, just months ago bustling with important activity, were dark and eerily silent. Betty could hear the explosions outside, and she crouched against a thick plaster wall. Above her head hung the official portraits of King George V and Queen Mary, and that was a comfort; she half convinced herself that with the personal protection of their Imperial Majesties, she would be safe.

Later that morning, as a calm interlude settled over the city, Betty made her way to her old apartment. Walking past the long queues of desperate people lining up at the bakeries and shops for the daily ration of bread and food, seeing the throngs of ragged children running in wild packs through the streets, she told herself that it would be foolish to expect things to be as she had left them. Still, she was unprepared for what she found.

The courtyard of the apartment house at Castellana 63 had once been an elegant entryway, a small, carefully manicured park with tall shade trees and bright flower beds. Now it had been transformed into a refugee camp. Pigs, hens, and even a few cows roamed indolently about. Families had plunked down their mattresses on what had once been a garden. Shouting children raced over the cobblestones. The sharp, slightly sickening smells of strange foods being cooked over open fires filled the air.

Upstairs, the embassy seal that Arthur had fixed with so much

162 · Howard Blum

confidence on the front doorpost the day they left for Biarritz had been slashed. She pushed the door, and it swung open; the lock had been removed. Cautiously, she crossed the threshold.

The clean white world Betty had so optimistically created two long years ago was a shambles. She acknowledged the obvious symbolism with a sad smile, and then grimly began a more comprehensive inspection. The Wells family silver, a wedding present from her mother, had been stolen. The rest of their belongings, however, were mostly still there; the thieves apparently had no use for ball gowns, morning suits, china, or books. As for the missing silver, Betty shrugged off the loss; she did not need any more reminders of her mother.

Waving a handful of pesos, she recruited one of the men camped out in the courtyard below to help repair the front door and get the apartment back into some kind of order. His name was Enrique, and he explained that he'd traveled up to Madrid after his family home was destroyed in the fighting down south. Betty, who had a sentimental streak, treated Enrique with kindness, and within a few hours he'd become devoted to her. "He seemed to gain satisfaction from protecting me," she recalled to Hyde, still somewhat mystified by this sort of simple and unwavering loyalty.

The apartment, Betty glumly told herself as she looked around, would be the base from which she would launch her search for Carlos. It was lonely, not very secure, and right on the front lines of a raging war, but it would have to do.

A pounding on the front door interrupted these uneasy thoughts. It was the embassy caretaker, with an envelope.

A Miss Fernanda Jacobsen of the Scottish Ambulance Unit in Spain, a group of volunteers working under the thin protection of the International Red Cross, wrote to welcome Betty to Madrid and offer shelter. If Mrs. Pack was willing to put up with their rough accommodations, the "boys" of the ambulance unit would be glad to take her in.

How did she know I'd arrived in Madrid? a puzzled Betty wondered. But in the next moment she solved the mystery—Leche! Once again she offered the minister, so cutting one moment, so gracious the next, her mystified thanks. And then, eager to escape her ransacked apartment, she went off to meet Miss Jacobsen and "the boys."

Fernanda Jacobsen, center, and two unidentified members of the Scottish Ambulance Unit in Spain.

A ROUTINE OF SORTS QUICKLY settled in. Betty spent her days trying to locate Carlos. It was a furtive, tedious search; she had decided that direct questions might place her lover in even greater danger. So she waved a false flag. She went to Republican ministries and to hospitals around the city and made inquiries about captured air force officers. She had concocted a story that the British government was trying to locate them, and shamelessly implied that the plan was to bring them before an international tribunal. It was a ridiculously fraudulent approach; it seemed absurd to her even as she spoke the words. But she never faltered as she offered it up to the authorities. And in the process the novice secret agent learned another valuable lesson: a coat of sincerity can whitewash even the biggest lies.

At nightfall Betty entered another world. Each evening the bombs would begin to fall. And there was Betty right in the thick of it, careening around Madrid with the ambulance crews. Shells pounded buildings, explosions turned entire blocks into flaming infernos, and the rickety ambulances, their sirens screaming amid the roar of destruction, rushed toward each new disaster.

Every night was its own adventure. A child pulled out of the flames of a burning building. The frantic hunt through the debris of what had once been a family's home for a grieving man's missing wife. The surgical wards already crowded with moaning victims as Betty, her heart overwhelmed but still outwardly resolute, helped carry in one more blood-soaked body. Then the all-clear siren and the sweet relief of a calming swig of Scotch with the boys, and a precious cigarette made from loo paper and a few scavenged shreds of tobacco. Betty had never been more scared, yet every tense minute energized her. In the process she picked up, she told Hyde, "good training in keeping cool . . . which helped me during my later life."

She lived this improbable, almost solitary way, only the ambulance boys for company, for nearly a month. It was as if she had never known any other way to live. She also had begun to suspect that these would be her last days. Charging around a blazing Madrid in an ambulance, she had learned very quickly to be philosophical about the prospect of her own death. Resigned, she decided that perhaps it would be better if in her twenty-sixth year it all came to a sudden end. She had given up any hope of finding Carlos, and without him, life, she told herself, full of her customary high drama, didn't seem worth living.

Then late one afternoon, just as she was preparing to go off for another hazardous night's run with the ambulance crew, Enrique appeared at the group's headquarters. "I have news, señora," the old man whispered conspiratorially into her ear. "About our friend."

Betty listened, and then let out a shout of pure joy. All at once she had found a renewed reason to live.

Carlos was in a prison somewhere near Valencia! He was alive!

WITH THE WELCOME SOUND OF the all-clear sirens echoing through Madrid, Betty started off the next bright morning for Valencia. Without any difficulty, she'd quickly recruited four of her new adventurous friends to make the long drive with her, and Miss Jacobsen had kindly offered the use of an ambulance. Just make sure to turn around and head straight back to Madrid once you deliver Mrs. Pack, she'd insisted.

It was late in the hot summer afternoon when the ambulance drove into Valencia. Betty had no plan, not even a specific clue as to Carlos's whereabouts. All she had to go on, she realized as she finally gave the mission some careful thought, was a rumor spread by an old peasant. How would Enrique know? She was sure he meant well, but now, mulling his information over, she began to question its credibility. Who were his sources? This was probably another wild goose chase. She'd been incredibly naïve to have run off in such sudden pursuit.

The immediate problem, though, was where to go. When nothing else popped into her mind, she told the boys to drop her at the chancery.

The ambulance pulled away, and she was left alone on the street with her small suitcase.

Then she saw John Leche coming up the block straight toward her like a man on his own mission. He'll order me to return to France, Betty thought.

"It's wonderful to see you again," said the minister, taking Betty by surprise. "But you look thin. Didn't they feed you? Come along upstairs and tell me about yourself."

Gin and tonics were poured, and Betty offered a glimpse into the harrowing nights she had experienced over the last month. Leche listened, asked a few sympathetic questions, and then in an instant his mood turned.

"I received a cable from the ambassador," he began with a new formality. "Sir Henry asked me to report on you. His orders were to make arrangements for your immediate return."

Betty said nothing.

Leche pressed on. "Well, I suppose I ought to think about getting you home now."

"I wish I knew why you are trying to chuck me out again," she snapped. "I need three or four more days at the very least in Valencia before I can even think of going home."

Leche rose from his chair and moved swiftly toward her. For all Betty knew, he was going to clamp handcuffs around her wrists and call for the chancery guards to drive her to the airport.

Instead he placed one hand tenderly on her cheek.

"Betty, are you going to be stupid forever? Are you blind? I haven't any intention of chucking you out. When I said home, I didn't mean your home in France. But home with me."

ON THE DRIVE OUT OF the city to Las Palmeras, Leche took Betty's hand. A long, thin finger traced a smooth path across her palm. "Tell me what is on your mind, Betty. You aren't going to evade me any more, are you?"

Betty knew what Leche wanted. Now he'd need to know what she wanted in return. If her mission were to have any chance, frankness would be the only way.

"No, John, I will not evade you—if you do not fight me. As to what is on my mind, it is this." She told him about Carlos, about her deep and complete love. It was her long search to find him that had brought her back to Valencia.

Leche became very still. He did not try to hide his disappointment. A tight mask fell over his face.

"Betty," he said at last, "tell me one thing. Is Carlos the only man you have ever loved deeply in the whole of your life?"

"Yes," said Betty. "Oh yes. I can say that with all my soul."

They drove in silence the rest of the way.

Leche ignored Betty during dinner. The attractive secretary had been restored to her place next to the minister, and Betty was seated far down the table.

Betty picked at her food. Perhaps her candor had been a mistake. She had thought it would win Leche's cooperation. He'd have seen through false promises, she'd believed. Now she decided she'd been foolish.

After the meal, though, Leche abandoned his pretty dinner companion and approached Betty. He suggested they go for a walk. He led the way, and they headed aimlessly down the beach as the waves lapped against the sand. The high night sky was illuminated by the diffuse glow of the bombs falling in the distance on Valencia. They strolled side by side, very close to one another, but in silence.

That afternoon Betty had said all there was to say. There was no longer any reason to talk.

Leche reached out for her hand. He held it tightly for a moment. Then he raised it to his lips and kissed her fingers, one soft kiss for each.

"I don't know how to let you go," he said.

After a while, he walked her back to her room. Betty closed the door, but through the window she could see him. He stood motionless, looking straight out into the deep, dark sea. At last Betty drew the curtain closed and went to bed.

Without Leche's help, she doubted she'd be able to find Carlos. She had taken a gamble, and she had lost. She fell into a fitful sleep.

"I don't know how much later"—Betty would vividly remember to Hyde while also trying to reach her own understanding of that night and all the other nights that followed—"but I wakened from a deep sleep to an exquisite anguish that I did not, at first, understand. My body had been moved and I lay wrapped in John's strong arms.

"We were both naked and his mouth was covering my face and throat with kisses that he pressed into my flesh as though to seal the contact. He was taller than I and my body fitted his like a built-in part of it, making us one welded substance in which I completed him from his shoulders down to his thighs."

Chapter 21

◆

AND SO THEY BECAME LOVERS.

"We made love every night after that, almost for as long as I remained in that part of Spain," Betty told Hyde, frank as always about sex. "He was a passionate man, very tender and kind."

But were they in love?

Betty's romances were mercurial. She could throw over everything on a sudden whim, only to decide in the clarifying light of a new day that it was a passing fancy. The fulcrum of her emotions went wildly up and down, exhilaration one day, tedium the next. At great risk, she could embark on an adventurous quest to rescue her "one true love," only to find herself beginning an intense affair with a man she barely knew.

"John Leche was never condescending or censorious," she stated to Hyde, trying to offer up a plausible explanation for the all-too-obvious inconsistencies in her life. He was "a friend and companion, and peaceful to be with when I wanted peace." That, she hoped, would serve as sufficient justification for her passion.

But even as Betty shared this rationale with Hyde, she knew it was hollow. She knew it was just one more cover story. She had run off to Ireland with him—another man! another betrayal!—to get to the bottom of things, to try to reach an understanding of her helter-skelter life, to come to terms with the many versions of herself she had presented to the world. As she goaded herself to find a deeper, more truthful explanation, a snippet of a conversation she'd had with Leche sprung up in her mind. The words resonated in her head as if she'd spoken them just moments ago. It was as close as she'd ever gotten, she now realized, to making an honest confession.

They were in bed, their desire spent, and Leche still could not let her go. He wanted more. "I want you to love me completely," he pleaded.

Betty considered what he was offering. At that moment, her life was in turmoil. She had a husband and a child in France; a lover locked in a Spanish prison; she was sharing her bed with yet another man; and a brutal war raged all around her. It would have been a great comfort to find some certainty, to put herself under Leche's total protection.

But as much as she tried to convince herself that she wanted that sort of constancy, she knew it would always be beyond her grasp. She could only offer small parts of the various selves that shaped her. In a burst of intimacy, an honesty that took her by total surprise, she confessed to Leche, "I could never love anyone completely. I am twenty-six already and the thing you mean is never likely to happen to me."

Now at fifty-three, a lifetime of experiences behind her, she saw that her prediction had proved true. Her heart could soar. Yet it would never find long-term fulfillment. A steady, companionable happiness would always elude her.

LECHE'S COMMITMENT, HOWEVER, WAS AS ambiguous as hers. He too had his own interior restrictions. It wasn't simply that he had a wife who had fled to her native Boston to avoid the dangers of war. Leche had never deceived Betty about that. But even as he professed his love, there was another unacknowledged presence in their relationship.

One morning as they were driving back to Valencia, Leche asked for her help. A small matter, he said breezily.

With the passing of the years, Betty now knew he had been following orders. The same people on Broadway in London who had been keeping an attentive eye on her activities in Spain had given Leche his instructions. She had no trouble imagining how it came about.

The Pack woman showed a bit of pluck in San Sebastian and handled herself jolly well in Madrid, she could hear the MI6 spymasters telling one another. But dodging bombs is one thing; staring into the face of some Spanish thug when you're armed with just a smile is another matter entirely. Let's see how she handles herself on an actual mission. Test her cool one more time before we rush in and propose marriage.

Looking back at it now, Betty couldn't work up any anger over Leche's disingenuousness. He'd helped push her farther along on the path to the Service—and that, after all, was the closest thing to a complete love she'd ever find.

"CAN YOU ACT?" LECHE HAD asked, seemingly out of the blue. They were driving to the chancery after a night together at Las Palmeras. "It would be useful if you could."

It struck Betty as a silly question. "You said I was acting the fool when I went to Madrid," she said dryly.

Leche made it clear that this was no joking matter. He needed— London needed, actually, he quickly amended, underlining the seriousness—to get a prisoner out of a Republican jail. He had already given the matter a good deal of thought, and come up with an escape plan—and it required Betty's help. "Will you spare a morning from Carlos to help me?"

"Of course I will, John."

The prisoner, Leche explained, was ill; how much longer he'd survive in jail was uncertain. It was essential that they move quickly. The man had done some favors for the crown over the years, and now it was time to repay him. His name was Luis Villada, the Marquis of Aruezza.

An old friend, Betty interjected, and Leche pretended to be surprised. The marquis had been part of the set she'd run with in Madrid before the war, she explained. A dancing partner, in fact.

Well, said Leche as if he were weighing the significance of this news for the first time, that could work in our favor. Unless, of course, the sight of a familiar face confused him. That could alert the guards, and things might get sticky. Was she still on board?

"Of course, John," Betty repeated without hesitation.

THE PRISON WAS A MAKESHIFT jail; before the war it had been a government office building. When the city's prisons had run out of space to house all the suspects being so diligently rounded up, the Republicans had started housing the accused anywhere they could.

The dim basement offices had been turned into cells—straw scattered about the concrete floor served as bedding, and a pail made do as a toilet. Despite the high emotions driving the war, security remained—or so Leche assured Betty—lax. There were squads of armed guards, but months of uneventful duty had left them bored and distracted. "Stick with the plan, and all will be fine," he promised as they approached the prison.

With the Union Jack flying from its hood and its diplomatic license plate, the chancery limousine was waved past the gate and into the courtyard. Leche instructed his driver to pull up to the front door of the red brick building. As if they were a couple out for an afternoon's walk, Leche took Betty's hand and led the way into the prison; tradecraft held that sneaking about attracted more attention than a casual stroll.

Once inside, he ignored the guards and strode officiously toward the stairwell heading down to the cells like a man who had come for an appointment. Betty followed, and in the process stored away another lesson: the key to playing any role is to act as if you're not playing at all.

When they reached the cells, Leche told her, "I'll keep the guards busy. You go see about our friend."

Leche flashed his diplomatic identity card and demanded to see the man in charge. He used, Betty couldn't help noticing, the same booming, intimidating voice he had employed when they first met. This time, though, it worked. The guards started scampering about, eager to do His Excellency's bidding.

Left on her own, Betty searched for the cell number Leche had given her. The door, she'd been told, would be closed but not locked; during the day the prisoners were allowed to wander about.

Betty found the cell quickly, but hesitated. She could feel the eyes of a dozen guards boring into her. If they caught a whiff of the fear oozing out of her every pore, she'd be finished. Taking a deep, calming breath, with the most casual of gestures, she opened the door.

"Dearest brother," she bellowed as soon as she entered the cell, just as she'd rehearsed with Leche. It was crucial to control the situation. She could not allow her old friend to betray her real identity.

The marquis stared at her in astonishment. Betty quickly enveloped him in a hug as she whispered into his ear: "Play along. Don't ask questions. I've come to save you."

He looked back at her, bewildered. For an unsteady instant Betty wondered if it was too late. The man in her arms was horrifyingly frail, a thin, pale presence hardly recognizable as the sleek dancing partner who had glided her across the floor at Jimmy's. Perhaps he was incapable of understanding what she wanted him to do.

Finally he nodded.

Howard Blum

"Papa and I have come for you," she said merrily, in a voice loud
enough for anyone in the basement to hear. "Just come along quickly."

She put her hand firmly around the marquis's waist to help him
to the door. At the same time she spoke in a low voice into his ear:
"Stay close to me. If the guards suspect any funny business, they
may get rattled, but they certainly won't shoot so near a woman."
Yet even as she spoke the reassuring words, she doubted them.
The guards wouldn't hesitate to shoot any prisoner trying to escape—or, for that matter, anyone assisting him.

Moments later they were walking together across the courtyard.
Her heels clicked against the cobblestones as she spoke brightly for
everyone to hear. "Oh, dearest brother, it will be so good to have
you home. Thank God the authorities realized this was a mistake."

It was a short way to the waiting car, perhaps fifty yards, but
it seemed miles. She could hear Leche hectoring the guards in
his stentorian His Majesty's official emissary's voice. Her arm remained tight around the marquis's waist; she was nearly carrying
him. Still, she feared the old man would not make it.

It required all her discipline to keep her eyes fixed on the distant car. Her every instinct was screaming to look up at the guards,
see if their rifles were raised, see if they were taking aim. Every
moment she expected to hear someone shout, "Stop them!" But
all she heard was Leche's loud, plummy voice and the clack of her
heels on the cobblestones.

Then they were huddled in the car's back seat, driving out
of the courtyard. The barrier was still down, and Betty suffered
through a terrible moment: they were trapped, she thought. She'd
be spending her days sleeping on a bed of straw in a cell next to
the marquis.

Leche, playing his role to the hilt, offered a crisp salute to the
attending guard. It was returned, and the gate was raised. The car
pulled swiftly away.

Leche hid the marquis in a safe house, refusing to tell Betty its location; the Republicans would be searching for their escaped prisoner, and if she didn't know where he was, even a brutal interrogation would be futile. But the Republicans never questioned Betty. Two days later, the marquis was aboard a British destroyer and on his way to France.

And Betty's praises were being sung by the spymasters in Broadway. The Service's recruiters had decided the Pack woman was a promising catch. Very promising, indeed.

Chapter 22

◆

BUT WHERE WAS CARLOS? WITH more brashness than ingenuity, Betty had succeeded in one swift operation in rescuing the marquis. Yet despite all her efforts, all her cunning and tenacity, she still had not managed to find Carlos. She'd spent day after long day running about Valencia, trying to get a hint of his whereabouts from the disdainful Republican authorities, yet it had all been futile. Every shiny shard of a clue turned out to be fool's gold. Every promising trail led to a dead end. She had even managed to get the lists of the inmates of the city's four principal prisons, only to discover that Carlos's name was not on any of them.

Despondent, Betty was beginning to believe that it no longer mattered. By now Carlos must be dead. Either he'd succumbed to the misery of his prolonged incarceration in a Republican jail; the marquis, a frail shadow of his once dashing self, had poignantly shown her what the ordeal could do to a man. Or just as likely, hands tied behind his back, he'd been marched to a wall, stood at attention, and executed by firing squad. Convinced she had failed, she was heartbroken.

But as every handler tells his novice agents, sometimes when an operation seems to be going wrong, when all else has failed, you need to fall back on every operative's most resourceful ally—luck. You must have faith that the clouds will part, and Providence will reach out its long arms and gently push you back on track. In Betty's case, though, Providence was an American general, and he grabbed her in an all-enveloping bear hug.

As Betty was heading back to the chancery after one more discouraging day, an unfamiliar dark car screeched to a sudden halt beside her. This was ominous enough, but in the next instant a short, squat man in a military uniform bounded out with surprising agility and, just as she was preparing to run, enveloped her in both of his strong arms.

I've had it, Betty thought. In the same unsteady instant she couldn't help wondering if it was the Republicans hauling her in for helping the marquis to escape. Or had the Nationalists, still convinced she was a spy, finally caught up to her?

She turned to confront her captor.

"Stephen!" she cried out with as much relief as joy. She was staring into the cheerful pink face of General Stephen Fuqua, US Army. The general was an old friend of her father's, a jovial southerner who had dropped out of West Point because, as he put it, he "cared more about fighting than books." Over the years he'd gone on to do his share of fighting, first in Cuba during the Spanish-American War and then in the Philippines. He'd been a guest at Betty's wedding, but she'd last seen the general nearly two years ago in Madrid, where he was serving as the military attaché at the American embassy. "But this is a miracle," said Betty, and at that moment it truly felt like one.

"Well, girlie, I couldn't ask for anything better on this side of paradise myself," said the general. "Come to my hotel and tell poppa everything."

Sitting in the dark hotel bar, gin and tonic in hand, Betty did just that. She had the general's attention as she spoke of nights spent racing through Madrid as the bombs fell. She boasted how she'd brazenly walked the marquis out of prison right under the guards' eyes. Finally, coaxed along by the gin, she divulged the real reason for her return to Spain—the long, futile search for Carlos. There was, after all, no reason to be discreet. The general was part of the prewar diplomatic set in Madrid; no doubt he'd heard the gossip about the British commercial attaché's wife and the Spanish Air Ministry official.

"I know where Carlos is," the general interrupted.

Betty stared at him pointedly. If this was a joke, she was in no mood.

Fuqua, though, went on with uncharacteristic gravity, a commanding officer reporting to his troops that all is lost. "He's in that big military jail out on the Barcelona road. It's the toughest joint in these parts. You can't try any Pimpernel stuff there unless you want to make the return trip in a hearse."

Betty couldn't think of anything useful to say.

"Why, they wouldn't even let you in unless you had a pass from Prieto himself."

Indalecio Prieto was Spain's minister of national defense. Starting out as an eight-year-old boy selling newspapers on the streets of Madrid, he had wound up owning the paper. He had a self-made man's brittle, confident assurance, and a dedicated socialist's fervor. The people loved him, and he loved them back. He was the most popular figure in the Republican government, and arguably the most powerful.

"Well," said Betty, "how about my going to Prieto? He's the boss now, and he's also in Valencia. What do you think?" It was a spontaneous idea, but as soon as she had shared it, Betty was convinced she'd hit upon a solution.

The general drank some more of his gin, staring into the mirror behind the bar, studying the reflection of Betty's face in the half-light.

Betty could only imagine, she related to Hyde, what was going through his mind. It was vital to her that the general believed she could succeed. She knew he had an eye for the ladies; he'll appreciate my allure, she decided. But more importantly, Betty wanted him to believe that she was her father's daughter, that she had inherited his intrepid spirit, his pluck.

"Sure," he told her as he drained his glass, "it's worth a try. You come up with a plan, and I'll do what I can to help." But he also warned, "You are getting into dangerous territory. Hell, I was at your wedding and I'll be damned if I'll go to your funeral."

Betty kissed the general on the cheek. She was certain Leche could arrange a meeting with Prieto. Her charm would do the rest. At last she'd be reunited with Carlos. She felt invincible. "Lunch with me at one tomorrow at the Ostero," she suggested to her savior. "We'll make a plan then."

That night, walking along the beach with Leche, she told the minister that she needed his help. She wanted an appointment with Indalecio Prieto.

Leche hesitated. He was the British chargé d'affaires, and Prieto was the Republican minister of defense. It would not be correct to ask for a personal favor.

"It's the only chance I've of saving Carlos," Betty pleaded. "Nothing else has worked."

Leche kept a stony silence. He knew what Betty was asking him to do was very wrong.

Betty moved closer to him, her hips pressing lightly against the fabric of his trousers. "I wish you were with me as I was with you for the marquis's rescue," she purred. "We synchronize so well. I love doing things with you."

"You must make it clear that you are coming to him in a purely private capacity," Leche said sternly.

"Yes," Betty agreed.

"Then I will do what I can."

Betty gave him a long, sweet kiss. And then another.

"And after you have conveyed to him clearly that you are not acting for our government," Leche continued when he'd finally pulled away from her embrace, "you may tell him that the British chargé d'affaires knows about your visit and the reason for it, and that he heartily approves."

LUNCH WAS OCTOPUS *arroz a la valenciana* washed down by frosty glasses of vodka. Once the general learned that Leche had agreed to help, he ordered another round to celebrate. "To success," he toasted. "To success," Betty echoed.

"I'll drive you round to Prieto's and wait while you do your stuff," the general offered. "Just watch your step. He's a pretty tough guy, this Prieto, but nothing like some of those Reds. Everything will be all right. You'll see."

After the long, lazy lunch, Fuqua drove Betty back to the chancery. As soon as the car pulled up, events seemed to prove his confidence justified. A secretary hurried over with a message that gave another boost to Betty's already soaring spirits: "His Excellency wants you to know that your appointment is for two thirty tomorrow."

"Hell's bells," the general exulted. "That's what I call liaison work!"

She hurried up the stairs to thank Leche, heading straight to the minister's private office. He was seated at his desk, poring over some papers, but he looked up sharply when Betty bounded in. She knew at once that something was terribly wrong.

"Here, read this," he said rigidly, rising from his seat and handing her a telegram. When she saw that it was from the embassy in Hendaye and marked "Most Urgent," her stomach dropped precipitously. Yet she forced herself to read on:

FOLLOWING FOR LECHE PERSONAL FROM

AMBASSADOR REPORT ON WHEREABOUTS OF MRS

PACK WIFE OF COMMERCIAL SECRETRARY BELIEVED
TO HAVE VISITED MADRID STOP ARRANGE FOR HER
IMMEDIATE REPEAT IMMEDIATE RETURN BY NEXT
AVAILABLE DESTROYER.

She did not know what to say. There was no way she would go
back to France until she had seen Carlos. The ambassador could
insist, he could demand that she return immediately repeat immediately. But she would not leave Spain until she had completed her
mission.

But what would Leche do? Without his help, she'd be unable to
see Prieto. If he obeyed orders and summoned the chancery guards
to escort her to a destroyer, she'd be powerless to resist. She'd be
sailing back to France by the morning.

"We'll have to send off a reply," Leche said, puncturing the silence.

"Stall on it," said Betty. It was the only strategy she could come
up with.

Leche, though, had another. "There is only one answer and it's
quite simple. You are staying here with me and that's all there is to
it. So you must decide about your feelings for me."

Betty had already decided. Leche was an interlude, not a commitment. But this was not the moment to make that clear. All her
instincts told her to be vague, to steer clear of both promises and
ultimatums. She needed the minister on her side for just a while
longer. She had to see Carlos. After she completed her mission,
there would be time to tell Leche that she was returning to France
and her husband and child.

"Say I'm in no danger and return is delayed on account of shortage of destroyer space," she suggested.

Leche considered. He could press the issue with Betty, but if he
did, he sensed that she would turn him down. She'd walk off and
leave him forever. And that would be unbearable.

"I'll cable the ambassador that there's no destroyer available," he agreed.

But even as he wrote the telegram designed to win her a reprieve, Betty understood that her departure was inevitable. She just wondered if Leche realized that too.

THE NEXT MORNING, JUST HOURS before her appointment with Prieto, there was a sudden change of plans. Leche wanted Betty to believe that the idea was his, but years later, and wiser with their passing, she would realize the instructions had come from the Secret Intelligence Service in London. No doubt he'd cabled the spymasters about her meeting with the foreign minister. If circumstances allowed, they must have decided, why shouldn't the Service come along for the ride too? By return flash cable Leche received his marching orders. And as if on a sudden whim of his own, he shared the request with Betty.

As Betty sat in his office, waiting for the general to arrive, Leche extracted a sheet of paper from the safe near his desk: a single-column typewritten list of the seventeen aviators being held in the same Republican prison as Sartorius.

"If Prieto seems favorable about Carlos," he said as he handed the thin sheet to Betty, "you can mention these people too. Otherwise forget about them. I trust your judgment."

Betty, however, soon found herself doubting not only her judgment but everything else about her mission. Parked with the general in the shadow of the hulking gilded *palacio* requisitioned as Ministry of National Defense headquarters, she suddenly felt that the challenge she faced was insurmountable. She had gotten her willful way with a doting assortment of fun-loving upper-class men, a string of diplomats, aristocrats, and playboys. But what flirtatious tricks could she try on a sullen, pure-hearted Marxist? Prieto, a no-nonsense true believer, would be immune to her playful charm. And then what would happen to Carlos? Perhaps her appeal would backfire. Once she mentioned her lover's name, Prieto, infuriated by her presumption, would make certain Carlos was never released.

"I'd rather face a firing squad then go in there," she said, sitting riveted to the car seat.

"If that's the way you feel," barked the general, finding his battle-cry voice, "you'd better be afraid of my kicking you out of the car. Anyway it's time to go now. Get the hell in there!"

And so Betty charged forward. She went through a gauntlet of suspicious secretaries and militiamen, having her credentials checked and studiously rechecked. Finally an officer in an elaborate uniform appeared to escort her up a long, winding staircase. He pointed to a closed double door at the top of the landing. The foreign minister is expecting you, he announced; and in the next instant, as if by some sorcerer's trick, he had vanished.

Betty walked into a vast, dark space. From out of its depths a small voice called out, "Prieto." For a bewildered moment Betty thought she was being greeted in some obscure foreign tongue; but then a short, chubby man approached with his hand extended, and she realized that the minister believed his name alone was sufficient welcome.

Graciously, he directed Betty to a plush chair. As if deeply weary, he collapsed into the armchair opposite it. "How can I be of assistance, señora?"

Betty looked at him carefully. She'd been foolish, she decided, to have been so anxious. Prieto was a fat, bald, tired man in a rumpled suit. If she could get a priest to consider abandoning his calling for her, she could cast a spell on this beleaguered official, with his double chin.

In a steady, firm voice, she announced that she had come to

ask for the release of Carlos Sartorius. She made sure to focus all the glow in her bewitching smile and her sparkling eyes on the minister.

"Excuse me, señora," Prieto replied. "Why are you so interested in this case?"

Betty weighed her response. Her instincts told her that Carlos's fate could depend on her answer. Every ploy she had previously tried in the course of her long quest had failed. Now she decided to rely on the only one that remained—the truth.

"For two reasons, señor el ministero," she began. "The first is because I love this man. The second is that through loving him I know all about him. And I know that he has never done anything against the Spanish government. He does not deserve to be in prison."

The minister looked down at the floor, his head sinking into his hands. It was the posture of a man who was bored, or tired, or perhaps both. Betty had been earnest, she had been sincere—and, she felt, her plea had failed.

As if rousing himself from a much-needed sleep, Prieto finally raised his head and looked up once again at the woman seated opposite him.

"I am very grateful to you for coming to see me," said the minister. "There are many things that are not brought to my attention."

With great effort, he pulled himself up from his chair. He rose in slow stages, like a man who had been awkwardly bent and had to take care as he straightened himself. "Is there anything else?" he asked once he was standing.

Betty had no idea of how the meeting had gone. Prieto was a puzzle. But the one thing she knew for sure was that she'd never get another chance. She reached into her purse and handed the minister the typewritten list with the seventeen names.

"These men are prisoners, too," she said. "Like Señor Sartorius, they have been wrongly imprisoned."

Prieto took the list and his eyes traveled over it with attention.

"Señora," he said, "you will understand that I can do nothing arbitrary. But I promise you that I will examine these cases carefully." Then a thin, coy smile broke through the mask of his face, and for Betty it was like the light of a thousand suns. "I think I can tell you to have good hope of their release!"

For a moment Betty was speechless. His encouraging words had taken her completely by surprise. Was her long battle nearly over? Could it have been this simple? Filled with an overwhelming joy, she somehow managed to put her gratitude into words.

The minister was escorting her to the door when, ever solicitous, he asked, "You are certain there is nothing else?"

Betty did not want to overplay her hand. She did not want to do anything that would jeopardize the release of Carlos and the other airmen. She did not want to discover the limits of Prieto's tolerance. But at the same time, she could not help herself.

"Yes, there is," she blurted out. "May I see the man I love and give him some hope too?"

With a mystifying silence, Prieto returned to his desk. He began writing. Betty wondered if she had finally overstepped the undefined bounds. Perhaps he'd decided he had put up with enough of her requests, and, at last angered, was preparing an order for her arrest.

He wrote quickly and then looked up at Betty. "You will need this," he said, and finished by signing his name with a flourish at the bottom of the page. He handed the sheet to Betty.

It was a pass allowing Señora Pack to enter the military prison to visit with inmate Carlos Sartorius.

"You may meet with him," said the minister. "Indeed, you should."

◆　◆　◆

WHEN BETTY WAS A YOUNG girl, her father had served as the commandant of a marine prison in Maine. Over the years the memory of that dark fortress had remained vivid in her mind. It still made her shudder. It was a frightful place, and she could not imagine a more lonely and horrifying fate than to be locked inside its thick walls. Then she saw the prison on the Barcelona Road.

On a flat, treeless highway, the only structure on a desolate plain that stretched to the horizon, the military prison stood like an ominous intruder. It was a boxy red brick building, stark and ugly.

The general's car drove under a smoldering orange late-afternoon sky toward the front gate as Betty's hopes gave way to despair. How could Carlos have survived inside this place? What had he endured? What price must he have paid? The prospect of seeing her handsome lover broken, reduced to something small and groveling, left her shaking. For a terrible moment she wondered if coming to the prison, her entire quest in fact, had been a mistake.

But then she was out of the car, striding confidently to the massive iron door. She waved the minister's pass about, and it proved as effective as any magician's wand—sentries snapped to attention, doors were unbolted and thrown open, and with great ceremony she was led into an empty room. Two chairs were brought in. Knees crossed, she sat in one of them and waited. And prayed.

Carlos walked slowly into the room.

For a moment Betty couldn't move. She just stared at him, overwhelmed.

Suddenly she was on her feet and rushing into his arms. He held her and she held him, and for a long while they were locked in this tight embrace. She wanted to say something, but couldn't find the words. Then she realized she was crying. And so was he.

At last Betty pulled away. "Let me see how you look," she said.

She had expected to find a different man, and indeed, Carlos was pale, thin, and had grown a long, unruly beard. But he still smiled like the mischevious lover with whom she had spent so many sweet afternoons in the Madrid penthouse. During the course of her long search she'd cherished the image of the man she first encountered on a tennis court at a Washington country club, and now, despite everything, the bearded, unkempt prisoner in his gray uniform caused the same flutter in her heart.

They talked and talked, though afterward Betty could not remember a word that had passed between them. All the time her mind was silently racing, shouting louder than their conversation: *He's alive! Soon he will be free! I did it!*

Then a guard appeared: their allotted hour was over.

"I believe that fate is with us," Carlos told her as they held one another in a farewell embrace. "It won't be long before I am free and we are together again."

The guard approached, and Betty pulled herself away. She was weeping violently. She did not try to speak.

As she was led into the corridor, she heard the door behind her slam with a heavy, echoing bang. Carlos was calling to her, "Adios! Adios! We shall meet soon."

His words grew fainter as she headed down the long walkway toward the main gate.

Betty did not call back to him. There was nothing more to say. She understood the firm boundaries that held her life, however passionate at any random moment, in place. She had done what she had set out to do, and now her time with Carlos was over.

"I won't let you go," said Leche.

"I have to go," Betty insisted.

In this newspaper article from 1965, Betty details how she rescued her lover, Spanish air force officer Carlos Sartorius, from a military prison.

Sixteen days had passed since her visit to Carlos, and each day she woke convinced that the day had come for her to return home. She had accomplished her mission. She had a husband and a daughter waiting in France. There was no reason to remain in Spain. And yet she had lingered. Leche was an enjoyable companion. They would walk hand in hand on the moonlit beach to the room they shared, and spend the nights in one another's arms.

But today she knew it was the end. She was neither surprised nor disconcerted. Her resolve was firm. She had seen a British destroyer lying off the port, and at that moment she made up her mind: she'd be on board when it steamed off.

"I don't know whether there will be room for you," Leche tried.

"Then I will stay on deck with the refugees," Betty said, unflinching.

Resigned, Leche drove her to the port. "Please," he begged as he helped her into the narrow launch that would take her to the naval ship. All Betty offered him was a soft kiss on the lips.

It was a short trip through a calm blue sea to the destroyer. Betty stood tall in the open launch the entire way, looking straight at the big gray warship. She did not look back, she did not turn to wave a last good-bye to Leche. There was no longer any point.

Chapter 23

◆

BETTY ARRIVED IN FRANCE ONLY to learn that Arthur was in trouble. Her loose-tongued husband had exceeded his brief, the Foreign Office had decided. He had behaved in a manner unsuitable for a representative of His Majesty's government.

"It has unfortunately come to our ears," a perturbed George Mountsey, the head of the Foreign Office, had cabled Sir Henry Chilton, the British ambassador to Spain, "that Pack . . . has created the impression both in official and unofficial circles that his attitude over the Spanish conflict is strongly biased in favor of the Franco regime. . . .

"It is obviously more prudent of any representative of HMG to be cautious in this respect. Unfortunately, I don't think Pack has been cautious."

Mountsey's critique banged huffily on for an exhausting thirteen pages. With each new reiteration of Arthur's transgressions, his rage appeared to build. Finally, as if throwing up his hands in disgust, he grumbled that the only solution was to shuffle Pack off to another post, to a country where there were "no live internal political issues to distract him."

To his credit, the ambassador did his best to defend Arthur. "It is a great pity that Pack who knows the ropes and everyone should be transferred," Sir Henry complained to Whitehall. But the Foreign Office remained adamant: Pack must leave Spain.

In the meantime, all Arthur could do was wait, a convicted felon before a hanging judge, as the Foreign Office mulled his sentence. Given Mountsey's raw anger, he was certain he'd be sent off to some remote, and no doubt entirely irrelevant, corner of the globe.

Betty took the news with a sigh of relief. It wasn't her madcap dash into Spain to rescue her lover that had torpedoed Arthur's career. Nor had her public carryings-on with Leche brought her husband down. Arthur, in fact, had put that embarrassing matter to rest in a stiff conversation shortly after their reunion in Saint-Jean-de-Luz. If Betty would never mention Leche's name again, neither would he. It was an agreement Betty readily endorsed; Leche, she had already decided, was out of her life. She was not eager to leave her beloved Spain, but at the same time she took comfort in the fact that despite Arthur's many proclamations that her antics would be his ruin, she was not in fact responsible for his comeuppance.

Or was she? Looking back, Betty came to realize that she had a larger role in her husband's supposed fall from diplomatic grace than anyone—herself included—had realized at the naïve time. She now understood that Arthur's public and conspicuously forceful upbraiding was a bit of smoke, as they called it in her new trade.

On confidential instructions from the Secret Intelligence Service, Whitehall had obediently strung out a paper trail to justify Arthur's abrupt departure from Spain in the middle of a civil war. The purpose of this deception, however, was not to get Arthur out of the country. It was the cover story that would allow a valuable MI6 asset to take up her new post. The spymasters had been not only impressed with how Betty got her way with Prieto, they'd been stunned. There had been no reason, neither political nor practical, for the minister to have cooperated. Yet he had. If she could charm that dour, doctrinaire old stick-in-the-mud, the feeling on Broadway was, there was no telling what else she might accomplish.

When Arthur's new assignment was announced, it was not,

as he had been given good reason to believe, to some diplomatic backwater. His new post was Warsaw, Poland. Just as Hitler was flexing his muscles, as the Führer's menacing intentions were becoming frighteningly clear, Arthur was being sent into the midst of the gathering storm. It was certainly not the sort of posting the Foreign Office would give to anyone "temperamentally unsuited" to deal with sensitive issues. But it was a sufficient bit of cover to get Betty and her unique talents into the thick of things without raising too many suspicions. She'd be the dutiful wife accompanying her diplomat husband, not the secret agent being put into position right at the Nazis' front door.

At the time, though, Betty did not understand the full significance of Arthur's new orders. She was more excited by the glorious news she had received from Spain: not only had Carlos been released, but so had the seventeen airmen on the list she had given Prieto. It was that triumph that filled her head when, along with her daughter and a Spanish nanny, she boarded the Warsaw Express in Paris on an autumn evening in 1937. As the night train chugged east, Betty had no inkling of the future that awaited her in Poland.

Part IV

Enigma

Chapter 24

◆

DRIVING DOWN THE WINDING ROAD that twisted through the green Wicklow hills, the steep valleys below dotted with brilliantly blue glacial lakes shimmering in the high spring sun, Betty was enchanted. It was their fourth day in Ireland, and Betty was must have thought that her instincts had been right: this *was* her spiritual home. "How lovely it all is," she told Hyde. "I would love to have a cottage here and come for several months of the year."

Later that afternoon, they stopped at the ancient churchyard in the even more ancient village of Drumcliffe. Hyde had insisted. When you come to Ireland, you must pay homage to Yeats, he explained.

William Butler Yeats's grave.

The poet's remains had been brought over from France after the war, and he had been reburied with honor in a simple grave. On a stark gray tombstone quarried from the local Sligo limestone an epitaph was carved. Anticipating his own imminent death, Yeats had himself composed it:

> *Cast a cold Eye*
> *On Life, on Death.*
> *Horseman, pass by!*

She stood by the grave and read the poet's words in a low, soft voice. Then she repeated them.

At that somber moment, her jaw throbbing, it was impossible to avoid the realization that her own death loomed. The dark horseman, she must have known too well, would soon stop beside her. He would not pass her by. She would never fulfill her blissful fantasy of settling into a quaint cottage nestled in the green Irish countryside. She had been deluding herself.

All she could do was complete her mission. While she still had the time, she could cast a cold eye on the life she'd lived and look for the answers she so deeply desired.

She walked in silence away from the graveyard. It was as if she was determined not to reveal her true thoughts. These were her secrets, her challenges.

Hyde, too, had, he would say, felt the epitaph speaking to him. He too was struck by Yeats's words. For him, they were an admonishment to put aside his own lingering regrets about the many turns his life had taken. He had one more chance. He could cast a cold eye on the recollections Betty was sharing and see where they led him, how they helped him understand his own predicament. There was much more to learn. It was not yet time for him to pass by.

Finally, he asked her to pick up the story where she'd left off days ago in the Shelbourne bar—her liaisons with the moody young Polish diplomat Edward Kulikowski, the romance that would be her first official operation for the Secret Intelligence Service.

Chapter 25

◆

I N THE AFTERMATH OF HER christening on a Warsaw golf course, Betty, now a full-fledged British secret agent, continued to cajole secrets from the still-unsuspecting Edward Kulikowski. But as the winter of 1938 drew to an end, both Betty and her superiors realized that this operation had outlived its usefulness. The young Polish Foreign Service officer had no new information to share. Betty's reports had grown thinner and thinner. It was time for a new assignment.

After consulting with London, Jack Shelley, her case officer and a modern man, gave it to her unembroidered, without hesitancy or embarrassment. The Service wanted her to spread her graceful wings, fly high into the upper air of Polish society, and, if the opportunity presented itself, seduce a more valuable source than Kulikowski, the ardent piano-playing minister's assistant.

Committed to the cause, and schooled by a lifetime of misbehaving, Betty went to work. Her colleagues in her new profession, trying to put a circumspect spin on things, called the liaisons in which secrets were whispered in bed "honey traps." The jargon helped them to remain untroubled by the morality of what they were asking a married woman—the wife of a brother Foreign Service officer, no less—to perform for the realm.

In Betty, they quickly discovered, they had recruited a queen bee.

She was very busy. In the uncertain spring of 1938, Poland, squeezed between Germany and Russia, was desperately trying to rustle up support for a "Third Europe," a confederation of continental nations that could shore up its small army when push inevitably came to a mighty shove. Great Britain was trying to convince the endangered Poles they'd stand by them, while at the same fawning time, they were scurrying to assure the Nazis that they'd gladly cut a deal to ensure "peace in our time." Each day there were new secret political developments, and Betty, after a night out on the town, and often a morning after, would deliver informative reports to Shelley.

Her husband was still recuperating in England from the debilitating stroke he had suffered on New Year's Eve at the end of their first year together in Poland. After taking him to England, Betty had traveled back two weeks later to Warsaw. Her return was Arthur's idea; he wanted the ambassador to believe that his illness was insignificant, and that he'd soon be joining his wife. But by now Arthur had been in a rehabilitation facility on the Isle of Wight for over ten months. His every day was filled with his own battles, his own struggles. He knew nothing about his wife's recruitment by the Secret Intelligence Service. He had no idea that while he lay in a nursing home, while his recovery dragged on and frustratingly on, a world away a procession of besotted diplomats passed through Betty's life.

Yet even as Betty threw herself into the task, she never expected that the matchmakers on Broadway would soon send her off to meet the next great love of her life. Nor, for that matter, had the spymasters in all their initial scheming imagined that their orders would lead to pillow talk that would help change the course of the coming war.

For Betty and her controllers, it began as one more routine assignment.

"Do you know Count Michal Lubienski?" Shelley asked at the end of one their debriefings.

Betty said she did not.

"We'd like you to get to know him."

◆ ◆ ◆

THE OP WENT INTO PLAY with a little help from the American ambassador. Anthony J. Drexel Biddle Jr. was the son of a mainline Philadelphia society baron who would be immortalized on both stage and screen as "the Happy Millionaire." And Tony was, among other accomplishments, a chip off the old good-time-loving block. Before joining the staid diplomatic corps, he had famously hosted a bash at the St. Regis Hotel in New York for the Belgian boxer he managed that ended with truncheon-wielding cops struggling to restore order as black-tied guests giddily wheeled pianos out of the lobby and fled down Madison Avenue carrying cases of champagne in their arms. And with vast and artful expense, he had opened the Casino in Central Park, only to have this freewheeling nightclub too raided by the police and padlocked. Tony Biddle knew how to throw a good party, and he loved doing it.

When the ambassador and his second wife, Margaret, the heiress to a mining fortune, heard their good friend Betty Pack ask over cocktails whether it wasn't about time they hosted another of their dreamy dinner dances, the couple immediately decided that it was a splendid idea. And when Betty coyly added that it would be divine if she could be seated next to Count Lubienski, the ambassador did not need further explanation. A little mischief was just the thing to get any party roaring.

On the night of the party, it was as if the strategists on Broadway had choreographed every perfect detail: the bright moon glowing in the calm summer sky; silver and crystal glittering in the candlelight on the tables; gardens of colorful flowers arranged in cut-glass bowls and vases; mounds of caviar and icy bottles of vodka. Champagne corks popped, and flutes were filled and refilled. The orchestra played soft, romantic melodies. The men were dapper and distinguished in their dark evening clothes. The women sparkled in their long gowns and jewels. And there was Betty in a dress that seemed sculpted around her every curve. Graceful, confident, and incredibly radiant: an elegant and resourceful spy.

With customary diligence, she'd done her homework before going off on her mission. It did not require much digging to understand why the Service was interested in the count. He was the *chef de cabinet* to Poland's foreign minister, Colonel Josef Beck, the perplexingly moody, stiff-necked diplomat who was the dominant force in negotiating Poland's political future. Lubienski would have access to all the confidential documents and the minutes of every secret conference that passed through the office. If Great Britain wanted to know what Poland was up to with the Nazis, or how the beleaguered country, despite all its dogmatic posturing, truly intended to find a way through the looming war, a look into Beck's office would be invaluable. Its files were a repository of diplomatic treasures. Betty fully understood the importance of the operation, and went off that glittering evening prepared to do whatever was necessary to ensure its success.

When she sat down at the dinner table next to the count, she was surprised by the man to whom she was introduced. He was a presence: a saber-thin aristocrat with a relaxed, easy charm, his eyes a languid Mediterranean blue, his hair thick and yellowish, a wheat field lit by the sun. Betty, always candid about such matters, told Hyde, "When I heard what his job was, I would have made a dead set at him, even if he had been as ugly as Satan. But happily this wasn't necessary."

After dinner when the party moved into the ballroom, the count, executing a rigid bow, asked Betty to dance. They danced together for most of the evening, and with each new melody he held her closer in his arms. They glided slowly across the dance floor, and Betty let herself be trapped by his tight embrace.

A portrait of Colonel Josef Beck, the Foreign Minister of Poland, taken on Sept. 1, 1939—the day Nazi Germany invaded Poland.

"Something is happening to me," he whispered into her ear as the band played on. "I must see you again. May I call you tomorrow?"

"I'd like that," Betty promised.

The next morning a large bouquet of pink roses arrived at her apartment. Attached was the count's engraved card.

At this juncture in any operation, it was standard tradecraft for the agent to apply the brakes. Let the target make the next move; let him believe he's in complete control, making all the decisions. But Betty was having difficulty following the rules. She didn't care how suspicious her ardor might seem. She knew she wanted to see Lubienski again, and the sooner the better. She made up her mind to call him; thanking him for the flowers would be a sufficient excuse. But before she could, a maid came into her bedroom to announce that there was a Count Lubienski on the telephone, asking to speak with her.

They went out to dinner that night. When they finished one bottle of wine, with a flick of the count's hand, another immediately appeared. Betty paid little attention to the food or the drink. They talked and talked for hours. It was as if they were a couple who had known each other forever.

As they were leaving the restaurant, the count told Betty that his wife and children were away. Off in the mountains on a summer holiday, he explained. Betty said that she was on her own, too; her husband was in England, recuperating from a stroke.

They agreed that they did not enjoy being alone. They pretended to be complaining about some annoying inconvenience their inconsiderate spouses had inflicted on them.

But each understood what the other was really saying.

Hand in hand, they went off to Betty's apartment. That night the count shared Betty's double bed. By dawn, when he sneaked off before the arrival of the maid, the operation had been launched. And so had Betty's next great romance.

BETTY HAD NEVER KNOWN SUCH a glorious summer. She felt as if she was doubly blessed: in love with a handsome, debonair aristocrat who loved her back, and at the same time inexorably devoted to the righteous cause she was serving. Her allegiance to the Service required her to betray the man she loved, but that was a duplicity on which she refused to dwell. The inherent conflicts in her behavior were, in Betty's mind at least, nonexistent simply because she refused to acknowledge them.

It was, she felt, the romantic honeymoon she had never had. "Nightingales are not born from owls," Lubienski had proudly told her, quoting the Polish proverb the nobility liked to trot out as sufficient justification for their entitled, gilded lives. Betty discovered that elegance was not just his inheritance but also his instinct: a way of life. Effortlessly, the count made each new day float by with grace and beauty.

Decades later, small, random moments would still be sweet memories in Betty's mind. There was a walk along the Vistula as the setting summer sun ignited the water with its red glow. A table for two at a small café on a cobblestone street in the Old City, a bottle of white wine chilling, platters stacked high with pink freshwater crayfish. Mugs of rich, thick mead in a dark, boisterously jovial tavern in the Painted Square. A night spent dancing slow and close across a nightclub floor, both of them completely content, each wishing the music, like their summer together, would never end.

The count would accompany Betty home, stay for a while, and then leave; he could not go into the ministry wearing the previous day's clothes. Yet as the dawn light lit up the Warsaw streets, he would return, letting himself into her flat with the latchkey she'd given him. He would undress, climbing back into the warm bed he had just left a few short hours ago.

Entwined, he would talk to Betty about the day ahead, about the stiff challenges he and his minister would be facing. As attentive and consoling as a priest in a confessional, Betty listened to his every word.

Beck was a difficult man to work for, gruff and sinister, and Lubienski needed someone to confide in. The count was candid and open-hearted with his secrets, quick to air them and eager to vent his anger. As he lay next to Betty, even as his hands caressed her, the stories poured out.

His own deep sense of honor affronted, Lubienski railed to Betty about the two contradictory paths Beck was simultaneously pursuing. The minister was in secret negotiations with Hitler, hoping he could forge an arrangement that would prevent a war, while at the same time he was working with Britain and France to finalize a treaty that guaranteed Poland's borders. Lubienski knew every detail, and he offered these without restraint. The ministry's contacts with Berlin, communiqués to the Foreign Office, the daily top-secret message traffic to and from the prime minister's office—Lubienski, a punctilious reporter, routinely shared it all. And there was more. Whatever else he might have come across during the course of his hectic day at the center of power—troop deployments, industrial outputs, economic indices, office feuds, even the latest gossip about who was sleeping with whom—he recounted to his confessor.

Lubienski knew he was revealing too much. And Betty was a foreigner; no, worse, the wife of a British diplomat. But any sense of caution, of discretion, had abandoned him. He wanted to tell her things, to open his heart to her. It had become important to him. By the time he left each morning at eight, he felt, Betty believed, unburdened, a man ready to face the new day's battles.

And no sooner would he be out the door than Betty would hurry to her typewriter. She would fill page after page with all she'd heard. Her instructions were to report everything. No remark was to be considered too banal, no gossip or rumor too irrelevant. The agent in the field simply gathered the raw intelligence. It would be the job of the wise old owls on Broadway, Shelley had firmly told her, to see where all the pieces fit.

As Betty's lengthy reports arrived twice a week in the diplomatic pouch, the analysts in London read them with excitement. They were elated. The Service had a source that was putting them directly inside the highest level of the Polish government. Now, when the Foreign Office played poker with Beck, they already knew what cards he held. They knew precisely what he was thinking, and what his next move would be.

And just when both Whitehall and the Service felt that their agent in Warsaw couldn't deliver intelligence more valuable than what she was regularly dispatching each week, Betty fooled them. It got better. Much better.

Chapter 26

◆

IDDEN DEEP IN THE BASEMENT beneath the army command post in the tenth-century city of Poznań was a room known, to the select few who shared its secrets, as the Black Chamber. It was here that a handful of students carefully selected from the Mathematics Institute at the University of Poznań, the school's best and brightest, worked under the demanding direction of Lieutenant Maksymilian Ciezki, the young officer who headed the Polish Army Cipher Bureau's German section.

Each day and long into the night, the team struggled to solve the same vexing problem: deciphering the encoded German military communications. But after two long years of harnessing their talents and ingenuity to the challenge, they could not break the cipher. Their mathematics could not, the frustrated young Poles acknowledged, perform the thousands and thousands of calculations necessary to get even a start on a solution.

The German engineers had adapted a 1920s commercial "secret writing mechanism to frustrate inquisitive competitors" called the Enigma to encode the nation's military and diplomatic message traffic. And the demoralized Polish team was now ready to concede that the original marketers had chosen an appropriate name: *enigma* was the Greek word for "puzzle."

At a glance, the Enigma machine seemed to look—and work— like a typewriter. However, when the operator hit a letter on the keyboard, this released an electric current that traveled back and forth through reflectors to a series of scrambling elements. The first letter in a word, *A*, for example, might come out as *Z*. And so on for each individual letter. The machine, in effect, translated sentences into a language that only another Enigma device—and one set that day to speak the identical tongue—could understand.

The scrambling elements were the inspired heart of the machines. There were three movable wheels, a miniaturized plug board that worked like a switching station in a telephone office, and a ring marked with the twenty-six cardinal letters of the German alphabet—omitted were vowels with umlauts—that ran around the rim of each wheel. Working in tandem, these mechanisms could transform the messages sent by the machine, awed cryptologists later estimated, into 150 million million million possible permutations.

Once encoded, the message would be transmitted in Morse code by a radio transmitter. Intercepting these signals was easy enough; the Poles, as well as the British and French, routinely grabbed Germany's message traffic out of the ether. But it didn't do them any good. Unless the recipient had another Enigma machine and, equally crucial, knew the designated daily settings for the device's internal scrambling mechanisms, deciphering the code was impossible. A message remained tightly locked behind an impenetrable wall of seemingly meaningless blocks of letters.

But then in December 1931, just as they were ready to throw up their hands in defeat, the Polish Cipher Bureau wranglers gained their first insights into how the machine worked. Mathematics, though, had very little to do with this preliminary breakthrough. Two other fundamental principles conspired to move things forward—greed and sex.

Hans Thilo Schmidt, a married forty-three-year-old official at the German Defense Ministry Cipher Office, had stumbled into an affair with his family's maid. It was a totally unexpected bit of excitement, and it only piqued his appetite. He began looking for other extramarital dalliances. And he found them—at an unanticipated price.

An interlude of courting, he discovered sadly, was required before he could coax fräuleins into the bedroom. Champagne-fueled dinners and gaudy trinkets were costing him a bundle. And piling on to that teetering mountain of bills, there was the love nest he had rented and ostentatiously furnished to set the mood for these assignations. A middling bureaucrat's salary could not stretch far enough to cover such an expensive hobby, especially when he was already supporting a demanding wife and two children.

Schmidt knew he would either have to give up his womanizing or find a way to make some extra money. With brisk pragmatism, he made his choice: he would earn a fortune by betraying his country.

Schmidt wrote a letter to the Deuxième Bureau, the organization that handled France's intelligence operations, declaring that he had important German government documents to sell. Weeks later, in a hotel room in a small Belgian town near the German border, he handed over to a French secret agent the manuals explaining how to operate the German army's Enigma machine.

In Paris, curious French cryptologists earnestly pored over the manuals, finally admitting defeat. The instructions, they complained, explained how to encipher a message, but gave no information that could be used to read a coded transmission.

In a rare fraternal gesture, the Deuxième Bureau charitably passed on the purloined manuals to MI6's man in Paris. Full of great expectations, he sent them across the Channel to the Government Code and Cypher School, located two floors below the Service's headquarters at 54 Broadway. After all, in the last war these wranglers had broken the previously "unbreakable" German code.

This time, however, they found themselves for once agreeing with the French: Enigma could not be cracked.

Yet this second defeat only fueled the resolve of the tenacious head of the Deuxième Bureau cipher section. He'd paid 10,000 marks for the manuals—the equivalent of about $50,000 at the time—and he was determined to get some return for his lavish investment. Some brainy Poles, rumor had it, were poking at the Enigma machine; he decided he might as well let them have a look too.

Still, it was with little hope that he took the manuals to Warsaw and hand-delivered them to the army major who headed the Cipher Bureau. Perhaps these might be helpful, the French spy suggested. Maybe they'd spark an idea or two.

After consulting with the young team working in the Black Chamber, the major reported back. His message was deliberately guarded; he was a soldier by training and a Pole by birth, and both had schooled him to distrust the French. A few things here that interest us, he said mildly. But what my boys really need is a copy of the current Enigma settings the Germans are using. Think you might be able to get your hands on that?

The request was passed on to Schmidt by his handler. More money was exchanged, and within the month the specified documents were sent by diplomatic pouch to Warsaw for the major's attention. Once they were delivered to the Black Chamber, the team eagerly went back into battle.

Working conscientiously, with a slow, methodical determination, they forged on. Over the next year, the French passed on additional manuals Schmidt had stolen, and more pieces were fitted into the puzzle. Soon the team's shaky guesses were replaced by firm hypotheses, and then, miraculously, by proven theories. They were beginning to understand how the machine performed its magic.

◆ ◆ ◆

IN THE AUTUMN OF 1932 a trio of the Chamber's most gifted young mathematicians were ordered to Warsaw. It was now agreed that there was only one way to break the code: they would need to build their own Enigma machine from scratch. In a secret facility hidden in the Kabachi Woods, ten kilometers from the bustle of Warsaw, they went at it.

Working around the clock, they constructed a prototype in about six months. But one machine, they soon realized, was insufficient; enciphered messages could only be accurately decoded after they were received by another machine with identical settings. But how could they predict the settings? It was impossible; the scrupulous Germans changed them daily. The practical solution would be to construct an Enigma device that allowed the encoded message to be simultaneously read through a variety of different settings.

This insight snuck up on Marian Rejewski, one of the team members, as, looking for some small comfort at the end of a tedious day, he was studiously licking the ice cream from a *bombe glacée* off a spoon. In tribute to this eureka moment, the *bomba* was christened in the winter of 1934.

It was a network of Enigmas, a group of machines wired together, their many wheels and rings adjusted to a range of settings. The broad theory was that once an encrypted message was typed into the *bomba*, the message would travel through the network until ultimately it was read by an interconnected Enigma with the corresponding settings. And after weeks filled with frustrating trial and error, it finally worked.

The Polish team had broken Enigma.

For the next five years, the Poles read the encoded messages sent by the German military.

They did not inform the French whose spy had, at great risk, on at least six occasions, passed on the manuals and settings essential to their understanding of the wiring of the machine. And despite assurances made to the British cryptologists, they never told them either.

The Poles kept their breakthrough a closely guarded secret.

BUT IT IS THE BUSINESS of espionage, as well as the nature of spies, not to trust anyone. The most rudimentary tradecraft assumes that every promise will be broken. And so while the donnish codebreakers at Britain's Government Code and Cypher School innocently accepted the Polish team's assurance that any Enigma discoveries would be swiftly shared, the Secret Intelligence Service was not so gullible. Their agents were covertly scurrying about, trying to find out whatever they could about Enigma.

The significance of the machine had first been brought to the Service's attention by several valued sources. But as the likelihood of a war in Europe built to a gloomy certainty, one intelligence asset reiterated, and then kept doggedly pressing in his assertive, self-important way, that the secrets of the Enigma machine had to be unraveled. It was, he insisted, the key that could unlock the Nazis' most carefully guarded plans. Among the many voices in the intelligence community preaching that Enigma would be of incalculable wartime value, William Stephenson's was arguably—and he would later be the first to make this self-serving argument—the loudest.

Stephenson was a Canadian who, with his inventions and a shrewd business sense, had made a fortune in electronics after World War I. He settled regally in London, bought a grand country estate in the Chilterns, and, still restless, eager for new worlds to conquer, cannily branched out into a variety of businesses.

In the 1930s Stephenson's investment in the Pressed Steel Company had him frequently shuttling off to Germany to buy steel. It was in the course of these business trips that he slowly came to a troubling realization: Germany was covertly allocating nearly all the steel it produced for the manufacture of arms and munitions. This was a violation of the Treaty of Versailles signed after World War I. But more importantly, he feared, it was indicative of the Nazis' intentions for a not-too-distant future.

Back in London, Stephenson shared what he had seen with the Industrial Intelligence Center, the government organization monitoring foreign nations' preparations for war. Major Desmond Morton headed the center, and the old-school soldier was impressed with Stephenson's well-documented report, as well as with the pugnacious self-made millionaire. The major, who knew everyone who mattered, made sure that Stephenson's detailed warning was passed on to his close friend Winston Churchill as well as the crown heads of intelligence who reigned on Broadway.

It was in this way that Stephenson—not unlike young Betty in her adventurous days in Spain—was recruited as an asset. He wasn't a British agent, but the spymasters gave him the opportunity to get deeper into the secret world: in the course of your travels in Germany, they said, if you see or hear anything that might be of interest, give us a holler; we'd be eager to hear it.

Stephenson had many contacts in Germany. He dined in feudal splendor at the schloss of Fritz Thyssen, the steel magnate who was one of the early supporters of Hitler. He strolled through the sinister gray streets of Berlin with Charles Proteus Steinmetz, the wary Jewish scientist's eyes darting about with suspicion, Stephenson would recall, as they headed down every block. He made sure his trips were busy, a whirl of factory meetings and black-tie dinners. He lived his cover. Yet he was always the secret agent, watching, listening. And so, without trying, he learned about Enigma.

It was a small indiscreet moment. One of his German hosts, bursting with *Gemütlichkeit* and fueled by schnapps, brought it up out of the blue. Remember those damn Enigma machines? he asked. Didn't you give them a look years ago, and then decide they weren't right for your organization?

Yes, Stephenson agreed, it was a bit too much fuss for the sort of messages we send. More trouble than they were worth.

Well, the German went on, as if amused. Guess who's using them now? The Wehrmacht! Retooled the machine, and now they swear by it. Encode all their communications with Enigma.

That so? Stephenson said mildly. And then the conversation turned in another, long-forgotten direction.

Like many successful men, Stephenson was convinced he could instinctively appraise the value of a secret as soon as he heard it, whether it was a stock tip or the odd snippet of gossip. And he was a patriot. He also had his brief; and quite possibly he was already envisioning his own dashing future as a player of the Great Game. When he returned to London, he enthusiastically passed on this nugget—small, but solid gold, he was convinced—to his new friend Major Desmond Morton, and then to the Service.

But Stephenson didn't consider his mission complete with a single report. He doggedly continued to lobby the spies on Broadway. He sent them missive after conscientious missive, arguing that the realm would be well served in the years ahead if it learned as much as possible about Enigma.

And so, with a behind-the-scenes chorus of sources raising brash voices in unison, with agents already traipsing about Europe on life-and-death missions hoping to discover some clues to the secrets of Enigma, it was inevitable that Jack Shelley, MI6's man in Warsaw, would be given the assignment too.

Lieutenant-Colonel Colin Gubbins, who as a general would direct the Special Operations Executive (SOE) skullduggery during the war, had come to Warsaw to instruct the Polish general staff about potential sabotage missions if the Germans invaded. His

schedule was crammed, rounds of intense meetings followed by
the formal dinners his gregarious military hosts insisted upon. Still,
Gubbins found a moment to meet with Shelley. As soon as the
two men sat down, he announced to the surprised spy that he had
brought instructions from London.

Find out, Gubbins said, repeating the words he'd been told,
everything the Poles know about Enigma. You are to consider this
operation a priority.

The next day Shelley met with his most productive agent. He
did not emphasize the significance of what he would ask her to
do; in truth, he did not grasp its promise. In his crisp Guardsman's
voice, he simply announced a new mission: Betty should collect
all the information she could about the Polish efforts to break the
German code.

*Canadian William Stephenson, working as an independent
asset, during his business trips to Germany, galvanized the
efforts of British intelligence to break the Enigma code.*

◆ ◆ ◆

IN THE BEDROOM, CUDDLED NEXT to Lubienski, Betty went to work. She did not get everything from the count at once; a lifetime of carefully nurtured instincts had taught her when to prick up her ears and when, with a lighthearted resignation, to allow things to move on. The rule in any honey trap was to tickle, but never to shove. When the target returned to bed, you'd have a second chance. And Betty's men always hurried back. And back.

Over time Betty filed an impressive series of reports. Many of the secrets she collected remain locked in the Service's vaults; intelligence agencies stubbornly hang on to even outdated cryptological information. Nevertheless, this much is known:

Working from classified documents that the unsuspecting count routinely brought home each night from Beck's office, and also blithely guiding their meandering pillow talk, Betty helped the Service monitor the activities of the Black Chamber team. She kept her controllers informed as the young Poles, sequestered in the woods outside Warsaw, received stolen Enigma manuals from the French and struggled to build a prototype. And it was Betty who first reported the startling news that the Poles were able to read Enigma traffic.

"We couldn't believe our eyes. Here was the missing link in the whole chain of our intelligence on Enigma. . . . And that is where [Betty] came in with the most unexpected results," one intelligence officer gushed, fulsome in his praise but careful not, even decades later, to reveal too much.

In July 1939, with the war only weeks away, the Poles finally got around to inviting two senior British cryptographers to be briefed on Enigma at their wrangler's workshop, as the espionage professionals called it, outside Warsaw. The Brits, though, were reluctant to make the trip. A meeting in January in Paris had been unproductive, the Poles alternatingly testy and tight-lipped. Yet encouraged by Betty's intelligence, the cipher experts put aside their misgivings and went to Warsaw. It proved to be well worth the effort. Not only did the Poles at last admit that they had broken the Enigma code, but they agreed to ship the British, through an agent in France, a replica of the Enigma machine.

And although she never knew it, it was thanks to her stream of reports on Enigma that Stephenson first heard about Betty. He had continued to offer the Service whatever stray scrap he could get hold of on the machine, but the information she was passing on, according to the confidences whispered to him, was in another league. Hers was, he was told, "vital."

Betty Pack was clearly an agent, the would-be spymaster told himself, of considerable talent. He made a mental note to remember her name.

THE HOARY PARABLE OF THE blind men and the elephant held, Hyde knew, a special place in the hearts of intelligence agents. From their first days in the secret world, they heard it from trainers and controllers. Just as the blind man could only appreciate the specific part of the elephant that he touched, recruits were lectured time after time, the solitary field agent can never truly understand the total significance of his mission. No single operation, no matter how daring, how costly, how consequential, is more than a small episode in a grand scheme. Intelligence is a communal enterprise.

In an operation as long-running and multifaceted as Enigma it would be a mistake, a sin of naïveté as well as arrogance, to crown a single operative with laurel. Enigma, to use the instructors' favorite analogy, was an elephant of mammoth and mysterious proportions.

By 1942 the British were decrypting 84,000 German messages each month. As the war raged on, Enigma gave the Allies a formidable advantage; they knew not only the location and strength of the enemy but also their strategy, how they intended to deploy their troops, planes, and ships, and when they planned to attack. As a grateful Dwight D. Eisenhower, commander of the Allied forces, wrote, "It has saved thousands of British and American lives and, in no small way, contributed to the speed with which the enemy was routed and eventually forced to surrender."

The history of Enigma offered many heroes—from the ingenious young Poles who first decrypted messages from the machine, to the British seamen who sacrificed their lives to rescue Enigma machines from sinking German U-boats, to the hundreds of bright minds like Alan Turing who labored at Bletchley Park, a Victorian country manor fifty miles north of London, to improve the rudimentary Polish *bomba*, keep pace with the many German adaptations to the machine, and decipher the nearly constant flow of German message traffic.

Yet Betty too played a crucial role. In the increasingly uneasy late 1930s, when the Service was desperate to learn whatever it could about the machine and the Polish attempts to crack the code, Betty, resourceful, persistent, and manipulative, provided invaluable intelligence. She was, Hyde realized, the spy England needed; and, as always, the woman she wanted to be.

Chapter 27

◆

I T WAS FIVE O'CLOCK ON a September afternoon in 1938 as
Betty, running late, hurried across Warsaw's crowded Central
Station to the Nord Express. Clouds of steam puffed from the
locomotive, but just in time she scampered up the small steps to
the first-class sleeping car. The train started to lurch forward, and
she followed the porter down the narrow corridor to the compartment where Count Michal Lubienski was waiting. She was on her
way to Berlin, and her next mission.

Two weeks earlier, the day's first light slipping through her bedroom curtains as they lay together, the count had told Betty that
he would need to go to Germany. Hitler had requested that Poland
send a representative to the annual Nazi Party rally at Nuremberg
on September 13.

But Beck, the count went on with mounting rancor, had decided
that it would be inappropriate for the country's foreign minister to
attend. For him, or for that matter any senior government official, to
be in the cheering throng waving their red-and-black swastika flags
could be construed as Poland's endorsement of Hitler. At the same
time, Beck did not want to offend the Führer by sending an inconsequential representative. He had, however, hit upon a solution.

By solution, the exasperated count explained, Beck means me.

The foreign minister's *chef de cabinet* would be of sufficient stat-
ure to placate Hitler without antagonizing Britain and France.

I have no choice, said the count. It's all been arranged. I'm to
have a private audience with Hitler after the rally. I leave for Berlin
in ten days.

Then he turned petulant. He didn't want to go; he would miss Betty too much.

Betty at once recognized the opportunity being dangled in front of her. She wouldn't, of course, be in the room when Michal met Hitler. She couldn't even accompany him to the rally. Her appearance at his side—the wife of a British diplomat!—would set tongues wagging in both London and Warsaw. And no doubt the Nazis, masters of hypocrisy, she judged sourly, would also find a silly reason to be offended by the count's showing up with his mistress.

Still, for a secret agent a trip into Nazi Germany would be a coup. Shelley's latest marching orders had been to get a handle on what the Poles thought Hitler was really up to. Last month Germany had mobilized 750,000 more men for military service. Maneuvers were already taking place along the Czech border. Were these only bold threats, designed to convince the British and French to yield to Germany's demands? Or were they the opening moves in an unstoppable battle plan—a dash into the Sudetenland, followed by a charge west across Europe? Here was Betty's chance to give London some answers. She'd put an ear to the ground in enemy territory, chat up a few Nazi bigwigs, and, not least, get the count talking about his meeting with Hitler while it was fresh in his mind.

"I'll miss you too," Betty told him. Thinking quickly, she proposed a solution. She would go with him to Berlin. When Lubienski went on to Nuremberg, she'd head to Prague. Wilbur Carr, the American ambassador, and his wife were old friends. They'd been begging her to visit. After meeting with Hitler, Lubienski could join her in Prague. They'd take the train together back to Warsaw.

The count hesitated. He was traveling to Germany on official business, a representative of the Polish government. Besides, he was a married man.

"The sleeping cars on the Nord Express are quite comfortable, I've been told," Betty suggested.

And so it was settled.

Betty informed her handler that afternoon, and Shelley was on board right away. It was an operational godsend. He'd be able to insert an agent into the heart of Nazi Germany. And she'd have bulletproof cover: her lover was on his way to see Hitler.

Yet at their scheduled debrief later that week, Shelley seemed on edge, Betty noticed as soon as she sat down. He went through the usual opening catechisms—Anyone follow you to the meet? Are you in any immediate danger? How long before you're expected somewhere else? Then, with that out of the way, Shelley gave her his news: since Betty was going to Prague, London wanted her to assist on a little job that was already in the works.

And now it was days later, and a steward was carrying champagne in an ice bucket into the compartment. With well-practiced skill, the count began to uncork the wine, and as the train chugged west through the autumn night to Berlin, he filled Betty's glass. She clinked her flute against his, but her mind was elsewhere, and speeding along as fast as any train. Betty was thinking about what she would need to do in Prague.

WAITING IN THE SHADOWS, NOT too far down from the unlit entrance of number 4, Betty surveyed the street. Her time in Germany had been brief, and offered disappointingly little operational intelligence. Now she was in Prague, it was after midnight, and the city was dark and quiet. No one would be out at this hour, Shelley had said. The job should be easy: a simple, uncomplicated burglary.

Yet now, on Hybernská Street, Betty was having a hard time accepting her handler's logic. The boulevard was too empty, too still. There was no sign of life. A policeman on patrol would take one look and wonder why this woman wasn't tucked in bed like the rest of the city.

Betty had a cover story ready, but it was perilously thin: she'd stormed out of the hotel after a quarrel with her husband; downhearted, she was aimlessly wandering about. How long would it take a suspicious policeman to poke that shaky tale full of holes?

But there was no turning back now. The operation had been launched. If all was going as planned, upstairs her accomplice had picked the lock on the front office door and was already making his way to the back room.

It didn't matter that her nerves were stretched thin, or that she imagined every dark shadow was cast by an approaching policeman. She had her assignment: Make sure no one enters number 4. Use your charm, or your guile, but keep any intruder on the street. And if that fails, if someone starts up the stairs, sound the alarm that the world was about to come to an end. Make sure your partner knows he'd better run for his life.

THE BACK ROOM ON THE second floor of 4 Hybernská Street was the private office of Karl Henlein, the head of the pro-Nazi Sudeten German Party (SGP). A small but rising star, Henlein was a former gym teacher who had found his true calling as a particularly nasty right-wing politician. He'd had a minor brush with scandal after a close friend was convicted of homosexuality, and for a while it seemed inevitable that he'd be charged too. But as concerns about Czechoslovakia's autonomy grew, Henlein had shrewdly catapulted himself to center stage. Almost overnight he had become too important a politician for the local authorities to dare to question his morals. One week Henlein would be meeting with Churchill, insisting that he alone could dissuade Hitler from annexing the Sudetenland. The next, he'd be conferring with

Ribbentrop, contradicting with a politician's easy practicality all the assurances he'd blithely given to the British.

Henlein—MI6 knew from an informant they'd bought inside the party—kept his most valuable papers, including his secret correspondence with the Germans, in a locked drawer of his desk in the back room. It was that drawer—bottom right-hand side, keyhole in the center—that was the target of the operation.

As instructed by Shelley, Betty had rendezvoused with her accomplice—to this day, no matter how much Hyde pushed, she steadfastly guarded the agent's identity—on the afternoon she arrived in Prague. She offered the prearranged word code, and with that formality out of the way, they quickly got to work.

With a flippancy that was all disguise, the agent briefed Betty on the mission. He sketched the layout of the second-floor SGP offices—front door with only a half-hearted lock; then a couple of biggish rooms where the party hoi polloi slaved; and finally, behind another locked door, was the private office of the great man himself. His desk was shoved close to a far wall plastered with a map of Europe. The lock on the drawer shouldn't give me too much trouble, he said with confidence. All Betty would have to do was babysit.

He took Betty for a stroll down Hybernská Street. They walked arm in arm; young love was always good cover. As he leaned in to give her a small kiss, he whispered into her ear that the squat building behind them was number 4.

Only one operational question remained: When to strike? A rally was scheduled in a couple of days, the agent explained. The headquarters would probably be crowded day and night as party loyalists prepared. Better to let things settle down, get back to normal. He'd send word to Betty at her hotel when he thought the time was right. There was no rush, he said lightly as they parted.

◆ ◆ ◆

BUT SUDDENLY THERE WAS A rush, and the plan had unexpectedly been set in motion.

Two days after Betty arrived in Prague, as a desperate Neville Chamberlain, the British prime minister, met with Hitler at the Führer's mountain retreat at Berchtesgaden, hoping to negotiate a peaceful solution to the Czech crisis, Henlein decided to reveal his true allegiance. Speaking at a feverish party rally, he thundered that Germany must take immediate control of the Sudetenland. The border territory, home to three million Germans, had been stolen from the Fatherland after the First World War, he said. It had to be returned.

With the crowd's cheers still ringing in his ears, and knowing the Czech police would arrest him for treason, Henlein immediately left for Berlin. He arrived wearing the black uniform of an SS colonel, and received a hero's welcome.

That evening, as the American ambassador hosted a dinner in Betty's honor, she was summoned to the phone. A doctor from Warsaw calling about your daughter, the butler explained.

It wasn't a doctor. It was her contact, and he reported that Henlein had unexpectedly fled to Germany just hours before. We have to move quickly, he said, before he asks one of his henchman to clean out his desk.

They were on for that night.

AND NOW BETTY, STILL IN her evening clothes, was waiting on the pitch-black street, ears straining for every stray sound, eyes searching about warily. What was taking him so long? She glanced at her watch, and then reprimanded herself. Instead, she tried to think of Michal. Or Arthur. Yes, Arthur; that'd take her mind elsewhere. She wanted to think about anything but the agent upstairs in the dark, struggling with his tools as he crouched by a desk across from a map of Europe.

She wanted a cigarette. Never had she wanted one so much. But the glowing red tip would signal her position like a beacon. How much longer? she kept asking herself. How many more minutes?

But just when she was certain she couldn't stand the tension one more moment, a hand grabbed her arm.

Come along, her accomplice whispered. Remember, we're a happy couple making our way home after a night on the town.

Which, a relieved Betty felt, was true in its way.

Arm in arm they strolled down the boulevard, oblivious to the thin drizzle that was beginning to fall on the old city.

"I WILL TELL YOU SOMETHING," the count said to Betty as they sat together a few days later in the seclusion of a first-class compartment on the train back to Warsaw. "I know we are going to part, you and I. And one day I feel we will meet as enemies."

Sadness choked his words. It was as if he was suddenly unable to talk. He had been drinking for a while.

In a moment he continued: "You must wear a white carnation on that day to show me that you won't kill me."

"What do you mean by that?" Betty asked, suddenly angered. "Do you mean that you are going to be on the German side?"

"I don't know," he said morosely, "but that is the way I see it."

He went on in this fatalistic way. In their meeting, the count revealed, the Führer had promised to support Poland's demands on Czechoslovakia. But Lubienski told Betty he believed it wouldn't end with that. Hitler had set his sights on Poland too. And when he struck, Poland would have no choice but to become part of the Reich.

As the train rumbled toward Warsaw, Lubienski continued telling Betty about his troubling conversation with Hitler. He spoke at first with a genuine venom, but his anger was quickly spent. He went on listless and resigned.

Betty silently committed every word to memory for the report she would send to London. She wanted to offer solace, but her heart wasn't in it. The sad truth, Betty believed, was that Lubienski had only an intimation, and a small one at that, of how bad things would soon get.

In her suitcase, packed among her negligees—that, she hoped, would be the last place even an officious border guard would look—were the documents from Henlein's desk. Among them was a map illustrated in bold colors. Each color represented another stage in Germany's three-year plan for the annexation of middle Europe.

In another newspaper tell-all, Betty detailed her seduction of
Beck's chef de cabinet, *Count Michal Lubienski.*

Chapter 28

◆

WHEN BETTY RETURNED TO WARSAW, she discovered that her own world was about to be upended, too. The count's wife had returned from her summer holiday. Now Betty and Michal's time together was curtailed; every rendezvous became a challenge. Already brooding over his country's future, Lubienski slid into a deeper despair. And Betty found herself worrying about the stability of her lover, as well as his continued usefulness.

In his agitated state, Lubienski decided there was only one honorable course. Life had to be lived honestly, or it was nothing! He could not remain captive to a loveless marriage. Driven by his passion, emboldened by his conviction, the count confronted his wife.

He was in love with Betty, he announced. He needed a divorce so they could marry.

Then, exhilarated by his display of courage, Lubienski hurried off to complete the next part of his redemptive mission. He informed the foreign minister of his intentions.

Beck listened. With a diplomat's instinctive courtesy, he let his aide ramble earnestly on. But his silence did not mean agreement, or even sympathy. He could not be bothered to try to understand Lubienski's anguish or his self-justifications. Who had time for love, for fatuous adolescent ardor, when Poland was on the brink of being crushed under Hitler's heel? When the count's monologue had finally run its course, he spoke.

Beck's words were not a chastisement but an ultimatum. His *chef de cabinet* could not become entangled with an American woman, the wife of a British diplomat. Either the count would abandon his plan to marry Mrs. Pack, or he would resign from the Foreign Office.

Lubienski was stunned. He had acted with honor, with a chivalry inspired by his love for Betty. In all his wishful rationalizations, he had never anticipated such a stern rebuke.

Nevertheless, he was prepared to sacrifice his career—and along with it his reputation—for Betty. Her presence, each new day, each new night, would be more than sufficient consolation. Once they were together, their love would be a refuge from a world careening out of control.

With a soldier's pride, he went to tell Betty what he had done. He imagined it would be a time for celebration, for toasts to their shared future. Instead, he discovered that he had been deceived. He did not know Betty at all.

To her credit, Betty did not pretend. She did not suggest distant possibilities or tantalize with false promises. After their time together, she felt she owed him candor. She wanted him to understand the woman she really was.

"I don't know what I'm capable of," she confessed flatly. "I'm a loner really. I come and I go. No bones broken, and no hearts either, I hope. I don't like broken hearts. I'm not sentimental at all."

Lubienski did not know what to say. He had never before seen this impenetrable side of Betty. He had believed their passion was love. And love was a full-pitched commitment—or it was nothing.

"Does that shock you?" Betty asked with a cruel bluntness. "Can you understand that? I have to be *free*. That you *must* accept."

Still, even while Betty, the hard-hearted lover, was telling sharp truths to the count, Betty the British agent was desperately trying to hold on to a valued source. It would be an intelligence disaster if Michal was forced to leave the Foreign Minister's office. The flow of the important secrets she was passing on to London must not be interrupted.

When the count, his imagined life with Betty collapsed in ru-
ins, suddenly asked for a favor, she felt she had to agree. It was utter
foolishness, the worst sort of mawkish sentimentality, but the spy
in her overruled any objections.

Later that evening, when it had been arranged for Mme Lubienski to be out, Betty appeared at the count's apartment. As he led
the way through his home, he pointed out his cherished possessions
and asked her to touch them. He wanted Betty's fingers on his
books, his chair, his pipe. He wanted to feel her presence on all that
he cared about. Even if she was not with him, he wanted her to be
part of his life. "There will be something of you always here," he
said, wanting to believe it.

Betty, for her part, was also trying to believe in something: that
they had still an operational future. She wanted to believe that in
spite of all that had happened, her mission had not been blown to
smithereens.

IT DID NOT TAKE BETTY long to realize she'd been deluding herself. The messenger was Peta Norton, and she was only too glad
to deliver the news. From Betty's first days in Warsaw, the wife of
the counselor at the British embassy had had it in for her. Was she
offended by Betty's promiscuous liaisons? Envious of the younger
woman's startling beauty? Whatever drove her animosity, she arrived at Betty's apartment determined to enjoy her victory.

Foreign Minister Beck has written to Sir Howard Kennard,
complaining about "your behavior," she explained with a restraint
that struck Betty as more gleeful than decorous. "The ambassador
wants you out of Poland. Immediately."

My behavior? Betty wanted to scream. What would this prissy
witch say if I told her my "behavior" has been encouraged, ordered in fact, by the Secret Intelligence Service? It took all her

professional discipline not to share that truth and enjoy a satisfying last laugh.

Instead, Betty played the scene as defiant. She could not possibly leave, she insisted. She needed to pack. And what about her child and Denise's nanny? Arrangements had to be made for them too. Confident that the intelligence service would quickly rush to her rescue, Betty marched Mrs. Norton to the door.

Then she rang Shelley, and used the code word for a crash meeting.

Her handler was enraged. "London thinks you're a star!" he declared. It was absurd. Ridiculous. How could they kick his best agent out of Poland when she was continuing to deliver prize material? Don't worry, he assured her. He'd have a talk with Sir Howard and work things out.

The next morning, a sullen Shelley delivered the verdict: there would be no reprieve. "I begged the ambassador not to let you go," he said, "but he is adamant."

Shelley went on grimly. "There is more in this than meets the eye," he suspected, and so he had asked some questions. It didn't take him long to discover that Beck's angry letter wasn't the only problem. Something else was solidifying the ambassador's resolve.

There was a story going around the embassy, he explained, that Betty was leaking secrets to the Poles. That was why Lubienski was so chummy: he was using Betty to get British intelligence, then passing it on to his pro-Nazi friends in the Foreign Office.

And, continued Shelley with apparent frustration, there was no way to refute that story without revealing the truth—that Betty was a British spy. And that, of course, was impossible.

The Service's hands were tied, he concluded. Betty had to leave.

Twenty-four hours later, on the morning of September 27, Shelley drove Betty to the airport. Tears in her eyes, she boarded the plane to Helsinki, the first stop on her way to London.

Once in the air, Betty, with her usual gallows humor, felt almost like laughing. "It was a fantastic situation," she told Hyde. "There I was, getting hold of top secret information which the ambassador himself couldn't obtain, and I was being banned from the country apparently on account of my association with the very man who was the principal source of that information."

Yet years later, as she told Hyde about her sudden expulsion from Poland, another realization struck her. It seemed so logical and so obvious that she could only wonder why it had not occurred to her at the time. The unknown source of the rumor buzzing through the embassy that branded her as a Polish operative? It had to have been, she now saw, Jack Shelley.

With Beck's letter stirring the pot, MI6 must have suspected that things were getting too hot for Betty in Poland. Even if her cover had not been blown, how long before Beck put two and two together and realized what was behind her attraction to the count? And if Polish intelligence brought her in for questioning, how long before she confessed or, worse, spilled the names of other agents, other ongoing operations? Betty now understood: the longer she remained in Warsaw, the greater a liability to the Service she became.

But—and this was the inspired part of Shelley's double-cross, as Betty now realized—if the Firm could find a plausible excuse for her suddenly leaving Poland *and* at the same time tar her as a Nazi sympathizer, her cover would survive without a scratch. In fact, in the eyes of the enemy, it would be reinforced. And Betty, whose husband's diplomatic posting to Poland would anyway soon come to an end, could go on to spy another day.

It was masterful, Betty now told herself. But at the time, her swift expulsion struck her as painful rather than shrewd. And even all those years later, knowing how things would work out, the missions she would have, she still couldn't find it in her heart to forgive Shelley or the Service for what they had done.

◆ ◆ ◆

IT WAS A SHAKY BETTY who arrived in England. She felt un-hinged. She had lost both her lover and her opportunity to help the Service. She could not imagine anything ever taking their place. Desperate and uncertain, she decided to reach out to her son. She wanted to believe that the boy, her flesh and blood, could make up for all she had lost.

Her trip to Dorrington to see Tony at the Cassells' was just one more disappointment. It had been three years since her last visit, and as soon as she arrived, she understood why she had been so lackadaisical: she felt nothing. She was Tony's mother, but that had created no tie, no inexorable bond. She had brought him into the world, and that was the start and the end of her involvement. Her son, she decided, could not fill any of her empty spaces.

With no place else to go, she returned to Arthur. Her husband was convalescing at the low-ceilinged white house they had shared in Saint-Jean-de-Luz. The temperate climate, he'd hoped, would be a balm while he waited for the Foreign Office to give him a new assignment.

Arthur was surprised to see Betty, but not nearly as surprised as she was by his reaction to her arrival. He knew about the count, but expressed neither indignation nor rage. Instead, he focused his anger on the way the Foreign Office had treated his wife. He viewed Betty's expulsion from Poland, particularly its unseemly speed, as a personal insult. Affronted, he cabled the ambassador.

"Why do you not allow my wife back in Poland?" he asked testily.

A terse reply swiftly came back: "It is in the interest of the Service that she does not return."

But Arthur, with time on his hands and perhaps also looking for a way to channel his repressed resentment over Betty's latest affair, persisted. He badgered the Warsaw embassy with a flurry of telegrams, each one another acerbic demand that his wife be allowed to return to Warsaw to pack up their furniture and possessions before his next posting.

Finally his pounding away brought a grudging response. "Mrs. Pack can return to Warsaw for a week provided she promises not to see anyone."

"ALL AGENTS LIE," BETTY GLIBLY rationalized, having sent word to the ambassador that she would accept his terms. She repeated the same flip justification when she shared the details of her return to Warsaw with Hyde.

Lubienski welcomed Betty at the airport, and in high spirits they went off to dinner to celebrate her arrival. But by the time she returned to her apartment—"with Michal, of course," she offered offhandedly to Hyde—the festive mood had soured. The brevity of their time together loomed over their reunion. The count would not let Betty sleep; each moment together was too precious to squander.

The next day, as Betty went through the motions of packing up, the count made a sudden decision: they must run off for as long as they could. They must make each day they had left theirs alone. It would be as close to forever as they would get.

It did not matter that the embassy had insisted Betty remain sequestered at the apartment until she left Warsaw. So what if someone was scheduled to come by each day to check on her? When Lubienski announced that he was taking her to the country, someplace where they could be alone, an inn with a big feather bed, Betty agreed at once.

But all too quickly their slow days in the countryside and their long nights in the big feather bed came to an end. Lubienski was in tears as he waited for Betty to board her plane. "Someday I will find you, even if it takes me twenty years."

Betty did not reply. She knew she would not wait twenty years for the count, or for any man, but there was no point in sharing this truth. She gave him a final embrace. Then, brisk and practical, a woman who had said many good-byes in her life, she turned and walked off without another word.

"And that," Betty told Hyde, "was the end of my first secret service mission and also the end of my big Polish affair."

But it would not be the end of her career. Before boarding the plane, she had met with Shelley. "Don't worry," he told her, "the Firm will contact you again no matter where you are."

This was the lover's embrace she truly craved.

BACK IN QUIET SAINT-JEAN-DE-LUZ, BETTY waited. She waited to hear where Arthur would be posted, and she waited to hear her next mission. The two were intertwined; Arthur, for better or worse, provided her cover. The wife of a British diplomat, she could travel nearly anywhere in the world without raising suspicions.

To help pass the long, empty days in the quiet fishing village, she spent a good deal of time with the new chargé d'affaires, Owen St. Clair O'Malley. He was the scion of an ancient Irish family, a roaring bull of a man with a rascal's contrarian charm; "swimming against the tide," he'd write with a mischievous pride, was how he made his way through both life and the Foreign Service.

Of course Betty loved him. But for once it was a pure, unencumbered friendship. O'Malley's wife was pretty, talented, and close at hand—that was one impediment. But another obstacle was her double life in Poland had left her exhausted. Nearly as much as her convalescing husband, she needed to recover, to prepare herself for the danger that lay ahead.

When the news came that Arthur was being posted back to

Chile to run the embassy's commercial department, Betty felt betrayed. Santiago was an ocean away from the momentous events that had already begun to surge across Europe. Santiago would be an exile. All her loyalty, all her devotion to the cause, and this was her reward? She was inconsolable. The world was rushing to war, but she was a spy without a mission.

Part V

The Long Way Home

Chapter 29

◆

A S IT HAPPENED, JUST AS Betty had finished telling Hyde about her easy, restorative days spent walking along the rocky strip of beach in Saint-Jean-de-Luz with Owen O'Malley, they found themselves in the seaside town of Mulranny. We're only a few miles from Rockfleet, Hyde suggested.

Rockfleet, Betty knew from all of the elaborate stories she'd heard in these strolls, was the O'Malleys' ancestral home. In its time buccaneering pirates, pugnacious nationalists, and esteemed peers of the realm had walked through its grand rooms. It was a house with a long, rich history, and she instinctively felt that because of her relationship with O'Malley, it was somehow tied to her own past too. Betty couldn't help but be curious.

May 13, 1963

The enclosed posy [Betty wrote to O'Malley, now in Oxford, later that day], *I picked on the lawn of Rockfleet this morning. . . . The housekeeper kindly let us in and I had the joy of sitting on your bed and looking out your front and side windows and imagining you there, as I have so often imagined you over the years. . . .*

The house is lovely in every way; the weather was wild Irish with mist and drizzle and white wavelets on Clew Bay. A brown hare hopped in the wind across the green grass outside the library, and

the wind blew hard and strong. But spring was there too, in the
apple blossoms trellised against the wall near the front door and in
the early flowers in the lawns. How glad I am to have seen it all
and to share this part of your life with you, too.

Back at the old railway hotel in Mulranny in the evening of
that cold, wet, and gusting day, they sat in silence over dinner. She
was, she'd later write, sorting through the day, linking it back to
her own past and inevitably bringing it all full circle. She'd come
to Ireland to search, to find the lucidity she needed, and despite the
jauntiness of her letter to O'Malley, an introspective shadow now
stretched across all she had observed.

In time, she shared a little of what had been filling her mind.

The element in her relationship with O'Malley that she so
deeply cherished, she tried explaining to Hyde, was the complete
absence of intrigue. It was as it appeared to be and nothing more—a
friendship. So much of her life had been calculation and deceit. In
the name of love, she had betrayed her husband. And in the name
of duty, she'd betrayed her lovers.

She wanted to know why they both, a pair of old spies and
unfaithful spouses, had made the expedient and amoral decisions
that had shaped their untidy lives. She asked why they had thrown
away their scruples.

There were many answers Hyde could have given. He might
have suggested that confusing passion for love was, in its too human way, an honest mistake. He might have turned defiant, making the specious case that their spouses were not harmed by their
philandering. Or, taking the lofty road, he might have argued that
moral ambiguity be damned. The work they did in the war was
invaluable, and wars are not won by playing by the rules.

Instead, Hyde chose to be more honest: "We are who we are. It is our nature."

It was not the explanation she had probably been hoping for. She might have preferred something more exculpatory, an insight that would've allowed her to forgive herself for the many acts she now regretted. Still, Betty gave his words some thought. And the more she considered Hyde's terse pronouncement, the more she'd later acknowledge she suspected he was right.

It's time for bed, she said at last.

Tomorrow, he reminded her, we'll need to pick up where you left off. You had just returned to Chile.

Chapter 30

◆

THE ART OF BUILDING A convincing cover, the MI6 spy-masters knew, had a single Golden Rule: Take what's already there and add more of the same. Done right, it was a long-running process. The deeper the layers of disguise, the more credible the new identity, and the smaller the likelihood it would raise suspicions once the agent was off in the field.

Yet there was one operational drawback: such deliberate invention required patience. For an agent like Betty, a woman whose restlessness was a constant ache, the passive discipline required was excruciating.

At the end of April 1939, when Betty arrived in Chile, she was already disappointed. Not only was it a return to a too-familiar turf where a high-spirited game of polo was her only chance for action, but she was consigned to this limbo just when Europe was about to explode. She yearned for more consequential sport.

Betty tried fitting in with the embassy crowd, but once again she was quickly raising eyebrows. A catty story—small, yet one of many that chronicled her unbridled streak—was soon being whispered at cocktail parties. Betty was strolling through downtown Santiago with Leslie Doublet, the wife of the local manager of the Bank of London, when a dress in a store window caught her eye. She went in to try it on. Mrs. Doublet followed her into the changing room, only to discover that, as Betty pulled the dress she had on over her head, she was naked. Shaken, Mrs. Doublet crisply suggested that Betty "ought to wear some underclothes." Betty dismissed the admonishment with a bemused laugh. "Phooey! There's a war on. I haven't got time to worry about things like that." That's our impish Betty, the gossip mongers had tittered, as a member of the embassy crowd cattily remembered decades later.

For Arthur, though, the return to Chile was just what he needed.

"Things do not look very hopeful in Europe," he wrote to his family in England not long after he received his new post, "so perhaps it is just as well for my health that I am going to the end of the world. . . . Denise and Betty are both very well and we are all together again for the first time in over a year."

But while Arthur might truly have had no inkling of the discontent building up in his wife, the Service was more realistic. They suspected that Betty's unhappy days with Arthur were drawing to a close (how indeed had the couple lasted this long?), and when the marriage collapsed, so would Betty's diplomatic cover. They would use this interlude in Chile to fashion Betty's new identity. Only when it was complete would they send her back into the fray.

Arthur Pack, left, in Chile, with Leslie Doublet—the wife of the local manager of the Bank of London, who stuffily told Betty she "ought to wear some underclothes."

◆ ◆ ◆

AMONG BETTY'S MANY TALENTS, IT was duly noted in the offices on Broadway, were her literary skills. Her reports from first Spain and then Poland had generated nearly as much praise for their narrative precision and style as for their content. In the flood of dispatches streaming into headquarters, Betty's always found an audience: they were a good read. Plus, her background file also included the intriguing fact that she was an author—or at least had been, as a young girl. And so the plan was conceived to reinvent Betty as a reporter. Journalistic cover, after all, was as tried and true—and nearly as bulletproof—as a diplomatic posting.

When the details of this scheme were shared with Betty, she jumped at it. She had been sitting on the sidelines in Chile for too long. Here was the chance, she explained to Hyde, "to do something for the war effort actively, wholeheartedly, and practically." Even better, it held out the promise of future important missions. Her desire to do something useful had taken on a new urgency: on September 1, 1939, the Wehrmacht had goose-stepped their way into her beloved Poland.

In Chile, most people read either *El Mercurio* or *La Nación*. Since *El Mercurio* was a conservative sheet, its articles and editorials sympathetic to Germany's expansionist ambitions, she contacted Carlos Prendis, the editor of the more liberal *La Nación*.

The tradecraft in her approach was well conceived. She appealed to the editor's sense of journalistic fair play: "We must have one paper in Chile on the side of the Allies," she suggested. And—her argument's clincher—she was willing to write her articles "for nothing, simply for the privilege of getting into print."

Prendis listened; considered; and then turned Betty down. There was a large German community in Chile, and many were wealthy manufacturers and store owners. It wouldn't make much business sense to antagonize such a deep-pocketed crowd, especially when his paper looked to them for advertisements and circulation.

"So," Betty confided to Hyde, "I set out to persuade him. I did it personally. I flirted with him, of course."

HER FIRST ARTICLE APPEARED UNDER the pen name of "Elizabeth Thomas"—Betty could no longer remember whether that was a caution the embassy insisted on to distance itself from the strident pro-Allied arguments she'd be making in a neutral country or whether the work name was her controller's invention—and it was headlined "The Polish Corridor."

"The frontiers of Poland became intolerable to Germany," Betty thundered, "not only because they were those of a strong independent state (any independent state with tempting territory is 'intolerable' to the Third Reich) but also because those frontiers were an obstacle to the Nazi program of world domination."

The piece ran on September 4, 1939. It was the day after Great Britain had declared war on Germany, and Betty felt like she was rushing into battle too.

Articles with the Elizabeth Thomas byline rolled off the presses of *La Nación*, and soon they were being picked up by the local English-language paper, the *South Pacific Mail*. "Hitler's Excuse for Latest Theft," ran the feisty headline on a typically dogmatic piece.

With the Service's approval, she reproduced the map she'd stolen from Henlein's office a year before. Betty never, of course, shared with her growing readership how she'd obtained the secret document, but that didn't matter. The story the map told was more than sufficient to grab their attention. It was a timeline for the proposed Nazi march across Europe: 1940—Yugoslavia, Rumania, and Bulgaria; 1941—France, Switzerland, Luxembourg, Holland, Belgium, and Denmark; and 1942—the Soviet Ukraine.

Making facile use of an "eyewitness" account the Service had passed on of the sinking of a German battleship, she wrote a long, impassioned article that built up to an anti-Nazi roar: "Today all that is left of the *Admiral Graf Spee* sticks up out of twenty-five feet of water in mute testimony of a government that does not know the meaning of either courage or honor."

"Elizabeth Thomas" was making quite a name for herself. And in the heated process she was also, to her combative pride, making enemies. The angry German community decided to fight back. Thomas Kreiser, a local journalist whose laborious sentences bulldozed on and on like a Panzer attack, was recruited to rebut her pieces. "The whole thing," Betty snickered, "mushroomed into an exchange of polemics. I would write and Kreiser would reply, and I would reply to his reply."

This war of words, to Betty's dismay, seemed as close to a fighting war as she would get. But at least it gave her a reason to get a gun.

The Elizabeth Thomas pseudonym was only a thin veil, and evidently a transparent one too. It wasn't long before both Betty and the British embassy were receiving anonymous letters warning that she'd better "stop writing or else."

Or else what? an increasingly frustrated Betty felt like shouting. You'll give me the chance to get into a real fight? Still, that was all the excuse Betty needed. She cajoled the naval attaché into giving her a revolver. With the acquiescence of the Service, he agreed. Now she filled her empty afternoons taking practice shots out the Chancery windows at imaginary targets and, even more fun, deliberately annoying the embassy staff in the process.

But taking potshots at nonexistent Nazis was only a small and rapidly fading pleasure. Trading barbs in print with the maddening Kreiser offered even less sport. Determined, Betty made up her mind to get back into the game.

♦ ♦ ♦

THE PARQUE FORESTAL WAS IN the heart of Santiago, a rich green oasis with paths rambling through stands of tall trees. The park's turn-of-the-century design was precise and formal, more Gallic than Latin in its inspiration. And as a homage to the parks in Paris, its landscapers had shaped a leafy allée that twisted along the Mapocho River. Over the years this had become a favorite trail for equestrians who enjoyed starting their day with an early morning ride.

It was here on a glorious fall morning, not long after the sun had risen above the Andes, that Betty cantered along. She was a natural rider, her seat perfect, her back straight, and her hands comfortable with the reins. Her riding habit—the fitted jacket, the tight jodhpurs—had been snugly tailored. She was a wonderful sight.

Betty continued at a decorous canter until at last she saw that the moment she'd been waiting for was at hand. She broke into a gallop. Her horse surged ahead effortlessly. Then, her timing perfect, she kicked him sharply with her spurs. The horse shied, and Betty tumbled to the ground. Exactly as she had planned.

Full of concern, Colonel Montagu Parry-Jones galloped over, dismounted, and offered his assistance. He was the military attaché at the British embassy, but Betty, who knew a bit about how things worked, had pegged him as the intelligence service's liaison in Santiago. Their paths had crossed at several parties, and she'd made a few well-practiced assaults. She'd sidle up close to the old Etonian, and Parry-Jones, every taut inch the soldier, would merely nod politely. A week earlier, though, after she'd blatantly confided to the colonel that she'd like to get to know him better, she detected a slight thaw in his military demeanor. Encouraged, wanting to believe that she'd found an avenue back into the secret world, she had devised this scheme to move things along.

And now here was Parry-Jones gallantly extending his hand as Betty sat on the ground, laughing her rich, throaty, uninhibited laugh and pretending she was embarrassed. "Well, we are getting acquainted," Betty said as she took his hand. In one strong motion, the colonel lifted her to her feet.

WITH THE COLONEL'S CONSENT AND encouragement, as well as the acquiescence of the spymasters in London, Betty began, as she would later coyly put it, to "snoop a little." Chile was brimming with cells of Nazi sympathizers, a fifth column of bankers, mine owners, and landed gentry who brashly schemed with the Abwehr. The government remained officially neutral, but these men were covertly working for the day when Germany could get its hands on Chile's treasure chest of oil and mineral deposits. They hatched plots galore, many fanciful, but some that sent shivers through the British embassy. It was Betty's job to infiltrate this nest of renegades, and to keep London informed about who they were and what they were up to.

There Betty would be at diplomatic dinners, country-club dances, and polo matches, always glamorous, always charming, always the sparkling focus of every man's attention—and always listening. She trained herself to remember every word she heard, and in the aftermath of these outings she'd return to the embassy. With Montagu-Parry's consent, she'd been given access to the windowless code room, where she'd hunker down at a desk and type out her reports.

Each one was, in its formal way, a model of the professional fieldman's laconic art; Jack Shelley had taught her well. She clearly identified sources, weighed their reliability objectively, and then pithily summarized what she had gleaned. If she had an insight about how a specific piece of intelligence fitted into the big picture, she'd offer this up too. But she made it clear that this was her own assessment, and even then she never guessed; she never—sin of sins in intelligence work—tried to oversell the product.

Betty kept at it. But all the time she kept wondering if London had decided to let her stand in the wings, only a bit player, if that, in the great drama that was unfolding. The dismal month of June 1940 saw a swift series of Allied catastrophes. Holland, Belgium, and France had fallen. England was now preparing to make a last stand, rallying its forces and its people for what its new prime minister insisted would be Britain's "finest hour." Yet there she was, writing her articles and typing her reports in the netherworld of Chile.

Then she received a letter from London. The official crest of the War Office was at the top of the stiff page, and the single-spaced sentences were perfectly typed and centered:

Should Mrs. Pack return to England, a representative of this Office would be interested in meeting with her and discussing how she might be of assistance in the war effort.

The crisp tone was guarded. There was no acknowledgment of her past services and, more disappointing, no guarantee of future employment in intelligence activities. Betty reminded herself that during the year since her arrival in Santiago she had begun to stake out a new life. Her husband was on the mend, and without the nearly constant operational demands that she had in Warsaw, she was able to spend time with her six-year-old daughter. Now she was being told to abandon her family and travel across the world to a besieged London, to meet an unnamed factotum in the War Office—a recruiter? a pencil pusher?—for a conversation whose subject had been left annoyingly vague.

"This was a good enough excuse for me," Betty told Hyde. Despite her renewed relationship with Denise, it did not trouble her to leave her daughter; she felt little maternal pull. And as for

Arthur, she simply told him that she was going. It would be useless
to persuade her to stay, she warned. Her mind was set.

Using some of what remained of the modest sum she'd inherited upon her father's death, Betty immediately booked a ticket on
a steamer bound for New York. Once she arrived in America, she'd
figure out how to get to London.

Chapter 31

◆

B ETTY WAS REBORN. SHE WAS now, according to the story she made it her business to spread about the ship, a reporter traveling to New York for a new job. If anyone doubted her credentials, she had a hefty scrapbook of clippings in her valise to prove it. But Betty's past caught up with her when, as much to her disbelief as to her indignation, the British minister to Peru tried to rape her.

She had sailed on the *Orbita*, a British ship that left Valparaíso's harbor on July 4, 1940. For many of the passengers, it was an apprehensive voyage. A force of German U-boats, the Gruppe Monsun (Monsoon Group), was aggressively patrolling the Allied trade routes that crisscrossed the Pacific, and the slow-moving *Orbita* would be an easy target for an enemy torpedo. But Betty, the eager spy, had other concerns on her mind: she spent the voyage trying to prove her worth.

It had been suggested to Betty—after all these years, she explained to Hyde, she'd forgotten who at the embassy had passed along the message, which, he knew, might or might not be true— that she book passage on this particular crossing. It'd offer a few choice opportunities for discreet reconnaissance. A stint as a watcher, she'd been advised, could be a first step in her return to the field.

On board was the Chilean delegation to the Pan-American Conference. They were traveling to Havana where an anxious Cordell Hull, the US secretary of state, had hastily convened the gathering to get a sense of whether the Nazis' blitzkrieg through

Europe had created new support for Germany in Latin America. Betty's assignment was to cozy up to the delegates on the ship, play the guileless reporter, and let London know before the conference began what they were thinking.

A sea cruise—the long convivial dinners, the open bar, the lulling rhythm of the ocean, the starry nights, plus the large operational advantage she held simply because there was not a single woman delegate—was a bread-and-butter assignment for Betty. Nevertheless, her diligence was extraordinary. Ready to show off her skills, she threw herself into the job.

Was any spy ever more productive in such a short time? Her thick report included informative sketches of each of the forty-five delegates, but she zeroed in with special acuity on the six men who, she had discovered, were in Hitler's camp. The six of them had already begun covert discussions with German intelligence and were determined to persuade the government in Santiago to abandon its neutrality and support the Nazis. And in addition to this coup, she'd somehow got two of the senior delegates to divulge in expansive detail Chile's entire agenda at the conference.

An agent who delivered product like that was certain to get noticed. From Lord Halifax, the foreign secretary, to the British ambassador to Chile, to the civil servants on the Latin American desk, Betty's report made the rounds. As one anonymous Foreign Office reader scrawled in the report's margin, "Mrs. Pack is a forceful American lady."

It would not be long, though, before the British minister to Peru would be able to give his colleagues firsthand testimony on just how forceful the American lady could be. If he dared.

COURTENEY FORBES, HIS MAJESTY'S MINISTER to Peru, was a paunchy, acerbic, self-important Eton and Oxford man, a tyrant with an annoyingly booming voice. Since his opinions were the only ones that mattered, he bellowed whatever was on his mind for everyone to hear. He also, in his self-confident way, considered himself a benevolent God's gift to womankind.

Given the constant swirl of diplomatic parties and receptions, it was only natural that now and again Betty would have crossed his path. He had liked what he'd seen. More intriguing, he liked what he'd heard: Mrs. Pack was not quite a lady.

It was a normal courtesy when a fellow British diplomat of sufficient rank or his wife arrived in any city for the local ministry to send a junior staffer to assist them, but when the *Orbita* docked outside Lima, Forbes decided he'd be the one to show up. The legation had been informed that Betty, en route to New York, would be on board, and he figured this would be his chance. He'd greet the glamorous Mrs. Pack in her cabin; and then, if the many whispered stories were true, anything might happen.

Betty, with the steady calm of the never-ruffled fieldman, described to Hyde what *did* happen:

I was wearing a diaphanous nightie when the ship docked and was still in my cabin. Suddenly there was a knock on the door and thinking it might be the stewardess I got up and opened it. To my surprise there stood His Britannic Majesty's minister. He came in, carefully locking the door behind him. Evidently the sight of me in my nightie was too much for him, since without saying good morning he proceeded to catch hold of my waist and throw me on the berth. He then attempted to rape me.

"I struggled for a few moments and then told him I would ring for the steward, which I promptly did. Fortunately for him, by the time the steward appeared Mr. Courteney Forbes had recovered himself sufficiently to invite me to lunch at the Legation in Lima.

She accepted. The hardworking spy gamely told herself that in the course of their lunch, there was no telling what morsels she might be served. And Forbes had, somewhat convincingly, promised "to behave myself." Besides, intelligence, she told herself, was a trade where you must on occasion sup with the devil. Her spoon would be long; she felt she'd able to hold him off.

Forbes was docile enough—at first. When Betty trotted out the cover story that she was "on her way to the United States to work as a journalist," he seemed to buy it. In fact, Forbes said her articles had been reprinted in the Lima papers, and he'd read them with interest. Next thing Betty knew, he was offering her a job. Stay in Lima and write in the legation's information section, he said. Her starting salary would be a munificent $480 each month—about as much, Betty realized, as the Foreign Office paid Arthur. Still, Betty perfunctorily turned him down; she had more pressing ambitions. And as she griped to Hyde, "Anyhow, I had a shrewd idea that the task Mr. Forbes had in mind for me included a stint in the bedroom as well as the office."

Yet while the conversation at lunch was merely bothersome, what followed would be an all-out disaster. When Forbes learned that she was on her way next to the Hotel Bolivar to meet Señor Paradol, a Peruvian diplomat she'd known during her happy days in Madrid, he insisted on accompanying her. Forbes knew Paradol, too; he'd like the chance to say hello. After he shrewdly reminded that he had a car and driver waiting, Betty acquiesced.

Later that afternoon they walked into the narrow lobby of the hotel. It was, as usual, hopping; when Lima's old guard went out for a cocktail, the barroom at the Bolivar was where they gathered. Waiting to greet them, stationed by the busy entrance so Betty wouldn't miss him, was the courtly Paradol.

In his booming, assertive voice, Forbes called to Paradol. He was loud enough for everyone in the lobby to hear, as well as, a cringing Betty imagined, the rest of Lima too.

"Well, here's your girl!" he bellowed in a surprisingly fluent Spanish. "You know I think she is a spy. She has left Chile, the Germans are after her, and she is on her way to the United States to do newspaper work, she tells me. But if it's newspaper work, she could perfectly well stay here with us, couldn't she?"

Betty laughed bravely and loudly. What a card! she announced to Paradol and everyone else who was now listening, she feared, with rapt attention. Gaily she took Paradol's arm, and they went off to have a jolly time, dining and dancing the night away.

Yet all the time, the carefree, smiling mask she'd put on concealed her utter panic. How could Forbes—a ranking British official!—have been so careless, so destructive? With a sinking heart she considered the consequences. All she'd worked for, destroyed in one reckless, fatal moment.

"One hardly likes to have one's cover blown before one even begins," she complained to Hyde, her cool understatement made possible only by the passing of the years.

ONCE BACK ON BOARD, BETTY did her best at damage control. She worried that Forbes's outburst had been passed on to her targets in the Chilean delegation, and she immediately went to work to assuage suspicions. She made sure it became well known that the minister had a mean-spirited motive to lie: Betty had spurned his aggressive advances, and he wanted revenge.

Her campaign proved effective. Her cover remained unblemished, even unquestioned. To everyone on board, she remained Betty Pack, foreign correspondent; when she left Chile, she also left behind "Elizabeth Thomas." She could still go up to anyone and ask practically anything. And who thinks twice about the covert motives of a reporter out to get a scoop? Especially when the eager scribe has a smile that makes the heart race.

When the *Orbita* docked in Havana, Betty was offered further operational opportunity to test her new cover. George Ogilvie-Forbes, the man who had godfathered her conversion to Catholicism in Spain, was now minister in Cuba, and he had a proposition. Would Betty like to stay in Havana for the conference's duration? There was another north-bound ship in a couple of weeks. In the meantime, she could stay in the legation as his guest, and, of course, keep her eyes and ears open to what was going on behind the scenes among the delegates.

If Betty had any doubts about this seemingly spontaneous, rather offhanded invitation to spy, they were put to rest when the local MI6 man—"our man in Havana," she joked to Hyde—came to call on her. His instructions were succinct: Betty was to pass on all the fruits of her labor to him; he'd make sure her reports got to London. In fact, he added pointedly, they were looking forward to them.

Once again Betty proved her worth. The Service had all manner of agents. There were operatives who could break into enemy headquarters and make off with the battle plans. Others who could ingeniously spike an ambassador's phone. And there were teams of scalphunters available for wet work, agents ready to cut a throat or put a bullet between the eyes. But there were few—arguably none—with Betty's soft, coaxing touch. Who else could spend a long evening dancing cheek-to-cheek in La Floridita with a crowd of lovesick delegates and in the morning write a perceptive report detailing the schemes lurking in each of her dancing partners' minds, the political maneuvers they had up their sleeves, their hidden loyalties? Who else could share a candlelit dinner with a virulent pro-Nazi, anti-British Argentine politico and have him spill the secrets that lay hidden in his soul? Who else could get the most truculent Marxist delegate to abandon the barricades for an evening, for the hope of a little human kindness?

Betty could. And London had come to appreciate the valuable gift they'd been given.

BETTY'S PLAN WAS TO SPEND a few weeks in the States. She'd do some shopping in New York, and then dutifully visit her mother and sister Jane in Washington. Once her time with Cora was done, she'd fly to Lisbon, and from there she'd make her way to London. Still, the wartime air route to Portugal was an ordeal. From Miami, it was on to Jamaica, and then, after a short layover, the Pan Am Clipper continued to Natal in Brazil and then crossed the South Atlantic, stopping next in Monrovia, Liberia. From there, a quick jaunt up the West African coast to Portuguese Guinea. And finally you landed at an airport just outside Lisbon, near where the Tagus River emptied into the Atlantic. The trip took four days and cost Betty $318.75 of her own funds; the British, after all, had written that they'd like to meet with her, not that they were buying her ticket.

Exhausted, Betty arrived at the Palace Hotel on the outskirts of Lisbon. She was looking forward to a long bath followed by a gin and tonic; or maybe, she corrected herself, she'd have that drink first. At the front desk, she signed the register. No sooner had she put down the pen than she looked up with complete surprise into a familiar face. Standing next to her was Colonel Montagu Parry-Jones—the very man who had helped steer her back into intelligence work in Santiago.

Parry-Jones played their encounter as the most fortunate of coincidences. He was returning to London for a new assignment, and now they could have a jolly time together in Lisbon as they waited for the next plane to England. What a spot of luck, he said. Purest chance.

Yes, Betty agreed. But her suspicious mind told her something else. She'd been at the game long enough to know that there are no accidents in intelligence work—only schemes. The colonel's showing up at her hotel was as unpremeditated as her fall from her horse just as he happened to be riding by. Betty had no idea what plan London was cooking—or, the larger issue, what role she would play in it. She knew it would be futile to ask Parry-Jones. For now, all she could do was put on her famous smile and suggest that the colonel might want to join her for the drink she'd been so anticipating.

The following day a small, tantalizing corner of the plot was revealed. Returning to the hotel after a pleasant afternoon in Lisbon with Parry-Jones, she found a cable waiting for her at the front desk.

Odd, she thought. Who knows I'm here? She'd made her travel arrangements at the last minute. She hadn't known when she'd be arriving in Lisbon—or, for that matter, where she'd be staying. How could anyone else have known? Unless it was someone, like Parry-Jones, whose trade it was to know all manner of seemingly unknowable information.

The mystery deepened when she read the cable. It was from Arthur. It wasn't just that, from his outpost in faraway Santiago, he had somehow managed to track her down. It was what he was asking: that she fly home straight away. As the embassy's commercial counselor, he'd be hosting a trade mission headed by Lord Willingdon, the famously haughty aristocrat who had been viceroy of India. He needed, he nearly pleaded, Betty's help. He wanted her to serve as hostess during Willingdon's visit.

His proposal left Betty astonished. Furious at her desertion, Arthur had not been speaking to her by the time she'd left. And even if they had been civil to one another, she couldn't imagine that her husband would've considered her presence beneficial to any diplomatic encounter.

Hadn't he ranted on and on about her "American morality"?

Hadn't he barked about her behavior at parties, the conspicuous attention she provoked? And now, when she was halfway around the world, he wanted her to give up her plan to go to London, turn straight around, and head straight back on another long, exhausting journey! And for what? To be reunited in a country that bored her silly, with a man with whom she could scarcely bear to speak? It was absurd. No, worse, it was mad.

Yet that night, as she shared a cocktail with Parry-Jones, it began to make sense. She suddenly understood how Arthur had tracked her down. And she suspected that the idea to summon her back to Chile had not originated with him.

After she had mentioned her mystification to the colonel, and in the process had shared a glimpse of her seething anger, he offered his own take on the situation. Full of calming reason, he told Betty that to return might make good sense, after all. As if the idea had just occurred to him, he suggested that it would offer an opportunity to resolve things once and for all with Arthur. At the moment she was still regarded—often warily—as the wife of a British diplomat. But people would see a single young woman differently. A divorced reporter would find all sorts of previously locked doors suddenly open. Imagine the kind of access she could have, the acquaintances she would make?

The colonel talked on, carefully hypothetical, but nevertheless the spymasters' curtains of subterfuge had parted. London, Betty understood, wanted her to put the finishing touch on her new cover.

The next day she cabled Arthur that she'd be coming home. "In the circumstances, I felt it was best to comply," she explained to Hyde.

Although she'd be heading back to where she'd started, Betty felt that she was on the final stretch of her long journey back into the dangerous life. It did not make complete sense to her; why had she been summoned, and then directed to return to Chile? But she tried to convince herself—it was the bewildered fieldman's constant rationalization—that the deskmen in London had their reasons, that they alone could see the big picture. Once she completed this final task, it wouldn't be long before she'd be living a cloak-and-dagger life behind enemy lines in Europe.

She could not have been more wrong. Other plans had been made for her.

Chapter 32

◆

A SMALL BRONZE PLAQUE WAS FIXED to the wall outside room 3603 in the Rockefeller Center building at 630 Fifth Avenue in New York: "British Passport Control." Behind the black door was a long counter manned by several knowledgeable clerks who would obligingly answer any questions regarding travel documents for England. At the end of the counter, jammed between a few straight-backed metal chairs and a waist-high bookcase empty but for a single shelf holding a pile of passport applications, was an unmarked door.

To enter, it was necessary to press a buzzer. A peephole immediately opened, through which the visitor would be scrutinized. If he met with approval, the lock would be released and the heavy door would swing open. Inside, as well as on the floor below, was a warren of rooms swarming with busy office workers, or so they appeared at a cursory glance. Their trade, however, was espionage. This was a den of spies. It was the headquarters of the British Secret Intelligence Service in America.

In June 1940 Colonel Stewart Menzies, the wily old-boy aristocrat who headed the Firm, had decided to send a man to New York to "establish relations on the highest possible level between the British SIS and the U.S. Federal Bureau of Investigation." "C," as the head of the Service was traditionally known, went outside his narrow circle of establishment cronies and intelligence professionals, the old Etonians who, like him, belonged to White's Club, rode to the hounds, and had inherited stately piles in the country. A scrapper was necessary, he decided, someone who would lower his shoulders, clench his fists, and punch his way if necessary through the restrictions of America's Neutrality Act. He selected a self-made millionaire, a Canadian businessman who had flown daring fighter missions in the last war and gone many rounds in the ring as an amateur boxer.

He was also encouraged in his choice by the new prime minister, Winston Churchill. Even more than Menzies, Churchill envisioned the head of the Service in America as an activist. To his way of thinking, the essential mission was to get the United States to contribute the arms and matériel Britain needed to fight on and, no less important, to help convince a reluctant America that the nation must ultimately join the fight against Hitler. A practical politician, Churchill wanted someone brash enough to get the job done, and at the same time canny and charming enough to get away with stepping all over the sensibilities and, if need be, even the laws of the host country.

Menzies chose William Stephenson, the forty-three-year-old part-time intelligence asset who had first entered the game by sharing the information he'd picked up during his prewar business jaunts to Germany. Churchill promptly seconded the choice. He met with Stephenson so soon after his election as prime minister that he'd not yet moved into Downing Street, and urged him to accept the post in America. "Your duty lies there," Churchill insisted. "You must go."

Stephenson not only went, but in his ambitious way he saw his duty as something larger than either Menzies or even Churchill had imagined. Starting from scratch, and spending his own money freely as well as resourcefully, he built a vast intelligence organization whose covert activities stretched across the Western Hemisphere. Its agents penetrated enemy-controlled businesses, embassies, and spy rings. Political warfare officers shamelessly spread propaganda to the American press and, with money to burn, set up pro-interventionist front organizations. It recruited and trained special operations agents for impossible missions in America and Europe. In Bermuda, its teams intercepted sacks of mail bound for Europe or America, wantonly steamed open any letter that caught their fancy, and scrutinized the contents. And its armed patrols policed British interests in the Americas against Nazi sabotage.

By the time Stephenson was done, he had built a formidable intelligence network that included espionage and counterintelligence missions that were normally restricted to either MI6, MI5, or the special operations units. An empire builder, Stephenson had all manner of inventive ops going on under his broad umbrella. He'd have, for example, a celebrated medium touring the country and making sure to sneak prognostications of spectacular Nazi setbacks into his act. And he ran Camp X in Canada, a backwoods training ground that taught derring-do secret agents all the dark arts. At full operational strength, he had over two thousand people—agents, staff, and assets—on the payroll.

The organization became, Stephenson would boast, "the only all encompassing integrated secret security organization that had ever existed anywhere, and myself the repository of secret information at all levels beyond that of any other single individual then involved."

Including J. Edgar Hoover. Yet the FBI potentate, who also knew a good deal about the accumulation of power, was, surprisingly, one of Stephenson's early supporters. At first he went tacitly along with British secret agents working in the United States. He even suggested the cover name for the group that Stephenson obligingly adopted—British Security Coordination (BSC). But as Intrepid—the organization's Western Union code name and cable address, the name Stephenson embraced, as well as the image, as his own—he with increasing frequency launched missions that played fast and loose with American law and trampled over the country's official stance of benign neutrality. Hoover turned hostile. He assigned his own agents to monitor what the British were up to. And if the Bureau caught BSC operatives in illegal acts, Hoover's no-nonsense orders were to slap on the handcuffs and haul 'em in.

Yet, the BSC had one important—definitive, arguably—supporter, President Franklin D. Roosevelt. "There should be the closest possible marriage between the FBI and British Intelligence," the president assured His Majesty's ambassador in Washington. And after Stephenson traveled to Hyde Park to give the intrigued president a remarkably candid briefing on what his organization planned to accomplish, neither Roosevelt's enthusiasm nor the Anglo-American bond was diminished. "I'm your biggest undercover agent," Roosevelt told Stephenson expansively.

It was a slyly appropriate endorsement. After all, the meeting had been arranged by a tireless amateur spy who, in turn, saw himself as the president's "biggest undercover agent"—Vincent Astor.

THE ROOM WAS A SMALL, very select club, a secret society of rich and powerful men who liked to play at being spies. Its name was a veiled reference to their covert meeting place, a dingy apartment at 34 East Sixty-Second Street in New York, with an unlisted phone number and an impressive collection of wines. The Room's keyholders all shared similar pedigrees, a provenance of recognizable family names, New England boarding schools, and Ivy League colleges. But the group's acknowledged driving force was Vincent Astor.

After the *Titanic* sank into the sea with his father, John Jacob Astor IV, onboard, Astor had dropped out of Harvard to manage the family's multimillion-dollar real estate empire. Yet soon he was looking for more excitement, and instinct and opportunity conspired to push him toward the secret life. Here was a trade that offered not just the opportunity to protect the gilded establishment world he'd been born into but also a rustle of adventure. A well-connected amateur could ply it as effectively, or so he innocently thought, as the diligent professional.

With Astor setting the tone and often the agenda, the monthly Room sessions were informal intelligence briefings. One member would report, for example, on his trip to China. Another would give an insider's report on the growing Japanese financial reserves at his bank. Astor would share what he'd discovered on his self-styled reconnaissance missions across the Pacific in his gleaming motor yacht, the *Nourmahal*. Notes of the discussions would be typed, and then Astor, with a gravity normally reserved for state secrets, would distribute the Room memos to his important friends in the federal government and in the Office of Naval Intelligence.

Playing intelligence agents proved to be enjoyable sport for these worldly men; they were as happily occupied as boys in a tree house frolicking with decoder rings and secret writing kits. But in 1933 their freelance ops abruptly took on a new significance— Franklin D. Roosevelt was elected president.

Not only was FDR one of their privileged own, part of the Groton, Harvard, Knickerbocker gentry, but he was also Astor's longtime friend. The new president soaked his paralyzed legs at the indoor pool on the Astor estate just down the dirt road from his farm at Hyde Park. When the pressures of his job grew over-whelming, he'd unwind with Astor and a tight circle of buddies, all members of the Room, on the palatial *Nourmahal*; "This is the only place I can get away from people, telephones and uniforms," the president would write. And like the Room's keyholders, Roosevelt too had a dilettante's fascination for the intriguing game of espio-nage. He encouraged diplomats, generals, and journalists to bypass normal channels and pass their confidential reports directly to the intelligence analyst-in-chief. He did not hesitate to let his friends into this operational circle too.

Vincent Astor and President Franklin Delano Roosevelt on the deck of Astor's yacht, the Nourmahal.

Astor, particularly, relished his new heady role as the president's very own secret agent. An entirely new way of living had swept away the tedium of his pampered life. What fun he had! There he'd be, the undercover yachtsman steering the *Nourmahal* around the Galapagos Islands to check out the rumor that Japanese ships were scouting the area for a covert base. Or he'd be playing the wireman with the yacht's direction finder as he voyaged across the South Pacific, hoping to locate, as he wrote to Roosevelt, "the Jap Radio stations in the islands." Or before taking on his next mission, he'd confidently share a bit of his tradecraft with his controller in the

Oval Office: "Tomorrow I start working on the banks, using the Chase as the Guinea Pig. Espionage and sabotage need money and that has to pass through the banks at one stage or another." And as director of the Western Union cable company, he could disregard privacy laws and use his lofty position to scour international cable traffic, uncovering a bounty of secrets. He'd forward to Roosevelt intelligence revealing the locations of Japanese gas storage facilities, burgeoning plots against the United States hatched by foreign agents in Mexico City, and the existence of a larcenous ring inside the Brazilian naval commission, a group of hustlers who routinely collected payoffs in return for the weapons they'd purchase in Washington.

Astor would detail his findings in meticulously organized reports, all designed to reinforce the personal nature of his small triumphs. But for optimal effect—and no doubt because proximity to power was a cherished part of the adventure—he made it his business to have frequent one-on-one debriefs with his controller. He'd meet with Roosevelt in Hyde Park or at the White House. The president would listen attentively, often offer words of encouragement, and, most gratifying, from time to time suggest new missions. Astor would jump at these presidential commands. And it wasn't long before the controller rewarded his agent's diligence.

A presidential directive appointed Astor area controller for intelligence activities in New York. It was by design a secret post; Astor was to remain on inactive naval duty, and his title was known only to the upper ranks of military intelligence. Still, he had an office and a staff in the Naval District Intelligence Office down by the Battery in lower Manhattan. And best of all, the gentleman spy now had official authority to play the game.

New York had always been Astor's playground, but he found it an even better place to be a spy. He rushed about the city, looking for new opportunities—and he made it his business to get acquainted with Bill Stephenson.

He had known the previous British passport control heads, Sir James Paget and Walter Bell. Both had been invited to speak at the Room. Afterward, always the fieldman, he had written to Roosevelt: "It occurred to me that Paget and Bell might from time to time obtain leads useful to us." As soon as he had heard Stephenson was coming to New York, Astor urged him to be his guest at his hotel, the St. Regis; "my broken-down boarding house," he called it with a millionaire's hollow self-deprecation. Then when Stephenson, a stranger to the bewildering corridors of American power, was looking for guidance, it was Astor who helped him find his way. All it took was one telephone call—and there was Stephenson sitting across from the president of the United States in Hyde Park and having a cozy chat.

It was only a matter of time before Stephenson and Astor, two well-heeled and keen neophytes in the secret life, developed their own special relationship. Working together, they launched what became officially known as the "Ships Observers' Scheme."

AN ADMIRING MEMO FROM THE chief of US naval operations detailed the official operational scope of their plan: "In cooperation with the British Intelligence unit in the Third Naval District, New York, New York, a plan for placing ship observers on American merchant vessels has been in effect for several months with excellent results. The plan involved cooperation between the British Intelligence and Naval Intelligence whereby certain ship observers placed on American vessels by British Intelligence were put under control of Naval Intelligence and certain additional observers were placed on American vessels by Naval Intelligence. Provisions were made for the mutual exchange of information."

And so when the *Excalibur*, an American Export Lines ship, sailed from Portugal for New York in October 1940, a quick-witted naval lieutenant was on board as an undercover observer. His name was Paul Fairly, but his officer's rank was part of his cover. He was a yeoman assigned to naval intelligence.

An experienced operative, Fairly had received high marks for his previous shipboard work as a watcher. He was also young, handsome, and oozing with confident charm. After mulling over several possible candidates, Vincent Astor had decided he was just the man he'd been looking for.

This mission, Fairly had been told, would be different from previous watcher assignments. It wasn't the usual eyes wide open, report anything on board that catches your attention. This op had a specific target.

The target had originated with Bill Stephenson. There was "a person of interest" to the Service sailing on the *Excalibur,* he had told Astor. She'd done a few things in Poland that had first brought her to his attention, and now he was thinking she might be of use to the BSC. Before he made the offer, he thought it'd be prudent to have someone look her over. He had big plans for her, but he didn't want to rush in without getting a better sense of who she was. He was a businessman by training, and he'd learned that due diligence was always a wise precaution.

Stephenson gave Astor a name, and Astor made sure it was passed on to Fairly.

The target was Mrs. Betty Pack.

The S.S. Excalibur *manifest with Paul Fairly's name.*
Stephenson, via Astor, had sent him to keep an eye on
Betty during the voyage from Lisbon to New York.

Chapter 33

◆

BETTY HAD NO IDEA SHE was being watched. But her operational lapse might be excused; she had other matters on her mind as the *Excalibur* sailed west across the Atlantic. An American millionaire had fallen in love with her, and after just two besotted days at sea had proposed marriage.

There were many good reasons why Betty might have discouraged this shipboard romance, why when he caught her by surprise with the first long kiss as they walked together on deck she should have thrown back her pretty head in indulgent amusement and, making sure there were no hard feelings, neatly extricated herself. One, of course, was that she was married. Another was that she had no time for diversions: Betty had to get back to Chile, tie up the loose ends of her life, and hurry back to Europe to fight a war.

But Betty couldn't help herself. Norman Whitehouse was a dashing cosmopolitan socialite, a man who shuttled between his homes in Newport and Paris, served with distinction from time to time on State Department commissions, played a fast game of squash, and danced like a stalking panther. "We had a mild flirtation," she confessed demurely to Hyde.

Yet the larger truth, she was beginning to understand even as she instructed Hyde to use a decorously expurgated version for his book, was that she needed to be in love. If she continually convinced herself that she was falling in love, then one day, she wanted to believe, it would actually be true. She would be at peace and would finally settle into an imagined happiness. Her restlessness would vanish.

Years later, older and growing wiser, she would understand her predicament. She hadn't had romances; she'd had adventures. But at the time, trying to believe in what she now knew was quite impossible, she did her best to convince herself that this shipboard encounter was something special. Once the *Excalibur* docked in New York, she let Whitehouse sweep her away to his redbrick mansion with the mansard roof in Newport. It was a comfortable household of chintz, fine china, and attentive servants, a setting where it was understood that evening dress would be worn at the dinner table. It was, she told her host, the sort of proper, gracious life her mother would've wanted for her.

Whitehouse, unaware of the long-running antagonisms that had kept mother and daughter at each other's throats, did not hear the bite in Betty's words; a stranger to her sarcasm, he took them as a compliment. Eager for any support he could find to reinforce his marriage proposal, Whitehouse quickly suggested Betty invite her mother up for a weekend. Perversely, Betty complied; she was looking forward to her mother's wide-eyed envy.

Like most of Betty's naughty schemes, it all went as she'd planned. A glance about the mansion set Cora's covetous heart beating. Suddenly full of maternal concern, she counseled Betty to divorce Arthur and marry this "divine man." If Betty had qualms about breaking the news to her husband—and this reminded Betty how little her mother knew her—then Cora would travel down to Chile and deliver the grim news herself.

Betty demurred, saying she was still uncertain. She needed time to think things through. Yet her daughter's hesitancy only added fuel to Cora's eagerness. "Just think of all the wonderful things you could do for me," she pleaded.

Her mother's raw logic brought Betty to her senses. As soon as the words were spoken, any possible long-term relationship with Whitehouse died. She was "talking like a madam," Betty snapped at Cora. Then Betty went off to thank Whitehouse for his hospitality and tell him it was time she returned to Chile, and her husband and daughter.

Betty and a deflated Cora left Newport the next day.

As the porters loaded Betty's luggage onto the train to New York, Paul Fairly watched from across the platform. He had been keeping an eye on Betty for a while now, and what had started as a simple stint of talent-spotting, a routine surveillance of a target his masters were considering for recruitment, had turned into something else. Something personal. He could not get Betty out of his mind. He looked at her, and he wanted to come out of the shadows and hold her very tight.

STILL, IT WAS WITH THE dispassionate control of a professional that Fairly finally made his approach. Mother and daughter were staying at the Ritz-Carlton in New York—Cora sullenly footing the bill—as Betty waited for the ship that would take her back to Chile, and he chose the hotel lobby for his initial pass.

Good tradecraft held that a crowded place was always fertile ground for an "accidental" meet; the proximity of bystanders helped the target to feel unthreatened. So when he saw Betty charging through the busy lobby in the resolute way he'd come to admire, and after a quick reconnaissance ascertained that her mother was nowhere in sight, Fairly decided the time had come. He bumped into her.

Fairly had worked out what he'd say days in advance, and he delivered the lines from his carefully memorized script: Oh, excuse me. Wait. Don't I know you? Yes, you were on the *Excalibur*. Small world. So was I.

Now that the words were spilling from his lips, he couldn't help feeling that they sounded absurdly transparent, the sort of coincidence that would send any experienced agent running at once for cover. But he improvised with a friendly grin, explaining that he was a lieutenant in the US Navy to show that he was harmless enough. When he asked Betty to join him for a drink, with hardly any hesitation, she agreed.

In the darkness of the cave-like bar, as he sat across from Betty in a booth in the rear, Fairly obeyed his orders. He told Betty the truth, or at least the version of the truth that his superiors had instructed him to share.

He confessed that their meeting was not an accident. He was a Naval Intelligence agent based in Washington. He was in New York on a mission: he had been sent to assist Betty. He would stay in touch with her while she was in Chile, and he would make sure she knew who to contact when she returned to New York. He'd been assigned the task of delivering Betty back into the secret life.

Once the official business was out of the way and the gin was flowing, Fairly moved closer to Betty. He looked directly into her vast green eyes and began to speak. This speech was unplanned and unrehearsed. But his message was clear: watching her from afar, he'd fallen in love with her.

Why was Betty so taken with his ardor? Was it his sincerity? His brash schoolboy's charm? Or was it—as she now suspected when she conjured up the barroom scene in her mind after so many years—that while everything else in her life had left her unsatisfied and confused, Fairly was offering her a path back into the one calling she desired above all else? He had come to give her another chance. He was summoning her back into the clandestine life. That was why his words, she now understood, had left her so susceptible, why she'd felt such a dizzying sense of rightness and well-being. He was her savior.

And that was why they became lovers.

◆ ◆ ◆

THREE DAYS LATER FAIRLY ESCORTED Betty onto the ship that would take her back to her husband and daughter. Since they had met they had hardly left each other's side. For Fairly, it had been double duty, and he'd served both his masters—the navy and his heart—with devotion. For Betty, who'd been traveling helter-skelter around the world, lurching from one caper to another, the interlude was a godsend. The promise of new horizons had quieted her uneasiness. At last she felt secure, released from the need to grasp at every stray opportunity or desire.

Even their farewell was more hopeful than sad. They'd agreed that it would be only a brief parting: Betty would return in a month, unencumbered and ready for duty. In the meantime, Fairly would make sure to keep his bosses in intelligence informed of Betty's travel plans. And they'd worked out a fallback procedure: if for any reason Fairly was unavailable—there was no knowing where his next mission might take him—then he'd let the right people know they could always reach out to Betty by leaving word at her mother's home in Washington. He knew his superiors, a socially well-connected clique, would be comfortable using that address as a mail drop; in fact, the sparkle of Cora Thorpe's pedigree would reinforce the rightness of the entire operation in their minds.

Betty, reassured, shipped off. Her future, she felt, was in good hands. Fairly had handled things the way Jack Shelley would've, and in Betty's world there was no greater compliment.

Her faith was confirmed by a cable that arrived as her ship passed through the Panama Canal. "Our friends have contacted your mother and wish to communicate with you," Fairly had written. It was, she decided, the first genuine love letter she'd ever received.

When her ship docked in Balboa, she hunted down the British

consul and after a good deal of persuasion convinced him to send a message to the Special Intelligence Service in London. I'm coming as soon as I wrap things up, she cabled. It was very important to her that the Service know their love was not in vain.

Then it was on to Chile. She tried to use the voyage to work out some way to give Arthur and Denise the hard news, but after writing a half dozen speeches in her mind, she rejected all of them. None seemed right. She'd just say whatever came into her head at the time; nothing, she understood, was going to make things any easier.

But first she had to stand by her husband's side and play the radiant diplomatic hostess. It would be her swan song in that role, and she put everything she had into her performance. As if they were the happiest of married couples, she accompanied Arthur to a swirl of receptions. Betty was always the dazzling charmer, the secret fantasy of many of the men who stared at her across the room or the dinner table. Arthur received the official praise for the success of Lord Willingdon's visit, but he knew that Betty's presence, her sheer, intoxicating glamor, had made it all possible.

When she broke her news, Arthur was devastated. "Why do you want to do that," he cried out as if in genuine pain, "now that we have come together again?" He was truly bewildered. He had assumed that Betty had had her "holiday" and had gotten "all this nonsense out of your system." After their many years of marriage, he still had no understanding of the strength of her demons, or of the ambitions that he competed with for her allegiance.

Betty listened, and turned cold.

"I have been unfaithful to you and I will give you a letter admitting it," she announced. "You can do what you like with it. You know that no two people could be more temperamentally incompatible than we are—in every way."

Arthur listened in silence; he understood that her mind was set.

Betty, relentless, continued: "I won't break up your diplomatic career. I'm not taking anything with me except my clothes. But I must go. I have a life of my own to lead."

She did not try to offer an explanation to her daughter. How could she say that while she cared about Denise, she loved the prospect of leading her own life, having her own adventures, more?

When she left Santiago at the end of the week aboard the train to Valparaíso, Arthur could not bring himself to go to the station to say good-bye. Six-year-old Denise remained home with her nanny too.

Betty had the spy's gift for never allowing guilt to interfere with self-interest. She felt only a sense of release as the train headed to the coast. Her old world slipped away, and she escaped.

A NAVAL LAUNCH SIDLED UP to Betty's liner as it entered New York Harbor. To her surprise, she watched as Fairly climbed onboard. This was the sign she'd been praying for during the long voyage north: her future was about to unfold.

He whisked her through customs with great authority, and then into the waiting naval car.

"Why all the VIP treatment?" she asked as they clasped hands in the back seat. She was impressed, and also suspicious. For a lowly lieutenant, Fairly seemed to have a good deal of official clout.

"It's British intelligence," said Fairly. "Seems they want to get ahold of you fast."

Betty was immediately excited. "Can you get in touch with some of your people and find out where this British intelligence outfit is located? I am getting tired of chasing around the world."

"That will probably not be necessary," Fairly said. Reaching into his briefcase, he extracted a thin sheet of paper and handed it to Betty.

She unfolded the page and read:

New York City

November 25, 1940
ATWATER 9-8763
Dear Mrs. Thorpe,
I wish to thank you for seeing me last Saturday in connection with your daughter, whom I am sorry to have missed.
Should you have any news from her which you wish to communicate to me, would you kindly ring the above number in New York City.
Yours sincerely,

J. Howard

Part VI

Washington

Chapter 34

◆

MONEY WAS ON HYDE'S MIND as they drove back to Dublin. Perhaps it was their visit the previous day to Rockfleet, the O'Malley homestead, that had brought the anxiety on. In the high-spirited aftermath of their walk through the house and around the ample grounds, he'd scribbled a quick postscript to Betty's letter to O'Malley: "We were entranced by Rockfleet and want nothing more than to take a long lease of it and settle there together." It had been a pretty thought the day before, but now reality kicked in. It wasn't just that he couldn't afford to lease a grand home like Rockfleet. As he drove along, the truth that pierced even the thick rain clouds gathered above Clew Bay was that he didn't know how he was going to live anywhere. He was nearly broke.

It wasn't that long ago that, swallowing his pride, he'd written a plaintive letter to Stephenson's secretary, a Miss Greene. He'd hoped to make the note sound like a routine follow-up about payments due for his work on *The Quiet Canadian*, but it wound up seeming rather desperate: "The sum I mentioned to you—£150 . . . —is less than half I have been getting as a Professor, and is really the minimum I can manage on to meet my commitments . . . as well as an invalid mother in Ireland." He was still waiting on that check.

Hyde also knew that things would only get worse on his return to London. His second marriage, or what was left of it, was falling apart. How could he afford another divorce? If he had to give up his home, where would he live?

His only hope, it was increasingly clear, was Betty. After days listening to her stories as they traveled through Ireland, he knew that his initial instincts had been right: the spy code-named Cynthia was money in the bank. He could spice up the tales Betty was telling him, and the glossy Sunday papers would clamor for the rights. He could already hear the newsboys: Read all about it! Sexy spy fights for king and country in her bedroom! It would be the big killing he needed to set himself right.

His barrister's mind started churning. What he needed to do was form a company with Betty. Otherwise, British taxes would gobble up the lion's share of the royalties. A right-sounding name popped into his mind: Cynamont, a combination of Cynthia and Montgomery. It had a nice corporate ring, he decided.

But would Betty appreciate the ingenuity of his scheme, or would she be suspicious? Would she think he was up to something underhanded, that the maneuver was meant not merely to defeat the taxman but to cheat her of her fair share?

That was the thing about spies, Hyde had learned over the years—they always suspected something. And with good reason: it was the only way to survive. Paranoia was the occupational disease of those who lived in the secret world. The cure, though, was worse. The day you let down your guard was the day you made your fatal mistake.

Add money to the equation, and your everyday spy's paranoia became a grade-one psychotic episode. Agents, like psychiatrists, look for motives, and money is far up on the list. If Betty got it into her head that he was stealing from her, he'd later remember worrying, there'd be no way he'd ever get her to relinquish that bit of foolishness. Not only would Cynamont never come into existence, their entire literary collaboration might fall by the wayside too. And then he'd be stuck at the bottom of the deep hole he'd dug, with no way out.

Looking for reassurance, he might have asked himself whether money was what really drove Betty. Would she focus on corporations, or how the pot was divvied up?

Like every handler, the textbook acronym MICE—Money, Ideology, Coercion, Excitement—had been hammered into his head during training. Those were the motives that drove recruits to take the big risks that came with the covert life. But greed had nothing at all to do with Betty's service. Ideology—doing her part to defeat Hitler—and even more, excitement—the thrill of living dangerously—were what attracted her. These were the keys to her character.

Perhaps if he stressed the patriotic importance of the story he wanted to tell and the uproar these previously classified tales would cause, that would convince Betty to go along with the rest of his plan, corporation and all. It would be a classic distraction ploy: get the target thinking about one thing, and they'll forget about another.

But as he drove toward Dublin, Betty sleeping next to him in the passenger seat, he decided it would be wiser to put off any discussion of profits and a corporation until they were back in London. He'd introduce Betty to his literary agent, and Iain could give her an objective view of things. Patience, in business as in espionage, was an operational virtue.

For now, though, his path was clear. The dogged journeyman reporter, he would keep Betty talking. He would extract the rest of her adventures, and they would give him a chance at a new, solvent life.

Chapter 35

◆

"M ay I speak to Mr. Howard?" Betty had dialed the Atwater number as soon as she entered her room in the Hotel Lexington. She hadn't even waited to take off her coat; ever since Paul Fairly had given her the note, she'd been like a Thoroughbred at the starting gate. All Fairly could do was sit mutely on the bed, watching and waiting.

Receiver pressed to her ear, Betty tried to be patient while someone went to find Mr. Howard. She knew, of course, that "Howard" was one of the Service's favorite code names; Jack Shelley had used it often.

"This is Mr. Howard speaking."

"Well, this is Mrs. Pack."

"Mrs. Elizabeth Pack? Why, we've been trying to contact you everywhere. Lisbon, Washington, Panama, Santiago—all over the place. But you've been one jump ahead the whole time. Anyhow, where are you now? I want to see you as soon as possible."

"I am here in New York, in the Hotel Lexington. To be precise, room 2215."

Fairly had gotten off the bed and now stood very close to her. The palm of his hand traveled softly up her back.

"Fine, I'll be right over," said Howard.

Fairly had begun to massage her neck slowly, his fingertips a steady caress. Betty swooned. She knew she had to get off the phone.

Apologizing, she told Howard that she had "some urgent business to take care of." She'd meet him in her room in an hour.

Even before she hung up, Fairly had started to undress her. She turned and embraced him. Locked together, they tumbled happily into the big bed.

EVERY HANDLER HAS HIS OWN "handwriting," his own style of dealing with his agents. Some assume a parental attitude, the concerned and benevolent patriarch who will sagely guide his charge through the secret world. Others play the hero: I've been there, done it all in my time, and expect nothing less than the same from you.

John Howard—his real name was John Arthur Reed Pepper, although Betty didn't know it at the time—was too young to assume a fatherly demeanor and too inexperienced to pass himself off as the veteran secret agent. Blond, blue-eyed, and boyish, he was a businessman Stephenson had recruited from one of his many corporations and turned into a spy.

Pepper was only a few years older than Betty and, without thinking too much about it, he handled their initial interview as if he were an upperclassman sitting down to talk to a prospective freshman. The BSC was a newly created branch of the Secret Intelligence Service, and he wanted to give the new recruit a sense, carefully edited, naturally, of what the organization would be doing in America. At the same time, he'd also be sizing up the candidate, seeing if she'd be right for what Stephenson had in mind.

Betty, for her part, unashamedly set out to sell herself. She had no doubt that Pepper was fully versed in her operational history; that was why the Service was interested in her, after all. Nevertheless, Betty was proud of what she had accomplished. With great enthusiasm—and a little reinvention to improve upon things when necessary—she went over all the old ground.

She talked about her years in Spain, her exploits during the civil war, building up to the time when, shaking with fear, she had worked with Leche to pull off the daring Spanish prison escape. Then she was back in tense prewar Europe, in bedrooms in Warsaw and on dark streets in Prague, working hand in hand with Shelley while passing on a trove of top-secret intelligence to London. And finally she was in Chile and then on to Cuba, writing articles, yet always watching and listening, making the most of her journalistic cover.

Shrewdly, she gave Pepper a hint of her family connections, how in her youth she'd been introduced to everyone in Washington who mattered, and still had access to the highest in the land. She also made sure he realized that although she was born in Minneapolis, she'd spent her formative years abroad; both her French and Spanish were faultless.

Betty was candid about her marital status, but at the same time presented things in the most favorable professional light. She was still married to Arthur, and that, she pointed out, gave her both diplomatic status and a British passport. And yet they were very much estranged; their divorce was simply a matter of paperwork. It would not be too much of a stretch to reinvent herself, using her maiden name; she'd be Elizabeth—Betty to her friends—Thorpe, freelance journalist.

Pepper listened attentively, all the time taking measure of the new recruit. Then it was his turn. The usual procedure was to be deliberately vague about what the operative would be asked to do. "It is the kind of thing that calls for courage and initiative," was the customary gung-ho explanation. A warning was also standard, though more to gauge the novice's reaction than because of any genuine concern for the trouble she might wind up in: "The Neutrality Act can land you in prison. In this work you cannot register as the agent of a foreign power, as the law requires; it would give the whole show away. And if you are caught, we haven't heard of you. You understand that?"

In Betty's particular case, Pepper also felt he needed to explore her loyalties. She was an American, and she'd be working as an agent for a foreign government. That could be a complication. He wanted to be satisfied that her allegiance to England ran deeper than her marriage—an unhappy one, at that—to a British citizen.

Painstakingly, he kept tapping at the same spot: "Our primary directive from the PM [Churchill] is that American participation in the war is the most important objective for Britain." He wanted to know if Betty, despite America's official stance of neutrality, would be willing to work toward that goal.

"Our best information," he continued, "is that the forces of isolation, a front here for Nazism and Fascism, are gaining, not losing ground. How do you personally feel about these forces? For example, the America First movement?

"Do you feel strongly enough on these matters to work for us in your own country? To spy on your fellow Americans and report to us?"

Betty was unruffled. "As you know," she said, "I've got a British passport. Even if you regard me as an American, it is the British cause I want to help. Or if you like, the Anglo-American cause, for I have a strong feeling that the United States will soon be in this thing up to the neck, same as the British."

For once she did not need to invent or improve upon the reality: her commitment to the defeat of Nazism was absolute. As for the personal risks she'd be taking, well, the truth was that it just made the battle so much sweeter.

After a spirited hour, it was settled. Betty was precisely the sort of agent the BSC was looking for as they established themselves in America. And intelligence work was what she'd wanted all along. Each would serve the other well.

"I think I can promise you," Pepper concluded, "that you shall work for us." His tone was formal, yet genial, as if he were an old boy accepting someone into his club; which, in its way, was the case. "But I am afraid I cannot tell you right now exactly what form the undercover side of your activities will take. In any case, I have to consult the chief about that."

"I see," said Betty, disappointed. She felt she had waited long enough; she wanted to rush off on her next mission. "Then what do you want me to do now?"

It was an obvious question, and Pepper had prepared his answer. He had simply been waiting to see if a deal would be made. Now that he was certain, he shared his plan: "I want you to go down to Washington and rent a house or apartment, a house for choice, in some good neighborhood like Georgetown. Where you will be able to work and receive people. And do some discreet entertaining."

Discreet entertaining. The words hung heavily in the room.

Finally Betty spoke. "And when do I start?"

"The sooner the better. As soon as you find somewhere suitable, let me know and I'll come down and see you and we can discuss the next move."

Now officially her paymaster, Howard asked, "How much money will you need? Of course we will pay the rent of the place and what it costs to live there."

Betty thought for a moment and then suggested an inconsequential monthly stipend. Things were at last working out just as she'd always hoped, and she didn't want to do anything that would jeopardize the opportunity.

"All right," said Howard, although he doubted the figure would cover her expenses. He decided he'd simply send a check each month for the amount he thought sufficient, the payment issued by a BSC cover account at a discreet Wall Street bank. "We'll see how it works out."

And he gave her some operational advice. "Don't be in a hurry. It may take a couple of months or even three before you are ready to begin operating."

Betty understood. She was eager, but she also knew cover needed time to take root and grow. Security was a genuine concern: America was officially neutral. And while the BSC had a tacit working relationship with US intelligence, it was an increasingly tenuous one. British agents caught working in the country faced the possibility of arrest or deportation. She'd need to take care not to attract the attention of the FBI.

There was one last matter to be decided. "And I shall call you—what?" asked Pepper. Standard tradecraft required that for security Betty needed a code name.

Betty's mind went blank. She could not think of any name that felt right.

"I've got it," Pepper announced, as happy as any father at a christening. "Cynthia! That's what I am going to call you. That's the name by which you will be known from now on in the Service."

At 3327 O St., her house in Washington, DC—as secure a house as any spy could want, Betty decided.

O Street in the Georgetown section of Washington was cob-blestoned and tree-lined, just a short stroll from the tow canal that guided traffic along the Potomac River. The house at number 3327 was a pretty, nicely proportioned nineteenth-century Georgian with tall dark-shuttered windows. There were high ceilings and polished wood floors and a small garden in the back that received a sliver of afternoon sun. But more important than her new home's charms were its operational qualities. Betty decided it was as secure a house as any spy could want.

The neighborhood was as quiet as a graveyard at night; anyone snooping around would be sure to attract attention. And the sitting room and master bedroom overlooked O Street; she'd be able to glance out the window and see who was coming. But best of all, the garden wall hid a door to an alleyway that exited onto Thirty-Third Street. A watcher monitoring the front door would never suspect that a back way into the alley existed. It was the perfect escape route.

Pepper sent Betty the $700 she needed for two months' rental deposit, and she moved into the house in February 1941. When they met later that week in New York, he gave Betty her march-ing orders: "Go out in Washington society and look up your old friends and acquaintances. You can say that you have become a newspaperwoman and are writing articles about the war. After all, you were doing that in Chile so it shouldn't be difficult."

Pepper was right; it wasn't difficult. She still had connections in Washington. Her mother continued to flit about town, always busy with luncheons and dinners. And her younger sister was also living in the city. Betty had not been very close to Jane; while Betty liked her cocktails, she felt Jane liked them too much. But Jane's husband owned the Roosevelt Hotel downtown, and Betty, the pragmatic agent, suspected that the day could arrive when she'd need a dis-creet hideout. And the Roosevelt was always filled with important people. A friendship with its owner, or at least his wife, might come in handy. She put aside her reservations about her sister and worked to renew their faded friendship.

Then almost overnight, or so it seemed, Betty's name appeared in the *Social Register*, the same book she'd studied with bewilderment as a young girl. It was what her mother had always wanted, although Cora would probably have been less approving if she knew her daughter's inclusion had more to do with tradecraft than any social ambitions. And after a discreet phone call suggested that people in the highest places would like things to move forward, the British Information Service gave Betty accreditation as a freelance reporter.

Yet as Betty prepared for her next mission, there was, as she candidly confessed to Hyde, one unanticipated "mishap." One that "might have seriously interfered with my work if immediate steps had not been taken." She was nearly three months pregnant with Fairly's child.

"I had learned a good deal since my marriage," she explained to Hyde with a philosophical practicality, "and made no amateur attempts to get rid of it as I had done before. This time I had an abortion. It cost me quite a lot of money and I was ill for a fortnight, but there were no aftereffects. I never told my lover in the U.S. Intelligence anything about it."

When she recovered, she was prepared to launch her new operational life in America.

Chapter 36

◆

BETTY HAD ALL SHE NEEDED: a convincing cover, a comfortable safe house for "discreet entertaining," years of derring-do experience in the field, a shrewd handler, and best of all, an evil adversary who needed to be crushed. The only thing missing was a mission.

It was a great moment in history. Britain was preparing to make what Churchill feared could prove to be a last stand. Betty was eager to join the fight, to do her part. Yet Pepper kept her standing on the sidelines. And what made the waiting so much harder—Betty now understood and conceded to Hyde—was that she needed to slay her own demons too. A terrible yet all-too-familiar restlessness swept through her as the long days in the house on O Street passed.

Each week she reported at a prearranged time to a room at the Ritz-Carlton Hotel in Manhattan. There she was debriefed by a shrewd and formidable woman who, although clearly American, spoke French as fluently as Betty did. Betty knew her only as Marion; not until years later did she learn her contact's full name, Marion de Chastellaine, or that the New Jersey native had earned a law degree at the Sorbonne and had lived in high style in Romania for many years with her businessman husband and their two children.

At the time, Betty had little interest in Marion's biography, even if it would have revealed a life as exotic in its way as her own, and that they both, although US citizens, had first attracted the attention of British intelligence because of their marriages to Englishmen. All Betty glumly knew was that each week she'd go to the trouble of flying—the train was too slow for restless Betty—up to New York, making the contact time to the minute, and then have nothing to report. Her debriefings were pathetically short. She'd spend the rest of the afternoon shopping, returning home to Washington loaded down with parcels and frustration. It was no comfort to Betty that Pepper, with by-the-book caution, was feeling out his agent, taking and then retaking her measure before turning her loose.

When Marion finally informed Betty of her first assignment, it was a genuine disappointment. Marion tried to make the mission sound like a risky cloak-and-dagger op: Betty was "to detect and uncover a female agent from a neutral country who was on her way to Britain to make pacifist propaganda for the Nazis." But Betty knew it was just a routine piece of watcher's work—keep a steady eye on the subject and report. Still eager for anything, she jumped at the chance.

Betty was the model operative. She followed the woman—her name long forgotten, and still redacted from the public official histories—around New York for several days. A stealthy, unobtrusive observer, Betty was never spotted. The typed reports she delivered to Marion demonstrated equally impressive tradecraft: she described the target's movements in detail, and precisely identified all her contacts.

The reports provided the British authorities in Bermuda with the evidence they needed. When the Spanish steamer *Marqués de Comillas* docked in Nassau, the target was marched off at gunpoint on suspicions of being an enemy agent. She would be interned for the remainder of the war.

And the agent code-named Cynthia had proved that she was ready to take on larger missions.

THE LETTER MIGHT JUST AS well have been written by a beleaguered relative confessing to a rich relation that he was down on his luck and would be mighty grateful for a helping hand. That the besieged correspondent was the British prime minister and the recipient was the president of the United States only made the plea more poignant.

The top-secret letter arrived at the White House on December 9, 1940, and it opened with a harrowing inventory of the beating Britain was taking—manufacturing plants destroyed by the Blitz, ships sunk by German submarines, empty warehouses once filled with munitions and arms. Then, after having so sadly set the stage, the prime minister confessed that the nation's future prospects, its chance to get on its feet and fight back, were jeopardized by an inconvenient reality—the treasury was nearly empty. "The moment approaches," Churchill wrote plaintively, "where we shall no longer be able to pay cash for shipping and other supplies."

Roosevelt received the letter with great sympathy. In his generous heart he felt that Britain must hold on, and that America would soon come to its senses and realize that the only moral course was to join the fight against Hitler. Yet in his politician's head, he knew that his hands were effectively tied. Even the president of the United States could not force pragmatic bankers to lend vast sums of money to a foundering nation with no convincing guarantees of repayment. Nor did he have the authority to order Congress to make outright gifts of war matériel to the British. He read and reread Churchill's note, only to keep returning to the same dispiriting conclusion. He had no choice but to turn the supplicant down.

Yet Churchill's plea for help remained on his mind. And after weeks of earnest mulling, the president stumbled onto a plan. With a breezy yet somewhat disingenuous geniality, he described his solution to Britain's desperate situation as if it were comparable to one neighbor lending a garden hose to another to save his burning house. "What do I do in such a crisis?" the president asked with rhetorical drama at a press conference. "I don't say, 'Neighbor, my garden hose cost me $15; you have to pay me $15 for it.' I don't want the $15. I just want my garden hose back after the fire is over."

Of course, FDR's solution would involve a lot more than an inexpensive garden hose. It would potentially supply hundreds of millions of dollars of war matériel. But the underlying principle, in the president's mind at least, was identical: the United States would send Britain bulging armories of weapons and munitions without charge. Then, after the fire was put out, Britain would either re-turn what it had borrowed or pay up.

But while the president's "lend-lease plan," as it quickly became known, had a righteous and appealing simplicity in his own mind, convincing a fiercely isolationist Congress to go along with it was another matter. Arming Britain, a largely Republican coalition of noninterventionist senators argued, would put the United States one step closer to fighting in a faraway war that was not America's problem. Refuting the president's logic, Senator Robert Taft of Ohio offered his own folksy analogy: "Lending war equipment is a good deal like lending chewing gum. You don't want it back."

The Service's spymasters, men who had taken to working in an underground bunker to escape the Blitz, knew only too well the danger Britain faced. The fires burning in London would be only the prelude to a greater conflagration if Hitler followed through on his plan to invade the island. The BSC was ordered to do whatever it could to nudge Congress toward the right decision. The covert manipulation of the levers of democracy in a neutral foreign coun-try—a nation they hoped would eventually come onboard as a fighting ally—was never an issue. With so much at stake, it was no time to be squeamish.

When Betty appeared for the next meeting with her controller, she was given the names of two of the most vocal and power-ful opponents in the US Senate to the passage of the Lend-Lease

Act—Democrat Thomas Connally of Texas and Republican Arthur Vandenberg of Michigan. Her assignment: Turn their minds and hearts around and get them to support the bill.

THOMAS CONNALLY WAS A VAIN man with many opinions and few doubts. He was proud of his silver hair and kept it long so that it flowed over his collar like a lion's mane. A bit of a dandy, he wore custom-tailored suits and shirts that required pearl studs rather than ordinary buttons. He was chauffeured around Washington in a limousine provided by his wealthy second wife, the widow of another US senator from Texas, Morris Sheppard. The press called him "flamboyant," and he took the appraisal as fulsome praise. And as chairman of the Senate Committee on Foreign Relations, he was the Democrat's chief spokesman on foreign policy.

He was dead set against the Lend-Lease Act. It was a matter of principle, one, in fact, of many deeply held and unwavering personal credos. He felt that sending arms and munitions to Britain would start a courtship that would ultimately end in a disastrous marriage: American troops would wind up fighting in Europe. And that would be just plain wrong.

Connally's worldview was summed up in a tale he told as he stumped across Texas in his reelection campaign. He had enlisted in both the Spanish-American War and World War I, but was never deployed overseas. "I've been in more wars and fought less than any living man," he joked with a self-deprecating humor time after time on the campaign trail. Now he wanted to ensure that a new generation of American boys would, same as him, not have to fight.

Betty, who always did her homework, knew that Connolly would be a hard target. Everything was working against her. He was firmly set in his ways; relished a good debate, especially if it put him head to head against the president; and, most discouraging of all, he apparently loved his wife. Still, she made it her business to get invited to a dinner party where she knew, thanks to Cora's idle chatter, that Connally would be a guest.

Radiant, glowing with a bubbly charm, she approached the senator. Within moments they were locked in conversation, Betty's eyes fixed on her prey with her usual deliberate attention. In her mind she was already plotting her next move. But Connally was too shrewd.

"You're an American turned British," he said with happy superiority. "I guess that means you're going to try to get us into the war. You're wasting your time, my dear—come over here and sit on my knee instead."

Betty would gladly have sat on his knee, at the very least, if it would've done any good. But she knew he was right; she was wasting her time. So instead she turned her attention to Senator Vandenberg.

Vandenberg, although a Michigan Republican, shared many of the same qualities as his Senate colleague from Texas. He was vain; "the only senator who can strut sitting down," was how one reporter described him. And he was adamantly opposed to the Lend-Lease Act. He had been active on the Nye Committee, which had investigated the munitions industry's profiteering in World War I, and he now looked back on America's involvement in that conflict as "a mistake." The country's entanglement in another European war would be, he insisted, an even greater error.

Yet there was one defining, and perhaps even crucial, difference between the two senators: Vandenberg was, famously, a womanizer. He was already carrying on with the wife of a British diplomat, Mitzi Sims; the joke making the rounds across Washington was that he'd become "the senator from Mitzi-gan." Betty decided that she should try to join the queue.

Vandenberg had known her mother for years, and one evening when Cora appeared at Vandenberg's house for cocktails, Betty came too. Cora was mystified by Betty's sudden desire to tag along, but she had long ago given up trying to understand her daughter.

Betty made it a point to spend most of her time talking to the senator, standing very close. The next time she met Vandenberg, she left her mother home.

There were other subsequent encounters with the senator. With great, if not typical, discretion, she refused to give Hyde any details of what went on between them. Yet she proudly pointed out that Vandenberg had stood on the Senate floor and announced his change of heart: he was voting for the Lend-Lease Act. "If we do not lead, some other great and powerful nation will capitalize on our failure," he proclaimed with a convert's ardor.

The bill was passed in March 1941. And Betty had done, she always felt, her small part for the cause.

Yet by the time the Senate vote was taken, Betty had already plunged into another urgent, and slippery, operation.

Chapter 37

◆

THERE IS AN ART TO making a martini; it was, Betty liked
to say, the only thing of any value that she'd learned from
her mother. The technique passed on by Cora put great
emphasis on making sure the gin was not "bruised" in the stirring;
the last thing you wanted, mother had gravely counseled daughter,
was to do anything to dilute the drink's kick. Over the years Betty
had taken this maternal wisdom to heart. She proudly served up a
very powerful martini.

Icy glass in her outstretched hand, she offered one of her expert
cocktails to her controller as soon as he walked in the door of her
O Street house. It was a chilly evening in February 1941, and Pepper had popped down to Washington, as he did a couple of times
each month, to touch base with his new operative. There was no
real agenda. The primary purpose of these meets, as any good case
officer knew, was simply to hold the agent's hand for a heartening
hour or so, letting him know that, though he might be alone in
the field, headquarters had not forgotten about him. He wanted
Betty to understand that while Marion conducted many of the
debriefings in New York, he was still her handler, the man both
running and watching over her. At the same time, Pepper would
be reassuring himself too; it's always valuable to take a fieldman's
temperature from time to time, to get a sense if he's jumping at
shadows or simply being prudently cautious.

Betty and Pepper had been sitting across from one another in
her living room for a while on that wintry night. The conversation
had meandered easily, and Betty, who could always talk to anyone,

had kept up her end. She treated Pepper warmly, but with a certain distance; he was her controller, after all. And the martinis had done their job to keep things comfortable, too. Before she knew it, the pitcher was nearly empty.

She had risen from the sofa to mix a new batch when, as if it were nothing more than a stray thought, Pepper asked, "I suppose you don't know anyone in the Italian embassy here?"

"Well, I used to," Betty said as she twisted open the cap on the bottle of gin. "In fact, I once had quite an admirer there. I was a schoolgirl."

Betty continued mixing the drinks with meticulous attention. As she went at it, she thought about mentioning that she'd been a teenager and he was thirty years her senior, and that he would travel all the way up to Massachusetts just to have tea with her. But she stopped herself; it sounded a bit preposterous, maybe even unseemly. Instead, she merely added, "He used to work in the naval attaché's office. His name was Alberto Lais."

Pepper jumped to his feet. "Alberto Lais!" he repeated. He was clearly excited; it was as if he could suddenly see Cynthia's next operation unfolding in his mind. "Why, he's the very man we are anxious to get hold of! He is an admiral now and he is the Italian naval attaché."

Betty brought the drinks over, and they began to plot.

WHY HAD ALBERTO LAIS, THE director of naval intelligence in Rome for the past three years, been transferred to Washington as the naval attaché? The story the Italians had circulated was that he was a ranking naval flag officer—*ammiraglio di divisione*, officially— and it was only fitting that their Washington naval attaché wear an admiral's stripes. But Stephenson and his team at the BSC, as well as the wise men on Broadway, had other suspicions: once a spook, always a spook. If the Italians were sending the man who had been head of naval espionage to America, it wasn't merely so that he could attend diplomatic receptions. Despite the cover, he'd be running Mussolini's intelligence networks in America.

That theory alone would have stamped Lais as a priority target. As soon as Lais arrived to take his new post, there were deskmen in the Rockefeller Center offices telling Stephenson that he should put teams of watchers and pavement artists on the admiral, and tap his home phone for good measure. The BSC needed to learn what he was really up to. Then abruptly any speculative interest in Lais took on a new operational importance.

In the late winter of 1940, a flash cable was received by Intrepid from SIS/London: the Admiralty "urgently" required the Italian naval cipher, a copy of which was known to be in the possession of the Italian naval attaché in Washington.

The cable did not bother to explain why the ciphers were immediately needed; it was not necessary. Even from his office in New York, Stephenson was aware of the dismal battle condition of the Royal Navy. Its ships, particularly in the Mediterranean, were spread perilously thin. If the Italian navy attacked in strength, it could very well result in a debacle. Having the ciphers—the ability to decode the enemy's messages and learn their intentions in advance—would allow the undersize Royal Navy forces to fight with a distinct strategic advantage. The power of such knowledge could not be overestimated. It could keep the British fleet afloat.

And now Pepper had learned that the BSC ran an agent with a longtime connection to Admiral Lais, the very mystery man— part-time diplomat, full-time spy?—who held the keys that would unlock many vital secrets. That night as the martinis flowed, he gave Betty her orders: Get close to Lais, get the ciphers, and, for king and country, do whatever you must do to accomplish the mission.

Of course, said Betty.

A younger Alberto Lais, when first appointed director of
Naval Intelligence in the Italian Ministry of Marine.

ALTHOUGH HER HEAD WAS STILL foggy from the pitchers of martinis, early the next morning Betty called the Italian embassy. She
identified herself as "an old friend" who wished to speak to Admiral Lais.

"Who is it?" he asked politely when he came to the phone.

"It's your Golden Girl," Betty merrily answered, at once trying to
spin her web. "I'm here in Washington and would like to see you."

The line went silent; for a moment Betty wondered if the connection had been broken. When at last the admiral spoke, it was in
a clipped, harsh tone she had never before heard him use.

"No," he said, the single world uttered as emphatically as a door slammed shut. "I am afraid that is impossible. Maybe it will be possible when peace comes, but not now. *Arrivederci!*"

Before she could say a word, Betty heard the phone go dead. Her mission was over before it had even started.

OVER THE NEXT UNSTEADY DAYS Betty lived in that particular circle of operational hell reserved for those agents whose high hopes and big plans have suddenly come crashing down. At first she had tried to plot ways to approach Lais, to engineer an "accidental" meet. But even as she played out those schemes in her mind—in a city like Washington where diplomatic receptions filled the calendar, there would be plenty of opportunities—she knew it would be futile.

Her only hope for success would be to get Lais alone, to rekindle what he had felt years ago for his "Golden Girl." She needed to make it clear to him that the teenager had abandoned her childish ways. A fully grown woman, she'd be interested in sharing more than a cup of tea and a slice of chocolate cake. But Betty could not imagine how a public encounter would allow her to move things along in this manipulative way.

Fortunately, as things worked out, Betty was not the only one suffering. The admiral apparently was experiencing his own bout of frustration. He knew his duty, but Betty's call must have triggered its own powerful demands. Did his head fill with previously dormant memories? Was his imagination racing? Whatever the deciding factor, later that week he ignored all the sound reasons that had counseled restraint and he called his old friend.

"It's me, Alberto," Betty heard when she answered the phone one morning.

"How did you get my number?" she wondered, genuinely

surprised. And she kept her larger astonishment to herself: *He had called! The operation was back on track!*

"Never mind," he said. "I want you to listen to me. I have been thinking very hard over our conversation the other day, and I have come to the conclusion that it will be all right for us to meet after all."

Betty knew better than to interrupt.

The admiral continued: "But it must be done very discreetly and without anyone knowing. Of course, it cannot be at the embassy or my own house or even a hotel, as it would be immediately known. Have you any suggestions?"

Have I any suggestions? Betty felt like shouting. But instead, as if it were a random idea, the last in a long list of possibilities, she said, "Well, you can come over to my place."

Lais considered while Betty prayed, not for the first time, to the operational gods.

"Yes," the admiral finally said.

"Well, that's fine," Betty said, her calm all artifice. "Come tomorrow night after dinner. My maid is going out and I shall be alone."

Chapter 38

◆

BETTY HAD CAREFULLY SET THE stage. A fire burned in the sitting room grate. A well-chosen bottle of full-bodied red wine had been uncorked to breathe; two crystal glasses flanked it on the bar table. After sorting through her closet for what had seemed like hours, she'd put on an off-the-shoulder black cocktail dress, neither too tight nor too low-cut. She did not want the admiral to think this would be too easy, yet at the same time she wanted to encourage his attentions. She wanted to look elegant, but not distant.

Just after nine o'clock the doorbell rang, and the op went into play.

"It's my Golden Girl and she hasn't changed a bit," the admiral lied as soon as Betty opened the door. He wrapped her in a warm, paternal embrace and kissed her on both cheeks.

He held her longer, though, than a father might. And Betty let him.

When he released her, she looked him up and down in a thoughtful appraisal. "You don't seem to have changed much either," said Betty, who also knew a good deal about lying. The truth, she silently observed, was crueler: balding, portly, and in his sixties, the admiral showed the passing years.

She linked her arm merrily in his. "Come along in," she said as she led the way into the sitting room, "and tell me everything. It seems ages since we met. My wedding, I think, was the last time."

"TELL ME EVERYTHING," BETTY HAD commanded, but what does a long-married man confide to a young woman? Invariably he pours out his heart, revealing a wife who doesn't understand him and a life of disappointment and unhappiness.

Over the next month, appearing two, sometimes three, times a week at Betty's home, Lais shared his version of this common middle-aged complaint. His wife Leonora was a good mother to their two children, he was grateful for that; but he "had never really loved her." He had married Leonora because she was "suitable," but after nearly three decades together this was small consolation. He was, he moaned, a very unhappy man.

Betty in turn shared a melodramatic and self-serving version of her own unfulfilled life. Her marriage to a cold-blooded man had been a failure from the start. It had taken her years to find the will to escape, and in retaliation Arthur now held their six-year-old daughter hostage. She rearranged the facts to present an image of a woman who was not just alone, but lonely. She wanted Lais to know that she needed a friend, a confidant, just as desperately as he did.

As she told her own sad story, Betty, thinking several operational steps ahead, began to unfurl a false flag. She made sure Lais believed that she had turned not just on her English husband but on Britain too. She had returned to Washington because she was an American. Her loyalty was to the Stars and Stripes, not the Union Jack.

She was certain this was exactly what Lais would want to hear. He had spent many convivial years in the United States. His wife was an American. It caused him great pain that Mussolini seemed determined to drive a wedge between Italy and the country that had become, he had told her with a gushy sentimentality, "my second homeland."

But England—that was an island for which he harbored a steely, unmitigated hatred. He still bitterly remembered how Britain had reneged on the promise it made in 1915 to grant his nation sovereignty over the Italian-speaking districts on the Istrian Peninsula and Dalmatia in return for Italy's entering the war on the Allied side. As did many of his countrymen, he found it an unforgivable betrayal. It was this enmity that Betty, casting herself as a patriotic American, the proud daughter of a distinguished family from the heartland, hoped to exploit when the time was right.

Between their shared problems, their mutual unhappiness, and their political sympathies, it did not take long for their renewed friendship to move into the bedroom.

THE DOUBLE BED WAS A battlefield where Betty had fought many engagements. An experienced veteran, she was rarely taken off-guard and rarely unwilling in the heat of combat to make whatever sacrifice was necessary. Nevertheless, the admiral's demands left her puzzled.

He'd have her sprawled naked on her bed, or for variety occasionally the sitting room sofa, lush and provacative like Manet's *Olympia* come to life in soft pink flesh. And where would Lais's fancy take him? He would cuddle, stroke, and fondle her for hours.

Perhaps she remained in his mind's eye the adolescent "Golden Girl," and intercourse was taboo. Or maybe age had trumped desire. But whatever the reason, Betty found this chaste routine as bewildering as it was unexpected.

Years later, it was all still a mystery to her. "Technically we weren't lovers," she told Hyde, barely concealing her astonishment. "All that we would do would be to sit on my sofa or lie on my bed. He would kiss and fondle me and whisper to me and pet me and hold me close and say that I was the only thing he had left in America. This was as far as our physical relations went. Although no doubt it could be called intimate, our relationship was sentimental and even sensual rather than sexual."

She never thought, though, to judge Lais. "Men can want very different things at different times," she explained to Hyde matter-of-factly. "It was my job to know what and when to do whatever would make them feel happy and comfortable."

All that mattered was the mission. No sacrifice was too great, too unseemly. As long as she succeeded, she had no regrets. Even today, Betty realized, she'd still throw everything over for something she believed in.

VALUABLE INTELLIGENCE, THOUGH, FROM THE Lais operation was slow in developing. The admiral was also a spy, and Betty was beginning to fear that he was too much of a professional to reveal any secrets.

Her handler, however, proved masterful. Pepper was encouraging and patient, two qualities that were essential in any case officer who sends his agent out into the field. Betty would show up for her weekly debriefings at the Ritz-Carlton Hotel in Manhattan— now that Lais was the target, Pepper had largely taken over from Marion—and he'd listen with rapt attention to summaries of her inconsequential conversations with the admiral. When she finished, glum and a bit defensive, Pepper nevertheless always had a word of praise. You've made contact, that's the important thing, he'd insist. These things take time. Espionage, he'd repeatedly lecture, his metaphor inspired by the weekends he'd spent gardening in Surrey in a previous life, is like tending a seedling. You keep watering and pruning, and wait and wait until it bears fruit.

Pepper also made sure to keep Betty focused on the prize. Before sending Betty back to Washington, he'd reiterate that the goal of this entire op was the ciphers. Where they were stored, who had access to them, how they could be smuggled from the embassy— the answers to those questions were her primary assignment.

In the meantime, his instructions were "to play along."

* * *

BETTY WAS TOUCHED BY THE admiral's gift. It was a silver trinket box, decorated with a delicate hand-carved filigree. The craftsmanship was exquisite. But even more affecting was the small, heartfelt speech the admiral made when he gave her the present.

They were in her sitting room one evening when, without prelude, he reached into his pocket and offered the shiny silver box. He wanted Betty, he said, to have something he treasured. He spoke earnestly, as a lover does to his beloved.

"I will treasure it with all my heart," Betty said, and at that moment she genuinely meant it.

But she was also a professional, and every instinct told her to take advantage of what had just occurred. The admiral's vulnerability was too promising an operational advantage to squander.

"But there is something else in your power to give me," she began cautiously, "which I would treasure equally, if not more so, my dearest Alberto."

"What is that, my dear?"

Betty rested her head on his shoulder; she wanted him to feel her warmth before she proceeded. Still, she hesitated. And when she finally spoke, the tremor in her voice, she'd tell Hyde, was not contrived. She was scared. The entire operation had been building to this moment.

Dusting off the cover story she'd prepared weeks earlier, she said an American friend in the Office of Naval Intelligence needed a favor.

The admiral looked at her quizzically, but said nothing. Betty suddenly wondered if his vaunted friendship for America was a ploy, one spy throwing a bit of disinformation at another. But she had gone too far to turn back.

The Americans badly need the Italian naval ciphers, she announced. She tried to make the words sound reasonable, but once she heard herself, she realized that was impossible.

Lais was stunned. His Golden Girl had asked him to commit treason.

"It will be a great help to my American friends," she tried again. "And so, I feel sure, to Italy in the future."

The admiral said he thought he should leave.

"Will I see you on Wednesday?" Betty asked.

He walked off without answering, the front door slamming behind him.

AT NINE WEDNESDAY EVENING BETTY made all the usual preparations. The fire burned. The wine was uncorked. But she did not know if the admiral would appear.

As she waited in the overheated sitting room, Betty found it easy to believe that he would not come. Perhaps, she feared, she would never see him again. Or, no less a possibility, he might send around a couple of gorillas from the embassy. They'd offer their own version of "discreet entertaining" as they demanded who she was working for, who really wanted the ciphers. Maybe, she began to worry, she should go to New York, get out of Washington.

Yet she sat on the sofa, waiting for the doorbell to ring.

When she heard the bell, a shiver of fear rushed through her. But she rose and went to the door.

Admiral Lais was standing on her doorstep. Alone.

They were in the sitting room, and Betty still was uncertain how things would go. The admiral was distant, even detached. He had not even kissed her cheek in greeting when he'd arrived. But he had come, Betty told herself. She found confidence in that. That surely meant something.

"I will try to do anything you want," the admiral, she repeated to Hyde, told her at last, his voice low with surrender. But, he explained, he could not give her the ciphers. It would be too large a betrayal.

Betty knew better than to argue. She just sat across from him looking gorgeous and desirable, his fantasy come to life.

What I can do, the admiral said finally, is give you the name of the cipher clerk in my office. He has daily access to the code books. What you do with his name is not my responsibility. The rest will be up to you.

Betty smiled sweetly. Then she rose from the sofa, took the admiral's hand, and led him into the bedroom.

Chapter 39

◆

S EATED IN AN ARMCHAIR IN the sprawling Art Deco lobby of the Shoreham Hotel across from the woods of Rock Creek Park, Betty waited. The admiral had given her the cipher clerk's name—Giulio (she could no longer recall his full name, and the case history has been sealed). Then the BSC boys had done their part: they had identified Giulio as a third secretary in the naval attaché's office, tracked down his apartment in the Shoreham, and provided Betty with a head shot of a somber-looking dark-haired man in his forties, courtesy of the US State Department files. The rest, they told her, would be up to her. And so now she waited.

There is an art to looking as if you're doing nothing when all the time you're on high alert; every watcher learns the skill, or else he doesn't survive. Betty, a natural spy, had the gift. She sat for hours in the Shoreham lobby, her face buried in a newspaper, and yet no one passed through the hotel's wide front doors without coming under her scrutiny. She was searching for a face that matched the State Department photograph hidden in her pocketbook.

Betty hadn't decided what she'd do after she made Giulio. She'd worked out several possible ploys, but in the end decided to take a good look and size him up before she settled on her move. All her experiences as a spy had taught her to follow her instincts, and before she could go down that path, she'd need to see Giulio in the flesh.

Then there he was, walking through the lobby, the somber, slightly world-weary man of the photograph. Up close he seemed even more washed out, already old beyond his years. One look told Betty he was not a bottom pincher. So much, she knew at once, for any fortuitous encounter in the hotel bar. And she immediately jettisoned any schemes to win him over in bed. She'd have to find another itch, another repressed yearning bubbling under his skin.

When in doubt, standard tradecraft holds, a direct approach is the card to play. "Direct," of course, like everything in the shadowy world of intelligence, is relative. Betty's quickly improvised scheme was to wait until Giulio was up in his apartment, knock authoritatively on his door, and announce that she was a journalist, writing a piece on the people behind the scenes at the Italian embassy. It was part of a series on the foreign service staffs in embassies throughout Washington, the people who did the nuts-and-bolts work while their bosses went to luncheons that lasted all afternoon and hurried off to parties as soon as the sun set. She'd close the deal by telling Giulio that Admiral Lais had suggested Giulio as the perfect person to interview. After that, she'd see how things developed. When the moment felt right—and she knew better than to make an operational timetable at this juncture—she'd steer the conversation around to the ciphers.

After waiting long enough for Giulio to settle in, Betty took the elevator up to the sixth floor and rapped on his apartment door. It opened, and all at once her plan fell apart—a woman stood there.

Somehow the BSC diggers had missed the fact that Giulio was married. The presence of a third person made things trickier; she'd need to dim down her usual flirty charm. But it was too late to retreat or devise another play. Soon Betty was sitting in the living room, making her earnest journalistic pitch to both Giulio and his wife.

As she'd hoped, he was intrigued. It was time, he agreed huffily, that the work he did was appreciated. After he heard that his boss, the admiral, had given Betty his name, any lingering reservations vanished. He'd be glad to answer all her questions.

Betty's next move was delicate; all that had occurred since she had entered the apartment had been leading to it. She realized that what she had to do could backfire, and then any hope of getting the ciphers would be lost. Yet she had to find a ploy to get Giulio alone.

And forget the bedroom, she once again told herself. Wife or no wife, Betty was convinced that sex wasn't one of Giulio's appetites. No, she decided, he craved another sort of attention. He reminded her of Arthur, a man seething with resentment, the civil servant who felt he'd never received the rewards or the recognition he deserved. Betty had never been able to summon up the will—or the kindness—to flatter her husband's yearning ego. But for the Service, and the cause, she'd gladly make this striving little man feel like one of the world's secret heroes.

As soon as Giulio's wife left the room, Betty made her pitch. It might be more useful, the conscientious reporter suggested as if it were a perfectly natural idea, if we could talk in private. Just the two of us, one on one. That way I could interview you in detail, and you could answer freely. I'm sure you have a lot to say. We wouldn't need to worry about being interrupted.

Giulio nodded noncommittally. But Betty chose to focus on the fact that he hadn't said no. So she took the next step:

I'd like it if you came to my house tomorrow night. We could continue the interview there. Then she wrote down her address on a piece of paper and handed it to him.

Giulio took it without a word, furtively stuffing it into the pocket of his trousers before his wife returned.

The next evening at the house on O Street, he talked and talked, and his audience's attention never faltered. Giulio was delighted; after all the dreary years as a bit player, he was finally at center stage. He looked forward to sending the finished article to his relatives in Italy, he told Betty. At last they'd recognize the important contribution he was making.

He returned later in the week, and Betty, in a moment of sudden inspiration, decided to cook dinner. It was nothing elaborate, just bowls of spaghetti and a bottle of red wine, but Giulio was appreciative. No one had ever focused such attention on him. All his life he'd been weighed down by self-doubts and insecurities, and now a glamorous reporter was treating him as if he were someone special. *"E la vita!"*—This is the life!—he exclaimed.

"How I wish I could live like this," he said, almost dreamily. His eyes traveled around the comfortable, well-appointed sitting room—a world forever beyond his reach.

Betty recognized his covetousness. She could feel the sting of his ungratified ambitions. And at that moment she knew she had him.

"It's perfectly simple to arrange," she said mildly. "You only have to do what I ask."

Then she told him: American friends needed the naval cipher code books. If he were willing to help, a "satisfactory understanding could be reached." He'd have the money "to lead this kind of life." She also added that he'd be helping Italy, but here her logic was so thin that she knew better than to offer any further explanation. She simply hoped it was a rationale, however specious, that he might find convenient. After all, no traitor liked to admit even to himself that he was in it only for the money.

When Giulio asked, "How satisfactory an understanding are you suggesting?" Betty knew she had succeeded. All that remained was the negotiation. And this proved to be simpler than Betty had anticipated. For a cash payment far less than the BSC housekeepers had authorized, the deal was made.

The actual exchange went so smoothly it left Betty with a feeling of anticlimax. While Giulio counted his money, in the next room the ciphers were photocopied. The original code books were returned to Giulio, who had them back in the embassy safe before anyone noticed that they had been removed.

The next day an armed BSC courier left New York to hand-deliver Betty's gift to the Admiralty in London.

ACROSS THE GLOBE FROM BETTY'S world, shortly before noon on March 27, 1941, Admiral Sir Andrew Cunningham, commander in chief of the Mediterranean fleet, suggested to his flag officer, Lieutenant Hugh Lee, that a round of golf might be just the thing to help him to relax. When Lee hesitated, the admiral made sure the lieutenant understood it was not a request but an order.

The admiral and his aide played eighteen holes at the Alexandria Sporting Club later that afternoon. They kept score, but that was a charade; the lieutenant was wise enough to know that junior officers never best commanders of the fleet. And anyway, that day they were playing for higher stakes.

The admiral, despite his earlier suggestion to the lieutenant, had not been looking for a brief diversion in the midst of a war that seemed to be going dangerously wrong. He had taken to the links to be seen. He wanted the enemy diplomats who made it a habit to hang around the Egyptian club to get the impression that the commander of the British fleet had nothing better to do that day than play a round of golf. And on the way back to the clubhouse, when the wily Cunningham spotted the Japanese consul—a diplomat MI6 had identified as an Axis asset—he laid the disinformation on even thicker. "Is everything ready for dinner tonight?" he boomed to his lieutenant. And Lee, by now aware of the admiral's ploy, played along. "Yes, everyone's invited," he improvised impressively.

But there was no dinner scheduled. Just like the round of golf, it was an attempt to lull the enemy into a complaisant confidence. At seven that evening Cunningham would furtively sail out of the harbor on the HMS *Warspite*, leading a flotilla of British warships to surprise and then destroy the Italian fleet.

And Betty had played a large—arguably crucial—part in the admiral's daring battle plan.

In the tense days leading up to his attack, Cunningham had received intelligence, as he guardedly explained to his vice admiral, "from a most secret source." This information revealed that on March 28 the Italian fleet planned to ambush the British troop convoys that would sail from Alexandria to Piraeus. Only now that he knew about the scheduled Italian attack, the admiral had conceived a bold plan of his own: "My intention . . . is to clear area concerned and so endeavor to make enemy strike into thin air whilst taking all action possible damaging him whilst he is doing so."

At 10:20 on the night of March 28, Cunningham spotted the Italian fleet near Cape Matapan, off the southern tip of Greece—precisely where he'd known they would be. He gave the order for the British vessels to turn on their searchlights: a nearly straight line of huge enemy warships was illuminated in the heavy darkness, their gun turrets pointing fore and aft as benignly as if they were on parade in a sea pageant. "Fire!" Cunningham yelled. The *Warspite's* fifteen-inch guns exploded, and quickly the other British ships joined in.

By dawn, orange flames were shooting up from the dark, oily sea, the hulking carcasses of huge ships lay crippled in the water, and a grisly flotilla of inert bodies drifted toward the horizon. Three Italian cruisers, two destroyers, and one battleship had been sunk, burned, or destroyed. More than 2,400 Italian sailors lost their lives. The sole British casualty was the pilot of a Swordfish torpedo bomber. The Battle of Cape Matapan was a staggering victory for the outnumbered British fleet.

Winston Churchill celebrated. A single battle, he declared as solemnly as if he were intoning a benediction, had put an end to "all challenges to British naval mastery in the Eastern Mediterranean at this crucial time."

For the remainder of the war, the Mediterranean remained a British sea.

BUT WERE BETTY'S PURLOINED CODE books the magic wand that had made this victory possible? Were the ciphers taken from the embassy in Washington used to decrypt the Italian admiralty's message traffic?

The reality—as both Hyde and Betty, seasoned professionals, knew—was that every intelligence operation has many heroes. The agent in the field gets his orders and does his best to complete his mission. But the fieldman never knows where his assignment figures in the scheme of things. It's up to the owls at headquarters to put together all the pieces collected from a multitude of covert sources. They are the ones sitting on the spy's Olympus and looking down omnisciently.

And although Betty was unaware of it at the time, teams of British wranglers working at the Government Code and Cypher School at Bletchley Park were also instrumental in deciphering Italian naval message traffic. In the days before the victory at Cape Matapan, they had finally broken the coded Italian messages being sent over the navy's Enigma machines.

Did Betty's stolen code books give the cryptologists the edge they needed to pry open the Italian code? Were they the missing piece that completed the puzzle? The final clue that, presto!, solved the mystery?

Or were the Bletchley Park discoveries simply icing on the operational cake? Did all the credit for the destruction of the Italian fleet, for the unknowable number of Allied lives saved as a result, for the subsequent successful Allied invasion of Italy, belong to the cipher sheets taken from the Washington embassy?

Hyde—a writer *and* a spy—knew only too well how difficult

it was to find the truth in a world where lies and deceptions were the accepted coin. Another rub: all the players had their own reasons for not telling the truth. Grudges, rivalries, pride, as well as the ingrained disposition of the intelligence professional to let secrets stay deeply buried—all this made getting at what actually had happened a difficult enterprise. Impossible, in fact, he was willing to venture. After all, who knew the answers to all the questions? Who stood above the raucous fray of a half-dozen or so competing agencies and possessed the objectivity to set things straight? Spies lie by inclination, and governments are in the business of endorsing these falsehoods. Truth inevitably falls by the wayside.

Consider, he told Betty, what happened after he included a brief mention of her manipulation of Admiral Lais in his book on Stephenson. The Italian ministry of defense quickly shot back a belligerent response. Full of haughty indignation, they insisted his account was a libel on "a man of the highest integrity and honor in whom the ministry had absolute faith." But if Lais *had* played a part in code books being taken from the embassy, then undoubtedly he was running his own intelligence operation: the cipher books passed on were counterfeits.

It was, a still bristling Hyde felt, the sort of dexterous response one might expect from a ministry reluctant to concede that one of its naval heroes had been seduced into betraying his country. Yet who could blame them for being so defensive?

In fact, Lais's behavior was so mind-boggling, Hyde confided, to Betty's utter embarrassment, that the classified "secret history of the BSC" that Stephenson had allowed him to read was still shaking its official head with wonder over the coup the spy named Cynthia had pulled off: "In retrospect, it seems almost incredible that a man of his [Lais's] experience and seniority, who was, by instinct, training and conviction, a patriotic officer, should have been so enfeebled by passion as to have been willing to work against the interests of his own country to win a lady's favor. But that is what happened."

Hyde staunchly believed that this top-secret history of the BSC offered the final say on the significance of Betty's role:

"It is a matter of history that they [the undermanned British fleet] were never so challenged, and that the Italian Navy was virtually neutralized and failed to win a single battle.

"This may have been largely due to the fact that British Intelligence had knowledge of the Italian Naval cipher."

And, the official BSC historians proudly boasted, Betty was the agent who single-handedly provided the intelligence that allowed the Admiralty to accomplish this incredible feat.

Chapter 40

◆

E VEN AFTER THE CIPHER COUP, the Lais operation remained up and running. The admiral continued to shuffle
off a few evenings each week to the house on O Street, and
Betty diligently trolled for any stray bits of intelligence he had to
offer. Lying naked next to him, she would from time to time pick
up a small nugget, say, about the deployment of the Italian fleet or
an intriguing snippet of embassy gossip. Yet unknown to Betty,
these encounters had attracted some unwanted attention.

To: Special Agent in Charge, Washington, D.C.

Re: MRS. ARTHUR PACK (was ESPIONAGE F)
Reference is made to your letter . . . in which you set out
certain information concerning subject PACK and request
authority to make an investigation of her. It is believed
that a discreet enquiry of Mrs. Pack may produce valuable
information and the same is authorized.
Very truly yours
John Edgar Hoover

Director

Betty would soon learn about the FBI surveillance on her home.
Unfortunately, she made the discovery at precisely the same time

that she unexpectedly picked up some startling intelligence from Admiral Lais. And in the scurrying panic that followed, the entire operation came very close to careening out of control.

IT WAS THE LONG, DARK night after the Battle of Cape Matapan, but Lais, who—incredibly—never realized he might have played a role in his navy's historic defeat, was consumed by another concern. He lay next to Betty in her bed, and that night her body did not tempt him. Instead, enveloped in a thick sadness, he began to sob softly.

Betty felt sympathetic. She had the intelligent agent's gift of caring about her target even while betraying him.

"What's the matter, Alberto?" she asked. "I can see there's something on your mind. Let me help."

"Oh, my dear one, indeed there is," he said, trying not to break into tears. "I've just received orders from Rome to put all our merchant ships at present in the United States ports out of commission."

Betty was immediately on alert. And as her mood shifted, the sympathy she'd felt only moments before was replaced by shrewd treachery. "Do you mean sabotage?"

Lais took a moment to answer, and when he did, he was calm, almost matter-of-fact. "Yes," he said, and then he explained. His words struck Betty as a confession: he wanted her, an American, to forgive him for what he had done.

The high command, he said, had come to realize that it was only a matter of time, and probably sooner rather than later, before the United States abandoned its increasingly thin pretense of neutrality and seized the Italian ships that, wary of British destroyers and submarines, had been stranded since the start of the European war in American harbors. They had played with the idea of ordering the interned vessels to make a run for home, but even as this was discussed, the admirals knew it would be suicide. The lumbering merchant ships would have no realistic chance of running the British Atlantic blockade. Caught between two equally unsatisfactory alternatives, the high command settled on a compromise strategy that seemed marginally better: they would scuttle the ships. Lais had been asked to make sure their orders were executed.

Betty probed carefully. Would you really be able to follow through? she asked. Destroy your own ships in American ports?

Lais sighed with weary resignation. He had already given the orders. Time bombs had been placed in the engine rooms of five ships anchored in Newport Harbor. They were ticking away as he spoke. And before leaving the embassy this evening, he had cabled the captains of Italian vessels anchored in ports throughout the United States with a list of instructions. He would not be surprised if at this moment crews were busily tearing the ships apart.

After he'd shared his secret, Lais, as if in a daze, got up and began to wander around the house. Perhaps he was looking for a distraction. Or maybe he just wanted to hide, to escape from what he had done.

Betty, though, was on full operational footing. "I could scarcely believe my ears," she told Hyde. She needed to telephone Pepper and Fairly. At once. Every second counted: time bombs were ticking. Yet it would be risky to do anything while Lais remained in her home. She had to come up with an excuse to make him leave.

The FBI provided it. For no sooner had Betty begun scrolling through a variety of possible scenarios in her mind than an agitated Lais hurried back into the room. He had happened to glance out the window and seen two men standing by the front door. The glow of a streetlamp had framed them perfectly: two big, beefy men in topcoats and hats pulled low on their foreheads.

"I'm sure they are from the FBI," he said anxiously. The admiral was convinced the G-men had somehow learned about the sabotage plot and come to arrest him. It never occurred to him that their target was the British secret agent Betty Pack. "You must get me out of here. If I could only get back to my embassy, I would be safe. They couldn't touch me there."

Betty turned out the light in the room and went to the window. With great care, she gently pulled back an inch or so of curtain and peered down into the street. And there they were! Two men who certainly had the dour, no-nonsense authority of FBI agents. Betty could've hugged them. They were the saviors she needed at precisely the moment she needed them.

The doorbell suddenly exploded with a loud, long ring.

"Hurry! Hurry!" Lais begged.

Now a fist began pounding an insistent tattoo against the front door. The peal of the bell continued too.

With a professional detachment, Betty ignored the constant noise, took the admiral by the hand, and led him to the rear of the house. Standing by a bedroom window, Betty revealed the escape route she'd mapped out months ago after moving in: a short drop below was the roof of the covered porch. From there, jump down and you're in the garden. A door in the wooden garden fence opened onto an alleyway that led straight to Thirty-Third Street. Hail a cab, and you'd be in the Italian embassy in minutes. And best of all, no FBI agent stationed by the front door would be any wiser.

Betty opened the window.

The doorbell continued to scream. The pounding on the door rumbled on, one loud bang after another.

But the admiral hesitated. He was in his sixties, and built like a teakettle. He wondered if he'd even fit through the window, let alone manage the jump from the porch roof down to the garden.

Now it was Betty's turn to say, "Hurry!"

The angry noise coming from the front of the house seemed to be growing more intense. Finally the admiral realized he had no choice. With some difficulty, he squeezed himself through the window. Moments later Betty heard him land in the garden with a dull thud. She looked out, but he had vanished, lost in the night's shadows.

Hurrying to the sitting room, she picked up the telephone and called Pepper at his home on East Fifty-Seventh Street in New York; she had memorized the number in anticipation of a night like this. He listened and then told her to call Fairly. As luck would have it, Fairly was still in his Washington office at Naval Intelligence. He took down all the details, asked a few questions, and then told Betty he would get on it right away.

By the time Betty put down the phone, the banging on the front door had stopped. She looked furtively out the window and saw that the two FBI men had left.

Only now did the evening's ironies run through her head. The FBI had come to question her about her activities as an enemy agent, only to stumble unknowingly upon another adversary who *was* really up to no good—who had just launched a sabotage operation in ports throughout America. And yet their sudden arrival could very well have helped to thwart the plot and win the day— which, as it happened, was what their so-called enemy agent had also been trying to do. Espionage, she told herself with a small chuckle, was a bewildering profession. Rarely was anything what it seemed to be. But that, of course, was part of what made it so exciting.

CHARGING UP THE GANGPLANKS, SQUADS of blue-coated US Coast Guard agents boarded the Italian ships. They raced through the vessels and caught the surprised crews in the midst of acting on Lais's orders. Acetylene torches that had been burning through rods and shafts were abruptly extinguished. Sledgehammers, chisels, and crowbars fell to the floor. Oil-soaked rags wedged between containers of flammable cargo were hastily removed.

Yet Fairly's urgent information had meandered through the naval and then the federal bureaucracies with a costly loss of momentum. By the time the boarding parties raided the ships, six of the Italian vessels had been effectively put out of commission, and another twenty would need extensive repairs before they could go to sea. The Coast Guard had succeeded in saving only two ships from any substantial damage.

But government agents did recover fourteen of the telegrams that had initiated the destruction. Each had been sent from the Italian embassy and signed by its naval attaché, Admiral Alberto Lais.

The following day, an angry US State Department decided that the government had the tangible evidence it had been hoping for. Federal authorities seized all Italian and German ships in US ports and immediately went to work refitting the salvageable Italian vessels. And a vindictive press had a field day.

Front pages were filled with banner headlines announcing the confiscation of the Axis ships. Incriminating photographs of the wantonly damaged Italian vessels illustrated nearly every outraged story. Readers across the nation picked up their newspapers and stared at the somber, pudgy face of the Italian naval attaché, the man identified as the mastermind of this destruction.

Americans were seething. Here was proof of illegal activity on US territory by a foreign diplomat, documented sabotage by alien operatives in the nation's harbors. A furious nation took one more step toward the decision that would bring them into war on the Allied side. Prime Minister Churchill had made pointedly clear that this was the BSC's primary mission. And working from her bedroom, secret agent Betty Pack had set it all in motion.

But at the same bittersweet time, Betty had also effectively put an end to her own long-running operation.

"Your Excellency," the US secretary of state wrote to the Italian ambassador,

> *I have the honor to state that various facts and circumstances have come to the attention of the Government of the United States connecting Admiral Alberto Lais, Naval Attaché of the Royal Italian Embassy, with the commission by certain persons of acts in violation of laws of the United States.*
>
> *The President has reached the conclusion that the continued presence of Admiral Lais as Naval Attaché of the Embassy would be no longer agreeable to this Government. . . .*
>
> *Cordell Hull*

It was agreed that Lais would leave the country a month later, on April 25. Still unaware of the part Betty had played in his expulsion, still needing the comforting presence of his Golden Girl, the admiral asked Betty to come to New York with him. He wanted to spend his last night in America with her.

Betty agreed. It was more a sentimental than an operational decision. Given the circumstances, she felt she owed him that much.

For propriety's sake, they had separate but connecting rooms in the hotel. During the day, when Lais went out for some last-minute shopping in Manhattan, Betty snuck into his room. She made a careful inventory of his luggage, describing each piece.

Color, size, manufacture, even the type of lock—all was meticulously recorded. She'd pass the list on to her handler, who would cable it to the BSC agents in Bermuda. When Lais's ship stopped in Nassau on its way to Portugal, the admiral would be kept busy while his luggage was covertly searched. It would be the last op Betty ran against him.

That evening Lais snuck into Betty's room. He lay next to her, kissing, stroking, petting. It would be his last chance, too, with his Golden Girl.

In the morning Betty left the hotel and took a cab to the pier where Lais was preparing to board the *S.S. Marqués de Comillas*. She walked toward the admiral but then came to a sudden halt. His wife and nineteen-year-old daughter stood next to him; they had unexpectedly traveled up from Washington to say good-bye. Betty stayed back, offering only a small, almost surreptitious wave of farewell.

But Lais could not be bothered with discretion. He hurried across the dock to Betty. And, as Hyde read in the official BSC history and Betty confirmed with a bemused shrug, "the lovesick Admiral spent his final minutes with her and ignored his tearful family."

And there was a coda to the operation. Betty handed the silver box Lais had given her to John Pepper, telling him to give it to his son. The trinket, Lais—none of it meant anything to her anymore. Unencumbered, Betty was already looking for a new adventure.

Part VII

Big Bill and Little Bill

Chapter 41

◆

O NCE AGAIN SITTING ACROSS FROM Betty in a booth at the Horseshoe Bar of the Shelbourne Hotel, Hyde realized that he had nearly come to the end of his complicated journey. He had spent an intense, exhausting week driving Betty around Ireland as she led him on a tour of her past lives. Now they were back in Dublin for one last night before their flight to London.

Yet there still remained one corner of Betty's wartime memories he needed to explore, and this would likely be his last chance. His tale would be incomplete without an account of the adventure that had prompted Stephenson, usually as parsimonious with his praise as he was with a pound, to christen Betty "the greatest unsung heroine of the war." It was a mission that had also left her American handler marveling that she had "changed the whole course of the war." Hyde, the enterprising author, knew he had to get Betty talking about her long-running operation against the Vichy French embassy in Washington.

But Betty seemed to hesitate. She had come to Ireland to get an understanding of her own life. But perhaps she was now feeling that some parts of her past should remain buried, thought about only with a secret pride. And there was her husband to consider, too. Charles had been very much a part of this episode. Betty had to have wondered whether he would appreciate the attention. She had betrayed him by running off with Hyde, but she still would have wanted, in her often contradictory fashion, to protect him too.

Hyde, however, had come too far to retreat. Yet he did not insist. Instead, he shrewdly led her down what seemed like a different

332 ·   Howard Blum

path. He picked his words carefully. "In spite of the very dramatic incidents in your life," he began, "I think you will agree that there is a great deal of hard work, a great deal of very anxious work and a great deal of planning before you can undertake any successful intelligence operation."

"Yes indeed," Betty said. "In this type of work you must forget yourself and simply live for your work and nothing else. I had put aside all thoughts of my two children. I could not allow myself to feel tired or ill. My whole being had to focus on the project."

Hyde listened, and then asked, "Would you take up this kind of work again?"

"Like a shot!" she exclaimed.

In these words, Hyde heard "an almost rapturous note in her voice." Hoping to take advantage of her complex feelings—a heightened introspection about what was now beyond her grasp? a passionate pride in what she had done?—he turned to a clean page in the notebook on the table.

He asked again about her Vichy operation. It was a memory that would put her back in touch with a time when she had lived in a deeper, more purposeful way. A time she still missed, and still deeply desired.

Now she talked without hesitation.

Chapter 42

◆

BETTY DID NOT HAVE TO wait long for her next mission, or, for that matter, her next romance. They came, as they so often did for her, in tandem. And it was all set in motion, Betty explained to Hyde in the resolute tone she unconsciously adopted when talking about her wartime work, late one unseasonably warm April afternoon in 1941, after her maid announced there was a gentleman to see her.

"A Mr. Williams, ma'am. I've shown him into the living room."

Betty did not know a Mr. Williams, and the sudden arrival of a stranger so soon after the Italian op put her on guard. The FBI had clearly taken an interest in her—Betty nearly stumbled over their amateurish watchers whenever she went out—and perhaps now they were ready to ask some hard questions. This possibility, though, was followed by a more terrifying thought. She'd made a lot of enemies in her work, only they'd start in with the rough stuff and save the questions for later, when she'd be begging for the chance to answer if they'd just stop. A hasty escape through the garden door seemed suddenly appealing. It had worked for Admiral Lais. But, she reminded herself, it had only bought him some time, and not much at that. No, she decided, she'd brazen this out. She'd confront the mysterious Mr. Williams, put on a show of implacable confidence, and see what happened.

She went downstairs and shook hands with a short, fit, late fortyish, rather dapper man in a well-cut tweed suit. He smiled at her confidently, and a small scar she hadn't previously noticed at the corner of his mouth twisted his face into something sinister. Who was this little man with the lopsided grin?

"How do you do, Mr. Williams," Betty said, gesturing for him to sit in a chintz-covered chair. "To what do I owe this honor?"

He brushed away her sarcasm with another lopsided smile. Then he said genially, "I'm from the New York office."

Betty decided he was lying. She had never heard anyone in New York mention a "Mr. Williams." And certainly her handlers would've alerted her to the arrival of a new contact. Either Williams was a G-man trying to trap her, or he was with the opposition, and neither alternative calmed her jangling nerves. She kept a loaded revolver in a drawer in her bedroom dressing table, and she cursed herself for not having brought it down. Betty decided she'd make up some story that'd allow her to scoot upstairs, and when she returned she'd at least have the gun in her purse.

She was just about to ask Williams to excuse her for a moment when he took her by surprise. "May I have a dry martini?" he asked. A mutual friend had raved about her martinis, he explained. Said you served a drink that packed a real punch. And once again he flashed his odd smile, but now it struck her as more coy than sinister.

As she mixed a pitcher—although less shaky than she had been moments ago, she too needed a drink—Williams went to work soothing whatever apprehensions lingered. "You did a good job of work with the Italian admiral. You may be interested to know that we got the naval ciphers all right. The chief is very pleased."

Betty listened and relaxed. She no longer doubted that Williams worked for the BSC, but she was beginning to suspect something else. She had the cunning, though, to keep this thought to herself.

After she handed the drink to Williams, she mentioned that it was her mother's recipe, and then trotted out her well-used line that it was the only thing she'd learned from Cora.

Once again he ambushed her. With a mock severity, Williams chastised Betty for not giving Cora her due. After all, he pointed out, hadn't she studied at the Sorbonne? Then there was another flash of the coy smile.

That clinched it for Betty. Only a few people in the organization would be privy to her personnel file, or, for that matter, would've gone over it with such a fine-tooth comb as to know where Cora had been educated. Besides, Williams didn't act like any handler she'd ever known; he wasn't trying to pass himself off as her best friend or win her approval. Williams treated her cordially, but with a certain distance. It was a remoteness, she judged, that came with rank. Betty was certain she knew exactly who he was. But if he wanted to toy with her, well, she'd play with him too.

"What is our chief like?" Betty asked, doing her best to make the question sound like one operative talking shop to another. "Do you know him well?"

"Yes," he answered, "I think I know him well," and—enjoying her game, and knowing she'd seen through his—added, "He is a terrible chap!"

"You can't mean that. I think he must be a rather wonderful person," she chided, but not as playfully as she'd imagined. In truth, it was what she wanted to believe. She needed the man she served to be worthy of her respect.

The banter continued, but when his glass was drained, Williams got up to leave. "I have a plane to catch. I must get back to New York tonight."

"Must you?" Betty nearly begged. The words rushed out before she'd thought about them. But she truly did not want him to go. She very much wanted him to like her. And now, recalling the unsettling exchange for Hyde, she had a further realization: she'd been once again searching for the father she deeply missed.

Williams, though, was suddenly all business. "John Howard

will be in touch with you about another job we want you to tackle for us. I can't give you any details now, but it is something really big this time. It will certainly be a feat if you can bring it off."

A moment later he was gone. Betty had no doubt that she'd spent the past hour drinking martinis with the master spy who ran British intelligence in the western hemisphere. And that William Stephenson had felt it was important enough to check her out himself, to do some personal talent-spotting, before he approved her next assignment. Betty hoped she'd passed the test.

"SO YOU HAD A VISIT from the chief," said Pepper when he came to see her several days later. "I gather you got on quite well."

Betty responded with a gratified smile: her suspicion had been correct. And even more heartening, Stephenson had inspected the goods and given his approval.

Then, just like that, the small talk was abruptly over. Pepper put on his wartime voice and proceeded to give Betty her next assignment. She was to penetrate the Vichy French embassy in Washington. The operational plan—admittedly vague, he conceded—was for Betty to do what she'd done time after time in the past: get close to key embassy personnel, then exploit these friendships. Rumors, gossip, secrets—especially secrets, Pepper emphasized—Betty was to collect it all.

As Betty struggled to get a handle on this unwieldy new mission, Pepper told her a bit about why it was so important. And in the process, he filled in the blanks of a story she'd previously known only in its broad strokes.

With the collapse of France in the summer of 1940, the country had been divided. Paris and the surrounding northern districts were placed under the harsh administration of the conquering Nazi forces. The central and southern provinces functioned, under Germany's ever-watchful eye, as a quasi-independent version of the former French state; it was known as Vichy France, after the town, celebrated for its palliative mineral water, that was now the seat of government. Marshal Henri Philippe Pétain, the military hero who creaked about as if he'd won his fame fighting with Napoleon rather than in the previous world war, was the ostensible leader of Vichy France, but he had no actual power. His job was simply to look like a sage, white-haired head of state, while all the time nodding with benign consent to whatever the Germans dictated. The real day-to-day authority rested with Admiral Jean Darlan; he had a finger in every pie, and he always made sure the Nazis were well served.

While Vichy behaved in every discernible way as a Nazi puppet state, Germany nevertheless allowed it to maintain France's overseas diplomatic missions and to continue to administer the country's far-flung colonial empire. A besieged Britain balked at the prospect of the Nazis using the cover of a Vichy embassy to get a foothold in London; His Majesty's government refused to establish diplomatic relations with Vichy. But the United States, still a neutral country, sent its representatives to Vichy and, in turn, gave accreditation to its legations. Vichy ran a consulate in New York and a busy embassy in Washington.

The BSC's hope, Pepper continued, was to get a look inside the Washington embassy and in the process find out what Vichy was up to in America, as well as elsewhere in the world. But the real coup, he said, his voice stiffening, would be to discover what plans Vichy had for the French fleet and the nearly $300 million in gold reserves it had sent for safekeeping to its Caribbean island colony of Martinique. If the French battleships were to be handed over to the Germans, the Service needed to scuttle those plans. And if the gold would be made available to the Nazis, an invasion of Martinique should be considered.

But there was also a part of the story that Pepper held close. He wanted Betty well briefed, but she didn't need to know that the prime minister had personally reached out from Downing Street to give this mission its initial operational push. In a sharp, testy memo to C, the head of the Service, Churchill had complained: "I am not satisfied with the volume or quality of information from both the occupied and unoccupied areas of France. . . . So far as the Vichy Government is concerned it is not creditable that we have so little information." C had passed Churchill's displeasure on to Stephenson, and the BSC head, searching for a solution, had found himself drinking a strong martini in Betty's living room. Once back in New York, he'd ordered Pepper to give the spy code-named Cynthia the mission.

"Will you try to do it for us?" asked Pepper firmly.

Betty did not hesitate. "You know I will."

BUT HOW? HOW WOULD SHE make her approach? And who in the embassy would she target? So much depended on her initial pass. The United States was not in the war. If she got burned, if an indignant Vichy diplomat filed a protest with the US State Department reporting that a British spy had cozied up to him, it wouldn't merely put an end to the operation; she'd wind up in federal jail, prosecuted as a foreign espionage agent. Or, no less likely, the Gestapo-trained Vichy goons who handled embassy security would come calling.

Questions and concerns filled her mind as soon as Pepper left. And as she juggled them, another realization stopped her short: this operation would be significantly different from all her previous assignments. In the past, Betty had set out to seduce someone she knew, and more often than not her prey was already smitten. Now she'd have to work her magic on a stranger, casting a spell so strong that he'd be willing to prove his love by committing treason. That was asking a lot, she feared, from a night or two of bouncing around in a double bed.

But, she reprimanded herself, there was no point in running through all the what-ifs before she'd even started. She was determined, Betty told Hyde with the willful pride she'd never lost, "not to let the side down."

With a professional's focus, Betty plotted her first small steps forward. She set out to get a sense of her potential targets.

The BSC files Pepper shared offered a quick history of the key embassy personnel. Gaston Henry-Haye, the ambassador, was— and here the Service happily quoted Secretary of State Cordell Hull—"a little man with ruddy cheeks and a truculent moustache who arrived with the taint of association" with the Nazi sympathizers who ran Vichy. George Bertrand-Vigne, the counselor, was a stuffy minor aristocrat who, the BSC analysts speculated, could be counted on to look at the world with a lawyer's deliberative caution. And Charles Emmanuel Brousse, the press attaché, was a much-married—the exasperated file had the marriage count somewhere between three and six—World War I flying ace who was the co-owner of an influential newspaper with a sizable readership throughout France's southern departments.

But the sketchy BSC files didn't offer the piquant intelligence Betty was looking for. So she traveled to New York—she knew better than to risk asking questions in Washington—and checked into the luxurious Pierre Hotel on Fifth Avenue. The Pierre was famously packed with well-heeled Vichy sympathizers waiting out the war, and Betty made it a point to bump into two old friends she had heard were in residence. Over drinks with a woman from Chile who was now married to a French count, and tea the next afternoon with another longtime acquaintance, an English woman married to a prosperous Vichy businessman, Betty received a more complete briefing.

At first Brousse, the press attaché, seemed to offer the most promise for the game she was hoping to play. "Oh, a real charmer," said her Chilean friend in response to Betty's seemingly casual question. "I don't know about now, but he was a member of the Anglo-French Intelligence Board," she added, referring to a joint military planning group the two countries had set up during the last war. "He is loyal to Vichy, as he is a serving officer, but he has no love whatsoever for the Germans."

But then Betty's English friend gave her the dirt on the ambassador. Henry-Haye, she whispered with catty delight, had a Frenchman's wandering eye. These days it had wandered to two mistresses whose affections he was merrily juggling. In addition to, of course, his long-suffering wife.

Betty shared a giggle over the randy ambassador with her friend, but at the same time her operational mind began churning. A plan swiftly took shape: using her old standby cover as a journalist, she'd set up an interview with Henry-Haye. Once in the room with the ambassador, she'd hit him with the full force of her high-voltage charm. Any man enjoying two mistresses, she told herself, should be willing to add a third. Especially if she made it quite clear that this was just the sort of liaison she was looking for, too.

On May 19, Betty, assuming her cover identity of Elizabeth Thorpe, called the embassy. She had rehearsed her lines all morning, and delivered them as soon as Charles Brousse, the press attaché, came on the phone: She was an American newspaperwoman who wished to help France. She wanted to write a series of articles on Vichy France's brave struggle through these complicated times, and she would like to start with an interview with the ambassador. How soon could one be arranged?

Brousse did not respond for a moment. All Betty could do was wait, and hope she had sounded both professional and sincere.

Another moment passed; the silence was unnerving. Growing

desperate, Betty tried another tack. Perhaps, she challenged, Captain Brousse wasn't, well, quite high up enough in the Press Department to make such arrangements.

An indignant Brousse shot back at once. "Of course I have the necessary authority! Will you come to the chancery tomorrow afternoon at two o'clock? Everything will be arranged and you will have as much time with the ambassador as you like!"

Captain Charles Brousse and his wife, Catherine, aboard the S.S. Exeter *as they arrived in America for Brousse's new post as press attaché to the Vichy French Embassy.*

Chapter 43

◆

ETTY CHOSE A TIGHT GREEN dress whose bold color came close to matching the deep emerald of her eyes. Usually that sort of advantage would have reinforced her confidence, but as her appointment at the embassy approached, her anxiety increased.

She decided to walk around the block before going up the steps to the front door; perhaps that would settle her nerves. She knew the neighborhood well. After her father's death, Cora had moved into an apartment just three doors down the street. Yet this afternoon she studied the embassy on Wyoming Avenue as if she were seeing it for the first time.

In a previous life, the embassy had been a comfortable private Victorian-style home, and it still retained its wide front porch, sloping roof, and bay windows. But another more businesslike story had been cobbled on, making the building look squat and misshapen. It was, she decided, a very ugly fortress.

Her nerves somewhat calmed and her resolve returning, she climbed the front steps. Yet as she walked through the door, Betty suddenly realized: she was behind the lines in enemy territory.

CHARLES BROUSSE, THE PRESS ATTACHÉ, greeted her with an apology. The ambassador, he explained with a diplomat's fulsome sincerity, had been unavoidably delayed. Would Miss Thorpe please accompany him to his office? They could get to know one another until the ambassador was available.

*The Vichy French Embassy, located on Wyoming
Avenue, as photographed in 1942.*

Their conversation was more a flirtation than an interview. Perched informally on the edge of his desk, his long legs crossed, Brousse was aware of the mischief in what he was doing. Without embarrassment, he studied her openly. It was a very deliberate inspection. Betty, alert and intrigued, welcomed his attention. She listened with rapt interest to his every word, at the same time making sure to signal her availability.

What did they talk about? With guile made all the more artful by her fluent, accentless French, Betty began by asking about the impressive display of ribbons on his suit. Brousse took the bait, recounting the wartime exploits that had earned him his Croix de Guerre and Légion d'Honneur rosette. Then with barely a

344 · Howard Blum

pause, Betty shrewdly maneuvered the conversation to more personal revelations. Here, too, Brousse was quick to brag, portraying himself as a debonair forty-nine-year-old Frenchman of a certain class. He dismissed his many marriages with an insouciant shrug, spoke candidly of his numerous affairs, and let her know that he had a connoisseur's appreciation for fine foods and good vintages.

Both of them realized full well that their meandering conversation was merely background noise. What mattered more was unspoken, but nevertheless filled the room: the attraction pulling them toward one another.

As it built in intensity, an aide entered to announce that Ambassador Henry-Haye was ready to see Miss Thorpe.

Gaston Henry-Haye, Vichy France Ambassador to the United States, with Charles Brousse on the right.

◆ ◆ ◆

THE AMBASSADOR WAS FURIOUS. HE had just returned from a session with Cordell Hull, in which the secretary of state acted like a stern headmaster admonishing a misbehaving schoolboy.

Henry-Haye had requested the meeting to protest the US seizure of French ships interned in American ports and, a more self-interested complaint, the recent flurry of critical newspaper articles about the Vichy embassy. He had marched into Hull's office expecting to receive at the very least a somewhat apologetic explanation; the traditional stiff courtesy between diplomats required Hull at the very least to display a modicum of chagrin. Instead, Hull fired right back. "The French Government at Vichy has gone straight into Hitler's arms," he railed. Vichy's "first thought," he snarled with genuine contempt, was "to deliver France body and soul to Hitler." The fierce upbraiding continued without pause for an hour. Too shocked to offer more than an occasional feeble rejoinder, Henry-Haye suffered through most of his lashing with a mute astonishment.

But now, safely back in his own office, the ambassador poured out everything he felt he should have said to Hull. As he ranted, Betty was the perfect audience. She listened to his every resentful word with sympathetic concentration.

"How dare they [the Americans] judge France when they themselves had never suffered invasion," Henry-Haye fumed. He ridiculed "American vulgarity and lack of civilized manners" and angrily justified his "difficult" mission: "France's future requires cooperation with Germany. If your car is in the ditch, you turn to the person who will help you put it on the road again. That is why we will work with Germany." On and on he went, in a monologue that lasted for a seemingly endless two and a half hours.

Betty was only too happy to let him vent. There was no better way to win the ambassador over than to sit back and listen, an adoring smile fixed on her face.

Finally Henry-Haye was too exhausted to continue. Yet although clearly spent, the gallant ambassador nevertheless rose from his seat and escorted Betty to his office door. Fixing her with a deep, meaningful look, he solemnly said he would be only too happy to see her again.

Brousse was waiting in the hallway. A perfect gentleman, he accompanied Betty down the embassy steps. They stood together on the street, and he bowed, kissed her hand, and said, "Au revoir."

"Au revoir," Betty replied before she turned and walked off. She felt an immense relief. Against all odds, she had completed the first part of her mission: she had made contact with Henry-Haye. But as she continued down the street, she found herself wondering whether it would be the ambassador or his press attaché who would make the next move. Either one, the practical spy decided, would suit her just fine.

A BOUQUET OF RED ROSES arrived the next morning, confirming Betty's hopes: the operation was moving forward. She hesitated, though, before opening the accompanying envelope. Which of the two Frenchmen had stepped into her trap? With a sense of delight that took her by surprise, Betty read Charles Brousse's name on the enclosed note. Even better, he'd invited her to lunch that day at the Carlton Hotel.

"I shall never forget that lunch," an uncharacteristically nostalgic Betty told Hyde as they sat in the Shelbourne. The champagne flowed, but it had only worked, she'd thought at the time, to give her a firmer operational advantage; "I must say I was in my most sparkling mood," she admitted. "As a diplomat's wife"—the many jurisdictional problems caused by Arthur's being in Chile and Betty's return to America, as well as the war, had put their divorce on hold—"who had seen a good deal of the world, I had a fund of anecdotes. I could tell a story well, and I always kept them short. I told Charles the most amusing of them—with a few naughty ones thrown in deliberately. My object was to make Charles believe that I was a woman of the world who would not be averse to being wooed and won by a handsome Frenchman, even though we were both married. At the same time, I had to be careful not to reveal who my husband was and where my real sympathies lay. It was a tricky business, I can tell you."

As the lunch continued and Betty went on gaily spinning her web, it got trickier. Brousse absently ran a single finger slowly up her arm, its tip tracing a smooth trail along her skin. The next moment he reached for her hand, cradled it gently, and then, as if it were the most natural of gestures, lifted it to his lips for a tender kiss.

And all the while Betty's operational soul was telling her to go slow, to play this next stage long. The higher the price, the greater the appreciation, went the spy's time-honored maxim. Tradecraft required that Brousse not get his way too soon or easily.

But her racing heart was sending Betty entirely different instructions. When Brousse caressed her, all her professional discipline nearly vanished. It took immense restraint not to return his touch, not to lean across the table and plant a long, deep kiss on his lips. So accustomed to being the one manipulating events, Betty found herself locked in a struggle with herself, each side of her mercurial nature vying for control.

When the long, leisurely lunch ended, Brousse asked if he could accompany Betty home. Yes, she agreed, at the same time trying to convince herself that her mind was not made up. Nothing had been decided by this small acquiescence.

Yet the moment the front door closed behind them, Brousse put his arms around her in a strong embrace. Suddenly, he lifted her off the floor and began to carry her up the stairs.

Howard Blum

"Charles, what on earth are you doing?" she tried, but her protest sounded hollow even to her.

"You'll see," he promised. "You have nothing to fear."

Their lovemaking was long, slow, and expert. His every gesture, his every touch, was skillful and precise. It was a power that ignited a greed in her for more.

That evening, after Brousse had gone home to his wife, Betty telephoned her handler in New York. "Johnny," she said in a voice that she hoped did not betray the complicated emotions she was feeling, "I think I can say it's in the bag."

"Wonderful," said Pepper. "But for heaven's sake, play it cool."

"Don't worry, Johnny, I will."

Betty hung up and sat on the edge of her bed, trying to convince herself that one more lie wouldn't make any difference.

Chapter 44

♦

THE TACTIC OF PRETENDING TO love someone in order to betray him was one that Betty had used with great success over the years. But setting out to betray someone she actually loved was something else entirely. It was, Betty began to discover, a much more precarious operation: she'd need to betray herself too.

Still, she did not turn away. Even as she fell deeper and deeper in love with Brousse, she went ahead with her mission to recruit him. She did not hesitate to deceive and manipulate, placing him in great danger. As she offered Brousse her affection, and yearned for his in return, Betty set out to coax him into being her agent.

Betty lived these two conflicting lives without regrets. Her wayward romances had taken her to some bad places, and this new affair was, she'd tell Hyde with total sincerity, the "complete love" she'd never before experienced. Yet it was also the "smoke," as the jargon of her trade put it, that gave her the opportunity to turn a high-ranking Vichy official into a traitor. It was Betty's gift—or was it a curse? she wondered as she shared this episode with Hyde—that while lying in Brousse's arms, she could feel blissfully happy. But no sooner was he out the door than she'd be typing a report transcribing all he had carelessly revealed during their passionate afternoon.

In the same day Betty could live two lives. And she'd never feel any conflict, any warring loyalties. For she had—and this insight, too, reached across the decades as she sat in the Shelbourne opposite Hyde—already pledged her allegiance, and after that nothing else mattered. She would sacrifice everything for the cause she served and the secret life she had chosen.

RECRUITMENTS, LIKE MOST SEDUCTIONS, PROCEED in stages, and so it went as Betty set out to make Charles Brousse her agent.

In the beginning they simply shared earnest confessions, the small revelations that lovers disclose to one another as they weave the fabric of their romance. Or at least that was what Betty wanted Brousse to believe. He would tell her about his loveless marriage to his wealthy wife, the great-granddaughter of John C. Calhoun, a former vice president of the United States. With unembarrassed candor he would admit that he counted on Kay to pay the bills; his assets were tied up in France, and he had a fondness for all the good things money could buy. Other times he would rant about Henry-Haye; in his eyes the ambassador was incompetent and, much more unforgivable to Brousse, an *arriviste*, the son of merchants who had the effrontery to think he was worthy to represent France. All these snippets would be dutifully included in the weekly reports Betty delivered to handlers in New York, but even as she typed, she knew they were of negligible intelligence value. Still, she was not discouraged. Experience had taught her that trivial divulgences can gather momentum, and that frank talk can become a habit. The road to treason is paved with small confidences.

But it was John Pepper, pressured by an impatient Stephenson, who pushed the op to the next level. He gave Betty a typed sheet of questions for Brousse. "I want the answers on my desk next week," he ordered.

Pepper was not demanding state secrets. He had carefully crafted his questions so that Brousse would be disclosing seemingly random scraps of diplomatic tittle-tattle—say, the names of his close contacts at the German embassy, or who was out of favor in his own embassy and who had the ambassador's ear. And Betty, of course, was never so clumsy as to directly question Brousse; it was not an interrogation. The art—and Betty's tradecraft was wonderfully instinctive—was to insert an inquiry into their conversation as if it were a small curiosity, nothing more than another fork in their meandering pillow talk.

Yet—and this was the part that kept every agent on full alert—Brousse had to realize on some level what was going on. Like any target who has not yet signed on, he might deny to himself that he was being played—but part of him would know. He must have suspected that the woman with whom he was falling in love was grooming him for treason.

But still he had a choice. He was not fully committed. He could walk away with no consequences; neither his ambassador nor his government would ever know. At worst, he could admonish himself that he'd been indiscreet.

At this crucial moment in every operation, all any fieldman can do is worry through the long, sleepless nights. Will the prey run for the hills, or will he come back for more? Everything depends on what happens next. And—a further complication for an anxious Betty—she not only wanted Brousse as her agent but desperately needed him in her life.

Yet after Brousse played innocently along, responding with no apparent hesitation to her questions, three silent days passed. He did not call, and Betty slept alone in her bed.

When Brousse finally returned, he brought Betty a present—or, more accurately, two presents. They were telegrams. Admiral Darlan, the head of Vichy's naval operations, had sent the first, to the embassy that morning. It requested a list of all British ships being refitted in American dockyards and the specific repairs scheduled. The second telegram was the response the embassy's naval attaché had sent just hours earlier. "From a good source," the attaché began, and he proceeded to rattle off the names of the British battleships, carriers, and cruisers in East Coast ports, the work being done, and the approximate dates when they would put to sea.

Brousse handed this gift to Betty with no explanation. He was reluctant to discuss what he'd done; any conversation would force him to face up to the treasonous act he'd committed. With purposefully delusional logic, he wanted to be able to tell himself that he was merely sharing some interesting information about his day at the office with the woman he loved. It was a rationale he clung to even as he knew it was a lie.

And in fact no further explanation was necessary. Betty knew the telegrams were pure intelligence gold. Here was proof that the Vichy embassy in Washington was working hand in hand with the Germans; the French navy surely had no tactical interest in British ships. More of a concern, the embassy was also clearly providing the Nazis with information that would allow their U-boats to ambush English ships as they steamed out of US ports.

The consequences, Betty understood, would be significant. As soon as the BSC cabled London, the Admiralty would change the redeployment schedule of its warships in American dockyards, and this time make sure the dates remained a closely guarded secret. And the Foreign Service would use this incriminating evidence to bolster its ongoing plea to the US State Department that restrictions on Vichy's operations in America were necessary.

Already looking to the future, Betty was confident that she had turned Charles. She would move on with his help to unlock the larger secrets that the embassy held. And no less a long-term blessing, she could count on her lover returning to her bed.

BUT AS IF PLAYING THREE roles—reporter, secret agent, and mistress—were not a sufficiently complicated juggling act, another of Betty's lives chose this inopportune moment to intrude. Her husband arrived in Washington.

Arthur had been summoned from Chile to participate in trade talks with Lord Halifax, the British ambassador to the United States, but he also found the time to call on his wife. Seated in the living room of the house on O Street, he piously announced that he was willing to offer Betty a second—or was it a third? a fourth?—chance. Struggling to find a calm and steady tone, he explained that, after much agonized thought, he was now able to forgive her transgression with the American naval lieutenant. He would forget about Paul Fairly, and that would be that. They could continue as man and wife.

Betty listened in silence. If Arthur had landed in a spaceship from another planet, he could not have been any more alien to the life she was now living. She found her cold, flat voice and slashed away at him mercilessly.

Paul Fairly? she repeated, as if it were the name of some obscure character in an ancient text, which to Betty's way of looking at things it was. She was no longer seeing him, she said (which was almost the truth: they still had a professional relationship; he remained her conduit to US naval intelligence). She had fallen in love with a Frenchman. He was married, and whether he would ever get a divorce remained uncertain. But regardless, Arthur should use the letter she'd already given him admitting to her affair with Paul to obtain a divorce. She would never, ever go back to him.

What about Denise? Arthur tried.

The question only hardened Betty's heart. It would be impossible to raise a daughter in Washington, she coolly replied. After all, America no doubt would soon be joining the war; Denise would be better off in Chile. When the fighting stopped and it was a safer world, then she'd see about negotiating a visitation schedule.

Arthur left their brief reunion convinced Betty had taken leave of her senses. She was running head-on from one passionate affair straight to another. She had no interest in her daughter; she hadn't even asked to see a recent photograph of Denise. And she was calling herself a reporter even though she had no job, nor had she published, as far as he could tell, any articles. She had become, he would write his sister, "impossible."

"Betty was living," he said, "in a world of make believe."

Which, as any spy could've happily confirmed for him, was the only world in which she'd ever really wanted to live.

MEANWHILE, IN ANOTHER OF BETTY'S turbulent lives, Brousse continued to cooperate, answering her more pointed questions, talking more freely about embassy matters. However, he remained only "semiconscious"; that is, he was aware of what he was doing even as he still guardedly maintained the illusion that he was not betraying his government. Each week Betty and Pepper discussed whether the time was right to make the pitch—to ask Brousse, in effect, to sign on the dotted line and become fully operational. And each week Betty convinced her handler to wait. They both knew that if they moved too quickly, if their timing was not perfect, Brousse could bolt. The operation would be blown, and along with it Betty's cover.

Then the moment they'd been waiting for unexpectedly came their way.

"Will you come back to France with me?" Brousse suddenly asked one evening as he lay in Betty's bed. "I can't leave without you."

It was July 1941, and their affair—and Betty's operation—was two months old. That day Brousse had been abruptly ordered home; the Vichy government had decided to abolish the press attaché's position. Henry-Haye had offered him a compromise, but it was a small one: from a private fund, the ambassador could scrape together $600 a month—half of Brousse's previous salary—and Brousse could stay on at the embassy, working as Henry-Haye's personal assistant. But a man with Brousse's refined tastes and high style could never get by on such a pittance, and given the rocky state of his marriage, he couldn't ask his wife to supplement his salary more than she was already doing. In fact, he suspected that Kay was getting ready to leave, and when she left she'd take her money with her. No, he told Betty, the only practical solution was for him to return to France. And he wanted Betty to accompany him. "I love you," he said solemnly.

Betty was elated. It filled her with joy to have the man she loved announce that he loved her too. But even as her heart soared, her operational mind was working at full speed. Here was a chance, she told herself excitedly, to go behind the lines in occupied Europe. She'd have perfect cover—the mistress of a Vichy diplomat. She'd be invaluable to the Service. And, oh, the adventures she'd have.

As soon as Brousse left, she was on the phone to Pepper. Yes, he agreed, it was a scenario that presented intriguing possibilities. But first, before anything else could be contemplated, the embassy op in Washington had to be played out. The moment had come, he concluded with an unwavering certainty, to make her pitch. "It's now or never."

"Now or never," Betty echoed, resigned.

She confronted Brousse and offered up a bounty of rewards in return for his allegiance. As she'd done with so many others, she waved a false flag. She knew Brousse detested Britain, the former ally that just a year ago had so mercilessly bloodied the French fleet off Oran. Betty suspected that if she asked him to spy for British intelligence, he'd turn her down flat. Instead, she looked her lover deeply in the eyes and, a stagy tremble in her voice, revealed her big secret: she was an American agent.

Before he could respond, Betty quickly explained that her activities were not aimed against France but rather against the Vichy collaborators, the likes of Pétain and Laval, foot soldiers for the Nazi invaders. Here was an opportunity, she insisted, her argument deliberately tapping straight into his patriotic soul, to restore French honor, to soothe the sting of defeat, and to make sure German troops never again goose-stepped down the boulevards of his beloved Paris.

And she was practical. Betty stated that the US Treasury would pay him for his efforts (although, of course, the money would be coming from London). The Americans would make generous monthly cash payments to supplement the meager salary Henry-Haye had offered. He could enjoy his well-heeled life in Washington for a while longer, and even better, he would no longer have to depend upon his wife's charity.

But in the end, perhaps her strongest argument remained unarticulated. She was tacitly offering Brousse the opportunity to continue their romance. Share my important work, Betty signaled as she sat across from him, her beguiling beauty casting its heady spell, and we can share a life.

Before the night was over, Brousse agreed. He would spy for the Americans.

For Betty, for the Americans, for France, for the money—whatever the reason, or reasons, once Brousse was on board, he proved to be an extremely valuable agent. He had a good memory, and he liked the game; he'd even go as far as to take notes openly as the ambassador read out the day's cables to the senior staff. He produced so much raw product that Betty was now making two or three trips each week to New York to deliver this windfall to Pepper.

But Pepper was a demanding handler. He told Betty that Brousse could do even better, and so she obediently went to work. By November she had persuaded her agent to pass on decoded copies of every cipher telegram the embassy sent or received. Novice but nevertheless gung-ho, Brousse also produced an impressively detailed daily written report, a catalogue of each day's secret goings-on inside the embassy.

There were mountains and mountains of raw intelligence for the BSC analysts to pore over. The movements of the French fleet; communications with French colonies, including Martinique, where the gold reserves were stored; the identities and activities of Vichy agents in America; Vichy's messages to the State Department and even to the president; assessments of US and British intelligence operations—the Service had knowledge of virtually everything that went on inside the embassy.

With a showman's flair, Stephenson compiled the troves of information collected from the embassy—while Brousse was the jewel in the BSC's crown, they had other sources, too—into a dossier and had it delivered to his new friend, Franklin Roosevelt. The president, who loved a good spy yarn, eagerly read it "as a bedtime story."

It was "the most fascinating reading I have had for a long time," the excited president let Stephenson know the next day. "The best piece of comprehensive intelligence I have come across since the last war."

EACH DAY WAS FILLED WITH risks. Brousse would peruse a cable marked "Secret," only to place it surreptitiously in his jacket pocket when he hoped no one was looking. Then he'd invent some excuse to leave the embassy and meet up with Betty. She'd get it photocopied, as Brousse paced anxiously, trying to think of anything but the ticking of the clock and what would happen if the ambassador requested that particular cable at that moment. The copy made, Brousse would hurry back to the embassy. All stealth, trying to ignore the piercing needles of fear, he'd replace the cable in its proper file.

They both dreaded "the Vichy secret police," as Brousse with a grave respect referred to the embassy security detail. If they were under surveillance, they knew their operation would be swiftly exposed. Brousse would be killed. And no less likely, Betty would vanish too.

The BSC did its part to protect its star source. When it covertly passed on the evidence to the *New York Herald Tribune*, leading to a startling series of articles with headlines like "Vichy Men Play Nazis' Game Here in Shelter of Embassy" and "Vichy Embassy Heading Clique of Agents Aiding Nazis," they made sure that Brousse was identified as a key conspirator in "the underground work of Vichy in the United States."

The BSC, which kept the specific activities and identities of its agents secret from the American authorities, also made it a point to pass on derogatory intel about Brousse to the FBI. "Brousse is the most evil element in the embassy and has a bad influence on the Ambassador. Haye is completely committed to the Laval/Darlan policy and Brousse works closely with him," stated a Bureau report with utmost certainty.

But these efforts to reinforce Brousse's cover earlier were of little operational consolation to an agent who each day took new, large risks. Each night as Betty and Brousse lay together, they found themselves wondering if a stray night noise could be the muffled sound of the Vichy secret police creeping up the stairs, and if this night would be their last. The danger intensified the excitement they shared in their every moment together.

Chapter 45

◆

I N A WORLD FAR REMOVED from the two lovesick spies, yet only blocks away—in the White House Oval Office—the prime minister and president, surrounded by their political and military chieftains, held a war council. At the tail end of December 1941, just two weeks after the attack on Pearl Harbor and America's entry into the war, Churchill had come to Washington to discuss strategy with his new ally. High on their agenda was how they would coordinate their common fight against the Nazis. And perhaps not unexpectedly, considering the complex egos, ambitions, and self-interests of the many participants, the conference soon became quarrelsome.

The confident American warlords envisioned the European war unfolding quickly and decisively. They wanted to launch an Allied drive within months, straight through France toward Berlin.

The English generals, still reeling from their army's desperate evacuations from France, Greece, and Norway, were more cautious. Even though Russia had stopped Germany's massive invasion just outside Moscow, they predicted that the attack had not run its destructive course. Hoping the Russians would inflict further damage on the German army, the wary British were opposed to a single large-scale campaign. First encircle the Reich, let the Russians conclusively repel the German invaders, and encourage the subjugated nations to rebel, they argued; then an Anglo-American force could charge into a tottering Germany.

Churchill endorsed this approach, vehemently arguing for a tactical first step code-named Super-Gymnast—a joint Anglo-American invasion of North Africa. Brandishing his cigar like a weapon, an impressed participant at the session would recall, he repeatedly reeled off the advantages of the Allies' beginning their military partnership with waves of troops landing on the sandy shores of Africa: Rommel's Afrika Korps would be trapped; the short, direct sea lanes through the Suez Canal would be reopened; American troops would get their baptism under fire in less harrowing conditions than they would in a massive attack through well-fortified France; fewer resources and not as much training would be required; Vichy might very possibly rethink its support of the Reich; and, the empathetic bottom line of his argument, the operation could be launched fairly quickly, with American soldiers providing support to the embattled Soviets within the year.

Unpersuaded, the American military officials continued to dismiss a North African invasion as a sideshow. By the end of the conference, the bickering participants felt that its code name of Arcadia, evocative of the pastoral paradise of Greek mythology, was pure wishful thinking. The Anglo-American partnership seemed to be falling apart even before it had marched off to war.

Nevertheless Churchill, tenacious and supremely confident, returned to London determined to prevail: if necessary, he'd convince Roosevelt to overrule his reluctant generals. He informed his advisers to prepare for an invasion of North Africa.

As the British war machine mobilized, the Secret Intelligence Service went to work too. The spymasters understood that surprise would be key if the invasion were to succeed. Knowing the movements of the French fleet in the Mediterranean would give the strategists an enormous advantage in planning the timing and locations of the Allied landings, and it would direct Allied air power to the location of the French ships. Intelligence would provide the tactical edge in a campaign that would determine the future course of the entire war.

In March 1942, C, using his personal cipher, sent a flash cable to Intrepid. A message from the head of service always received immediate attention, and the BSC wranglers went to work decoding it as soon as it came in. A half hour later Stephenson read the crisp decrypted message: the Admiralty "wished to obtain a copy of the French naval cipher, a copy of which was used by the Naval Attaché in Washington."

Stephenson read it twice in rapid succession, and when he was done he was still shaking his head with wonder and, he'd later concede, a bit of rage. Why didn't London ask him for something easy—say, the key to the bullion depository at Fort Knox or a tap on the president's private phone line? He couldn't help believing that Sir Stewart Menzies, who he felt had always dismissed him as Churchill's man in America, a well-connected amateur who should never have gotten the job, was setting him up to fail. Imperious London might "wish to obtain," but he lived in the real world of armed guards, steel doors, and locked safes. How was the BSC going to extract the ciphers—every nation's most closely guarded secrets—from Vichy's well-guarded embassy? And, a further complication, while America had gone to war against the Axis powers, its relationship with Vichy was still officially "neutral." The Washington embassy would also be protected by the FBI.

He met with Dick Ellis, the MI6 professional who had been sent over from London to be his second-in-command, and with John Pepper. After feverish hours of brainstorming, they were no closer to an operational plan. The Vichy embassy, they forlornly agreed, was impregnable. The only hope, and a depressingly small one, would be if the agent code-named Cynthia could use her hold on Brousse to get into the cipher room. But even if Brousse and she were willing, they still didn't have any idea of how the mission would proceed. The best they could come up with was London's ploy: simply announce to Betty that they wished to obtain the cipher, then stand back and let her sink or swim.

In the second week of March 1942, Betty opened the door of her room at the Manhattan Ritz-Carlton to a visibly tense Pepper. He hurried through the standard questions, and after making sure that Betty felt she was in no immediate danger, that no one had followed her from Washington, he put it to her without further preliminaries: the naval attaché at the Vichy embassy in Washington had the code books used for communicating with the entire French fleet. "Well, Betty," he asked abruptly, his usual English courtesy abandoned, "can you get hold of them for us?"

Betty had no idea if she could. She knew nothing about a possible invasion of North Africa, nor did she need to know. All she knew was that it seemed like an impossible mission—and that was enough. A great challenge was all the motivation she required.

"Yes, I can. And I *will*," she promised.

"YOU SHOULD CALL ME MORE often in the afternoon," Brousse said mischievously after greeting Betty with a long, tender kiss. She had telephoned as soon as her plane from New York landed in Washington, and Brousse, tingling with amorous anticipation, had hurried over.

Betty pulled away from his embrace. She tried to find her operational voice, the one she used when she addressed Brousse as his case agent, not as his lover. "But it is not for *that* I need you, but something else," she said flatly. Then she explained how "our American friends"—the lie came easily—had asked her to obtain the naval ciphers, and she'd agreed. But as soon as she spoke the words, she realized how absurd they were. It was a mission without any realistic hope of success.

"You can't be serious, *ma cherie*," Brousse answered. "Or else they are lunatics. *C'est de la folie.*" It really wasn't worth discussing, and anyway he had other things on his mind.

"Listen to me," Betty said with surprising force. The anger that suddenly spilled out was aimed not just at Brousse but also at her handler and, not least, herself, for foolishly accepting the assignment. "I have never been more serious in my life. There's a war going on, and if you, who swear you love me, will not help me, then I will either work alone or with someone else who *will* help me."

Brousse chose to ignore her outburst; his mind remained fixed on other matters. "It is plain that you are tired or ill. You should go to bed," he tried. "Yes?"

"Bed!" Betty, who knew a bit about seduction, snapped. She wouldn't be so easily diverted. "I am talking about the naval ciphers. And I will tell you straight that if I find anyone who will help me, I will pay any price and you must not blame me afterwards."

Whether his patience had worn thin, or by now he'd come to realize that there was little chance of leading Betty to the bedroom, Brousse finally exploded. "But you are asking the impossible of me," he bellowed. "You don't understand the precautions that are taken to guard the ciphers."

The code room, he explained, was a stronghold. He couldn't simply walk in and "borrow" the naval code books unnoticed. There were two thick books, each about the size of a Washington telephone directory; it would be impossible to slip them casually into his suit jacket pocket, as he did with a cable.

Besides, he wouldn't be allowed into the code room. There were strict rules restricting entry. Even the cipher clerks could only get into the facility when it was necessary to decode an incoming message or encode an outgoing one—and then only with the supervision of the chief cipher officer. Except for the ambassador, the naval attaché, and the embassy counselor, the room was off limits to the rest of the embassy staff.

At night, he continued wearily, the cipher books were locked away. The diplomatic ciphers went into a safe in the code room; the naval ciphers, in a safe in the naval attaché's office. There were impressive locks on the doors to both rooms, and an armed night watchman accompanied by a snarling dog patrolled the floors. And if that were not sufficiently discouraging, there was the Vichy secret police force, and they were a ruthless and very professional squad, he reminded her. One never knew when they might send a team to check up on things, or, for that matter, what alarms they might have covertly installed.

"I can tell you right now that you have promised to do the impossible," an exasperated Brousse concluded. "Mon dieu! Ah, les femmes!"

"Les femmes," Betty shot back at him, but without her previous sharpness. She was wise enough to realize there would be no easy solution, and for the time being she might as well step away from her role as the demanding case agent.

"That may be your trouble, darling," she said brightly, suddenly playful. "If you had not had so many women in your life, you might be able to discriminate and recognize in this one a woman of good sense who does not admit the impossible."

Betty wanted to make sure he recognized what made this woman so different. She stuck her hip out jauntily, a pinup's pose. It was an ironic gesture, but not entirely.

Brousse looked at her with new attention.

"Why, it's even impossible for me to be angry with you," she purred. "Though you refuse me this small thing and look at me with those reproachful brown eyes of yours."

Brousse smiled, and then he kissed her. This time Betty returned his passion. And now that she had concluded the briefing, when he took her hand she could not think of any reason not to follow him into the bedroom.

♦ ♦ ♦

BY THE TIME BETTY ARRIVED in New York for her next scheduled meet with her handler, she still had not come up with a plan.
But she did bring some news. With the lease on her Georgetown
house about to expire, she'd decided to move to an apartment across
town in the Wardman Park Hotel. It had many operational advantages: a short stroll away, just over the Connecticut Avenue bridge,
was the Vichy embassy; there were several exits, one onto Woodley
Road, another onto Connecticut Avenue. The FBI's watchers had
grown increasingly attentive since the United States had entered
the war, so these would come in handy when she needed to sneak
off; and while this was not entirely a professional concern, Brousse
and his wife lived in the hotel, which meant her asset—and her
lover—would be just an elevator ride away.

Pepper, without any further discussion, approved the move;
he'd arrange to have the rent money paid to Betty each month.
And with that bit of housekeeping swiftly out of the way, it was
Pepper's turn to share his news. He had to spend several months
in Europe, and therefore Betty would be assigned a new handler.
Yet before she could digest this development, Pepper in the same
breath revealed an even greater surprise: her new handler would
be an American. His name was—and Betty, of course, knew this
was a work name—"Mr. Hunter." Then, sounding like a repri-
manding parent, Pepper instructed Betty to remain in her room.
Mr. Hunter, he added as if suddenly realizing an explanation was
necessary, would appear shortly. And then, with only a perfunctory good-bye, Pepper left.

Alone in the hotel room, Betty tried to make sense of what had
just happened. She knew that the Americans, with a good deal of
guidance from Stephenson, had five months before Pearl Harbor
set up their own gung-ho intelligence organization, its name deliberately as bland as the BSC's—Coordinator of Information (COI).

Her reports from the Vichy embassy, she had been told, were routinely passed on to them. But were the Americans also interested in the naval ciphers? Would this mission still be a priority? And "Mr. Hunter," what would he be like? An agent alone in the field, Betty had to be able to turn to her handler with confidence, to call on a mentor's wisdom or, if the situation demanded, a friend's reassurance. In a dangerous business filled with deceptions, her handler was the one person she needed to trust.

A knock on the door interrupted these anxious thoughts. It was Betty's way to make snap judgments, and, always mercurial, dismiss them just as easily. But that afternoon, as soon as she opened the door, her doubts were set permanently to rest. One long, appraising look at Hunter—his real name, Betty would learn in time, was Ellery C. Huntington—and she decided he'd do.

Standing in the doorwell, illuminated by a shaft of light from the hallway, Huntington looked tall, broad, and formidable. He had a commander's presence. In one former life, he had been a star quarterback at Colgate. In another, he'd moved on from Harvard Law School to Wall Street, enjoying a lucrative career dispensing wisdom to corporate clients, many of whom had gotten into particularly sticky jams. And although he was a relatively ancient forty-eight, as soon as America had entered the war he appealed to his squash-playing buddy General William Donovan, the head of COI, for a job. He'd been accepted immediately, just as swiftly given the rank of colonel by the War Department, and then sent for a crash course in the dark arts of espionage at a secret training camp in Virginia, the facility modeled by Donovan after the one the BSC ran deep in the Canadian woods. Now he was chief of the newly established security branch of the COI. Betty was his first asset, and the operational linchpin of his first assignment: the Americans too wanted the Vichy naval ciphers.

In October 1941, two months before Pearl Harbor, Donovan—

once again influenced by Stephenson—had met with the president and presented a bold plan for US spies to infiltrate North Africa. Roosevelt, despite his genuine fondness for cloak-and-dagger missions, hesitated; America was still neutral. But only weeks after the nation committed itself to war, the president, no longer seeing any reason for restraint, gave his approval. Covert operatives infiltrated sandy beachfront towns, ordered to gather intel and prepare sabotage ops in readiness for the moment the Allied invasion of North Africa—soon to be rechristened with the new code name of Torch—got the green light. And in the same week that the BSC asked Betty to obtain the ciphers, Donovan received a similar communiqué from "the highest possible military level": "We have reason to believe they [the Vichy embassy] are handling information for the enemy. We want to be able to read their cables."

Yet as the leaders of America's military and burgeoning espionage establishments began clamoring for the ciphers, one prudent voice counseled for some operational caution. Donald Downes, head of the COI's rough-and-tumble Special Activities branch (a position he'd continued to hold when by presidential directive the COI in June 1942 morphed into the Office of Strategic Services), warned of "the calculated risk" in a mission that blithely targeted the embassy of a still officially neutral nation.

"An embassy is foreign territory," he sternly reminded his masters. "Entering a foreign embassy clandestinely and 'borrowing' code books was full of risk for everyone concerned. . . . If we failed, if someone was caught inside the embassy and talked, an international incident of great moment would result."

But rather than let his cautionary words rein in the operation, Donovan and his counselors came up with a plan designed to give America cover—"plausible deniability" was the spymasters' phrase—if the entire mission came crashing down in scandal. The two Bills huddled—Donovan was universally known as "Big Bill,"

Stephenson as "Little Bill," and they were of such like minds on most things that wags speculated that the Creator no doubt had fashioned the lumbering Irish American first and then used whatever was left to assemble the scrappy Canadian—and they quickly formulized the shared operational scheme. From the shadows, an American would pull the strings, while out in the field, ready to take sole blame if the Vichy security forces caught them in the act, would be the British operative and her asset.

Huntington, who had the lawyer's skill of dancing around troubling facts, gave Betty the big picture without dwelling on the background details. A Tennessee native, he had, despite his years up north for college and then on Wall Street, a soft southern lilt; Betty liked to hear him speak. He made sure that his agent understood that although she had a new handler, her mission had not changed. In fact, he emphasized, her assignment was, if anything, more crucial than ever. As if arguing to a jury, he kept repeating the same summation: she'd now have the noble opportunity to serve the two countries to which she was inextricably tied—Great Britain, the land she had married into, and America, the country of her birth.

Betty listened, but in truth what he said that afternoon was of little consequence. Huntington had her allegiance as soon as he'd entered the room. In his balding, middle-aged way, she confided to Hyde, he reminded her of another military man and lawyer she adored: her father. "I knew right away," she said to Hyde as they sat in the Shelbourne bar, "that I'd follow him anywhere. He had my complete loyalty from the start."

Chapter 46

♦

WITH A RENEWED SENSE OF purpose, Betty returned to Washington. Huntington's briefing was still ringing in her ears, and she was more determined than ever to snatch the ciphers. She decided, for no apparent reason other than it suited her purpose, that Charles had been too pessimistic; there *had* to be a way into the embassy. And on the morning of her first day back, she confidently set off to do reconnaissance.

She had already worked out her fallback in case she drew the attention of the Vichy security guards or, no less an enemy, the FBI. She'd explain that she was on her way to her mother's apartment—the address, conveniently, was just doors away—and the prospect was so troubling that she found herself dawdling. But all the time, of course, she'd be studying the building. Charles had drawn a rough layout of it, and now she'd try to see with her own eyes how the pieces fit. It was with a professional's scrutiny that Betty began to circle around the embassy block.

As she approached from Connecticut Avenue, Betty spotted what had to be, if Charles's sketch was accurate, the code-room windows. They were off to the building's side, and even better, away from the street. The location of the naval attaché's office window, however, was more of a mystery. According to Charles's diagram, it too was on the ground floor. But where it was supposed to be, at the rear of the building, there was now an addition. The only window she saw was high above this new wing, a daunting ten feet off the ground at least. Still, this had to be the attaché's office, where he had his safe. But how would she get up to the window?

Jump? Climb? Either would require a lot more dexterity, Betty suspected, than she could muster.

Continuing her stroll, she discovered a gravel path that stretched back from the street, parallel to the rear addition. It led to a rickety building used, a glance told her, as both a garage and a toolshed. In the dead of night, she wondered, would someone carrying a ladder down the path attract attention? Would it seem plausible that the ladder was being returned to the shed? Would anyone walking down the nighttime street take it into his head to wander down this dead-end path? And if he did, in the pitch-dark would he notice a ladder leaning against the side of the building?

Yet even as she asked herself these questions, part of Betty already knew the answers. Climbing up a ladder into the attaché's office would be, she firmly told herself as she completed her recon and headed toward her mother's apartment, entirely too insecure. Even if she got lucky and no one spotted the ladder, what about the alarms that would undoubtedly start clanging as soon as she jimmied the window? And she still would somehow have to break into the safe. No, there had to be a way that offered a better chance of success and less risk. The operation might have the tacit endorsement of one faction of US military intelligence, but if she was caught climbing in through a foreign embassy's window, the FBI would make sure she spent the rest of the war in an American jail. If, that is, she survived the Vichy security force's interrogation.

Disappointed, Betty concluded that she had to find another plan. Her mind wandered, and as she reminisced over her conversations with Charles, something snagged her attention. He had named the embassy personnel who had access to the ciphers, and now she reviewed this small list once again in her mind. One by one, she summoned up the names, and one by one she swiftly dismissed them. To attempt to persuade any of them to commit an act of treason would, her instincts shouted, lead to disaster. Neither her charms nor a bankroll of cash would be enough. And these were not merciful men.

But as she grappled with this discomfiting fact, a new possibility floated up into her mind. Perhaps there *was* a man who not only had access to the ciphers but also might very well want to help the Allies. Yes, she tried hard to believe, her thoughts spurred on as much by desperation as conviction, he might very well feel he had a good reason to cooperate.

Betty abruptly decided she'd visit her mother some other time. Instead she hurried off to find a telephone. She needed to call Brousse.

"HE IS A BEAR WHO has lived for the past twenty years with his work," a testy Brousse argued as soon as Betty brought up her plan to approach Charles Benoit, the recently retired chief cipher clerk. "He arrives in the chancery, says good morning to no one, and goes straight to the code and cipher rooms." Brousse was nearly pleading. He wanted Betty to understand that this was not only a futile idea; it was a dangerous one. A crusty longtime bureaucrat like Benoit would run straight to the ambassador to report her approach.

But Betty had convinced herself that there was reason to be hopeful. In April, the doddering Marshal Pétain had been shoved up a notch in the Vichy hierarchy to the purely titular position of chief of state. Pierre Laval, a Nazi sympathizer in his heart as well as in his deeds, became the new premier, and life in Vichy France began more closely to resemble life in the Reich. With this ominous shift, five members of the embassy staff resigned; they could not in good faith work for a state, even one run by Frenchmen, complicit in the Nazis' dirty work.

Charles Benoit had been one of these. But although he no longer officially worked at the embassy, he remained the expert who was summoned from time to time to deal with problems in the code room. He still had access. And, with only his recent resignation to support her eager theory, Betty believed she could persuade Benoit to take his moral convictions a step further.

Brousse, however, dismissed this as pure folly. "No arrangements could be made with Benoit," he said decisively. But Betty was adamant, and finally he surrendered. With an audible sigh, he announced that he'd find the clerk's home address; the talk around the embassy was that Benoit had retreated to his downtown Washington garden. In retirement, Benoit was tending roses with the diligence he'd once devoted to the ciphers.

Betty liked the idea of calling on Benoit at his home. Though her arrival would be unexpected, it would still be less threatening than if, for example, she bumped into him on the street and started up a conversation. He'd at least feel in charge, able to control the situation. Always let the target think he's running the show—that was the rule. If Benoit felt reassured, that could only work to her advantage.

But first she had to get past the front door. The next afternoon, taking care to dress primly and turn down her usual dazzle as much as possible, Betty arrived at a snug multifamily house at the end of a shady block on Chesapeake Street. She had rehearsed what she'd say when he opened the door, but the words that earlier in the day seemed dramatic and enticing suddenly struck her as contrived. Floundering, she tried to think of another opening that might convince him to invite a stranger into his home. But no idea came to her. Anyway, she told herself, it was too late to deviate from her script.

"I must speak to you on a matter of grave importance to France," she announced with somber authority in her impeccable French as soon as Benoit opened the door.

He stared at her quizzically for a moment. Then, to Betty's immense relief, he asked madame to please come in.

Benoit led her to a gloomy little room, and he stood at polite attention until his guest took her seat in one of the two armchairs flanking a long sofa. As he settled into his chair, fitting comfortably into its well-worn depths, Betty had a chance to study him. He was a short, elderly man, his round face gray and weary, but he sat with his back straight as a soldier's, giving him a remarkable dignity. Betty at once knew it would be a mistake to offer him money, or to try to charm him. She would stick with her plan.

Small talk would be of little help, she sensed, so she came out with it at once. "I work for American intelligence," she said in French, and unlike the last time she'd said this to Brousse, it now was true.

Benoit looked at her, confused and perplexed, and she took advantage of his bewilderment to continue in her rapid French. "Our desires and aims are the same as yours," she said. "We want you to help France because we know that by doing so you will also be helping the Allied war effort."

He fixed her with a hard, chilly stare.

Betty let the silence continue. She wanted him to ask the inevitable question.

"What do you want me to do?" he finally demanded.

Betty once again did not hesitate or attempt to dance around what she had in mind. If Benoit decided she was being coy, if he felt she was holding something back, he'd end the conversation. So Betty told it to him straight: she wanted his help in obtaining the naval ciphers.

Benoit's face collapsed into a frown of disapproval. And then, overwhelmed, he started to cry. "I am very confused," he pleaded. In just moments, Betty felt, he seemed to have aged a decade, perhaps even two. "I have had no time to think," he went on through his tears. "Everything has happened so quickly."

Betty could not help but feel sorry for him. But at the same time all her training was telling her that Benoit had not turned her down. Her request was still out there, still dangling in the gloomy little room.

So she persisted. "It is in your power to prove how much the traitors in the French Government are helping the Germans. To turn the ciphers over to us would be the greatest service you could perform for your unhappy country."

Once more a thick silence stretched between them, and Betty did not dare puncture it.

"Excuse me, madame, but everything is so confusing. Everything has happened so quickly," he muttered at last. Then he repeated his words as if in a trance. "Everything is so confusing. Everything has happened so quickly."

Betty was ruthless. "Surely your loyalty is to the French people," she attacked. "Not to a government of traitors."

Benoit cradled his gray head in his hands. His agony over the decision he was so desperately trying to make had left him undone.

When he found his words, he spoke not in anger but with despair. "I cannot," he said in a soft, but steady voice. "I have a long record of loyalty to my chiefs. All of them have written me letters. The codes and ciphers have been my responsibility, my personal responsibility. To guard them has been my duty. Loyalty is loyalty." He repeated in his firm whisper, "I cannot."

Betty had the wisdom to concede defeat. She knew nothing she could do or say would convince Benoit to betray his concept of honor. And, to her surprise, she found that part of her couldn't help but admire his resolve. She thanked him for his time and then saw herself to the door.

She had failed. Now she would have to come up with a different ploy. But when she was back in her apartment, picking up the phone to ring Brousse, another, more chilling thought occurred to her: What if Benoit felt it was his duty to inform the ambassador? How long would it be before the FBI—or perhaps the Vichy security thugs—were pounding on her door?

Chapter 47

◆

BUT FEAR, BETTY REPRIMANDED HERSELF, is an indulgence. She would not allow the mission to be further delayed by her dread, or her shame, or her helplessness. She had no control over what Benoit would or would not do; she would push those anxious thoughts aside. What she could do instead, she told herself with pride, was find another way to grab the ciphers. She would rush straight ahead with a new plan.

She chose not to discuss this fresh idea with Brousse; he'd only try to dissuade her. And she also decided not to inform Huntington; she hoped to surprise him, to present him with the ciphers as a grand, totally unexpected present. The time for hesitation, for delicacy, had passed.

Determined, she decided that if she could not persuade Benoit, then she would find a more tractable target. She set her sights on the man who had replaced him as chief cipher officer, Count Jean de la Grandville. She made up her mind to strike the next day.

Long afterward, a more reflective Betty would look back on what she did and acknowledge both her impetuosity and her regret to Hyde. "Too much zeal, perhaps, and it was in my nature to be headstrong," she conceded with sorrow.

COULD TWO MEN CHOSEN FOR the same job have been more different? While Benoit was aged and weary, a plodding by-the-books factotum, young Grandville was another sort entirely. Blessed at birth with a grand family heritage and movie-star looks—with his toothy smile and dark wavy hair, he was often compared to the matinee idol Jean-Pierre Aumont—Grandville had strutted his way through life. Vain, preening, and self-possessed, he had the haughty confidence of a man who has little doubt that the world is his oyster. He was no friend of the Nazis—their fanaticism struck him as unseemly—but unlike Benoit he never felt that serving Laval's regime jeopardized his own sense of honor. Grandville conveniently twisted the facts to suit him. To his way of thinking, it was possible to be both a good Frenchman and loyal to Vichy. In fact, there really was no other choice.

Yet while there appeared to be little likelihood of appealing to the count's shifting patriotism or opportunistic morality, Betty thought she'd found other openings. Two snippets of gossip about Grandville that Brousse had casually passed on had convinced her that he'd be pliable. First, Brousse, with an indulgent laugh, had mentioned that the young count fancied himself a lady's man. And now that his wife had been exiled to the country as she waited to give birth to their second child, Grandville was eagerly taking advantage of his new freedom. Lurid stories about his many liaisons were flying around the embassy.

But that was not all. Exhibiting a genuine sympathy, Brousse had also told Betty that the count was in pretty much the same straits as he was: that is, broke. The Grandville money was firmly tied up in wartime France, and Washington was an expensive city; the count barely got by on a junior secretary's stipend. And the arrival of a new child, Betty slyly presumed, could only make a difficult financial situation worse.

In Betty's mind, then, her next move was clear. If the count could be bedded or bought, she could play this operation out to a successful conclusion; she had mounted reassuringly similar ops time after time, and all had been intelligence triumphs.

That evening Betty picked up the phone, boldly dialed the

count's home number, and, adding a new alias to her growing list, identified herself as Mrs. Elizabeth Branch when he answered. Then, before Grandville had a chance to hang up, she made her pitch.

"I wish to see you most urgently on a matter of interest to you," Betty announced in her faultless French.

It was wartime. He was a diplomat in an increasingly unpopular embassy; the security personnel repeatedly warned the staff to be wary of approaches by enemy agents. But his wife was away, and for once he had nothing planned for the evening. And the mysterious Mrs. Branch had a lovely voice. He could not help wondering what she looked like.

He was alone, he said. If Mrs. Branch would like, she could come over right away.

An hour later Betty was sitting opposite the count in his living room. If Benoit had been there too, he might not have recognized Mrs. Branch as the woman who had appeared at his house the previous day. It wasn't just Betty's attire, although she had purposefully chosen a snug dress that clung to her curves. Nor was it the flowery perfume that floated around her in an aromatic cloud. What had transformed her was the way she presented herself. She looked at Grandville with a new, intense alertness. There was a playful intimacy in her smile, in the ebullient gestures of her hands, in the way she casually sprawled on the sofa. All that had been diminished the night before, tonight was enhanced. With her long legs crossed, her green eyes shimmering, and her naughty, throaty laugh carrying things along, her sensuality filled the room. It was a calculated performance, and an effective one.

She began, though, with an appeal quite similar to the one she had used with Benoit. She was an American agent working in the interests of France, she said. But as she continued, her tone swiftly became more personal, as if she was coaxing a favor from an old and very dear friend, not someone she'd just met. "Why do you remain on the side of Laval instead of joining the cause of freedom? I can sense your true feelings," she said, leaning closer toward him.

"I am a career diplomat," Grandville countered, "and as such am in the habit of taking instructions from my government. I have no choice in the matter."

His tone, though, Betty noted, was more defensive than confrontational. And he had not asked her to leave. So she pressed on. "But in your heart you think France should come first, over and above these considerations."

He nodded mildly, as if he were agreeing. Encouraged, Betty decided to push on. "If you wish to accept this view, then I am in the position to offer you the means of helping your country."

"What exactly do you mean, madame?" Grandville asked, suddenly testy.

Betty realized she had reached the moment when it was everything or nothing. Either slink away or plow forward, knowing that any second the entire operation could blow up in your face. But she felt a heady confidence, certain that what she had to offer would persuade the suave, absurdly handsome egotist sitting smugly across from her to commit treason. As if it were a perfectly natural request, she asked for his help in obtaining the naval ciphers. They would be used, she stressed, against the Nazis and to benefit France. Then, without waiting for a response, she went on with an almost apologetic note in her voice, as if it were bad manners to raise a subject as banal as money. Still, she explained that she'd been authorized to offer "a considerable sum of money if he would perform this patriotic service." A monthly retainer could also be arranged if he were to keep her informed of any changes to the codes.

The count sat motionless in his chair, as if frozen by his thoughts. Finally he stood up and walked over to Betty.

"You are nice," he said, caressing her cheek with his hand. "You enchant me. But you are too young to bother about such serious things. When may I call on you tomorrow?"

"You are nice, too." Betty laughed, trying to keep things steady. But she was on guard: Grandville's manner was disturbing. Was he being impish or calculating? Betty was not sure. Equally confusing, he had not so much dismissed her offer as deflected it. Yet he did want to see her tomorrow.

She continued to flirt, but now with a strategic restraint: "You will only enchant me *if* you bother about serious things! You may call me at the Wardman Park after six o'clock in the evening—but only about serious things!"

An icy March drizzle fell as the count accompanied a wet and shivering Betty back to the hotel. They said their good nights in the lobby, and it was agreed that he'd telephone tomorrow. But in her warm apartment, even after she had toweled her hair dry and changed into wool pajamas, she found that she could not stop shivering. She lay in bed wondering if she had made a terrible miscalculation.

IT WAS AN AMBUSH, AND Betty did not like that at all.

From the start, it had been a tedious day. She left much later than usual for her weekly meet with her BSC handler in New York; Charles had called just as she was about to go to the airport and said he was coming over with something "that would interest our American friends." Then, on the flight back to Washington, a storm suddenly erupted, and her plane was forced to land in Baltimore. She waited impatiently for the next plane to Washington, only to be finally told that all scheduled flights had been cancelled. She had no choice but to take an annoyingly expensive taxi the forty or so miles back to the Wardman Park. It was after nine when, exhausted and bedraggled, Betty walked into the lobby.

And straight into an angry Grandville. He had been waiting for hours, and he was clearly bristling. "I have things to say to you," he bellowed threateningly.

People in the lobby were turning to look at them. Betty did not want to have a discussion with the count in public; for all she knew, FBI agents were watching her at that moment. And she certainly didn't want Brousse to see them together; his jealousy would only make things more problematic. But at the same time she was reluctant to ask the count up to her apartment. It was not just that she was totally spent after the long day. She was scared. Grandville continued to glower at her, his resentment honed to a sharp, intimidating edge.

But she'd have to take her chances with the count. Operational security was the most important concern. Let's go to my apartment, she said quickly. We can talk there.

Upstairs, the count's anger broke loose. He had discovered that Branch was not her real name. He now knew she was Mrs. Elizabeth Pack, the wife of a British diplomat. If she had deceived him about her identity, how could he trust her about anything else? How could he be sure of her?

"How can you be more sure than you already are?" Betty echoed. She had hoped to suggest that his question was absurd, but she knew her response rang hollow; she'd been caught. "You have my word that I am an American agent, and I have made a straightforward proposition to you," she continued with stagy indignation.

Grandville frowned. "I appreciate all that," he said. "But you know intimacy forms a bond like no other. I think there should be this bond between us."

Betty did not want a bond. She wanted the ciphers. Until the count handed over the codes, or at the very least promised that he would deliver them, there was no reason to bed him. It wasn't just her mood; desire had little to do with her reluctance. It was prudent tradecraft: sex is a reward, not an inducement. You pay your asset *after* he delivers, never before. Of course it was a rule she'd broken from time to time. But on those occasions either she was the one doing the manipulating, or the prospect of a bit of frolic had seemed enticing. She saw neither advantage nor pleasure in a dalliance with the count.

"All I am after is the ciphers," she said with what she hoped sounded like resolve. "As for anything else, it is besides the point and means nothing to me."

"It means nothing to you, but it means something to me."

Suddenly the count rose and took Betty in his arms. He kissed her, and when she didn't respond, he kissed her again. Betty thought about pushing him away, but she also feared that she'd be driving off her one chance to obtain the ciphers. She told him to stop, but he kissed her with more passion. His hands moved over her. All her training, all her instincts, told her it would be wrong to let this go any farther. She wanted to fight him off, but she also wanted to keep the operation alive.

Without really thinking about it, she found herself returning his kisses. She told herself she could be either a lady or a spy. She could not be both.

When he led her into the bedroom, she followed obediently, but not willingly.

"I closed my eyes and hoped that this, like so much else that I wanted to do, would be for England," she told Hyde, hoping to convince herself too.

AFTERWARD, MOROSE AND BITTER, BETTY lay wrapped in a tight cocoon of still-warm sheets. In her adventurous life, she had taken lovers for many reasons—for her country, for her pleasure, or simply for the reckless hell of it. But this had been something different.

Something untoward. As Grandville lay on top of her like a conqueror, as he moved inside her with a harsh fury, he had been punishing her. He had no intention of getting the ciphers, she realized. He wanted revenge for the lies she had told him, for her attempt to manipulate him. For the first time in her life she had a feeling of self-disgust, as if she had somehow sinned against her own very broad notion of honor.

Grandville, meanwhile, was getting dressed. The room was strangely quiet. Then suddenly he started to talk, his back to her. He addressed the reflection in the bedroom mirror in front of him; now that he was done, there was no reason to speak to her directly.

He would not cooperate, he told her firmly. He was "torn by doubts." In fact, he continued, he felt it was his duty to inform the ambassador that an American agent had contacted him. That she had asked him to steal the naval ciphers.

Despite her low mood, Betty knew she had to act. She had to steady a situation that was careening out of control. "We need to talk. We should meet again," she suggested, detesting herself.

The count turned to face her. "Yes, I could come by some other evening," he said. "When?" The prospect clearly pleased him.

Betty did not want to set a date. She did not want to go to bed with him again. But it was the only way she could think of to save the mission. Before she could say anything, the phone rang.

Glad for a reprieve, she picked up the receiver.

"I'm coming right over," she heard Brousse say before he quickly hung up.

Chapter 48

◆

BETTY HAD ALWAYS KNOWN HER many deceptions might someday catch up with her, but she'd prepared herself for tragedy, not a French farce. Yet here she was, trying to rush one lover out of her apartment and down the stairs before another lover stepped out of the elevator. Frantically she threw on her clothes, as she pleaded with the count to hurry. She loved Brousse, yet she had matter-of-factly betrayed him. Betty herself had difficulty understanding or condoning what she had done, and she couldn't imagine that Brousse would even try.

To her relief, the count quickly vanished out the apartment door, and Betty convinced herself there was reason to hope the two Frenchmen would not meet in the hallway. When Brousse marched into the apartment a moment later, ignored her offer of a cocktail, and stormed directly to the bedroom, she realized she'd been deluding herself: there had been no logical reason for hope at all. She had no doubt that Brousse and Grandville had met outside her apartment.

Charles shoved the bedroom door open. He stood at the threshold as if not daring to go any farther and stared out at the tangible proof of his suspicions—the unmade bed, the tangle of sheets. It looked to Betty as if he was trying to inhale any lingering scent of their coupling. Suddenly he let out a scream like a wounded animal. And then he came at her.

With one strong, harsh slap, he knocked Betty off her feet. Betty tried to get up, but Brousse would not let her. She lay on the carpet and he bent over her, slapping and punching away in his fury. The sounds he made were terrible and primitive. In a feeble attempt to protect herself, Betty raised her hands, but Brousse knocked them away roughly. He continued to hit her until all his rage finally seeped out of him.

Betty lay prostrate on the floor, in great pain. At last she managed to pull herself to her feet. She staggered to the sofa and fell into the cushions. After a moment, she raised herself up and sat with her head in her hands. Still huffing from his exertions, Brousse stood by the drinks table, pouring a large whisky.

Neither had spoken. It had all raced by so quickly, and now that it was over, what had happened still remained beyond their grasp.

The silence grew until it became impossible.

Brousse began to apologize, but Betty cut him off. She spoke carefully, with the perfect calm of a resigned anger.

"So far as our personal relations are concerned," she said, "you had every right to give me this beating. I shall remember it to the end of my days."

Then she paused to gather her thoughts. It was the end of a long, eventful night, and she needed to make things clear to herself as much as to Brousse. Grandville had not simply taken advantage of her susceptibility. She had let him bed her not on a whim, and certainly not out of desire, but because she was struggling to hold on to her mission. She needed to remind herself of that, as at the same time she wanted the man she loved to understand that there was an operational logic, a morality even, to her betrayal.

"I do not belong to you or anyone else, not even to myself," she explained. "I belong only to the Service."

She let that truth, however uncomfortable for both of them, linger. It was an articulation of her one unshakable article of faith, and she was glad she had said it. When she continued, she spoke with renewed confidence.

"When I promised to get the naval ciphers, I asked for your help. You were not in a position to give it, and I told you that I would work with anyone who could help. You were forewarned, and anything that I have done was in the line of duty."

She concluded with a stony ultimatum: "I respect your *amour-propre* as a man, but if this is going to interfere with me, then we will have to part at once."

She could, if necessary, live without Charles. But she knew she could not survive without the gratification that came from her work, her life in the secret world.

BETTY COULD NOT FACE RETURNING to the bed where she'd just been with Grandville. She told Charles to leave, and then she left too. Her mother was away, and she hoped to find some peace in the quiet of Cora's empty apartment.

But sleep would not come. She lay in the guest bedroom, her restless mind filled with a clutter of doubts, fears, and suspicions. She thought of Stephenson, of Pepper, and of Huntington, and how she'd let all of them down. She thought of the ciphers locked away in a safe just blocks away, still taunting her, still beyond her grasp. She was afraid that Grandville would deliver on his threat. He would run to the ambassador, bellowing that he'd been approached by an American agent. Charles, she glumly predicted, would inevitably be caught up in the investigation, and just as likely the BSC and the Americans would be implicated too. Her rashness would pull everything down. It was all her fault.

When Betty finally dozed, she had a dream. She was climbing a high ladder through a fog up into the naval attaché's office. She slipped easily through the window, located the safe, and it opened immediately to her touch. A flock of white carrier pigeons carried the ciphers away on her command. They flew like a band of angels through the blue heavens and landed peacefully on Stephenson's windowsill in New York.

Her wonderful dream was suddenly interrupted by her mother's maid shaking her awake. Mrs. Pack, you have a visitor, she explained. I tried to tell him you were sleeping, but he would not listen.

Betty rubbed the sleep from her eyes and saw Charles standing at the foot of the bed.

"It's time to come home," he said tenderly.

Not much later they were walking together back to the Wardman Park Hotel. Too much had happened, Brousse realized, for an apology to be sufficient. And, in truth, while he regretted striking Betty, he could not get the torturous knowledge that she had shared her bed with Grandville out of his mind. Still, he also knew he needed to be with Betty: he loved her. Searching for the words that would make things right, he solemnly asked that she please forget everything that had occurred last night. It was the best he could offer.

"That I cannot do," she said. "But I readily forgive you." She loved him too. "You must believe me: I am very sorry I hurt you."

Betty gave him her hand and he took it. Hand in hand, they strolled on toward the hotel.

As they walked, Betty told Brousse about her dream. It was, she was convinced, a sign: there *was* a way to get the ciphers. "I am going to try to work out something," she vowed.

But although she remained determined, a new concern troubled her. "I think that Count Grandville is capable of turning me in to the ambassador. I have a nasty intuition about this. It would be catastrophic if I were to be compromised." Unashamedly she pleaded, "Everything depends on you to get me out of trouble."

Brousse was glad for a chance to begin to make things right. "It is not difficult to outwit an imbecile like Grandville," he said confidently. "I promise you can rely on me."

◆ ◆ ◆

THERE WAS NO PRETENSE OF discussion. From the start it was an interrogation, an inquisition designed to keep Brousse squirming on the rack until he confessed. As soon as he took a seat in Ambassador Henry-Haye's office later that day, the ambassador began growling.

Do you know Mrs. Elizabeth Branch, alias Mrs. Elizabeth Pack? he demanded. Are you aware she is an American intelligence operative? Are you aware she is trying to obtain our ciphers? Has she approached you? Has she mentioned Count de la Grandville to you? Do you know, he asked, at last revealing the climax to which he'd been building, that she approached Grandville? That she offered him a fortune for our ciphers?

Brousse was prepared. He sat back amicably, completely at ease, a man with nothing to hide. He let the angry ambassador rant. Only when Henry-Haye was done did he begin to answer. He spoke without hesitation and without reproach.

Of course he knew Mrs. Pack, he volunteered with genial frankness. They lived in the same hotel, after all. She was an American woman of good family; her people were very well connected. He had seen her at parties from time to time, and she was always in the company of very senior American officials. He knew nothing about her being a spy. But he counseled caution. Given how delicate the embassy's relations were with the Americans, it would be reckless to make accusations to the State Department without sufficient proof. There could be unfortunate repercussions.

Henry-Haye considered this advice, until finally Brousse interrupted his thoughts.

"There is something else, Monsieur Ambassador. If I may speak in total candor."

Of course, Charles, said the ambassador.

A natural actor, Brousse hesitated. When he finally found his

voice, it was as if it was only after a great internal debate. His reluctance was palpable.

"Monsieur Ambassador, it troubles me to tell you that young
Grandville cannot be trusted. He is indiscreet."

The ambassador ordered him to continue.

Grandville has been spreading stories about your relationships
with Mme Picot and Baroness Zuylen, explained Brousse hesi-
tantly, as if embarrassed.

Impossible! insisted Henry-Haye. There are no stories to tell,
he lied.

Brousse quickly agreed. Nevertheless, he felt he had no choice
but to recount all the false tales Grandville was maliciously spreading. He made it clear that each salacious detail he uttered caused
him great personal pain.

"Rumors," the ambassador said stiffly.

Again Brousse agreed emphatically. Still, he was sorry to say, it
did show how inappropriate a person like Grandville was for the
heavy responsibilities that went with running the code room.

Later that afternoon, Grandville was unexpectedly summoned
to the ambassador's office. With a terse authority, Henry-Haye informed the count that he would no longer be serving as chief cipher
officer. In fact, he was banned entirely from entering the code room.

UNKNOWN TO BETTY, HER ILL-CONSIDERED actions had one
further repercussion.

"The youngest of my attachés"—Henry-Haye wrote indig-
nantly to the secretary of state's office—"now in charge of the code
office, Count Jean de la Grandville, has been approached at various
times, by a certain Mrs. Branch, known also under the name of
Elizabeth Pack, who resides at the Wardman Park Hotel and who
has insisted to obtain delivery of the secret codes of this embassy."

But even if Betty had been aware that the US State Department knew of her intrigues, it wouldn't have slowed her down. It wouldn't have mattered to her that the diplomats, although ostensibly on the same side as the OSS, might very well have tried to scuttle what they perceived as an ill-advised espionage operation. It was too late. There was no longer any possibility of her backing away. She was committed to getting the ciphers, and she was prepared to take any risk. The success of the mission would be her vindication.

Chapter 49

◆

TRUST WAS A RARE AND elusive quality in the shadowy world Betty inhabited; yet, paradoxically, it was always at the forefront of every operative's mind. Desk man, case officer, agent in the field—it preoccupied them all. Whom could they put their faith in? Who might be quietly plotting to betray them? It was not a casual speculation: their survival depended on the choices they made.

And now, as the discussion of an Allied invasion of North Africa grew more specific and the mission to steal the Vichy ciphers took on a new urgency, both the British and the American spymasters found themselves agonizing over the same question: Can we trust Charles Brousse?

Their doubts were not provoked by anything Brousse had done; to the contrary, he had delivered product that exceeded their expectations week after week. What worried them, though, was their own deception: Betty had told her asset that she was an American agent, and he was being paid from the coffers of the US Treasury. What would happen if, or just as likely when, he discovered that his paymasters were the detested British, and the theft of the ciphers was a joint British and American operation? Would Brousse walk off in disgust? Or, even worse, in his fury would he help his Vichy cohorts set a trap? Catching the Brits in the act of burgling a foreign embassy, they could imagine him gloating, would be appropriate vengeance for the lies he had been told. Agents routinely sold out friends for greed or ambition; revenge, the spy chiefs knew too well, was an even hotter motivation.

Both Stephenson and Donovan agreed that before the mission went any further, it was necessary to make Brousse fully aware of the operational details. They'd let him hear that he was working for both America and England, and see how he took the news. Before they went behind enemy lines, they needed to know they could trust the asset who'd be leading their agent—and, no less a worry, the two intelligence agencies—into harm's way.

Betty knew what was in store for Brousse, yet without any qualms she once again set up her lover to be blindsided, bringing him along as instructed to meet her contact. If the wise men felt they needed reassurance before things could move forward, then she was on board with that decision too. She would not let this operation fall apart.

The meet was held on neutral ground, in a safe house in Washington rather than Betty's apartment, and Huntington ran the show. There was, by his design, no drama. Instead, in his soft, avuncular southern voice he matter-of-factly let Brousse know the previously undisclosed facts about "our"—he chose the pronoun deliberately; he wanted Brousse to feel he was part of the team— "joint operation." Then he sat back and waited for an outburst of Gallic rage.

There was none. Brousse accepted this reality with a philosophical passivity. A new logic, after all, superseded his old antagonism. A world war was raging; France had been overrun by waves of Nazi invaders; and England, whatever its previous sins, was now formally America's ally in a war to save Europe. He was on the side of any nation fighting the Nazis. And there was something else pushing him to march off to war with the perfidious Brits: the woman he loved was a British agent.

To demonstrate that he was not secretly nursing a grudge over the disingenuous way he'd been treated, when the conversation strayed to the war in the Pacific, Brousse volunteered that he might be able to help. During his vacation in Japan in February 1939, his wife had given him a motion picture camera as a present, and he couldn't put his new toy down. He had shot extensive footage between Shimonoseki and Kobe in the Seto Inland Sea; mostly a banal tourist travelogue, he conceded, but the reels also included a detailed look at all the islands, bays, and inlets. Would the Americans be interested? he asked Huntington.

It was just the sort of intelligence the US Navy needed. To the analysts' greater joy, the films turned out to deliver the genuine goods; "exceedingly interesting," judged the navy in its official report. And in the months ahead the reels would often inform America's naval strategy as its warships advanced toward Japan.

Brousse's generous, well-timed gift firmly put to rest whatever lingering suspicions remained. The cipher mission, both the British and American espionage establishments decreed, could now proceed.

One not insignificant problem, however, remained. There was still no operational plan.

BETTY DIDN'T DARE TELL HUNTINGTON that a dream had inspired her. Even if she left out the part about the flock of carrier pigeons flying off with the code books, she had no doubts about the contempt with which the level-headed lawyer would treat such an admission. Instead, she presented her strategy as if it had been shaped solely by good tradecraft and diligent reconnaissance.

Every attempt so far has failed, she began. And now that the ambassador has been alerted, any pass at embassy staff will be a walk through a minefield; there's no one we dare approach. "We shall have to do it ourselves in a direct manner," Betty concluded definitively.

"What have you got in mind?" Huntington asked.

"Burglary."

"How would you propose going about it?" he asked, still lost.

"The ciphers are kept in a safe in the code room. This is on the first floor, with a window overlooking a small stretch of tree-shaded lawn."

Huntington nodded; she wasn't telling him anything he didn't already know.

Betty's words now spilled out in one breathless speech, as if she hoped that if she talked rapidly enough, the flaws in her plan would go undetected. "If I could find out the combination of the safe, I could get into the office through the windows with the help of a ladder. I could then pass the cipher books out the window to our people and hide inside until they photographed and returned them. On a dark night it would be easy."

"Easy!" Huntington shot back. Facile solutions made him suspicious. And Betty's climbing in through the window seemed "rather crude."

Yet at the same time he also thought Betty was on to something. There was no hope, he agreed, of getting anyone already inside the embassy to play ball. The spies would need to steal the ciphers on their own.

All they had to do was come up with a plan for a perfect crime.

NOW, AS THEY PREPARED TO move forward, they went on operational footing. Code names were assigned: Brousse was B.10; Betty, E.11. And heightened security went into effect.

"I am from the exterminating company," the technician sent from Donovan's shop—a ferret, as he was called in the trade—announced to Betty when she opened her door in the Wardman Park. He was dressed in overalls, scrupulous in his pretense that he was looking for "bugs"—which, in the jargon of his profession, he indeed was. On hands and knees he crawled under the bed, through closets, and behind curtains. He lifted rugs and carpets. He picked up her telephone, looked at the underside of the console, and still not satisfied, unscrewed the receiver and carefully examined the wiring. A couple of hours later, he shared his professional opinion. "Everything is O.K.," he told agent E.11. "You got no bugs."

Convinced that there were no covert microphones in the rooms, Huntington designated the apartment as the mission's tactical headquarters. The next day he brought over seemingly innocuous cardboard boxes packed with equipment—high-speed cameras, lights, and lenses—that could be used to photograph material. Then the practice sessions began. First Betty, then Brousse, went through the strenuous ordeal of learning how to photograph a document. There were, or so it seemed to the two neophytes, dozens of details—the brightness of the camera bulb, distance from the object being photographed, the speed of the film, and on and on—to know. And Huntington was a stern taskmaster. He wanted everything to be perfect. Only when they both could routinely shoot a document with speed and accuracy, when they had "the touch," as he put it, did he put an end to the training sessions.

And throughout these busy, furtive days, recon remained a constant preoccupation. Brousse, his heart racing madly, contrived a thin excuse to spend an afternoon in the embassy file room. Huntington had given him specific instructions on what to look for, but it wasn't easy; there was little method or rationale to the way documents had been filed. His hunt required great patience, and as the minutes passed, he kept imagining that a vengeful Grandville or one of the security thugs would come bursting through the door and demand to know just what he was doing.

Despite his fears, he kept at it until he located everything Huntington had requested: floor plans of the embassy, the precise layouts of the code room and naval attaché's office, and the purchase invoice that revealed the make and model of the attaché's safe. He hastily shoved the documents into his briefcase and, all the time feeling as if he were carrying a ticking bomb in his shaky hands, walked out of the embassy. He delivered them to Betty's apartment, where, now an expert, she photographed them. Late that same afternoon Brousse was back in the file room, the documents were replaced, and his world at once looked a lot less gloomy.

But Huntington, still trying to come up with a feasible plan, needed more intel. And so he sent Brousse on another mission. There was secret agent B.10 calling on the naval attaché in his office. Brousse had worked out a cover story to explain his rare visit, some rigmarole about French ships the Allies had interred, and to keep it convincing he kept his earnest questions going for a while. But suddenly, and with great annoyance, he interrupted the conversation to complain that the office was hot as a steam bath. Indeed, beads of sweat were rolling down his face convincingly, but they were more from his nerves than the heat. Then, before the attaché could beat him to it, Brousse jumped from his chair and strode to the window. As he raised the sash, he was filing away valuable information: there was no lock or latch on the window, and no alarm went off when it opened. Moments later he brought the conversation to a rather abrupt end, thanked the confused attaché for his time, and hurried off to tell Huntington what he'd learned.

Betty, meanwhile, was active too. On one of her weekly trips to New York Huntington brought a visitor to her hotel room, a short, balding man with a happy smile fixed on his face. He enthusiastically pumped Betty's hand as if they had just concluded a very profitable business arrangement, and at the same time her handler introduced his guest as "The Georgia Cracker." He was a professional thief, Huntington explained.

He told Betty she'd be working with the Cracker—later she'd discover he was Canadian; the only time he'd spent in Georgia was in prison, before Donovan arranged his pardon—and Huntington wanted them to get to know each other. And so they talked. Betty was, as always, charming, and the Cracker was confident. He had seen the purchase invoice for the safe, and he was certain it wouldn't be a challenge. "It's a Mosler with a click-click com lock, probably four wheels," Betty would always remember him saying, his broad grin still on his face. "I reckon I can crack it in about fifty-five minutes."

Huntington, though, still wasn't prepared to give the green light. The thought of both Betty and the Cracker climbing up a ladder in the middle of the night and then jimmying open a window left him uneasy. We need to find a better way into the embassy, he told them firmly. Disheartened, Betty tried to argue, but quickly realized it would do no good. The Cracker, simply glad to be out of jail, didn't say a word. His eager smile never faded.

Although disappointed, Betty didn't give up. Searching for inspiration, she made a point of walking by the embassy when she was on her way to her mother's in the evening or heading home at the end of a day. She had no notion what she was looking for, yet she'd fix her gaze on the building with the intensity of an artist staring at a blank canvas. That was how she came to meet the night watchman.

Whenever she passed, she'd call out a friendly "Bonne nuit," and he took to waving back at the pretty woman. One evening he approached and introduced himself; his name, Betty learned, was André Chevalier. Quickly pulling an alias from her long list, she said she was "Miss Elizabeth Thomas."

Now that they'd met, Betty would from time to time bring him a coffee or a container of hot soup. It was a gesture inspired by good tradecraft rather than kindness; Betty thought it might come in handy to have an ostensible reason for wandering around the embassy grounds at night. The watchman could assure any suspicious FBI agent—the G-men remained determined to lock up any foreign agents working in neutral America—or Vichy security officer that Miss Thomas was his friend.

With a burst of professional pride, she told Brousse about her cultivation of the watchman. He agreed; it made sense. But even after he left Betty and returned to his own apartment in the hotel, he found that her new friendship with Chevalier remained on his mind. He wasn't sure why; he certainly wasn't jealous. But it kept intruding. Even as he wished it would go away and let him sleep, he lay in bed wide awake, still thinking.

And then he had it.

It was after midnight, but he didn't hesitate. He tiptoed into the living room so he wouldn't wake his sleeping wife and picked up the phone. "Tell the American," he announced in a mysterious whisper to Betty, "we must see him right away. I have an idea."

IT WAS AN IDEA, HUNTINGTON would later say with both admiration and wonder, only a Frenchman could have conceived. But at first he only found himself growing annoyed as Brousse rolled it out with a showman's flair—slow, deliberate, and archly dramatic.

What if, Brousse began as the three of them met in Betty's apartment, he was to confide to Chevalier that Miss Thomas was his girlfriend?

A good cover story was built on reality, and Betty, Huntington reasoned, would have little problem passing herself off as Brousse's paramour. Go on, he ordered, cautiously intrigued.

And what if, Brousse continued, he was to complain to the watchman that he had no discreet place to take his lover? She lived with her parents, and he had a wife.

Huntington wasn't sure where this was going, but he'd heard nothing so far he could object to. Chevalier would know Brousse was married. And anyone who lived in Washington was aware that the wartime city's hotels were overcrowded; rooms by the day were impossible to come by.

And what if, Brousse asked, triumphantly removing the final veil, he appealed to Chevalier, one Frenchman to another, to allow him to bring Miss Thomas to his office at night so they'd have a place to be alone?

Huntington gave it some thought, his lawyer's mind looking at the idea from all angles and trying to find a flaw.

But Brousse continued. What true Frenchman would not want to help *l'amour* along? And as further inducement, he'd offer the watchman some money for his troubles. They'd have access to the embassy at night. The rest would be easy.

Once again, Huntington doubted anything about this op would be "easy." And while he could find a few dozen flaws in the plan and even more uncertainties, he also knew the clock was rapidly ticking. The date for the North African invasion had not yet been set, but he suspected it would be soon. Getting the ciphers was crucial.

"Okay," he agreed at last. "It's worth a try."

ROUTINE, WENT THE MAXIM, WAS a friend to any operation. The more things seemed to be moving along as usual, the greater the chance for any mission's success. And so Betty and Brousse conscientiously went to work establishing a routine with the watchman.

Early in June Brousse made his pitch to Chevalier. A handful of dollars was hastily exchanged, and the bemused watchman announced that he'd be glad to make the nighttime embassy available for their trysts.

The two of them began arriving arm in arm every night. They would settle into Brousse's office or, looking for variety, move to one of the two ground-floor salons, where there was a comfortable divan. And the sounds of their passion would echo through the halls of the dark, deserted embassy. The clamor reinforced their cover, and happily no acting was necessary. Chevalier began to look forward to their visits; they lightened the monotony of his long, dreary shift.

It was three weeks after they had begun their trysts at the embassy that Huntington called Betty and uttered the code word for a flash meeting. She arrived not knowing what to expect, but was only too glad to hear his news: the night for the burglary had been set.

It would be in three days, on June 19, a day chosen, Huntington explained, because it coincided with Winston Churchill's arrival in Washington. The FBI would be preoccupied, and the Vichy security force would not be expecting anything to occur that might derail the talks between the prime minister and the president. But what he didn't share with Betty was his knowledge that one purpose of this conference would be to select a date for the invasion of North Africa. The secrets the codes would unlock were suddenly vital.

He ended the briefing with a frank, lawyerly warning. "You must know the rules. If anything goes wrong, don't involve us. You and the Georgia Cracker may be picked up and even go to jail for a while, but that's all in the game. From now on, you're on your own."

"Good luck," he concluded gallantly, but the words seemed discouragingly hollow to Betty's ears.

Chapter 50

◆

W HEN THE CAB LEFT THE Wardman Park on that June
night, the sky was already ominously dark, and in the
course of the short ride to the embassy a hard rain had
begun to fall. The Georgia Cracker was at the wheel, and Betty
and Brousse sat in the back. Two bottles of champagne were cradled in the Frenchman's arms. Betty had two doses of Nembutal
in her purse—one for the watchman, and another for his Alsatian
dog.

"Wait for us," Brousse instructed the driver when the taxi pulled
to a stop on Wyoming Avenue. He spoke loudly, hoping that anyone lurking in the shadows would hear. Then, hand in hand, the
two lovers ran through the rain and up the embassy steps. Brousse
rang the bell.

"As soon as Chevalier opens the door," Huntington had told
them in his usual anxious way, "show him the champagne. Let him
know you're celebrating, and you want him to join in. Everything
depends on that."

Brousse greeted the watchman as if he were an old friend and
delivered the lines from Huntington's carefully written script: It's
the anniversary of the day Miss Thomas and I met, and we hope,
André, that you'll be kind enough to join us in a celebratory toast.
Out of habit rather than for any covert reason, Brousse had selected
the vintage with some consideration. He'd normally have treated
the champagne with more respect, but tonight he raised the two
bottles high and shook them like billy clubs to get the watchman's
attention.

Chevalier said he would be delighted. He suggested they share a toast in the privacy of his basement office—precisely what the spies had hoped he'd say. A good deal depended on the watchman not wanting to get caught with a drink in his hand while on duty.

Downstairs in the small, stuffy room, Brousse twisted the cork from one bottle, gaily making a production out of the effort. At the same time, Betty went down the hall to the water cooler to find three paper cups. She passed the big Alsatian lying stretched by his water bowl, and the dog jumped to his feet and began barking menacingly. Chevalier quieted him with a brusque command, but that didn't give her much comfort. The dog was a terror.

Betty returned and arranged the paper cups in a row on a table across the room. She took the open bottle from Brousse and began to fill them, one at a time.

It's important, Huntington had said, to establish the etiquette early on. Let the watchman see that Betty's the one pouring the wine. When she'd first heard the instructions, that had seemed reasonable enough. Only now her hand was shaking as if she suffered from palsy. She feared she'd splash more on the table than in the cups.

She managed to fill the cups, and brought them over to the two men.

Brousse made his toast. Though Betty smiled brightly at her lover as he spoke, she didn't hear a word. Her mind was focused on what she'd have to do next. This had been the dry run. Everything that followed would be what really mattered.

As soon as the cups were drained, Betty announced that it was her turn to make a toast. She wanted to thank M. Chevalier for all his kindness.

Even if the watchman was reluctant to have another drink, Huntington had correctly predicted, he couldn't turn down a toast in his honor.

Betty returned to the table. She checked to make sure Brousse had positioned himself in front of the watchman. He had; it wasn't much of a screen, but it would have to do.

"Don't hesitate," Huntington had warned. "Make your move and keep on going." Which Betty now decided was the stupidest thing she'd ever heard. How would she be able to do anything if her hands were paralyzed? It wasn't her fault that she'd been suddenly stricken by some immobilizing disease. Certainly Huntington would understand.

But all at once she'd recovered, and to her own amazement, she was opening her purse. She reached in and grabbed one of the tiny vials filled with Nembutal. Then she stopped. The champagne first, she remembered Huntington saying. She filled the cup; checked once again to see that Charles had Chevalier locked in conversation; and then she emptied the powder into the wine.

There might be a few grains of undissolved powder in the liquid, Huntington had explained. But no one would notice unless he was looking for something. And if the watchman was on the alert, then it would already be too late. At the briefing Betty had not found her handler's candor very reassuring, but now this memory left her at a complete loss. She was shaking. Never had she had it this bad.

Trying not to stare at the faint traces of the drug floating in the champagne, she handed the cup to Chevalier.

She'd prepared a short toast, but the words she'd rehearsed had vanished. Still she managed something, and then the cups were again raised.

Betty watched as Chevalier gulped it all down. Had he tasted the drug? Was he suspicious? She imagined him reaching for the revolver in his shoulder holster. She could hear him shouting the command for the Alsatian to attack. But Chevalier merely continued beaming at the couple with a paternal affection. Betty at last gratefully drained her cup too. Never, she told herself, had she needed a drink so badly.

Then they waited. It was a celebration, and naturalness was the foundation of good cover. "Act like you're having fun," Huntington had said, and Betty now realized that *act* was the operative word.

As instructed, Betty was the first to leave. With a demure tactfulness, she explained that she wanted to go upstairs to freshen up. As she walked out to the hall, she paused to pet the Alsatian. But instead, making sure to keep her back to the watchman, she dropped the powder into the dog's water bowl.

Dogs have a different metabolism than humans, Huntington had explained. A much larger dose will be required. So Betty had prepared herself: it would take a few moments to empty all the drug into the Alsatian's bowl. But she had not anticipated the noise it would make. The powder pelted the water like a driving rainstorm. She was certain Chevalier would rush over to investigate. But when she was done, she looked back and saw that Charles and the watchman were laughing heartily at some small joke.

Upstairs, Betty once again waited. She tried not to, but she could not help checking her watch. What was taking so long? Had Donovan's medical team miscalculated the dosages? Or maybe Nembutal was not even the correct drug. Dozens of unsettling thoughts ran through her mind. And it kept growing later.

Charles finally appeared and announced that Chevalier was asleep.

And the dog? Betty feared the big Alsatian more than the armed watchman.

Charles assured her that he was dozing like a puppy.

STANDING AT THE EMBASSY DOOR, Betty clicked the flashlight on and quickly off again. She waited a moment, and then repeated the signal.

The Cracker left the taxi and hurried up the embassy steps.

Betty led him to the door protecting the code room. Brousse waited in the front salon; he was the babysitter. His job was to keep the watchman occupied if he awoke earlier than expected, or, if someone else showed up, to sound the alarm. If he couldn't keep anyone from heading to the code room and discovering what Betty was up to, he had his fallback prepared. He'd be the shocked lover, the man who'd been played for a fool by his mistress, the secret agent.

The lock on the code room door seemed formidable, a big steel device. But the Cracker impressed Betty by dealing with it handily. He unscrewed the bolts holding the lock in place, and then gently extracted it from the door. When he turned the handle, the door opened.

The way to the naval attaché's office was a complicated maze in the darkness, but Betty had studied the floor plans. She guided them forward without delay. Minutes later the Cracker was seated on the floor in front of the attaché's safe.

The Cracker studied the safe and then complained that it was older than he'd been led to believe. It could take a while to open.

Taking command, Betty urged him to get started. This was not the time for misgivings, and anyway they'd know soon enough if there was a problem.

In the pitch-dark room, she aimed her flashlight at the dial. Suddenly a cone of light illuminated the circle of numbers.

"Write this down," the Cracker ordered. He read off the number where the dial had been set; he would need to return to that position before they left. Then he went to work.

With a stethoscope dangling from his neck, the instrument's bell pressed against the steel safe, the rubber earpieces in his ears, he patiently turned the dial, listening for the sound of the tumblers falling into place. What he heard confirmed his initial instinct; this could take some time. The tumblers of old safes glide rather than click sharply, and these were quite worn.

Betty watched in complete silence; she knew better than to disturb him. She did her best to hold the flashlight steady, but it soon felt like a dead weight in her hand.

"Four left five," the Cracker called out after a while.

Betty wrote it down.

The next setting came more quickly: "Three right twenty."

Suddenly there was a noise. Someone was coming! But it was only Brousse, checking to see how things were proceeding. "Get back!" she snapped at him brusquely, and he immediately retreated. She felt ashamed of her rudeness, but he had scared her, and worse, he had left his post.

"Two left ninety-five."

The one good thing about having to keep the flashlight steady, Betty told herself, was that she couldn't raise her hand to read her watch. Still, she didn't need to know the exact time to realize that it was getting late. Very late.

"One right two."

And an eternity later, a triumphant whisper: "Now I've got it."

The Mosler door swung open, the flashlight illuminating the cipher books on its shelves. The prize was within her grasp.

But Betty's triumph was short-lived: when she looked at her watch, she saw that it was after 2:00 a.m. The code book would need to travel to the Wardman Park, be photographed page by page, and then returned—all before the watchman woke from his drugged sleep or the morning cleaning crew arrived, just before dawn. Huntington had warned that the ciphers must be back in the safe and the two agents on their way home by 4:00 a.m. Any later, and they'd run the risk of being discovered.

Betty took a moment to think. Should she take the chance, try to get the codes photographed and the mission completed in less than two hours? Perhaps the Nembutal would remain effective for longer than had been promised. Perhaps the cleaning crew might not arrive precisely on time. It would be close, but if she was daring, maybe she'd succeed.

But if the cipher books were not returned to the safe, or if she was discovered, or if there was no time to put things back as they were and someone became suspicious, then all would be lost. The codes would be changed, and this time they would be placed under armed guard. Everything risked and nothing accomplished. And she would never get another chance.

She instructed the Cracker to close the safe.

Yet no sooner had Betty given the order than she told him to stop. She reached into the safe and ran her fingertips across the cover of each book. It was a lover's caress. And it was also a silent promise: she would return to hold them in her hands. At last she slammed the safe shut.

"Let's get out of here," she told the Cracker.

"TELL THEM FROM ME THAT I never in my life laid eyes or fingers on such tantalizing reading material," she told the Cracker as the taxi pulled up in front of the Wardman Park. As had been planned, he'd leave the taxi at the airport and then catch the next flight back to New York. When he made his report, Betty wanted to make sure the deskmen understood how close she had come. She had touched them! They had almost been hers!

Up in her apartment, both she and Brousse found sleep impossible. It wasn't simply that the dangerous night had left them too energized, although that was surely part of the reason for their restlessness. But Betty was also bereft; she felt she'd let the Service down.

Brousse, though, was now anxiously running through all the

things that could still go wrong. The watchman would wake up with a tremendous headache and realize he'd been drugged. Someone might notice that the code room lock had been tampered with. The naval attaché would go to his safe and decide things just didn't look right. As the litany of fears flooded his mind, he tried to prepare himself for each one. He pictured himself arriving at work. Suddenly two security goons would be at his side, pinning his arms behind his back and dragging him off to a brutal interrogation. How much could he endure before he revealed that Betty was in on it too?

At eight o' clock he decided he'd return to his apartment, shower, and dress in a clean suit. He told Betty he'd go off to work as usual, but he'd meet her back at her apartment at noon to let her know the mood at the embassy. He didn't bother to tell her that if he didn't return, she'd very likely never see him again, and she'd better vanish at once. He realized there was no point in articulating what they both understood only too well.

As soon as Brousse was out the door, Betty picked up the telephone and started to dial. Pepper had recently returned from his mysterious trip to London, and she decided to appeal to him rather than Huntington. Johnny had been running her longer. He knew her better. He'd have more confidence in her ability—or so she desperately hoped.

I want another chance, she told Pepper when he answered. She explained that since she now had the safe's combination, the rest of the op would proceed swiftly. She wanted to go back in that night.

Pepper said he needed to think about this. He'd get back to her. Just wait by the phone, he instructed.

By "think about this," Betty knew he meant that he had to talk to Stephenson. And that Stephenson would undoubtedly confer with Donovan. And Donovan would ask Huntington what he thought.

Betty had no idea how long these discussions would take. Yet she had no choice; she had to wait. Still, that didn't make things easier.

She sat across from the telephone staring at it, wishing for it to ring.

Three long hours passed before Pepper called back.

You can't go tonight, he declared as soon as Betty got on the line. She started to protest, but Pepper cut her short. The feeling is that tonight will be too soon, he said. You must be exhausted, and you'll need your wits about you. It'd be better to get some rest, to regroup, before the next attempt.

Betty insisted that she was fine. She didn't need any rest.

I predicted you'd say that, Pepper said. But what about Brousse?

Betty suddenly realized she had forgotten about him. All that had mattered was her getting another chance at the ciphers.

But before she could think of anything to say, Pepper continued on. "It's a go for tomorrow night," he said. "June twenty-first."

Betty began to thank Pepper, but again he interrupted her. There's something else, he said. The Cracker won't be coming along this time. One more unauthorized person inside the embassy only increases the risks. You and Brousse get caught—maybe you can talk your way out of it. But the Cracker wouldn't have a chance. Anyway, now you know the combination. You can open the safe. Correct? he challenged.

Betty agreed. She could handle the safe. This time there would be no problems, she reiterated. But once she hung up the phone, she worried that Charles might not share her confidence. In fact, he might not even be willing to make another attempt. Then she looked at her watch and saw the time. It was past noon, and Charles had not returned. She found herself wondering if she should start packing.

She waited, as she knew she would. The operation had been rescheduled. She couldn't run.

When Brousse finally arrived, he brought, he said excitedly, "good news." Everything at the embassy was as usual—no security alert; no naval attaché shouting that his safe had been opened; even the watchman had greeted him with a jolly "Bonjour" and a conspiratorial wink. They had gotten away with it, an elated Brousse told Betty.

Betty decided she would take advantage of his ebullient mood to share her news: they would be going back in to steal the ciphers the next night.

Impossible! he boomed. They'd never get away with drugging the watchman again. He'd suspect something. Besides, how would they persuade him to join them for a drink? It would seem far too much of a coincidence, ludicrous even, for them to bring in champagne to celebrate another occasion so soon. Or, he said with irony, perhaps Betty intended to explain to Chevalier that she'd been mistaken about the date of their anniversary, that they'd celebrated it two days too soon.

Patiently, Betty let him rant. When he'd finished, she told him that she agreed; they could not risk drugging the watchman again. This time they would wait until Chevalier finished his rounds and retired to his basement office to sleep. It was, she said, the only way.

"That's all very fine," said Brousse. "But supposing he appears while you are in the code room."

"Tell him that I am in the toilet. Then, if he has the indecency to look for me there, he will find me back with you on the divan in the hallway, be ashamed of himself, and go away."

Brousse considered. It might work: if Chevalier came upstairs, he'd send him off to look in the restroom while Betty scampered out of the attaché's office. But something else now troubled him. The longer we wait for the watchman to settle in for the night, he challenged, the less time the Cracker will have.

Betty had known all along she would need to tell him; now was as good a time as any. The Cracker won't be joining us this time, she said.

Then who—

Betty cut him off. She'd open the safe. She had the combination; it would be simple.

Brousse erupted, offering a dismal litany of all the things that could go wrong. Betty had to listen to him, he pleaded. She had to heed his warnings before it was too late.

Once again Betty had the wisdom not to try to rein him in. She let him vent—and when he was done, she went to work.

Betty played all her cards. She dismissed the dangers. She reminded him that they'd already had "a dress rehearsal." With great and sincere eloquence, she spoke of his "patriotic duty," how France needed his help in its time of need. And shrewdly, she saved her most persuasive argument for last. "I'm counting on you," she pleaded to her lover.

In the end, Brousse could not summon the will to resist. He agreed to return to the embassy the next night.

It had been difficult enough the first time, when Betty had not fully anticipated the torrents of fear that would flood through her when she entered the embassy. But this evening it was impossible to delude herself into believing there wasn't anything to worry about.

She arrived hand in hand with Charles after midnight, trying to lose herself in her role as his charming, besotted companion. Chevalier greeted them in the front hall, and this evening he had his Alsatian with him. Betty ad-libbed, saying what a splendid animal he was, and that only encouraged the watchman. As proud as any parent, he went on and on about the dog, its pedigree, its rigorous police training. "One never knows," the watchman speculated, when the dog would be called on to attack an intruder. Betty listened with, she'd remember, a smile glued to her face, all the time trying not to imagine the ferocious animal's sharp teeth sinking into her arm.

At last Chevalier, full of a coy familiarity that Betty, she complained to Hyde, found unseemly, said the couple had not, of course, come to talk to him. He would retire downstairs to his office and give them some privacy.

The two spies sat on the hall divan and waited. They did not embrace; in truth, the thought never occurred to them. They simply stared at the ornate clock on the marble mantel. When a half hour had passed, Betty announced that she had waited long enough. The watchman had to be asleep.

While Brousse kept guard in the hallway, she made her way to the code room. As efficiently as the Cracker, she removed the lock on the office door. It swung open at her touch.

Once inside the attaché's office, she took the slip of paper with the combination from her purse and went to work.

She spun the dial attentively, making sure she landed on the settings the Cracker had detected. It took only a few moments to reach the final stop. Eagerly, she pulled the handle.

It would not budge.

She decided she must have misread one of the settings she'd written down two nights before. Confidently, she spun the dial again, this time even more careful to land on all the correct numbers. She was certain that when she pulled the handle, the old Mosler would now swing open.

It didn't.

She tried again and again, spinning the dial through the correct combinations time after time. It was tedious, and frustrating, and completely humiliating, but she couldn't get the safe to open.

After each attempt, she'd tug at the handle, but the door would not move. The only thing she could do was keep trying. But then it grew too late.

She returned to the front hall and, her voice breaking with despair, told Brousse they had to go.

He looked at her, perplexed.

"The damned thing won't open!" she moaned.

Chapter 51

◆

BLINDFOLDED, TRAPPED IN A WORLD of darkness, Betty heard the crash of waves breaking and the rush of water lapping against the beach, the sounds magnified in her ears. But her concentration was broken as a harsh voice ordered, "Again!" Obediently she pushed everything else out of her mind and reached out. Her fingers touched cold steel. With infinite gentleness, she slowly twisted the unseen dial of the safe.

It was the day after her second aborted mission, and it was unfolding as a day full of surprises. It had begun with a crash meeting with Pepper at his Manhattan apartment on East Fifty-Seventh Street. He'd cut off Betty's agonized apology in midsentence. "Don't worry," he said. "I understand the article you are dealing with is very temperamental and is apt to behave unpredictably." It was just what Betty'd wanted to hear, even though she still felt incredibly stupid to have made such a mess of things. Yet before she could thank him for this small kindness, Pepper abruptly announced that they had to go.

The cab drove downtown, but Pepper still had not told Betty where they were heading. Betty considering asking, but she assumed he had his reasons for all this mystery, and anyway she'd know soon enough.

On lower Broadway, not too far from the southern tip of Manhattan, Pepper ordered the driver to pull over. Then he turned to Betty. "Hop into that black car standing by the curbside." He pointed to a roadster parked at the corner. "And come back to the apartment before you catch the Washington plane."

Betty crossed the street and got into the front seat of the black car. The intrigue was making her nervy, and she was ready to bark at the driver, demanding to know just what was going on. But when she turned toward him, she saw that it was the Georgia Cracker.

"I've never been so glad to see anyone in my life," she said with genuine emotion; the lingering disappointment over her failure had left her devastated and vulnerable. "How I wish you had been with me last night."

The Cracker wore his habitual smile, and his words were also cheery. "I don't like that piece of junk myself. Why do you suppose they don't get themselves a new one?"

Betty made a joke about French thrift. It was a small remark and not a particularly witty one, but for the first time in days she felt like laughing. Since the decision was made to enter the embassy, she had lived with an unremitting tension, and her two failed missions had only made things worse. Her nerves were badly frayed, but sitting next to this capable man with his perpetual smile, she felt as if she might be able to escape all her doubts for a while.

As they headed out of the city, Betty, more exhausted than she realized, fell asleep. The Cracker drove in silence, glancing admiringly from time to time at the brave woman sitting next to him. At that moment, he'd later confide to his BSC bosses, he felt very protective of her, and wanted to do all he could to help.

When the car stopped, Betty awoke. As she opened her eyes, she felt as if she was still caught up in a dream. They were parked on an empty beach. The waves were crashing. The sand was smooth. And the sky was wonderfully blue and bright.

The Cracker saw her bewilderment and explained that they were on Long Island, a place called Jones Beach. He got out of the car and Betty, still mystified, followed. She wondered where they were going.

But they weren't going anywhere. The Cracker swiftly removed the roadster's back seats revealing what he had hidden on the floor—a safe. Betty stared at it, and recognized that it was her nemesis: a Mosler identical to the one she'd failed to open.

He ordered Betty to get into the back of the car. "Now," he instructed, "do exactly what you did the other night—and I mean exactly."

She spun the combination, and at once he began shouting with great indignation. No! No! he chastised. You need to take your time, "feel" the dial, listen to the tumblers falling before you proceed to the next setting.

And with that, her tutelage began. She lay uncomfortably curled on the hard floor of the car, the smell of the ocean in her nostrils, the summer sun beating down, willing her mind to shut out everything but the dial of the safe. She soon lost track of time. Everything faded away but the hard voice of the Cracker pushing her on, keeping her at it until she had the "feel." Then, when he finally announced that he was satisfied, he blindfolded her.

In the darkness, the combination numbers she had memorized were irrelevant. She had only her touch to guide her. It was a very tactile, oddly sensual exercise. Her long fingers expertly twisted the steel dial back and forth until it felt satisfyingly right. She had the gift; it did not take her long to master this thief's trick.

"You want a job," the impressed Cracker told her, "you can be my assistant."

When, late in the afternoon of that same long day, they returned to Pepper's apartment, the Cracker assured Pepper that Betty didn't need him anymore. She could open the safe on her own.

Good, agreed Pepper. It's settled: the mission is on for tomorrow night.

But for the first time in her operational life, Betty refused. She would not go back into the embassy without the Cracker.

She had not changed her mind about the mission. She still passionately wanted to get the ciphers. And her reluctance wasn't a case of nerves, although the prospect of furtively breaking into the attaché's office a *third* time was utter hell. It was two other realizations that forced her to dig in her heels.

First, this would be her last chance. It would be foolhardy to count on the watchman's good-natured indulgence any longer. He was bound to grow suspicious—if he hadn't already. If she didn't land the ciphers this go-round, it would be too dangerous to try again.

And second, there was Charles. She had called on all her wiles to persuade him to go back into the embassy for a second attempt. It would be a struggle, and far from a sure thing, to convince him to return for a third shot at the prize. But even if she could somehow manage—Charles did love her, after all—Betty knew he'd balk if the Cracker wasn't along to unlock the safe.

Pepper didn't like it. If the Cracker was caught, he'd eventually be tied to the BSC. The last thing he—and Stephenson, as well as, for that matter, Churchill—wanted was a scandal involving British spies in America. Still, Betty was adamant, and the good case officer always lets the agent in the field be king (or, he silently corrected himself, in this case, queen); the agent taking the risks decides the safest course. Pepper was still not enthusiastic, but he ultimately agreed. The Cracker would handle the safe.

Later on the night of that same seemingly never-ending day, Betty was back in Washington, meeting with both Huntington and Brousse. On the plane ride from New York she'd rehearsed her arguments, but she never had to use them. When Huntington, who had spoken earlier with both Pepper and Donovan, announced to Brousse that there would be "one final attempt" tomorrow night, the Frenchman greeted the news with stoic dignity. In the last war he had flown many perilous missions; it was as if he thought it would be inappropriate, shameful, and demeaning to refuse the American colonel's order. He merely nodded in acquiescence.

Then Brousse turned to Betty. "Never a dull moment with you," he teased. "I am probably the only man alive who spends both his days and his nights at his office in order to satisfy his lady love."

IT WAS SHORTLY AFTER MIDNIGHT on a warm, starry twenty-fourth of June when the two lovers walked from the Wardman Park toward the embassy. The Washington streets were empty and quiet at this hour, and the only sound in the night was the staccato click of Betty's high-heeled shoes against the concrete sidewalk. But as soon as they turned the corner of Connecticut Avenue, Betty decided that things were not right.

A car was parked down the block from the embassy. Its lights and engine were off, but there were two people in the front seat. In the darkness, it was impossible to distinguish anything other than vague outlines. Lovers, Betty tried to believe. But if they were, they had chosen an odd spot for their date, particularly when the more secluded tree-lined roads of Rock Creek Park were nearby. And as she continued, she saw another car parked across the street. More lovers? What were the odds of that? Now she was certain. She knew, as any agent about to go into enemy territory would know, that it was a trap.

The passengers in the two parked cars must be FBI agents, she whispered to Charles. As soon as we have the ciphers, they'll swoop down. Nothing would make the G-men happier than catching a pair of BSC agents in the act.

Brousse argued that this was an American operation, too. But Betty dismissed that quickly. Hoover would love to embarrass the OSS.

"What do you want to do?" Brousse asked gravely.

Betty took a quick look at the two parked cars, and then at the front door of the embassy just yards away. "Let's proceed," she said uneasily.

Brousse used his key to open the embassy door; this might convince the FBI teams in the cars, if in fact that was who they were, that he was a diplomat authorized to enter the building.

But once they were inside, Betty grew even more certain that they had walked into a trap.

There was no sign of the watchman or his dog. That was very unusual. Chevalier must have heard them enter; they had deliberately not lowered their voices, keeping up a pretense of gay chatter, and had made a point of walking noisily to the divan in the front hall salon. He normally would have come to investigate or, if he recognized their voices, simply to exchange pleasantries. And what about the dog? The Alsatian should've begun barking as soon as they'd opened the door. The silence was unnerving.

They sat on the divan and waited. Perhaps Chevalier was busy or in some distant part of the building. Could he possibly not have heard them? But the longer they waited, the longer the sounds of their merry, contrived conversation filled the empty embassy and the watchman still did not appear, the more Betty grew convinced that he was part of the plot. The plan, she decided, was for Chevalier to burst in after she opened the safe. He'd signal the FBI agents, and then they'd come charging through the door and catch her with the code books in her hands.

Her mind was racing. She had to do something, or the mission would end in disaster. And she had to do it *now*.

Suddenly she jumped up from the divan and began pulling her dress over her head. She tossed it on to the floor.

Brousse stared at her with astonishment.

Now she had wriggled out of her silk slip. She hurled it away, and it landed next to the discarded dress.

"Have you gone mad?" Charles asked, anxious and confused.

She continued to undress, pulling down her stockings. "I don't think so," she said as the nylons were added to the pile on the floor. "But we shall see."

"Suppose someone should come in!" Brousse pleaded. "What are you thinking?"

"I am thinking just that," Betty answered as she unhooked her brassiere. "Suppose someone *does* come in!"

She pulled down her panties, and with one foot gracefully kicked them toward the rest of the clothes.

She stood naked except for the strand of pearls around her neck. She held herself easily and confidently. She had no modesty, no inhibition.

Now that she had undressed, she explained her strategy more fully to Charles. "What are we here for?" she demanded rhetorically. "We are here to make love. Yes? All right. Who makes love with clothes on if they can be taken off?"

He still did not understand, so Betty tried to clarify things further. "I am not suggesting that we actually make love, God help us, only that we give the impression. If you wish to help me, you will get up and start undressing yourself too!"

Her voice was sharp. She needed him to understand that every moment mattered. If her instincts were correct, Brousse would have to hurry.

Brousse still had not grasped Betty's plan, but he trusted her. He took off his jacket, undid his tie, and removed his shirt. He was unfastening his belt when the door opened.

A bright cone of light scanned the room, coming to a sudden halt when it focused on Betty. The light held steady, illuminating her nakedness.

"Oh là-là," said Betty in a voice more playful than shocked. She tried to cover herself with her hands, but her modesty was halfhearted and careless. She wanted the watchman to get a good long look. Whatever suspicions had been brewing in him, it was important that he now understood the couple had entered the embassy with only one thing on their feverish minds.

"I beg your pardon a thousand times, madame," muttered the watchman uneasily as he finally extinguished the flashlight. "I thought . . . didn't rightly know . . ." Flustered, he hurried off, closing the door behind him.

Betty waited a moment to let her eyes grow accustomed to the darkness. Then, a peal of triumph in her voice, she told Charles, "There *was* method in my madness."

IT WAS ALMOST LIKE HER dream. There was the ladder leaning against the windowsill, but now it was the Cracker who was climbing in.

As soon as she'd been convinced that the embarrassed watchman had fled to his basement office, Betty had put on her slip—nothing more; she wanted to be able to undress in a hurry if he reappeared—and made her way to the code room. She removed the lock and followed the now-familiar path to the attaché's office. The window opened easily, and she pointed her flashlight out into the darkness. One short burst. Then another. And minutes later the Cracker was standing next to her.

The safe opened on the Cracker's first try.

She looked inside and saw the two code books. "Thank you," was all she could say. She spoke to the Cracker, but she was also offering her gratitude to all the gods watching over her from their operational heaven.

The books firmly in one hand, the Cracker scurried down the ladder, and Betty watched him disappear into the night. One of Donovan's men hurried to remove the ladder, pausing only to flash Betty a thumbs-up, before he too vanished.

And then the waiting began.

According to Huntington's plan, it would take three hours for the books to be photographed; a lab had been set up in apartment 215B at the Wardman Park, and a team of specialists was standing by. By 4:00 am—no later, he promised—they'd be delivered to the front door of the embassy; so close to dawn, that'd be more secure than using the ladder. Then Betty would return the volumes to the safe. But for now all she could do was wait.

Betty smoked one cigarette after another. She stared out the window, and when she thought she saw a shape in the bushes, she tried to believe it was an OSS babysitter and not an FBI agent getting ready to sandbag the code books before they could be returned to the safe. Hearing the watchman's radio playing downstairs, she tried to lose herself in the music. But when it stopped shortly after two, she couldn't make up her mind whether this was a reason to relax, a sign that Chevalier was going to sleep, or if he'd turned it off because the embassy security thugs would now be crashing through the door. She even considered making love to Charles; at least it would help fill the time, distract her from looking at the clock. But in the end, all she did was wait. And wait.

Then it was 4:00 a.m.; the sun would soon rise. She had dressed, and now she stood by the front door waiting for the OSS operative to deliver the two volumes. She searched the street. There was no sign of the two cars that had been parked when she'd entered the embassy a lifetime ago. That gave her some encouragement. But then she began to wonder if the G-men had departed only to carry out a raid on the team in the Wardman Park. She had no answers, only anxieties.

It grew later, the thin daylight strengthening. Soon, Betty knew, the cleaners would arrive, and then there would be no chance to replace the ciphers. If the books weren't back in the safe—if, in fact, there were any reasons for suspicion—the Vichy admirals would immediately order that the codes be changed. And then the two books would be worthless, as irrelevant as yesterday's discarded newspapers.

At 4:30 Betty asked Charles if they should leave. If something had gone wrong, they would accomplish nothing by remaining in the embassy. They should flee before they were arrested. If they stayed clear of the Wardman Park, the OSS would put them up in a safe house, she suggested. Brousse listened, but said nothing. He knew she was talking without conviction; she was simply trying to keep herself occupied. He knew she would never leave.

Ten minutes later Betty saw a man hurrying up the embassy steps, the books clutched under his arm. He handed them to her without a word, and she softly closed the door. It was crucial not to wake the watchman. They had come so far, but everything still could be lost. She rushed back to the attaché's office, the prize clutched tightly in her hands.

Betty was about to put the books back into the safe when she hesitated. Spontaneously, she held one of the volumes up to her lips and kissed it. She repeated the gesture, pressing her lips quickly against the other book. It was a solemn moment, the gratifying fulfillment of a promise she had made. Carefully she laid the books on their proper shelves, making sure they were facing the same way as when they'd been removed. Then she closed the safe.

It was just after 5:00 a.m. when Betty and Brousse, hand in hand, lovers in love with each other and the world, walked down the embassy steps.

When they arrived at the Wardman Park, they did not think about going to sleep. There was something they had to do first. Betty knocked on the door of apartment 215B.

To her surprise, Paul Fairly, the naval intelligence agent who had helped engineer her recruitment, and a man who had once been her lover, opened the door. Yet the coincidence provoked not a stir in Betty's heart; her partings were always resolutely final.

Fairly welcomed them with great ceremony. They had, he exulted, pulled off quite a coup. Then he explained his presence: he was in charge of the photographic team.

The small apartment was packed with equipment—lights, cameras, tripods, and a mess of cables. Technicians and operatives were busily roaming about. And drying on tables, on the cushions of chairs, and down the length of the sofa, spread across the carpet in orderly rows, everywhere Betty looked, it seemed—were the photographs of the ciphers.

She had done it. They had the codes.

She stared at the pages, unable to speak.

Her thoughts were interrupted by a tap on her shoulder. Betty turned, and for a moment didn't recognize the man standing in front of her. Then she realized it was Huntington, now wearing a US Army colonel's summer uniform. She had previously only seen him in his spy's mufti of suit and tie, but in honor of their victory, he felt he should abandon his disguise.

He too seemed overwhelmed by the moment, unable to find anything to say that expressed the magnitude of all that he was feeling. At last he announced rather helplessly, "Colonel Ellery Huntington is at your command."

Betty answered instinctively. "And I am at yours, sir."

They both laughed with embarrassment, realizing how formal their words sounded. But the sentiment was heartfelt, a pledge between loyal comrades-in-arms.

And then John Pepper appeared. He had come down from New York so that he could personally deliver a copy of the ciphers to Stephenson. "Good work," he said officiously. "You are a credit to us all."

Betty did not answer. She stood there mutely, as if at attention,

swelling with the powerful pride that came with the knowledge
that she had accomplished something of great importance.

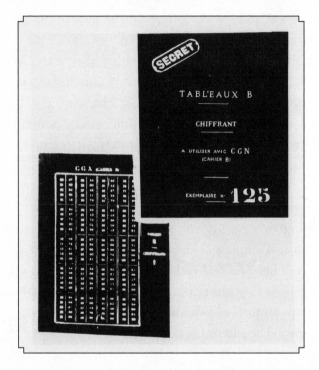

The cover and an interior page from the Vichy Naval Cipher
Book, which Betty stole from the Embassy in 1942.

TWO DAYS LATER THE CIPHERS were in the hands of the wranglers at Bletchley Park. They quickly put them to good use: they
were the missing pieces of a complicated puzzle that in time would
help the Enigma team decipher the entire Vichy code system. And
while the cryptologists labored in England, the OSS immediately
employed the code books to unlock Vichy naval communications
throughout the world. Vichy messages to the German high com-

mand, to their diplomatic missions throughout the western hemisphere, to their warships at Toulon, Casablanca, and Alexandria—all were read by American intelligence hours after they had been dispatched. The Vichy intercepts—as the thousands of collected messages became known to the busy wranglers—were a trove of classified secrets.

But arguably the stolen ciphers' greatest operational use was in the days leading up to and during the invasion of North Africa. Cloak-and-dagger teams of undercover OSS operatives took up their positions behind enemy lines before the first assaults, aware of what the Vichy forces knew—and, just as valuable, didn't know—about Allied operations. Thirty-three thousand Allied troops landed on the beaches east and west of Algiers, guided by intelligence gleaned from Vichy's top-secret messages. Allied bombers and warships pounded the French fleet at Casablanca and the coastal batteries with devastating accuracy, in large measure because the attacks' planners could read enemy communications. American soldiers poured down from the dusty hills of Saint Cloud to drive nine thousand French defenders out of Oran in a bold assault that would have been much more difficult without the codes. The entire Allied force, in fact, charged into North Africa fortified by the reassuring strategic knowledge that the Vichy government and the French intelligence service had no idea of the impending invasion.

A grim year earlier the Axis forces, seemingly unstoppable, had been advancing on all fronts. But after the exhilarating success of the North African invasion, as Churchill would write, "There was, for the first time in the war, a real lifting of spirits."

"Now this is not the end. It is not even the beginning of the end, but it is, perhaps, the end of the beginning," he told the House of Commons. In North Africa the course of the war had dramatically changed.

And what role had Betty played in these events?

Not quite five months after the night when Betty stood naked in the parlor of the Vichy embassy and opened the naval attaché's window to the Georgia Cracker, she found herself sitting next to Huntington on a train heading to New York.

The newspapers that week, in early November 1942, had been filled with jubilant dispatches from North Africa. Huntington picked up his copy of the *Washington Post* and handed it to Betty solemnly, as if bestowing a medal. She glanced at the paper, and then back at him, perplexed. So he explained.

"American and British troops have landed in North Africa, and have met with practically no enemy resistance," he said. "The reason there has been no resistance is a military secret. But I think that you should know that it is due to your ciphers. They have changed the whole course of the war."

Chapter 52

◆

BETTY WANTED A NEW POSTING. She still had the Vichy
op going; Brousse was delivering product regularly, and
she continued to bring it to her handlers in New York; but
her operational heart was set on a European assignment. And she
figured now, in the heady aftermath of her coup with the ciphers,
was the time to get it. With espionage chiefs in London and Washington singing her praises, Betty believed this would be as good
a moment as any, maybe better in fact, to renew her request to be
sent into occupied France.

There was also a tactical reason spurring her on. She needed to
get out of Washington. The FBI was closing in. Betty was convinced the Bureau had tapped her phone; she could hear a telltale
echo whenever she picked up the receiver. Their watchers, too, had
grown increasingly aggressive. She couldn't leave her apartment
without spotting the somber men in fedoras. And it wasn't just the
paranoia that creeps up on a spy stirring these suspicions. Her FBI
file—Bureau No. 65-43539—grew thicker each day with new and
often perplexed reports:

"Confidential information has just been received that Mrs. Pack
is now using the name of Mrs. Powers"; "The Military Intelligence
Division is presently conducting an investigation on MRS. PACK . . .
and has a plainclothesman staying at the hotel in connection with her
present activity"; "She has moved to a room [at the Wardman Park]
other than formerly occupied and is now living under an assumed
name"; "very well dressed and well groomed and . . . well educated";
"It appears there is something fishy about the whole matter."

Betty, of course, had not read the Bureau's dogged surveillance reports, but after her agitated sister Jane called to complain that two men had asked questions about her, she felt the persecution had gone on long enough. Weren't they all on the same side, fighting the same enemy? Furious, she telephoned the FBI's Washington field office, introduced herself, and snapped that if they had any questions, she'd be glad to answer them. She would be at her mother's apartment at ten the next morning. I'm sure you can find the address, she said with an icy sarcasm, and then hung up.

The next morning two special agents drank coffee from Cora's china cups and listened with astonishment to Betty's carefully expurgated story. Her mood had now steadied, and it was with her customary charm that she revealed a small corner of her professional life. She explained that she was a British agent attached to the Office of Strategic Services and provided the G-men with the names and telephone numbers of high-ranking officials who could confirm this improbable assertion. "I am working in America's interest just as you are," she concluded, confident that her candor would put an end to the Bureau's unnecessary harassment.

Betty was wrong. In her naïveté, she did not understand the petty jealousies and institutional antagonisms swirling around wartime Washington. Hoover, who before America's entry into the war had treated Stephenson as a comrade, now viewed him and his BSC operatives as foreign agents illegally usurping the Bureau's charter. "Does J. Edgar think he's fighting on Bunker Hill against us Redcoats or hasn't he heard of Pearl Harbor?" an exasperated BSC official complained after a testy meeting with the FBI chieftain. And Big Bill was no better than Little Bill in Hoover's envious eyes. Donovan was another enemy, another specious claimant to the intelligence throne that should be his alone.

Hoover's hostility toward these competitors—which, deep in his angry soul, was precisely how he viewed both Stephenson and

Donovan—was reinforced by the State Department. "Why should anybody have a spy system in the United States?" challenged Adolf Berle, assistant secretary of state, as the BSC activities grew more aggressive. And the OSS, although authorized by the president, was no less an irritant to the pin-striped suits at Foggy Bottom. "One of the most important things to be controlled is Donovan," a senior State Department official fumed. "He is into everybody's business, knows no bounds of jurisdiction, tries to fill the shoes of each agency charged with the responsibility for a war activity."

Caught up in this raging internecine political war, intelligence fiefdoms battling each other for ascendancy, Betty didn't have a chance. She remained a casualty, a hapless victim of collateral damage. Her earnest—and ill-advised, her superiors admonished—confession to the FBI had no effect on the Bureau's surveillance. Her telephone still echoed, the stolid watchers still lurked in the shadows. She grew convinced that she might very well wind up in a federal jail, convicted under the uncomfortably broad statutes of the Espionage Act of spying for a foreign power. She needed to hightail it out of Washington. Her chances for survival behind enemy lines in a shooting war, she told herself, might actually be better than if she stayed here much longer; and even if that was a bit of an exaggeration, she was certain she'd have a better time. With renewed determination, Betty intensified her lobbying for an overseas posting.

STEPHENSON WAS NOT ONLY WILLING but had a plan. He contacted Donovan and laid it out to his fellow spymaster. He wanted to send Betty to England, give her a short course in radio while at the same time brushing up her small-arms and hand-to-hand combat techniques, and then parachute her into France to work with the Resistance. Behind the lines, with her faultless French and her wiles, she'd be just the sort of daring and accomplished agent the OSS Special Operations could use.

Donovan agreed—but after giving it some additional thought, he told Stephenson he had another idea. On her own Betty would undoubtedly be a valuable asset, he conceded. However, Betty and Brousse working *together* in France would be even better. His R and A—research and analysis—boys had gone through the files, and he excitedly shared what they had found.

Brousse had unique access to the upper echelons of both the Vichy authorities and the Nazi occupational forces. In the south, his family's chain of newspapers gave him widespread contacts in business and politics, and, in another stroke of luck, he had a network of reporters on the family payroll to do the digging if the Allies needed specific operational information. He had also lived in Paris for thirty-eight very social years; he knew nearly everyone who mattered in the city, and those he didn't know, it wouldn't be hard for him to meet. His pedigree was impeccable: his father had served in parliament, and twice been minister of finance. And not least, his loyalty to Vichy and the Nazis could not be questioned. While other diplomats had resigned, he had, despite a reduction in pay, continued to serve the Pétain-Laval government. The grateful Vichy leadership would enthusiastically welcome Brousse upon his return home.

With worldly Betty at his side, with all her charm, all her cunning, all her daring, Brousse could accomplish great things. As a team they could uncover important secrets, provide incalculable support for the inevitable Allied invasion. They'd be agents-in-place in the enemy's well-protected citadels, spies who could saunter through the corridors of power. It would be an unprecedented intelligence coup for the Allies.

Stephenson agreed, but he couldn't help pointing out one not very small problem: Betty needed a bulletproof cover. Brousse's return to France would seem plausible enough, but how would he explain Betty's presence at his side? It was well known, of course, that Brousse was married; however, that was not what was troubling Stephenson. A mistress would not, in itself, raise any eyebrows; despite the Nazis, some things would never change in France. But Brousse arriving hand in hand in wartime with an American mistress, who was married to a British diplomat to boot—that would set off alarms. The Gestapo would immediately put Betty under the microscope, and their surveillance would undoubtedly be a lot more intensive than the FBI's. Could Betty withstand such scrupulous scrutiny while at the same time functioning as a spy?

Possibly, Stephenson suggested without enthusiasm. But in the end both spymasters glumly agreed it would be a long shot. With so much at stake, it was not a gamble they could prudently take— unless Betty was protected by a more imaginative biography, a history that hid her American roots and her British husband.

The discussion then turned to an evaluation of Betty's French. Just how good was it? It was one thing to be fluent, but that did not guarantee that Betty could pass as a Frenchwoman. And even if she could, they'd still need to invent a convincing explanation for how she'd met Brousse and how she'd happened to find herself in America. But since this was the most promising pretext they could come up with, the OSS Special Operations (SO) unit was asked to concoct such a cover story.

Working out of their E Street offices on Washington's Naval Hill, a stone's throw from the Lincoln Monument, the SO strategists racked their brains, and when they still weren't satisfied they brought the inventive R and A eggheads into the discussions. Several busy weeks passed. By the time they threw up their hands in frustration, they had invented over a dozen detailed legends, as cover biographies were known in the profession. Yet when each of these histories was held up to the light of intense analysis, holes became apparent. Each seemed more transparent than the next. The Gestapo would swiftly rip apart Betty's legend, and then they'd gleefully get to work on her.

It was at this low point, just when the general feeling was that it might be wiser to dust off the original plan, to insert Betty into France as a solo operative, that an idea popped up. In all the subsequent excitement, the identity of its originator was lost; in time both the SO and R and A units would claim credit. But regardless of the source, it was universally agreed that it'd been inspired by a casual, rather mean-spirited observation: Betty was young enough to be the old goat Brousse's daughter.

When the catty laughter stopped, the operational significance of the barb began to sink in, and they hurried off to search the files. The confirmation they were hoping for was there, more or less: Brousse was fifty, and Betty almost thirty-two. Chronologically, it would be a stretch, and a long one at that, for Brousse to have fathered a daughter in his late teens. But, as was quickly pointed out, Betty didn't look thirty-two. She had the trim, athletic figure and smooth skin of someone much younger. She could easily pass for a woman in her mid-twenties. And now the math came out right: Brousse could indeed have a twenty-five-year-old daughter.

Encouraged, they scurried back to the files and found real gold. Brousse's wife Kay had been married before—several times, actually. When wed to Shaw Waterbury, she had given birth in 1913 to a daughter, Catherine. And in a genuine stroke of luck, the kind that every successful op needs, the burrowers learned that Catherine Waterbury had died as a child. If she had lived, she'd have been twenty-eight. And Brousse's stepdaughter. Now that, they cheered, was certainly a role Betty could convincingly play.

Betty had recently been assigned a new OSS handler, Donald Downes, a well-connected Yalie who had knocked around the Balkans and the Middle East for naval intelligence before the war and was now moving up fast in the hierarchy; Huntington had been sent off to North Africa to direct a network of penetration teams. It was Downes's job—ironically, a year earlier he'd been the loudest voice against Betty burglarizing the Vichy embassy—to run this scenario past Betty. When he did, she jumped at it. She asked no questions. Betty simply made it clear she'd do whatever was asked, and more, for that matter, to get an assignment in occupied France.

Next, with a chorus of conflicting feelings singing in his head, Downes girded himself for his meeting with Brousse. Yet to his credit, it was with an impressively impassive face that Downes informed the Frenchman that he'd need to pretend that the woman with whom he was head-over-heels in love was his stepdaughter. And by the way, simply as a matter of operational security, Downes continued with rigid self-control, Brousse would also need to convince his wife that the glamorous woman playing their child was an American secret agent and not his mistress. When he had finished, Downes happily pretended that the scenario made perfect sense. It's just a matter of careful tradecraft, he said, of making sure you act with fatherly restraint in public with your stepdaughter.

"Tradecraft," Brousse echoed back, indignant. He saw things differently. He had to ask his wife to let an American agent assume the identity of her dead child; and at the same time conceal from her the fact that this woman pretending to be her daughter was actually his mistress. He wouldn't do it. He couldn't approach his wife, and even if he found the nerve, Kay would never go along with anyone posing as her beloved and deeply mourned daughter. The entire scheme, he flatly declared, was "impossible."

Downes tried to argue, but his heart was not in it. He knew how absurd it sounded. He had run his share of ops in his time, but this one was an impossibly long shot. It was tough to convince Brousse of its feasibility when he could hardly convince himself.

But Betty had more arguments, and more resources, at her disposal than any OSS man, no matter how many years he'd spent slinking around the world orchestrating sinister plots. She went to work on Brousse, and after one night together he grudgingly agreed "to think about it." After their next night together, he went off to speak to Kay.

Brousse had already been authorized to reveal to his wife that he'd been working as a US agent; the hope was that, since Kay was an American, she'd take comfort from the fact that her husband was not the Nazi stooge he pretended to be. And when she expressed joy and relief at this turn of events, the plan was for him promptly to roll out everything else—the entire scheme to infiltrate an American agent into France as his stepdaughter. Then, if Kay seemed intrigued, he could bring her too into the operational loop; that is, offer her the role of a subagent in the "family" network. Which would mean, he grumbled to himself, his wife would be taking orders from his mistress.

But it was wartime, and Betty was urging him on, and so he worked up the nerve to make his pitch to Kay. And just like that, she came on board. To Brousse's total surprise, she had no qualms about her daughter's name being used. And as for the prospect of becoming a spy, she immediately decided that was precisely the jolt her boring life needed; she'd even accompany Brousse to France if necessary. Brousse listened with a stunned bewilderment, yet finally found the presence of mind to praise Kay for her patriotism. And, more importantly, he found the discipline not to imagine what would happen if Kay ever discovered that the woman from whom she was taking orders was sleeping with her husband.

Once Kay was conscious, as they say in the trade, the operation picked up steam. A key plot point in the legend the OSS was concocting was that Catherine had been living in California with her husband, but he'd just died; that would explain why the Brousses'

Washington friends had never met her, and why she'd suddenly returned to her mother's home. To sell this story—and it would need to pass muster not just at DC cocktail parties but also for the Gestapo—they needed a name, a real name, of someone recently deceased, a man about Catherine's age who'd been living across the country. The R and A burrowers went back to digging, and once again they unearthed a rich vein: Lieutenant John Gordon, US Navy, thirty-two, a resident of northern California, had been a recent combat casualty. The SO forgers quickly produced a slew of genuine-looking documents—wedding license, passport, driver's license—that identified Betty as "Mrs. Catherine Waterbury Gordon."

Now the rest would be up to Betty, the new war widow.

IT CAUSED BETTY GENUINE PAIN, but she had her wonderful blond hair cut short and then styled into a simple, severe cut. When Downes was still not satisfied, she gave in and had it colored a dark, leathery shade of brown. The finishing touch was a pair of horn-rimmed glasses. "I wore no make-up, a simple black dress and made myself look as plain as possible," she told Hyde, as if still amazed at her sacrifice.

But the mousy disguise served two important and, at the same time, complementary purposes. It reinforced the legend that she was in mourning, still laid low by her husband's sudden death. And, of no less operational significance if this mission was not to blow up in their faces, it established Betty in Kay's eyes as a drab and rather pathetic young thing, all the glamor and fun long ago squeezed out of her. She was certainly not the sort of female to whom her husband, despite his notorious womanizing, would ever be attracted.

As further cover, Catherine Gordon rented an apartment

across town at the Roosevelt Hotel. Her brother-in-law, who owned the hotel, was too discreet to ask any questions. He simply found Betty a suite of rooms and apparently kept his thoughts about her new name and look to himself. At the same time, Mrs. Pack, also known to the staff as Miss Thomas, kept her place at the Wardman Park.

The Brousses did their part too. They took Catherine in tow, shepherding her around town and introducing their daughter to their wide circle of friends and acquaintances. Each new cocktail or dinner party filled Betty's handlers with trepidation; it seemed very likely that someone would notice that the sullen young widow had a striking resemblance to the vivacious Betty Pack. But no one ever did. And the reviews for the trio's performances were consistently raves: That poor young girl, so terribly sad. And yet what a comfort it must be to have such a caring mother and such a doting stepfather.

Brousse, in the meantime, had efficiently worked things out with Henry-Haye. He complained to the ambassador that he could no longer afford to live on his diplomatic pittance. He and his wife would be returning to France, and since she was at odds and ends, taking his grieving stepdaughter with him. Henry-Haye was solicitous; he understood Brousse's predicament and thanked him for his faithful service. As for the decision to bring Mrs. Gordon along, that only further demonstrated, the ambassador observed with admiration, just how loyal and honorable a man Brousse was.

Everything, then, appeared set to plant this family of spies in France. Betty was excitedly counting the days when she'd be an ocean away from a city full of people who knew her, and she could safely shed her lackluster disguise, morphing out of her chrysalis into the resplendent butterfly she'd been in a previous incarnation. But just as Stephenson and Donovan were congratulating themselves, just as they were anticipating the intelligence rewards they would soon reap, events intervened that decisively put the operation on hold.

And the irony was not lost on the two frustrated spymasters that it was the Allies' possession of the Vichy ciphers—Betty's great triumph—that was responsible, in many large ways, for this mission's falling so precipitously apart.

Chapter 53

◆

I N THE FIRST GRAY LIGHT of dawn on November 8, 1942, as US warships steamed close to the shore of North Africa and tense troops huddled on deck waiting to storm the beaches, the distinctive patrician voice of President Franklin Roosevelt suddenly blared over the public address system.

"We've come among you solely to destroy your enemies and not to harm you," the president informed the surprised inhabitants of the Vichy-controlled territories about to be invaded. "Do not obstruct, I beg of you, this great purpose." In a hesitant French he concluded, "Vive la France éternelle."

But the president's imploring words did not persuade many of the 120,000 Vichy soldiers pledged to defend North Africa to throw down their arms. And as German divisions moved in to bolster the besieged French positions, Pierre Laval realized he could no longer maintain any pretense that his government was not totally aligned with the Reich. He promptly broke off Vichy's diplomatic relations with the United States.

In retaliation, Secretary of State Cordell Hull brusquely announced that he had "sent Henry-Haye back his passports." The Vichy diplomatic corps would no longer be welcome in the United States. And Roosevelt, in a radio address the next day, made sure the nation understood how contemptible the Vichy crowd were. "Laval is evidently speaking the language prescribed by Hitler," the president said scornfully.

Yet the more the US officials castigated the Vichy diplomats, the louder their promises to roll up the welcome mat, the more

Betty felt like rejoicing. The punishment a stern secretary of state was dishing out—expulsion from America—was precisely what she wanted. It would provide even better cover than the earlier tale the OSS had dreamed up. Brousse's suddenly taking it upon himself to return to France would've worked. But now, with the fresh imprint of Uncle Sam's boot on his bottom, he'd get a hero's welcome when he returned—and have a hero's access to power. Best of all, it would undoubtedly speed things up. She imagined it'd only be days before Hull's minions rounded up the senior embassy staff, shoved them onto a boat, and with good riddance sent them off to France. And there she'd be, the mournful stepdaughter standing by her parents' side at the liner's railing as America faded into the horizon. It would all be happening very soon.

Brousse, the seasoned diplomat, however, saw things differently. He warned Betty that the successful invasion would have further repercussions. And he was right. With the Allies entrenched in North Africa, Germany needed to shore up its southern flank. On November 10, waves of gray-uniformed Nazi infantry marched as if on parade into Vichy France and announced they were taking control.

One immediate consequence of this sudden occupation was that the members of the American diplomatic mission were now stranded behind the lines in enemy territory. And the vengeful Nazis made it clear they were in no hurry to send them home. According to their realpolitik, in a world at war, diplomatic immunity offered only a tin shield at best. The Americans were rounded up, interned in Lille, and treated more like captured prisoners of war than accredited representatives of a foreign power who happened to get caught in the wrong place at the wrong time.

By the end of the week there was no longer any talk from Hull or anyone else at the State Department about swiftly giving the Vichy diplomats the boot. Rather, these Frenchmen had become valuable bargaining chips. Not a single Vichy diplomat would be allowed to leave the United States, the State Department announced, until a deal for an exchange—our emissaries for yours—had been worked out between the two governments.

At a hastily arranged meeting held at Catherine Gordon's apartment in the Roosevelt, Downes counseled patience. Six months at the most, he promised, and the exchange would be concluded. Cover intact, you'll be operating in France. Brousse, who knew only too well how even the simplest of diplomatic negotiations could wind laboriously on and on, was less optimistic. But his misgivings were nothing compared to Betty's. She was devastated. And now when she moped about as the doleful Mrs. Gordon, there was no need to act.

PERCHED ON A GREEN HILL above Pennsylvania's Lebanon Valley, the Hotel Hershey was, millionaire candy maker Milton Hershey proclaimed, his "proudest achievement." He ruled the seemingly feudal town of Hershey as magisterially as any lord, and when at the height of the Great Depression the idea popped into his head that a hotel should be built to house visitors to his domain, he handed his architect a postcard of a cozy, thirty-room Mediterranean seaside resort. "I want this," he demanded. He got something much grander—a hundred and seventy rooms, tall towers anchoring each flank, a cupola sitting like a crown on the massive roof, and a gurgling interior fountain as well as stables, lush gardens, and a nine-hole golf course, all surrounded by acres of woods crisscrossed with riding trails.

When the State Department began hunting for a place to store the entourage, three hundred or so strong, of Vichy diplomats and their families until the time came to show them the door, the Hotel Hershey was high on the list. It had, the Foggy Bottom search committee decided, a lot going for it. The hotel was not the sort of pricey big-city establishment that would infuriate the taxpayers who'd be picking up the tab; a cyclone fence could be erected around its distant boundaries and guards discreetly posted so that the internees would not feel like they were captives in a prison; and (in what turned out to be spurious logic) the comfortable accommodations would persuade Vichy to treat the interned Americans with similar consideration. There was also something else: the Hotel Hershey was one of the few places in the country willing to open its doors to the vilified French families. "I shall be very happy to have these people as our guests," Joseph Glasser, the hotel's general manager, assured "my dear Mr. Secretary" in an effusive letter just days after he was approached by the State Department.

There was no need for much additional negotiation. The US government swiftly agreed that the taxpayers would pay the hotel $7.50 a day for each adult, and $4.00 daily for each child and the thirty-eight guards. The price included both room and meals; alcohol was prohibited.

The restriction infuriated Henry-Haye. It was an unnecessary cruelty to deprive his staff of wine with their meals, he said. State, however, held firm, more or less: the Vichy oenophiles could order from the hotel's extensive wine cellar, but they would have to reach into their own pockets for any bottle that caught their fancy.

Nevertheless, even with access to the hotel's cave, Brousse didn't want to go. He didn't want to leave Betty, and he didn't want to postpone his mission to France.

Now it was Downes's turn to lay down the law. Finally losing his temper, he found the steely voice he'd used in a previous life to send his overseas assets off on dicey missions. Everything depended on Brousse traveling with the rest of the senior embassy staff to Hershey, he snapped. All the credibility Brousse had earned by refusing to resign would be squandered if he and his wife evaded internment. Here was an opportunity to reinforce his cover.

Downes had spent time in the perilous Balkans, and from this hard-won knowledge he reiterated the wisdom every agent in the field took to heart: operational security is always a wise investment. Six months spent at Hershey, he said, will pay dividends when you're in Paris and some Gestapo thug is giving your dossier the once-over. You'll be congratulating yourself for not having been impetuous, and me for stopping you.

But once Brousse had finally resigned himself to spending six tedious months at Hershey with his wife at his side, Betty demanded that she go too. Her argument made sense: Catherine Gordon would also benefit from being carted off by the vengeful Americans; when she arrived in France, her internment would be a badge of honor. What made less operational sense, Downes realized, was the possibility that Ambassador Henry-Haye, who Betty had interviewed two years earlier, might after seeing her day after day begin to wonder why Mrs. Gordon looked so familiar. Another cause for concern: Betty, Brousse, and his wife stuck in a hotel for months on end seemed like a ménage à trois destined for an unhappy ending.

Downes, though, kept those fears to himself. Instead, he simply raised a very real problem: Catherine Gordon would need to make a formal request through the State Department to join her parents. She couldn't just show up; she wasn't a member of the embassy staff and while she was the Brousse's child, she was also an adult.

Preempting what he knew would be Betty's next argument, he forcefully made the case that it would be unwise "to pull some strings." Another rule he had learned during his time in the cold was that everyone talks. If the OSS asked a favor of State, he lectured, it would be bound to leak. Someone would inevitably say something about how the spooks had infiltrated an agent into Hershey. No, he concluded firmly, file the proper papers and let them work their way through the system. The process, he said with his customary reassuring optimism, would move swiftly along. Even

Cordell Hull would not be so uncompromising as to keep an impoverished and grieving American war widow from her parents.

On November 17, under a bright autumn sun, a cavalcade of black limousines loaded down with luggage and families made the three-hour drive from Washington to the hotel. A report in the *Washington Evening Star* observed that "among the group was Charles Brousse, Press Attaché, and his Georgia-born wife. In his lapel Mr. Brousse wore the rosette of the Legion of Honor awarded him with gold leaves for valor in World War I."

Their daughter Catherine Gordon was not with them. And as for Betty Pack, she had her own problems. She had just discovered she was pregnant.

AS THE BROUSSES SETTLED INTO their suite at the Hotel Hershey, Betty lay in a room in Washington's Garfield Hospital. Only days after she'd realized she was pregnant, she had started bleeding profusely. She had miscarried. Rushed by ambulance to the emergency room, Betty needed multiple transfusions. She spent the next eight days in the hospital.

Weak and pale when she was released, she nevertheless immediately resumed her efforts to join her "parents" in Hershey. During the long, vacant days lying in her stiff hospital bed, she had thought of little else. She genuinely missed Brousse, but at the same time she also wanted to shore up her Catherine Gordon identity. Taking up residency at the Hotel Hershey, all her instincts told her, would be the first crucial step in her long journey to France.

Dutifully, she filed the necessary application to the Department of State:

MOTHER	Catherine Calhoun Graves Brousse
FATHER	Shaw T. Waterbury

DATE OF BIRTH   January 28, 1913
PLACE OF BIRTH   Washington D.C. Columbia Hospital

I have been widowed and have also lost my mother and
foster-father through their internment at Hershey. We have
always been very close and this separation has come as a
great shock to the three of us. My mother is not in good
health, depends on me for many services that I have long
been accustomed to do for her. I, in turn, depend upon my
parents for maternal and moral support.

After composing this sentimental piece of fiction, she sat back
and waited. But Betty was never a woman who could summon up
much patience, and with so much hanging in the balance, she was
particularly antsy. She pestered Downes, and when he only dished
out his usual platitudes about the virtues of discipline, she decided
to go over his head. She dexterously cajoled her way into a meeting with William Kimbel, Donovan's personal assistant. And like
many men before him, Kimbel swiftly melted under the glow of
her charm. The next day a tactfully worded letter went out from
William J. Donovan, director of the Office of Strategic Services,
to Frederick B. Lyons, executive assistant to Adolf Berle, assistant
secretary of state.

December 22, 1942

Dear Mr. Lyons:
At my request, I understand that Mr. Kimbel had discussed
with you a matter concerning a certain young lady to be
permitted to go to Hershey and later to proceed with the
French to France in the diplomatic exchange. I should

greatly appreciate your making it possible for this to be accomplished.

Sincerely,

William J. Donovan

But the letter, despite its guarded tone, was read as a threat, and more significantly, an impotent one. The imperious State Department, chafing at the swashbuckling OSS chieftain's intrusion onto their turf, curtly let it be known that the process had its rules: Mrs. Gordon's application would be dealt with in due time.

When an embarrassed Kimbel shared this disappointing news with Betty in an awkward meeting in his office, her reaction was to sulk. But by the time she'd returned home, she was once again thinking like a professional. She decided the time had come to take the initiative. She packed her bag and drove north to Pennsylvania.

At seven on a cold, dark December evening she arrived at the gates to the Hotel Hershey. Edgar Innes, the special agent in charge of the guards, was summoned, and he sat with Betty in her drafty car as she poured her heart out. And what a poignant story she told! She was the lonely, pregnant widow of a US naval officer who had been killed in action in the Pacific, and she desperately needed the warm support of her parents. And if that wasn't reason enough to let her in, she concluded by pointing out that tonight was Christmas Eve. Had the agent no compassion? Could he really say "Bah humbug" to a pregnant widow who just wanted to be with her family during the holidays?

Innes could. He had his orders, and at this late hour on Christmas Eve he couldn't reach anyone in Washington with the power to countermand them. Betty was refused entry.

But in this Christmas story there was a room at the inn—the

Hershey Community Inn. Holed up in her room for the holidays, she had nothing to do but make telephone calls. Betty reached out to anyone she could think of—in the OSS, the BSC, the State Department. She even managed to have a brief conversation with a sympathetic but powerless Ambassador Henry-Haye.

Finally, on December 27, all her beseeching had some effect. Special Agent Innes brought a visitor to the Community Inn— Kay Brousse. Betty spent the next two hours talking to her lover's wife.

BETTY RETURNED TO WASHINGTON BRISTLING with frustration. She was unaccustomed to things not going her way, and she'd always been restless. Fueled by this volatile mix, she continued knocking on official doors and writing imploring letters. And Brousse now joined in too. He missed Betty, but his resentment was also stirred by what he perceived as ingratitude for all his dangerous covert service to America. His letters—to State, to the OSS—not only revealed too much about secret operations, but were also, in the bewildered assessments of many ruffled government officials, a bit loony. "The fact that I cannot speak with her," railed Brousse, re- ferring to his stepdaughter, in one of his many impassioned appeals to the State Department, "drives me furious! I ask only one thing: to have Catherine Gordon here or to be free . . . I have reached the *last limits* of suffering."

And finally State surrendered, although whether the avalanche of emotional letters had broken their stony resistance or the wheels of bureaucracy had simply finished spinning was never made clear. All a grateful Betty knew was that on February 8—three long months after the embassy officials had been hustled off—she re- ceived the permission she'd been demanding. A memo was issued granting Mrs. Gordon the right to join her parents in Hershey, but, it emphatically also pointed out, all hotel expenses would be her own responsibility, and like the other internees, she could not leave the premises without authorization.

Betty—now calling herself Catherine Gordon-Brousse—did her best to settle into the hotel's languid routine. She kept up her disguise, dialing down her glamour and playing the sorrowful widow. She played her role so skillfully that Henry-Haye never had any second thoughts about the Brousses' sad child. But, as Downes had presciently feared, the tricky situation was a bomb waiting to go off. And then Betty, who needed danger to keep her spirit alive, lit the fuse.

One morning in June, Kay wandered unsuspectingly into Catherine's room—only to discover her husband and his stepdaughter lying naked together in bed.

Kay rushed at Betty, determined to kill her. In her rage, she might have succeeded if Brousse had not somehow managed to push Kay, still kicking and screaming, out into the hall. As he anxiously propelled his wife down the corridor toward their suite, Kay, in a voice loud enough for everyone in the entire town of Hershey to hear, or so it seemed to an agonized Brousse, continued to yell. "My daughter is not my daughter," she bellowed. "She's a spy!"

Naturally, the State Department took notice:

"Mr. and Mrs. Brousse"—according to the official memorandum filed—"had a bout which lasted for several rounds. Unlike most French arguments, it was more than verbal. Rocks were hurled. Apparently it was scandalous. The noise . . . was heard throughout the hotel. If only rocks and bits of furniture I would not worry but I have fears that real weapons might possibly be employed and we are apt to have something serious on our hands."

And a shocked Ambassador Henry-Haye heard too. He summoned Brousse, and while he didn't know whether he should charge his aide with incest or merely espionage, he certainly knew something was not right. Brousse, remembering how he had handily deflected Grandville's accusations, hoped that a distraction strategy might work a second time. Even as the ambassador asked his questions and demanded answers, Brousse went on the offensive. He charged that Henry-Haye's loyalties were "to a traitorous extent" pro-American. And he kept punching away, accusing the ambassador of "machinations with American officials to the detriment of France."

It was a long and heated row. As the two men continued to go at it, the State Department received a frantic report: "The Ambassador and Mr. Brousse are in the midst of a violent personal controversy in which Mr. Brousse is the aggressor . . . there are lots of antagonisms and animosities and some rather lurid details which appeared."

But this time it was an argument that Brousse could not win. There was too much to explain. Betty, full of a weary resignation, had begun packing even before Brousse returned from the meeting. She knew her cover had been blown.

That afternoon a still seething Kay Brousse was driven to the Waldorf-Astoria Hotel in New York. Mrs. Gordon—or whoever she really was—was ordered by the agent in charge to return home. Betty drove off, but she had no intention of going back to Washington. She checked into the nearby Community Inn. Their future as a covert team in France might be finished, but she still wanted to be close to Brousse.

For the next several nights, as stealthily as any agent sneaking into enemy territory, she'd creep past the guards and then scurry through the woods. Protected by the dense shadows that stretched over the hotel's golf course, she'd meet up with Brousse. The countryside alive with the buzz of night noises, the two lovers would lie in each other's arms on the fairway's freshly cut grass.

One evening after she had slunk past the guard post, an agent stepped out of his hiding place in a stand of trees.

He had no idea who he had caught. He suspected the woman was just down on her luck and looking for a place to sleep for the night. He threatened to arrest his captive and throw her in jail for vagrancy.

"I have ten dollars in my purse," Betty insisted. "I am not a vagrant."

"What are you then?"

"Simply a naughty girl."

He let her go. The next morning the naughty girl and former spy drove back to Washington.

STILL, BETTY TRIED TO GET back into the game. She appealed to Stephenson, who always had a soft spot for Betty; courage mattered a great deal to him. On November 22, 1943, Mrs. Catherine Gordon was granted a visa to leave the United States.

Betty arrived in London believing that she was on the road back into the secret world. She yearned to be sent into Nazi-occupied Europe as an assassin. She was assigned to one of the Service's cloak-and-dagger units run out of a small house on London's Dorset Square, and for a while the SOE strategists gave her infiltration into Europe serious consideration. But as the plans proceeded, the word came from several sources that Betty's cover was irrevocably blown. The Vichy diplomats had made a full and very incriminating report on her activities at Hershey.

Deeply disappointed, Betty returned to America. The negotiations between France and the United States had been completed, and the diplomats had been freed months ago. The Frenchmen had returned to their homes. Brousse, however, was waiting in a New York hotel for Betty.

Betty and Charles moved into the spare bedroom in Cora's apartment. Betty now proudly wore, as her impressed sister would recall, "a fabulous bracelet made of huge stones." It was an engagement present from Brousse, but their wedding date remained vague, since both of them were still married to other people. Their divorces, they told themselves, would come to pass once the war was over. The Allied troops had landed in Normandy and were now marching relentlessly toward Berlin, but precisely when the hostilities would finally stop was anybody's guess. In the meantime, the couple made plans to travel to Europe. Brousse dreamed of returning to a liberated Paris.

It was just after they had booked passage on a Spanish ship sailing from New Orleans for Portugal that Betty received a call from the White House. President Roosevelt wanted to meet her. Whether the president had heard about her adventures from Stephenson or Donovan, or perhaps both, was never made clear. But Betty passed a pleasant hour in the Oval Offices sipping martinis with the president. He liked a good spy story, and she certainly had plenty to tell.

Chapter 54

◆

WHEN THE COUPLE ARRIVED IN the French border town of Hendaye in the last week of October 1944, Betty could not help but feel that her life had come full circle. It was here, after all, that her adventures in the secret world had begun to gather speed. Yet despite this momentary pang, she refused to concede that those adventures had run their course. The fighting in Europe had not officially concluded; the Service, she told herself, might once again call on her talents.

It was not until a month later, when the couple was living in Paris, the newly liberated city slowly shaking itself back to life, that Betty finally came to terms with her retirement. Brousse's sister-in-law—"a flashy woman, a gypsy type, very beautiful," she told Hyde—had come up from her home in the south, and they met her for lunch at the Ritz.

Betty had not wanted to go; Charles had confided that this sister-in-law had been the mistress of the Gestapo officer in charge of the Pyrénées-Orientales region. Only after he explained that he hoped to use her contacts to speed the release of his younger brother from a concentration camp did Betty relent.

The Ritz was a sorry place, with none of the splendor that Betty remembered. There were no flowers on the table, the menu was woefully limited, and there wasn't even a *carte des vins*, just an apologetic waiter who offered only a choice of "rouge ou blanc." Yet, paradoxically, the cellar was well stocked with champagne—the Germans had apparently insisted it must always be available—and Brousse ordered bottle after bottle. That helped lift Betty's spirits.

So perhaps it was the free-flowing bubbly that led the sister-in-law to make her revelation. Or maybe she'd intended all along to give Betty a warning.

"You are the woman who was posing as Kay's step-daughter," she blurted out. "You were a spy. We know all about you. I even had your description. You fit it exactly, eyes, hair, everything else." Then she continued on with a slow precision. She knew "the whole story"—how Betty had seduced Charles and coerced him to infiltrate her into the Vichy legation. She had heard it from the Gestapo. They had Betty's photograph, and had been looking for her.

At the end of their conversation, Betty had to inhale deeply. There was no possibility of her being any use to the Resistance; all doors back into the secret life had been slammed shut. She finally understood that her war was over. Betty returned to the apartment on rue des Marroniers filled with the uneasy realization that she would now need to live in the real world.

IN THE YEARS THAT FOLLOWED, Betty tried to adjust to peacetime. But it was not in her nature. She could handle danger, but the banal demands of everyday life, of running a home, of being a wife and a mother, left her reeling. Still she tried. She kept making promises, to herself and to others. But in the end she could not find the will—or any reason, really—to keep them. Without a cause she could believe in, Betty was lost. Everything seemed insubstantial. And much worse, in her own eyes she, too, seemed to be less than she'd once been. She deeply missed being Cynthia.

In November 1945 Arthur Pack committed suicide. He had planned to remarry once his divorce from Betty was finalized, but as he'd explained with calm logic in a letter to the Foreign Office, "It would be unfair to any woman to allow her to marry a man of 55 years whose health is liable to crack up at

any moment and leave her stranded with a paralytic husband."
He was also unhappy with his recent posting to Buenos Aires,
and while he'd been told he could return to his former job in
Santiago, he declined. The new ambassador was John Leche,
one of Betty's old lovers, and the prospect of serving under him
was too grim. Convinced he'd run out of alternatives, he held
the muzzle of a revolver against his right temple and pulled the
trigger.

Betty tried to remember her husband with affection. "I will always love him," she wrote his sister Rosie. "He was a great man."
But by the time she sat down to write another letter to Rosie, her
mood had hardened. "Arthur was a taker and not a giver," she
stated. And she'd settled on an explanation for having left him: "I
was finally obliged to take account of myself and decided that unless I did something positive to remedy the situation both Arthur
and myself might disappear and leave our two children orphaned."
It was not the truth, or even close to the complexity of feelings that
pushed her into a procession of betrayals, but Betty did her best to
convince herself it was that simple.

With Arthur's death, she had no choice but to deal with another circumstance the war had given her a convenient excuse to
ignore—her children. She made arrangements for Denise, now
ten, to live with her in Paris. "I will never leave her. She will never
be alone," Betty pledged. As for her son Tony, now fifteen, whom
she had not seen for eight years, she would let the Cassells continue to raise him. "It would be a disservice to Tony to bring him
here," she wrote Rosie without further explanation. Years later
she offered a bit more to Hyde: "A wholesome, happy life with his
foster parents should not be shattered. The emotional stability that
Tony had was more important than my own emotional longings."
Although no longer in the trade, Betty could still transform rationalizations into truths.

Tony Pack, photographed in 1951.

Denise was a sullen, unhappy child who was convinced she was tormented by ghosts. She lived with Betty and Charles in Paris for two strained years. When Brousse's divorce was finalized, and the couple, after a small and deliberately muted wedding, moved into their storybook castle, Denise came along. But Betty's patience for her difficult daughter had run out. She dismissed the young girl as "selfish, ruthless, and completely hard-boiled." Despite the assurances she'd given, Betty could find no reason to put up any longer with the responsibilities of motherhood. Without remorse, she sent Denise off to America to live with Cora.

Tony finally came to Castelnou. The visit had been put off for years; either the castle's renovations were not completed, or Betty had the flu, or now was simply not the right time. At last he took the initiative. He was a newly promoted lieutenant, on leave from some tough service in Korea, and he was spending his holiday traveling through France. He made it seem like an accident, as if he'd just happened to find himself down south, and when he telephoned his mother, she agreed to meet him at the train station.

It was an unsentimental reunion. He stayed on for a few days, but he could find little in common with the stranger who was his mother. "Her idea of enjoyment," he observed with censorious bewilderment, "was to drive into Perpignan every evening and go from club to club where there were loud jazz bands and parties." He also had the suspicion his mother was "slightly odd in the attic"; after all, she'd confided to him that she conversed with the two huge hunting dogs that followed her devotedly about in a "dog language" that she alone among humans knew.

His mother was no less judgmental. She found her son to be narrow-minded and introverted, the stuffy personification of a stodgy middle-class Englishman. But it wasn't Tony's fault, she said graciously. She blamed the Cassells, and doubted whether she could ever forgive them.

Then suddenly, or so it seemed to a stunned Betty, "it was later than one thinks." Arthur had committed suicide. Denise lived in America and, now married, was largely out of her life. Tony had been killed in action. Cora was dead. Her old lovers had moved on. And she was dying.

The castle, as well as her steady life with Charles, was no longer a refuge. It had become something small, and she was beginning to believe, quite mean. She felt imprisoned.

Then, miraculously, along came Hyde from out of her past to rescue her. She ran off with him hoping to understand herself, to pierce through all the deceptive layers that overlaid her tumultuous journey of the past half century. She needed to make sense of it all, or she'd never find peace, either in this world or the next. "You don't bargain with death," she told herself. But nevertheless she found herself pleading, begging to be allowed to complete this final mission.

Betty Pack, photographed at Castelnou the year before her death in 1963.

Epilogue

Return to the Keep

◆

R ETURNING TO LONDON, HYDE CONTINUED to set their
schedule. Betty was swept up in a swirl of almost constant activity. There was a trip to the Victoria and Albert
Museum, a long stroll through a springtime Hyde Park, lunches
and dinners where he invited his many friends, and, on Betty's
insistence, several afternoons devoted to shopping. But although
their time was crowded, Hyde had his priorities. On their second
day in the city, he brought Betty to a lunch with his literary agent
Iain Thompson. Hyde, the wary professional, wanted to make sure
that the details of Betty's collaboration with him were carefully
established.

Betty went with some trepidation. As she had told her stories
to Hyde, she could not help feeling that her tales would be of
little interest to anyone else. She feared that her memories were
like the faded photographs in the family album Cora had been so
fond of trotting out: possibly intriguing to relatives, but tedious
to those who had no personal connection to the faces and places
in the snapshots. But sitting in the restaurant, she listened with
mounting excitement as Thompson reiterated what he'd previously
told Hyde: readers, he predicted, would be eager to relive Betty's
wartime exploits. The proper format, the agent suggested after a
few moments' thought, would be a series of articles in the popular Sunday press; either the *News of the World* or the *Sunday People*
would be possibilities.

Betty was unfamiliar with the English papers. She was not
aware of how the feisty mass circulation sheets relished putting a

provocative, often colorfully sensationalistic spin on the news. But sitting in the restaurant, she was carried along by both men's enthusiasm for the project. Without much consideration, she matter-of-factly agreed to the arrangements Hyde and his agent outlined. She'd write her memoirs as a series of newspaper articles, Hyde would rewrite them, and they'd split the income equally. If the articles provoked interest, and there was sufficient material, Hyde would then rework her memoirs into a short book. And when he shared his idea about forming a company to protect the potential profits from taxes, Betty went along with that too; "a stroke of genius," she'd subsequently write Hyde.

A few days later, at a lunch with Sam Campbell, an editor at the *Sunday People*, a deal negotiated by Iain Thompson was quickly finalized. The paper would publish a series of six articles based on Betty's memoirs and then "polished" by Hyde. The fee, a stunned Betty learned, would be an extraordinary 12,500 pounds, the money to be paid upon publication into the soon-to-be-established Cynamont corporation. This windfall was undoubtedly additional confirmation of the seemliness of the mission that had taken her to Ireland, even if she had to leave her husband and run off with another man to fulfill it.

The following day Hyde arranged one more lunch. Colonel Howard Ellis—known as "Dick" to members of the espionage establishment on both sides of the Atlantic—had been both his and Betty's wartime boss, the nuts-and-bolts professional MI6 had sent to America to assist William Stephenson with the operational details of running the BSC. Ellis was now retired from the Service, but he had once worked as a "weeder" for MI6—one of the men who decided what secrets in the files still needed keeping—and he'd given Hyde's manuscript of the *The Quiet Canadian* the bureaucratic shove it needed to get around the Official Secrets Act and be cleared for publication. Hyde hoped Ellis, although he no longer had that job, could offer advice on how Betty's articles could be published without the Service raising any objections. Hyde worried that any mention of ciphers, even those used decades ago, would put the secretive spymasters on high alert.

Hyde chose a French bistro in South Kensington not far from the tube station. He wasn't particularly fond of the food, but they knew him, and he could always get a table in a quiet alcove in the rear. He hoped to get down to business quickly and extract some practical advice from his former colleague. But as the talk turned to the old days, and both Ellis and Betty seemed so glad to be once again in each other's company, he realized this would be more a reunion than a working lunch.

He listened as Betty and Ellis chatted happily, the two of them reminiscing about a time when they had lived with a level of intensity that they'd never achieved again. And sitting there quietly, feeling the odd man out as the two relived the wartime missions they'd mounted together, Hyde's mind wandered.

He thought of what he had learned about Betty in the course of their travel and talks in Ireland. Betty had found her path—inevitably, he genuinely believed—into the secret world because it had offered her a way to subordinate the mercurial passions that ruled her life. She had needed something to steady herself—her "vast restlessness," she had called it—and then had the good fortune to stumble into a profession she could fully embrace. And it had been a perfect match; she lived easily with all the ambiguities of her adopted trade.

As the lunch went on, Hyde found himself thinking how much he enjoyed Betty's company—the simple pleasure of being with her. But he also realized the attraction was tied to their memories of a dangerous and vital time when they had both worked to help the Allies win the war. Now what was he doing? Shuttling half-heartedly from one hastily conceived project to another simply to cover his pile of bills? Giving excuses to his wife as he went off to Ireland with another woman?

He was beginning to understand that if he were to reclaim the lofty ambitions of his youth, he'd need to refocus his life before it was too late; he was, he reminded himself, fifty-six. And hand in hand with that self-knowledge, he also realized that it was time Betty returned to France. Their time in Ireland had served as a bridge to their common pasts, a time when they both had lived in the covert world. But it was a relationship that had no future.

As it happened, Betty came in her own way to a similar conclusion several days later. Concerned about whether the articles could use the names of Betty's lovers, or whether pseudonyms would be necessary, Hyde had begun to track down some of the men who had played a role in her life. In his investigation, he discovered that Michal Lubienski, the count with whom Betty had shared a passionate romance in prewar Poland, was living in London with his wife. When he informed Betty, she immediately picked up the telephone.

Count Lubienski, Betty was told by the servant who answered, was out of the country on business. Betty swiftly put down the receiver, not bothering to leave a message or even her name. And as soon as she did, she felt relieved. In that instant she understood that it would be better to leave the past in the past. Her mission had been completed. It was time to go home.

On their final morning together, Hyde accompanied Betty to the airport. They walked through the terminal toward the departure gate where the plane to Barcelona would be boarding, and Hyde recalled another walk they had taken, down Madison Avenue in wartime Manhattan. When they'd parted, he had said, "I expect we shall see each other soon." It had been two decades before he'd fulfilled that expectation. But today he knew better than to make any predictions. He had come to suspect that Betty's health was more fragile than she pretended. And in that moment Hyde, while sorrowful, at the same time felt an uplifting appreciation for what she had shared with him, and how she had reconnected him to his own memories of his service in the shadows during World War II. He looked at her and was suddenly reminded of something Stephenson had said: Betty was "the greatest unsung heroine of the war."

When he said good-bye, Betty simply nodded. Then she turned and, without a word, walked off. Hyde was not insulted. He knew that was her defense, the resigned way, time after time, she had concluded every chapter in her life. He watched her walk purposefully down the runway leading to the plane, until at last she had disappeared into the crowd of passengers, in his eyes still the bewitching spy.

ON THE FLIGHT TO BARCELONA, and then in the hired car to Castelnou, Betty had time to think, and the solitude to focus. She looked back at her trip through Ireland and the journey she'd simultaneously taken back into her own past. She had revisited a lifetime of experiences, and now even if everything she had done still did not make sense to her—she would say she knew better than to trust solutions that were too tidy—she had arrived close enough to the truth.

There had been a continuity of purpose in all her experiences. She had not cared what anyone else had thought. She had not worried about what seemed appropriate or acceptable. It was a way, a nature, that had left her with many regrets; there was, after all, no justification for the mother she'd been, for the damage she'd inflicted on her children. The most she could say in her own defense was that she'd succeeded in channeling her wayward character into something substantial, into a cause she believed in. And looking back, it was a commitment, Betty now recognized, that still filled her with pride. Her final mission had restored her faltering faith in the life she had lived.

As the car began to climb the winding road leading up to the castle, Betty wondered how Charles would greet her; would he even be waiting for her when she returned? She had betrayed him, but she hoped he'd realize it was insignificant. She didn't expect that he would understand what compelled her to leave, but she very much wanted him to forgive her. She needed him, and she found that realization very comforting.

Yet when the car pulled into the courtyard and she saw Charles standing there, she was afraid to let her spirits soar. He, too, seemed uncertain, staring at the vehicle as if trying to decide whether he should approach. But as Betty got out of the back seat, he was there to take her hand.

She held on tight to him, and they walked to the heavy wooden door. Betty stepped over a stone threshold worn flat by the centuries, and as she entered the dark castle, the aromatic scent of burning logs in the hall fireplace welcomed her back. Grateful, she disappeared into her home.

HYDE BELIEVED IN DUTY. AND now he had come to Washington to pay one last debt to Betty. As he had feared, he never saw her again after their afternoon together in London. Betty's cancer had spread viciously. Just weeks after she'd returned to Castelnou, she had sent a grave yet sober assessment: "I do hope I can live another year before the pain gets too bad. Anyhow I will stick it as long as possible before becoming a screaming nuisance."

Despite her illness and nearly three arduous months spent in a cancer clinic receiving chemotherapy, she had continued to work on her memoirs. She wrote by hand from her hospital bed, and a secretary typed the drafts of the chapters and sent them on to Hyde. As her illness progressed, she reluctantly decided she'd be unable to send Hyde anything more than notes for the introductory article the paper wanted and the remaining chapters. When the series ran in October 1963, she had misgivings. "The articles have all been rewritten by 'The People' to conform to their style," she complained in a letter to a daughter of a wartime colleague. "I never wrote anything so bragging and conceited . . . it makes me blush."

Betty died less than two months later, on December 1, 1963, in a clinic in Perpignan. She was buried in the park just beyond the castle's stone walls, under the shade of a cedar tree. "I am crushed to death," Charles wrote to Hyde.

With Charles's consent, Hyde went ahead and turned Betty's memoirs into a book. *Cynthia* was published in March 1963, but it was a slapdash work, eviscerated by the Official Secrets censors, filled with pseudonyms, and based on little more than Betty's incomplete memoirs and her cursory notes. It never proved to be the financial success Hyde had hoped. But the experience, in an unanticipated way, served to refocus his life. He married again, settled into a cottage in Surrey with his new wife, continued writing, and, now happy and productive, enjoyed greater commercial success. He was working in 1972 on a book about Soviet espionage when he learned that Charles Brousse had died. A fire had raged through Castelnou, and Brousse was discovered in the charred remains of his bed. The authorities suspected that he'd fallen asleep without turning off his electric blanket, and a spark from the blanket had set off the fire. But this was only a theory; the cause of the fire that destroyed the castle was never firmly established. Denise's death, Hyde also had learned, was another mystery. She had married, worked at *Newsweek* for a while, and then suddenly died. Colleagues at the magazine suspected suicide.

CHATEAU DE CASTELLNOU
PAR THUIR (PYR.-OR.)
TÉLÉPH. 77 THUIR

Decembre 9 1963

Mon cher ami

Votre télégramme, dont je vous
remercie, me trouve avec le
cœur broyé par la douleur.
Avec un courage surhumain
Betty a combattu la mort
jusqu'à la dernière minute
je l'ai aidée du mieux de mes
moyens.
Vous la connaissiez admirable
ment. C'est pourquoi votre
télégramme me va au cœur.
Votre dévoué
Charles E. Brousse

*Brousse's letter to Hyde, sent December 9, 1963,
conveying the news of Betty's death.*

And now, nearly two decades after Betty's death, Hyde stood in
the dim light of the bar at the Wardman Park Hotel. The hotel had
been renovated many times since Betty lived her clandestine life
here. Yet the new corporate owners were proud to acknowledge
the hotel's moment in history: Betty's portrait hung on a dark red

wall. It was the photograph that had been snapped moments after the twenty-three-year-old curtsied before King George V at the Buckingham Palace New Year's honors ceremony.

There was, however, no identification. Most revelers in Harry's Bar assumed it was simply a photograph of a glamorous woman, a model with a tiara nestled in her hair. Which was precisely how the professionals who had fought their own secret wars, who had also served in the shadows, wanted to keep it. In tribute, they would come to drink a silent toast to Betty's memory.

Hyde ordered a martini. He must have smiled as he remembered how proud Betty had been of the ones she poured. He raised his glass toward the photograph, but hesitated as he brought it up to his lips. Yes, she had flaws. And yes, her life had been very messy; there were boundaries she had crossed, acts that he would not even try to explain away or condone. But at a time when the world was in peril, she had joined the battle, fought bravely for the cause she believed in, and had a hell of a time doing it. What more can anyone ask out of life? He took a long, satisfying sip of his drink.

A Note on Sources

C AMBRIDGE UNIVERSITY'S CONNECTION TO ESPIONAGE is notorious. Staining its long, high history is the well-documented ring of Trinity College graduates who had served as long-term penetration agents—"moles," in the jargon of the intelligence trade—for the Soviet Union. And as someone whose reporting life has been largely spent peering into the covert world, I had read my fair share of the many admonishing accounts detailing the treacheries of Kim Philby and his co-conspirators. However, it wasn't until I walked through the formidable Great Gate and onto the grounds of Trinity College that the magnitude of their betrayals became something real, almost tangible.

Standing by the fountain in the Great Court, my eyes swept from the Clock Tower toward the Gothic chapel and around a Tudor panorama of turrets, towers, and ancient stone. What a rarefied world of privilege and tradition! As I continued on, ambling with a wide-eyed awe through the college's gilded spaces, the motives and perhaps even the depths of the Cambridge spies' treason became less remote. Their decisions, I began to suspect, owed as much to aesthetic judgments about a way of life as to philosophical and political arguments.

These empirical insights were still filling my mind when later that afternoon as a dusting snow began to fall I walked out of Trinity and headed across the River Cam to Storey's Way. My destination was the concrete and brick modernist halls of the university's Churchill College. I was going to the college's Archives Centre to forage through the extensive papers and documents another spy, Harford Montgomery Hyde, had left to the university upon his death in 1989.

His bequest included personal papers covering his war-time service in MI6, the British Security Coordination, and the mountains of research material he had gathered for his many books on espionage. But even more tantalizing, Hyde had left the college what has become known in intelligence circles as "the Cynthia Papers." He had amassed this collection while he was writing his breezy 1964 biography of Betty Pack, the spy who had operated under the code-name Cynthia, and it has remained largely an unmined treasure trove. There were the crinkled foolscap typewritten pages of the memoirs Betty had dictated as she knew she was dying, her earnest and thoughtful childhood diary, the archly sentimental book she'd authored as a young girl in Hawaii, boxes filled with the candid, often blunt letters she'd written and received over the years, and even her address book, the neat entries all in her elegant cursive script.

In the long days ahead as I made my way through this archival mother lode, a literary ambition that had first begun to take form in my mind as I had walked through and looked about Trinity College became clearer. I would use these splendid riches to shape a spy story that was not confined simply to biographies, clandestine activities, and the background thunder of world historical events. I would dig deep into this firsthand source material and in the process make my narrative into something less remote. I'd use my characters' own words—their own private thoughts, in fact!—to reveal human motives and the chaos of the interior reality of their lives. I would write a book that told, in part, a story about the decision to become a spy and what it was like to live in such perilous psychological territory. I had, after all, the source material.

I would not write an academic history; that sort of narrow, tightly buttoned narrative held no attraction for me. And yet I would tell a true story. I had the evidence; there were memoirs, letters, diaries, transcribed interviews, government documents, and contemporaneous newspaper articles. There would be no inventions in my account. I had the goods to write a non-fiction spy story where I could relate what my characters were saying, doing, feeling, and even thinking accurately as well as vividly.

Therefore, when quotation marks bracket any dialogue in this book this is an indication that at least one of the principals was the source. Further, when a character reveals what he is thinking or feeling, I found this too in a memoir, diary, a letter, or a previously published interview.

And yet even as I read with mounting interest the papers in the Churchill College Archives, I understood that Betty and Hyde were fallible. Memories—*all* memories—are prey to evasions and self-exculpations and spies are just like us—only more so. It seemed likely that people who lived with subterfuge and deceit would play fast and loose with the historical record and would not think twice about subjectively tinkering with the events, large and small, in their own lives. And so when I left Cambridge, I dug deeper.

Particularly valuable were the National Archives in Washington, DC, and their collection of OSS Papers and Diplomatic Records; the Federal Bureau of Investigation files on Mrs. Elizabeth Pack and Vincent Astor; Columbia University's Butler Library which houses W.J. Donovan's "A History of Espionage"; the Franklin D. Roosevelt Library, Hyde Park, N.Y., and its files on Vincent Astor, Adolf Berle, Ernest Cuneo, and wartime intelligence matters; the U.S. Army Military History Institute, Carlisle, PA, where the William J. Donovan Papers are stored; and the Public Record Office, Kew, England, whose files further revealed the activities of the British Foreign Office leading up to and during the war.

I found additional objective reporting and analysis about the far-ranging events shaping my narrative in the small library of books that focused on female spies and on World War II—its battles, intelligence activities, and diplomatic maneuverings. Again,

A Note on Sources

since this is not an academic account, I don't find it necessary to mention in this source note all the volumes that helped inform my narrative; a somewhat more extensive bibliography follows. Any reader, however, who is intrigued by Betty, both her life and the turbulent times in which she lived, would, I believe, enjoy settling in with the following works I found invaluable:

Cast No Shadow, Mary S. Lovell's meticulous account of Betty's life, published in 1992, tells a comprehensive story while also offering intriguing interviews with Arthur Pack's family and his friends; I am deeply indebted to her original and tenacious research. Another key resource was H. Montgomery Hyde's, *Cynthia*. It's a bit breathy, reading more at times like a bodice-ripper than a spy's operational biography, but nevertheless it offers compelling insights into both Betty and Hyde. And two other of Hyde's books—*The Quiet Canadian* (published as *Room 3603* in America) and *Secret Intelligence Agent*—provide firsthand accounts about wartime intelligence work in America as well as his own revelatory and frequently affecting reminiscences. Further, Elizabeth P. McIntosh in *Sisterhood of Spies* gives a gripping view of what it was like to be a woman working as a spy in wartime, historical territory also diligently covered by the more workman-like *Women Who Spy*, by A.A. Hoehling.

Another primary resource was the British Security Coordination's *Official History*. Written in 1945 at the request of Sir William Stephenson as the war was winding down, it used the extensive top secret BSC operational records to create an intentionally dramatic and often purposefully aggrandizing account of the organization's inventive and wide-spread intelligence activities. It remained classified—although a few purloined photocopied versions had been circulated among intelligence professionals—until 1998 when it was published in England and then the United States. It's a revelatory, often entertaining read—its BSC agents/authors included the English writer Roald Dahl and the Canadian journalist Tom Hill—and it helped inform as well as encourage an unfolding sense of drama in my tale.

There are shelves of books on intelligence activities in the Second World War, but of all the volumes I consulted let me offer a few to which I kept returning. Thomas F. Troy, a staff officer in the CIA, first wrote about the British Security Coordination and Sir William Stephenson in a classified 1974 issue of the CIA's journal, *Studies in Intelligence*. This long essay became the basis twenty years later for his book, *Wild Bill and Intrepid*. It's a wonderful read—scholarly, argumentative, and full of an intelligence insider's perceptions. Also valuable was Joseph E. Persico's *Roosevelt's Secret War*, a groundbreaking study of the president as case agent-in-chief. And although filled with extravagant claims and adventures that owe more to the imagination than the historical record, *A Man Called Intrepid* by William Stevenson offers an engaging (albeit often speculative) account of Betty's adventures. Further, a very readable and comprehensive account of British intelligence is told in Nigel West's *MI5: British Security Service Operations 1909-1945* and *MI6: British Security Operations 1909-1945*.

I also found myself returning to several newspaper and journal articles as I wrote this story. David Ignatius, a longtime *Washington Post* writer on intelligence issues (and a gifted novelist to boot), wrote a 1989 article for that paper, "Britain's War in America: How Churchill's Agents Secretly Manipulated the U.S. Before Pearl Harbor," that I found essential. William Stephenson's aura as Intrepid was roundly punctured by H.R. Trevor Roper's caustic essay, "Superagent," in the *New York Review of Books*, John Le Carre's essay, "England's Spy in America," in the *New York Times Book Review*, and Timothy J. Naftali, "Intrepid's Last Deception," in the journal *Intelligence and National Security*. Also, the History News Network's hyperlinks on its website, *The Honey Trap: The*

True Story of Madame Elizabeth Brousse was a most rewarding resource, and its investigation into the role of U.S. Naval intelligence operative Paul Fairly was particularly valuable.

Finally, my writing and research was shaped by conversations with intelligence agents, some serving, the majority retired, on both sides of the Atlantic. Thanks to my discussions with men who knew Hyde and had read the still classified operational case files on Betty, I was able to get closer to my characters, and to the truth about what actually happened.

The primary sources for each chapter of this book follow.

Chapter One

Cynthia Papers, Churchill Archives Centre, Churchill College [CP]; H. Montgomery Hyde, *Cynthia* (New York: Farrar, Staus, and Giroux, 1965) [Cynthia]; Mary S. Lovell, *Cast No Shadow* (New York: Pantheon Books, 1992) [Shadow]; Elizabeth P. McIntosh, *Sisterhood of Spies* (New York: Dell, 1999) [Sisterhood]; Castelnou.com; Château de Castelnou official site; Ina Caro, *The Road from the Past*, (New York: Mariner Books, 1996); Thomas N. Bisson, *The Medieval Crown of Aragon: A Short History* (Oxford: Clarendon Press, 2000); Citation of Award of Military Cross to Lieutenant Anthony George Pack, King's Shropshire Light Infantry Archives.

Chapter Two

CP; Cynthia; Hyde Papers, Churchill Archives Centre, Churchill College [HP]; Correspondence with Kathleen Cockburn, first quoted in *Shadow*; H. Montgomery Hyde, *The Quiet Canadian* (London: Constable, 1962) [Quiet]; *The Sunday Times Magazine* (London), October 21, 1962, p. 25; H. Montgomery Hyde, *Secret Intelligence Agent* (New York: St. Martin's Press, 1982) [Agent].

Chapter Three

CP; HP; Shadow; interview with Nigel West; Hotel Gavina official website; Hyde, Secret Intelligence Agent; Thomas F. Troy, *Wild Bill and Intrepid* (New Haven, CT.: Yale University Press, 1996)[Wild Bill].

Chapter Four
HP; CP; Cynthia; Shadow; Sisterhood.

Chapter Five
Cynthia; HP; CP; Michael O'Sullivan, Bernard O'Neill, *The Shelbourne and Its People* (Dublin: Blackwater Press, 1999).

Chapter Six
CP; HP; Shadow; Cynthia; Public Record Office at Kew [PRO]; Quiet; William J. Donovan Papers, Carlisle, PA, "British Recruitment and Handling of Agents"[DP]; Richard Deacon, Nigel West, *Spy!* (London: BBC,1980)[Spy]; Nigel West, introduction, *The Secret History of British Intelligence in the Americas, 1940-1945* (New York: Fromm International, 1999)[BSC]; F.H. Hinsley, E.E. Thomas, C.A. Simkins, and C.F.G. Ransom, *British Intelligence in the Second World War* (London: HMSO, 1988)[Hinsley]; Frank C. Roberts, ed., *Obituaries from the Times* (London: London Times, 1951); Nigel West, *MI5: British Security Service Operations 1909-1945* (New York: Stein and Day, 1982) [MI5]; Nigel West, *MI6: British Secret Security Operations 1909-1945* (New York: Stein and Day, 1983) [MI6].

Chapter Seven
HP; CP; Cynthia; Shadow; Secret; Obituary, "George Cyrus Thorpe," *Washington Star*, July 28, 1936; Nancy Whipple Grinnel, *Carrying the Torch: Maude Howe Elliott and the American Renaissance* (Lebanon, NH: University Press of New England, 2014).

Chapter Eight
HP; Shadow; CP; Cynthia; Betty Thorpe, *Fioretta* (Honolulu: Advertiser Publishing, 1922); *www.madamebrousse.com* "Honey Trap: The True Story of Madame Brousse."

Chapter Nine
CP; Shadow; HP; *Washington Post*, November 18, 1929, p. 8; *Washington Post*, November 21, 1929, p. 8; Spy.

Chapter Ten
CP; Cynthia; Shadow; Arthur Pack letter to Rosina Rivett, quoted in Shadow; Public Record Office, and Foreign Office Archives, Kew, London [PRO]; *Washington Post/New York Times*, February 8, 1930; *Washington Post*, April 30, 1930, p. 8; *Washington Evening Star*, April 29-30, p. 4.

Chapter Eleven
CP; Shadow; Cynthia; PRO; HP; Lovell interview with Rosina Rivett quoted in Shadow; Rex Doublet letter to Rosina Rivett, January 11, 1946; Lovell interview with Lady Campbell-Orde; *The Times*, London, January 15, 1932, p. 11.

Chapter Twelve
HP; Cynthia; CP; James Joyce, *Ulysses* (New York: Vintage, 1986); Cork Historical and Archeological Society, "The Martello Towers of Cork Harbour," July, 2012.

Chapter Thirteen
HP; Cynthia; CP; Shadow; PRO; *Who Was Who*, 1920-2008 (Oxford, U.K.: Oxford University Press, 2008); Obituary, Sir Henry Chilton, *The Times*, London, November 22, 1954.

Chapter Fourteen
Cynthia; CP; HP; Shadow; Spy; PRO; The Esoteric Curiosa, "The Anecdotal Lord"; George Malcolm Thompson, *Lord Castlerosse, His Life and Times* (London: Weidenfeld & Nicolson, 1973); MI5; MI6; Max Aitken Beaverbrook, *Politicians and the War 1914-1916* (London: T. Butterworth Limited, 1928); Beaverbrook, *Politicians and the Press* (London: Hutchinson, 1932); Anne Chisholm and Michael Davie, *Lord Beaverbrook: A Life* (New York: Knopf, 1993).

Chapter Fifteen
CP; HP; Shadow; Spy; Anthony Beevor, *The Battle for Spain* (New York: Hachette, 2012) [Beevor]; Tom Buchanan, "Edge of Darkness: British 'Front-Line' Diplomacy in Spanish Civil War, 1936-1937," *Contemporary European History*,

vol. 12, No. 3, August, 2003 (Buchanan); British National Archives, Bodleian Library Special Collections, Oxford University; Geoffrey Cox, *Defense of Madrid* (London: Gollancz, 1937); Helen Graham, *The Spanish Republic at War, 1936-1939* (New York: Cambridge University Press, 2002) [Graham]; Frank Jellinek, *The Civil War in Spain* (London: Gollancz, 1938) [Jellinek]; Sir Raymond Carr, *The Spanish Tragedy* (New York: Phoenix Press, 1977) [Carr]; MI6; PRO.

Chapter Sixteen
Carr; Graham; Jellinek; Preston Paul, "From Rebel to Caudillo: Franco's Path to Power," *History Today*, July 1986; *New York Times*, October 16, 1936; Cynthia; CP; Shadow; Hyde; Buchanan; *New York Times*, "Hendaye Now Center for Envoys to Spain," August 2, 1936.

Chapter Seventeen
Cynthia; CP; HP; Shadow; PRO; Spy; Jellinek; Carr; Graham; L. Trask, *The History of the Basque* (London: Routledge, 1997); Beevor; Buchanan; MI-6; Hinsley; Obituary, "George Cyrus Thorpe, *Washington Star*, July 28, 1936.

Chapter Eighteen
Cynthia; Hyde; Shadow; HP; PRO; Buchanan; Henry Taprell Dorling, *Blue Star Line at War* (London: W. H. Foulsham, 1973); www.saint-jean-de-luz.com; "Viscounty of Altamira," *www.digplanet.com*; "Goya and the Altamira Family," metmuseum.org/2014/goya; Jellinek; Granham; Eric R. Smith, *Relief Aid and the Spanish Civil War* (Columbia, MO: University of Missouri Press, 1993); Teofilio Ruiz, "The Transformation of the Castilian Municipalities," *Past and Present*, November, 1977; Josep Carles Clemente, *The Red Cross During the Spanish Civil War, 1936–1939*, reviewed in *International Review of the Red Cross*, February, 1994; Carr.

Chapter Nineteen
Graham; Carr; Jellinek; Cynthia; HP; CP; Shadow; PRO; Buchanan; "Valencia Under the Bombs," YouTube.

Chapter Twenty
Carr; Jellinek; CP; Cynthia; HP; Shadow; "British Embassy in Madrid,"

The Times, London, May 27, 1939, p. 11; PRO; University of Warwick Records Centre, "The Scottish Ambulance Unit in Spain and the Spanish Civil War"; Martha Gelhorn, *The View from the Ground* (London: Granta Books, 1990); Buchanan; Granham.

Chapter Twenty-One

Cynthia; CP; HP; Shadow; PRO; MI6; Hinsley; Buchanan; Carr; Jellinek; "Spanish Civil War Prisoners and Prisons," pamphlet collection, Hoover Institute, Stanford, CA [Prisons]; Spy; Agent; BSC.

Chapter Twenty-Two

Cynthia; Shadow; HP; National Archives and Records Administration, Washington, DC [NA]; *www.arlingtoncemetary.net/sofuqua/htm*; Stephen Ogden Fuqua, *Americans Wanted* (New York: Smith & Durrell, 1940); Prisons; Carr; Jellinek; Graham; Buchanan; Hugh Thomas, *The Spanish Civil War* (London: Penguin Books, 2003); Indalecio Prieto, *Remembrances and Perspectives* (New York: Spanish Editions, 1938); PRO; MI6; Hinsley; *Portsmouth Herald*, "Naval Prison Plans Dead in the Water," February 2, 2001.

Chapter Twenty-Three

PRO; MI6; Shadow; Cynthia; CP; HP; Sir Ivone Kirkpatrick, *The Inner Circle* (London: Macmillan, 1959); Lord Stang, *Foreign Office* (London: George Allen & Unwin, 1957); Buchanan.

Chapter Twenty-Four

Cynthia; CP; HP; Shadow; *www.sligotourism.ie/attractions/w-b-yeats-grave*.

Chapter Twenty-Five

Cynthia; CP; Shadow; Spy; MI6; Hinsley; David L. Hogan, "President Roosevelt and the Origins of the 1939 War," *The Journal of Historical Review*, vol. 4, 1989; Norman Davis, *God's Playground: A Short History of Poland* (New York: Columbia University Press, 1982); Jerzy Lukowski and Hubert Zawadzki, *A Concise History of Poland* (New York: Cambridge University Press, 2006), Walter Drzewieniecki, "The Polish Army on the Eve of World War II," *Polish Review*, 1981; E.D. Wynot, *Warsaw Between the Wars* (New York:

East European Monographs, 1983)[Warsaw]; Edward Baltzell, *Philadelphia Gentlemen: The Making of a National Upper Class* (New York: Free Press, 1958); "Foreign Service Athletic Christian," *Time* Magazine, August 8, 1935; Roy Rosenzweig and Elizabeth Blackmar, *The Park and the People* (Ithaca, NY: Cornell University Press, 1998); Stanislaw Mackiewicz, *Colonel Beck and His Policy* (London: Eyre and Spottiswoode, 1944) [Policy]; Henry L. Roberts, "The Diplomacy of Colonel Beck," *The International History Review*, January, 1981 (Diplomacy); Anna Cieciala, "The Foreign Policy of Jozef Beck," *The Polish Review*, vol. LVI, 2011 [FP]; BSC.

Chapter Twenty-Six

Hugh Sebag-Montefiore, *Enigma* (Hoboken, NJ: John Wiley, 2000)[Enigma]; Hinsley; MI6; David Kahn, *Seizing the Enigma* (London: Weidenfeld, 1996); F.H. Hinsley and Alan Stripp, editors, *Codebreakers* (New York: Oxford University Press, 1993); Wladsylaw Kozaczuk, *Enigma: How the Poles Broke the Nazi Code* (New York: Hippocrene Books, 2004); Quiet; HP; William Stevenson, *A Man Called Intrepid* (Guilford, CT: The Lyons Press, 2000) [Intrepid]; Agent; John Winthrop Hammond, *Charles Proteus Steinmetz: A Biography* (New York: The Century, 1924); Peter Wilkinson and Joan Astley, *Gubbins and SOE* (London: Leo Cooper, 1993); Spy; F.W. Winterbotham, *The Ultra Secret* (New York: Dell, 1974).

Chapter Twenty-Seven

FP; Diplomacy; Policy; Cynthia; CP; HP; Shadow; Michael Burleigh, *The Third Reich* (London: Macmillan, 2000); Ladislas Farago, *The Game of Foxes* (New York: David McKay, 1971); William L. Shirer, *The Rise and Fall of the Third Reich* (New York: Simon & Schuster, 2011); PRO; Wilbur J. Carr Papers, Library of Congress, Washington, DC; MI6; Hinsely; Karl Dietrich Bracher, *The German Dictatorship* (New York: Praeger, 1970); Czechoslovak Office of Foreign Affairs, *Two Years of German Oppression in Czechoslovakia* (London: Czechoslovak Publications, 1941); BSC; Agent.

Chapter Twenty-Eight

Cynthia; HP; Shadow; PRO; Policy; Diplomacy; FP; Warsaw; Spy; BSC; Hinsley; MI6; Stanley Cloud and Lynne Olson, *A Question of Honor* (New

A Note on Sources

York: Vintage Books, 2004); Shelia Mulloy, *O'Malley: People and Places* (Dublin: Ballinakella Press, 1986)[O'Malley].

Chapter Twenty-Nine
Cynthia; HP; Shadow; CP; *www.discoverireland.ie/arts/culture-heritage/rock-fleet*; Agent; *www.mulrannyparkhotel.ie/aboutus*.

Chapter Thirty
Hinsley; MI6; Spy; Cynthia; CP; Agent; Shadow; HP; PRO; "The German Embassy in Santiago," www.pasch-net.de; "Chile During World War II," YouTube; Arthur Pack letters quoted in Shadow; Interview with Margaret Owen quoted in Shadow; *South Pacific Mail*, September 21, 1939; National Monuments Council, "Parque Forestal" (Santiago, Chile: National Monuments Council, 2000); Intrepid.

Chapter Thirty-One
CP; Cynthia; HP; Shadow; NA; Cordell Hull, *The Memoirs of Cordell Hull* (New York: Macmillan, 1948)[Hull]; PRO; Agent; MI6; Hinsley; Spy.

Chapter Thirty-Two
BSC; Intrepid; Quiet; HP; Wild Bill; NA; Ernest L. Cuneo, "The British and Sir William," Cuneo Papers, Hyde Park [Cuneo]; Franklin D. Roosevelt Papers, Roosevelt Library, Hyde Park, NY [FDR]; Gilbert Martin, *Winston Churchill: The Wilderness Years* (London: Heinemann, 1983); David Ignatius, "Britain's War in America," *Washington Post*, September 17, 1989 [Britain's War]; Timothy J. Naftali, "Intrepid's Last Deception," *Intelligence and National Security*, July, 1993; Thomas Troy, "CIA's British Parentage," Tenth Annual Meeting of the Society for Historians of American Foreign Policy, August, 1984[Parentage]; MI6; Spy; Hinsley; Anthony Cave Brown, *The Secret Life of Sir Stewart Graham Menzies, Spymaster to Winston Churchill* (New York: Macmillan, 1987); Jennet Conant, *The Irregulars* (New York: Simon & Schuster, 2008) [Irregulars]; Thomas E. Mahl, *Desperate Deception: British Covert Operations in the United States, 1939-44* (New York: Brassey's, 1999)[Deception]; Sisterhood; Jeffrey M. Dorwart, "The Roosevelt-Astor Espionage Ring," *Journal of the New York State Historical Society*, July, 1981 [Ring]; Kermit Roosevelt Papers, Library of Congress; Jeffrey M. Dowart, *The*

Office of Naval Intelligence (Annapolis: Naval Institute Press, 1979) [ONI]; Astor Papers, FDR Library, Hyde Park [Astor]; Federal Bureau of Investigation, Washington, DC, File on Vincent Astor; Joseph E. Persico, *Roosevelt's Secret War* (New York: Random House, 2001)[Secret War].

Chapter Thirty-Three
Cynthia; CP; HP; *www.madamebrousse.com*; Shadow; ONI; PRO; Ring; Astor; BSC; Secret War.

Chapter Thirty-Four
HP; Cynthia; CP; Quiet; Shadow; BSC; Deception; Britain's War; Hinsely.

Chapter Thirty-Five
Cynthia; CP; HP; Agent; Quiet; BSC; ONI; Irregulars; Intrepid; Wild Bill; Deception; Britain's War; Hinsley; FBI File: Mrs. Elizabeth Pack; Washington Social Register, archives; Irregulars.

Chapter Thirty-Six
Cynthia; CP; Hyde; Sisterhood; BSC; A.A. Hoehling, *Women Who Spy* (Lanham, MD: Madison Books, 1993); Shadow; History Television "Family Secrets: Marion de Chastelain" (transcript); "The True Intrepid," *The Guardian*, London, 2000; Parentage; Britain's War; Intrepid; Quiet; Agent; FDR; David Brinkley, *Washington Goes to War* (New York: Knopf, 1988)[Washington]; William McNeil, *America, Britain, and Russia* (New York: Oxford University Press, 1953); "Bill to Aid Britain Strongly Backed," *New York Times*, February 9, 1941; "Lend–Lease Shipments: World War II," Chief of Finance, War Dept., December 31, 1946; Conrad Black, *Franklin Delano Roosevelt, Champion of Freedom* (New York: Public Affairs, 2003); William Langer, *The Undeclared War* (New York: Harper Bros., 1953); George Green, "Connally," Texas State Historical Association; Thomas E. Hachey, "American Profiles on Capitol Hill: A Confidential Study for the British Foreign Office in 1943," *Wisconsin Magazine of History*, Winter, 1973–74; "Michigan's Vandenberg," *Time* Magazine, April 29, 1937; Lawrence S. Kaplan, *The Conversion of Senator Arthur H. Vandenberg: From Isolation to International Engagement* (Lexington, KY: University Press of Kentucky, 2014).

Chapter Thirty-Seven
Cynthia; CP; HP; Shadow; Washington; Enigma; David Brown, *The Royal Navy and the Mediterranean* (London: Routledge, 2002); BSC; Intrepid.

Chapter Thirty-Eight
Cynthia; CP; HP; Washington; Enigma; Shadow; BSC; Intrepid.

Chapter Thirty-Nine
Cynthia; NA; Shadow; HP; BSC; Intrepid; Washington; Enigma; Jack Greene and Alessandro Massignani, *The Naval War in the Mediterranean* (London: Chatham, 1998); Royal Navy website, Battle of Cape Matapan; Anthony M. Scalzo, "Battle of Cape Matapan," *History Magazine*, June, 2000; Mavis Bately, "Breaking Italian Navy Enigma" in Michael Smith, *The Bletchley Park Codebreakers* (London: Biteback Publishing, 2011); James J. Sadkovich, "Re-evaluating Who Won the Italo-British Naval Conflict 1940-2," *European History Quarterly*, October, 1988; Agent; Quiet; PRO.

Chapter Forty
FBI File: Mrs. Elizabeth Pack; Shadow; Cynthia; CP; HP; Washington; BSC; Intrepid; Quiet; PRO; NA; Sisterhood; ONI; Hull; Enigma.

Chapter Forty-One
Cynthia; HP; Quiet; Shadow; CP.

Chapter Forty-Two
Intrepid; Quiet; Cynthia; CP; Shadow; BSC; Sisterhood; Spy; NA; Douglas Boyd, *Voices from the Dark Years: The Truth about Occupied France 1940-1945* (New York: The History Press, 2014); Jean-Pierre Azema, *From Munich to Liberation, 1938-1944*, part of the Cambridge History of Modern France (New York: Cambridge University Press, 1985); Simon Kitson, *The Hunt for Nazi Spies: Fighting Espionage in Vichy France* (Chicago: University of Chicago Press, 2008); Colin Smith, *England's Last War Against France: Fighting Vichy, 1940-1942* (London: Weidenfeld, 2009)[Smith]; Charles Cogan, *Oldest Allies, Guarded Friends: The United States and France Since 1940* (New York: Praeger, 1994)[Cogan]; Julian G. Hurstfield, *America and the French Na-*

tion, 1939-1945 (Chapel Hill, NC: University of North Carolina Press, 1986) [Hurstfield]; Hull; *London Times*, "Libel on Former Ambassador," March 16, 1966.

Chapter Forty-Three

Cynthia; HP; BSC; Intrepid; Sisterhood; NA: OSS Papers, Vichy Intercepts; Hull; Quiet; Shadow.

Chapter Forty-Four

CP; Cynthia; Shadow; BSC; Quiet; Intrepid; Washington; Hinsley; MI6; NA: Vichy Intercepts; Divorce Papers, Pack vs. Pack, May 14, 1945, Somerset House Archives, London; FBI File: Vichy.

Chapter Forty-Five

FDR; Rick Atkinson, *An Army at Dawn: The War in North Africa, 1942-1943* (New York: Henry Holt, 2002)[Atkinson]; Russell Brooks, "Casablanca–The French Side of the Fence," *U.S. Naval Institute Proceedings*, September, 1951; Henry H. Adams, *1942: The Year That Doomed the Axis* (New York: Warner, 1973); Robert Dallek, *Franklin D. Roosevelt and American Foreign Policy, 1932-1945* (New York: Oxford University Press, 1979); David A. Walker, "OSS and Operation Torch," *Journal of Contemporary History*, 1987 [OSS Torch]; BSC; Intrepid; Quiet; PRO; Wild Bill; Peter Wright, *Spycatcher* (New York: Viking Penguin, 1987)[Spycather]; Chapman Pincher, *Their Trade Is Treachery* (New York: Bantam Books, 1982) [Pincher]; Cynthia; Shadow; HP; Sisterhood; DP; Anthony Cave Brown, *Wild Bill Donovan: The Last Hero* (New York: Times Books, 1982)[Hero]; Anthony Cave Brown, *The Secret War Report of the OSS* (New York: Berkley, 1976)[Brown]; U.S. War Department. Strategic Services Unit. *War Report: Office of Strategic Services*, 2 vols. (Washington: GPO, 1949) [OSS War Report].

Chapter Forty-Six

Cynthia; HP; BSC; Shadow; Sisterhood; Intrepid; Quiet; Washington; FBI File: Mrs. Elizabeth Pack; NA:Vichy Intercepts; *New York Herald Tribune*, August 31, 1941, p. 1, and September 1, 1941, p. 1.

Chapter Forty-Seven
Cynthia; CP; Shadow; Sisterhood; Washington; Cogan; Smith; Hurstfield; BSC; Intrepid; Quiet; FBI File: Mrs. Elizabeth Pack; NA.

Chapter Forty-Eight
Cynthia; CP; Shadow; NA; BSC; Quiet.

Chapter Forty-Nine
State Department Papers: Charles Brousse File; Cynthia; BSC; CP; Shadow; NA; Spy; Sisterhood; Quiet; DP; OSS War Report; Washington; FDR; Atkinson.

Chapter Fifty
Cynthia; BSC; Shadow; State Department Papers: Charles Brousse File; CP; Sisterhood; Intrepid; Quiet; OSS War Report; Washington; Wild Bill.

Chapter Fifty-One
Cynthia; CP; Shadow; HP; BSC; Sisterhood; OSS War Report; DP; Butler County Historical Society, "Mosler Safe Company"; State Department Papers: Charles Brousse; ONI; Atkinson; OSS Torch; Intrepid; Quiet; Winston Churchill, *The Second World War*, vol. 4 (London: Cassell, 1951).

Chapter Fifty-Two
FBI File: Mrs. Elizabeth Pack; NA; Shadow; Wild Bill; State Department: Adolf Berle Papers; Intrepid; Quiet; Cynthia; CP; Agent; OSS War Report; DP; Hero; Brown; State Department Papers: Charles Brousse; BSC.

Chapter Fifty-Three
Atkinson; Hull; NA; FDR; Cynthia; Shadow; BSC; Intrepid; CP; Erika Dreifus, "A Golden Prison in Pennsylvania, The Hotel Hershey 1942-43," *Pennsylvania History*, vol. 69, Summer 2002; State Department Papers; Charles Brousse; *www.hersheyarchives.org/essay/details*; OSS War Report; *Washington Evening Star*, November 17, 1942; Catherine Gordon Declaration to State Department, December 28, 1942; DP; FBI Files: Mrs. Elizabeth Pack; Quiet.

Chapter Fifty-Four

Cynthia; CP; Shadow; HP; *South Pacific Mail*, Pack Obituary, November 8, 1945; Rosina Rivett Letters and Interviews quoted in Lovell.

Chapter Fifty-Five

Cynthia; CP; HP; Shadow; Wild Bill; *The People*, September, 29, 1963 and December 8, 1963; Spycatcher; Pincher.

Acknowledgments

WHEN I SAT DOWN AT my desk to write this book the pond outside my writing room was just beginning to freeze. By the time I had finished a pretty sturdy draft, the pond was sprinkled with lily pads and more than an entire year's worth of seasons had passed outside my window. Yet I felt as if I had worked in a whirlwind. Ensconced on my hilltop in front of my computer, I barely noticed the months flying by. And now that the book is done, I realize that this sort of joyful focus was only possible because there were a lot of people I could depend upon, and to whom I, from time to time, was able to reach out.

Lynn Nesbit, my agent and friend, was a constant source of wisdom. She's wise, prudent, and very loyal. I count on her and her friendship immensely. And in her office, Stephanie Koven was always working diligently on my behalf, Lenore Hoffman put up with my pestering, Bennett Ashley helped me navigate a few tight corners, and Hannah Davey did her best to help deflate each new crisis.

At the end of each day, when I re-read and then edited my pages, I was guided—and intimidated—by one constant thought: what would Claire think? Claire Wachtel, my editor at Harper-Collins, is every writer's dream—perceptive, demanding, and thorough. Working with her, having her edit my books, makes my work better. Jonathan Burnham, HarperCollins's publisher, was also a very involved and hands-on presence throughout the entire process. He's a smart, careful reader and an astute publisher. Also at HarperCollins, I benefited from Hannah Wood's many kindnesses and shrewd judgments, and Kate D'Esmond and Leigh Rayner's dogged attention.

Bob Bookman is a very untypical Hollywood agent. He's erudite, well-read, and a true connoisseur. For decades I have enjoyed his friendship. He was also, once again, responsible for bringing this book to the attention to the people who are now working to make it into a movie. At Sony Pictures, both Hannah Minghella and Lauren Abrahams have been early and enthusiastic supporters of this book and the movie it will be. And Mark Gordon, working along with Sara Smith, has been a diligent and thoughtful producer.

Alan Hergott, who's been my friend and attorney for years, and the tenacious Eric Brooks worked hard to make sure all the "i"s were properly dotted as the movie deal moved forward.

At *Vanity Fair*, both Graydon Carter and Dana Brown were early advocates of this book. I'm thankful for their many kindnesses.

And whenever I stepped away from my desk, I was fortunate to have many good friends I could turn to. My sister Marcy was always there for me, eager to offer advice, help, and a laugh or two. And I also counted on John Leventhal and Bruce Taub, buddies since our childhood basketball days; Susan and David Rich; Irene and Phil Werber; Sarah and Bill Rauch; Beth DeWoody; Ken Lipper; Pat and Bob Lusthaus; Bob Mitchell; Scott Silver; Betsey and Len Rappoport; Arline Mann and Bob Katz; Christopher Mason; and Claudie and Andrew Skonka.

My children—Tony, Anna, and Dani—fill me with pride. It's exciting and a blessing to see them make their accomplished way in the world.

And for so many things, both large and small joys, I'm grateful to Daisy and Ivana.

Bibliography

Adams, Henry H. *1942: The Year That Doomed the Axis*. New York: Warner Books, 1973.

Alsop, Stewart and Thomas Braden. *Sub Rosa: The OSS and American Espionage*. New York: Harcourt, Brace and World, 1964.

Andrew, Christopher. *Her Majesty's Secret Service: The Making of the British Intelligence Community*. New York: Viking, 1986.

Atkinson, Rick. *An Army at Dawn: The War in North Africa, 1942-1943*. New York: Henry Holt, 2002.

Azema, Pierre. *From Munich to Liberation, 1938-1944*. New York: Cambridge University Press, 1985.

Baltzwell, Edward. *Philadelphia Gentlemen: The Making of a National Upper Class*. New York: Free Press, 1958.

Beaverbrook, Max Aitken. *Politicians and the War 1914-1916*. London: Thornton Butterworth, 1928.

Beevor, Anthony. *The Battle for Spain*. New York: Hachette, 2012.

Berle, Adolf A. *Navigating the Rapids 1918-1971: From the Papers of Adolf A. Berle*. New York: Harcourt, Brace, and Jovanovich, 1973.

Bisson, Thomas N. *The Medieval Crown of Aragon: A Short History*. Oxford: Clarendon Press, 2004.

Black, Conrad. *Franklin Delano Roosevelt, Champion of Freedom*. New York: Public Affairs, 2003.

Boyd, Douglas. *Voices from the Dark Years: The Truth About Occupied France 1940-1945*. New York: The History Press, 2014.

Bracher, Karl Dietrich. *The German Dictatorship*. New York: Praeger, 1970.

Breitman, Richard, and Timothy Naftali. "Report to the Interagency Working Group on Previously Classified OSS Records." National Archives, College Park, MD, 2000.

Brinkley, David. *Washington Goes to War*. New York: Knopf, 1988.

British Security Coordination, *The Secret History of British Intelligence in the Americas, 1940-45*. New York: Fromm International, 1999.

Brown, Anthony Cave. *Wild Bill Donovan: The Last Hero*. New York: Times Books, 1982.

——— *The Secret War Report of the OSS*. New York: Berkley, 1976.

Brown, David. *The Royal Navy in the Mediterranean*. London: Routledge, 2002.

Buchanan, Tom. "Edge of Darkness: British 'Front-Line' Diplomacy in Spanish Civil War, 1936-1937," *Contemporary European History*, vol. 12, no. 3. August, 2003.

——— *"C" The Secret Life of Sir Stewart Menzies*. New York: Macmillan, 1987.

Burleigh, Michael. *The Third Reich*. London: Macmillan, 2000.

Butler, Josephine. *Churchill's Secret Agent*. London: Blaketon Hall, 1983.

Caro, Ina. *The Road from the Past*. New York: Mariner Books, 1996.

Carr, Sir Raymond. *The Spanish Tragedy*. New York: Phoenix Press, 1977.

Chalou, George C., editor. *The Secrets War: The Office of Strategic Services in World War II*. Washington, DC: National Archives, 1992.

Chisholm, Anne, and Michael Davie. *Lord Beaverbrook: A Life*. New York: Knopf, 1993.

Churchill, Winston S. *The Second World War*. Vols. 1-4. London: Cassell, 1951.

Cieciala, Anna. "The Foreign Policy of Jozef Beck." *The Polish Review*, vol. LVI, 2011.

Cline, Ray S. *Secrets, Spies and Scholars*. Washington, DC: Acropolis, 1976.

Cloud, Stanley, and Lynne Olson. *A Question of Honor*. New York: Vintage Books, 2004.

Cogan, Charles. *Oldest Allies, Guarded Friends: The United States and France Since 1940*. New York: Praeger, 1994.

Conant, Jennet. *The Irregulars*. New York: Simon & Schuster, 2008.

Cork Historical and Archeological Society. "The Martello Towers of Cork Harbour," July, 2012.

Costello, John. *Days of Infamy: MacArthur, Roosevelt, Churchill—The Shocking Truth Revealed*. New York: Pocket Books, 1994.

——— *Love, Sex and War*. London: Collins, 1985.

Coville, John. *Winston Churchill and His Inner Circle*. New York: Wyndham, 1981.

Cox, Geoffrey. *Defense of Madrid*. London: Gollanz, 1937.

Cuneo, Ernest L. "The British and Sir William." Typescript. Cuneo Papers, Hyde Park, NY.

Czechoslovak Office of Foreign Affairs. *Two Years of German Oppression in Czechoslovakia.* London: Czechoslovak Publications, 1941.

Dallek, Robert. *Franklin D. Roosevelt and American Foreign Policy, 1932-1945.* New York: Oxford University Press, 1979.

Darling, Arthur B. *The Central Intelligence Agency: An Instrument of Government to 1950.* University Park, PA: Pennsylvania State University, 1990.

Davis, Norman. *"God's Playground": A Short History of Poland.* New York: Columbia University Press, 1982.

Deacon, Richard. *A History of the British Secret Service.* London: Granada, 1980.

———, and Nigel West. *Spy!* London: British Broadcasting Corp., 1980.

Dorling, Henry Taprell. *Blue Star Line at War.* London: W.H. Foulsham, 1973.

Dorwart, Jeffrey M. "The Roosevelt-Astor Spy Ring." *New York History,* vol. LXII, No. 3, July 1981.

——— *The Office of Naval Intelligence.* Annapolis: Naval Institute Press, 1979.

Dreifus, Erika. "Golden Prison in Pennsylvania: The Hotel Hershey 1942-43." *Pennsylvania History,* vol. 69. no. 3. Summer, 2002.

Drzewieniecki, Walter. "The Polish Army on the Eve of World War II." *The Polish Review,* 1981.

Dunlop, Richard. *Donovan: America's Master Spy.* Chicago: Rand McNally, 1982.

Farago, Ladislas. *The Game of Foxes.* New York: David McKay, 1971.

Ford, Corey. *Donovan of OSS.* Boston: Little Brown, 1970.

Fuqua, Stephen Ogden. *Americans Wanted.* New York: Smith & Durrell, 1940.

Gelhorn, Martha. *The View from the Ground.* London: Granta Books, 1990.

Gilbert, Martin. *Finest Hour: Winston Churchill 1939-1941.* London: Heinemann, 1983.

——— *Winston Churchill: The Wilderness Years.* Boston: Houghton Mifflin, 1982.

Graham, Helen. *The Spanish Republic at War, 1936-1939.* New York: Cambridge University Press, 2002.

Greene, Jack, and Alessandro Massignani. *The Naval War in the Mediterranean.* London: Chatham, 1998.

Grinnel, Nancy Whipple. *Carrying the Torch: Maude Howe Elliot and the American Renaissance.* Lebanon, NH: University Press of New England, 2004.

Hammond, John Winthrop. *Charles Proteus Steinmetz: A Biography.* New York: The Century, 1924.

Haswell, Jock. *Spies and Spymasters.* London: Thames & Hudson, 1977.

Hinsley, F.H., and E.E. Thomas, C.F.G. Ransom, and R.C. Knight. *British Intelligence in the Second World War.* London: HMSO, 1979.

—— and Alan Stripp, editors. *Codebreakers.* New York: Oxford University Press, 1993.

Hoehling, A.A. *Women Who Spied.* Lanham, MD: Madison Books, 1993.

Hogan, David L. "President Roosevelt and the Origins of the 1939 War." *The Journal of Historical Review,* vol 4. 1989.

Hull, Cordell. *Memoirs.* London: Hodder & Stoughton, 1948.

Hurstfield, Julian G. *America and the French Nation, 1939-1945.* Chapel Hill, NC: University of North Carolina Press, 1986.

Hutton, J. Bernard. *Women Spies.* London: W.H. Allen, 1971.

Hyde, H. Montgomery. *Cynthia.* New York: Farrar, Straus, and Giroux, 1963.

—— *The Quiet Canadian: The Secret Service Story of Sir William Stephenson.* London: Hamish Hamilton, 1962. Published in the U.S. as *Room 3603: The Story of the British Intelligence Center in New York During World War II.* New York: Farrar, Straus, and Giroux, 1963.

—— *Secret Intelligence Agent.* New York: St. Martin's, 1983.

Ignatius, David. "Britain's War in America: How Churchill's Agents Secretly Manipulated the U.S. Before Pearl Harbor." *Washington Post,* Sept 17, 1989.

Irving, David. *Churchill's War: The Struggle for Power.* Perth, Australia: Veritas, 1987.

Jellinek, Frank. *The Civil War in Spain.* London: Gollancz, 1938.

Jones, R.V. *Most Secret War.* London: Hamish Hamilton, 1978.

Kahn, David. *The Codebreakers.* New York: Macmillan, 1968.

—— *Seizing the Enigma.* Boston, MA: Houghton Mifflin, 1991.

Kaplan, Lawrence S. *The Conversion of Senator Arthur H. Vandenberg: From Isolation to International Engagement.* Lexington, KY: University Press of Kentucky, 2014.

Kimball, Warren F. *Churchill and Roosevelt: The Complete Correspondence.* Princeton, NJ: Princeton University Press, 1934.

Kirkpatrick, Sir Ivone. *The Inner Circle.* London: Macmillan, 1959.

Kitson, Simon. *The Hunt for Nazi Spies: Fighting Espionage in Vichy France, 1940-1942.* London: Weidenfeld, 2009.

Kozaczuk, Wladsylaw. *Enigma: How the Poles Broke the Nazi Code.* New York: Hippocrene Books, 2004.

Langer, William. *The Undeclared War.* New York: Harper Bros., 1953.

Lash, Joseph P. *Roosevelt and Churchill.* New York: Norton, 1976.

Le Carré, John. "England's Spy in America." *New York Times Book Review,* February 29, 1971.

Lewin, Ronald. *Ultra Goes to War.* London: Pen and Sword, 2008.

Lovell, Mary S. *Cast No Shadow: The Life of the American Spy Who Changed the Course of World War II.* New York: Pantheon, 1992.

Lowenheim, Francis L., and Harold D. Langley, Manfred Jonas, editors. *Roosevelt and Churchill: Their Secret Wartime Correspondence.* New York: Saturday Review Press/Dutton, 1975.

Lukowski, Jerzy, and Hubert Zawadzki. *A Concise History of Poland.* New York: Cambridge University Press, 2006.

Mackiewicz, Stanislaw. *Colonel Beck and His Policy.* London: Eyre and Spottiswoode, 1944.

Mahl, Thomas E. *Desperate Deception: British Covert Operations in the United States 1939-44.* New York: Brassey's, 1999.

Martin, Gilbert. *The Wilderness Years.* London: Heinemann, 1983.

McIntosh, Elizabeth P. *Sisterhood of Spies.* New York: Dell, 1999.

McNeil, William. *America, Britain, and Russia.* New York: Oxford University Press, 1953.

Mullay, Shelia. *O'Malley: People and Places.* Dublin: Ballinakella Press, 1986.

Murray, John. *A Spy Called Swallow.* London: W. H. Allen, 1978.

Naftali, Timothy J. "Intrepid's Last Deception: Documenting the Career of Sir William Stephenson." *Intelligence and National Security.* July, 1993.

O'Sullivan, Michael, and Bernard O'Neill. *The Shelbourne and Its People.* Dublin: Blackwater Press, 1999.

Paul, Preston. "From Rebel to Caudillo: Franco's Path to Power." *History Today,* July, 1986.

Pearson, John. *The Life of Ian Fleming.* New York: McGraw-Hill, 1996.

Persico, Joseph E. *Roosevelt's Secret War*. New York: Random House, 2001.

Pincher, Chapman. *Their Trade Is Treachery*. New York: Bantam Books, 1982.

Prieto, Indalecio. *Remembrances and Perspectives*. New York: Spanish Editions, 1938.

Rejewski, Marian. "Remarks on Appendix I to *British Intelligence in the Second World War*, vol. I by F.H. Hinsley," *Cryptologia*, January, 1982.

Roberts, Henry L. "The Diplomacy of Colonel Beck." *The International History Review*, January, 1981.

Rosenzwieg, Roy, and Elizabeth Blackman. *The Park and the People*. Ithaca, NY: Cornell University Press, 1998.

Ruiz, Teofilio. "The Transformation of the Castilian Municipalities." *Past and Present*, November, 1972.

Sadkovich, James J. "Re-evaluating Who Won the Italo-British Naval Conflict 1940-2." *European History Quarterly*, October, 1988.

Sebag-Montefiore, Hugh. *Enigma: The Battle for the Code*. Hoboken, NJ: John Wiley & Sons, 2000.

Shirer, William L. *The Rise and Fall of the Third Reich*. New York: Simon & Schuster, 2011.

Smith, Colin. *England's Last War Against France: Fighting Vichy, 1940-1942*. Chicago: University of Chicago Press, 2008.

Smith, Eric R. *Relief Aid and the Spanish Civil War*. Columbia, MO: University of Missouri Press, 1993.

Smith, Michael. *The Bletchley Park Codebreakers*. London: Biteback Publishing, 2011.

Smith, R. Harris. *OSS: The Secret History of America's First Central Intelligence Agency*. Berkeley: University of California Press, 1972.

Stafford, David. *Camp X*. New York: Viking Press, 1986.

Stang, Lord. *Foreign Office*. London: George Allen & Unwin, 1957.

Stevenson, William. *A Man Called Intrepid*. Guilford, CT: The Lyons Press, 2000.

Stuart, Graham H. *The Department of State: A History of Its Organization, Procedure, and Personnel*. New York: Macmillan, 1949.

Sullivan, Brian P. "The Intelligence Career of William J. Donovan." *Rockefeller Archive Center Newsletter*, Fall, 1993.

Thomas, Hugh. *The Spanish Civil War*. London: Penguin Books, 2003.

Thompson, George Malcolm. *Lord Castlerosse, His Life and Times.* London: Weidenfeld & Nicolson, 1973.

Trask, L. *The History of the Basque.* London: Routledge, 1997.

Trevor-Roper, H.R. "Superagent." *New York Review of Books,* May 13, 1976.

Troy, Thomas F. *Wild Bill and Intrepid: Donovan, Stephenson and the Origin of the CIA.* New Haven, CT: Yale University Press, 1996.

———— "CIA's British Parentage—and the Significance Thereof." Society for Historians of American Foreign Relations, George Washington University, Washington, DC, August 3, 1984.

———— *Donovan and the CIA.* Frederick, MD: University Publications of America, 1981.

U.S. War Department, Strategic Services Unit. *War Report: Office of Strategic Services.* 2 vols. Washington, DC: GPO, 1949.

Walker, David A. "OSS and Operation Torch." *Journal of Contemporary History,* 1987.

West, Nigel. *MI5: British Security Service Operations 1909-1945.* New York: Stein and Day, 1982.

———— *MI6: British Secret Intelligence Operations 1909-1945.* London: Weidenfeld and Nicolson, 1983.

Wilkinson, Peter, and Joan Astley. *Gubbins and SOE.* London: Leo Cooper, 1993.

Winterbotham, F.W. *The Ultra Secret.* New York: Dell, 1978.

Wright, Peter. *Spycatcher: The Candid Autobiography of a Senior Intelligence Officer.* New York: Viking, 1987.

Wynot, E.D. *Warsaw Between the Wars.* New York: East European Monographs, 1983.

Credits

424: Churchill Archives Center, Papers of Harford Montgomery Hyde, HYDE 02 011

454: Personal collection

456: Churchill Archives Center, Papers of Harford Montgomery Hyde, HYDE 02 007

466: Churchill Archives Center, Papers of Harford Montgomery Hyde, HYDE 02 007

Index

Italicized page numbers indicate photographs and illustrations.

Altamira, Viscount Augustin, 140–
141, 143, 144, 150, 151–152
Aruezza, Marquis Luis Villada, 171–175
Astor, Vincent
background, 264–265
intelligence work of, 265–269, *266*
Avedillo, Viscount Don José de
Yanguas Messia, 147–148

Beaverbrook, Lord, *109*
recruits Betty for intelligence
work, 108–110, 118
Beck, Joseph, *202*
Lubienski and, 227–231
Lubienski reveals information
about, to Betty, 201, 204–205
sends Lubienski Germany,
218–220
Bell, Walter, 268
Benoit, Charles, 371–375
Berle, Adolf, 429, 444
Bertrand-Vigne, George, 339
Biddle, Anthony J. Drexel Jr., 200
Biddle, Margaret, 199
Black Chamber. *See under* Poland
Blanding, Don, 59
Bletchley Park, 217
Italian navy codes and, 318
Vichy navy codes and, 424–425
British Security Coordination (BSC)
Betty and, 269, 285–289
FBI and, 261, 263–264, 289
Italian navy codes and, 300–321
Italian navy plans in US and,
321–328
Lend Lease and, 261–262,
295–298

Roosevelt as supporter of, 264
see also Vichy French embassy entries
Brousse, Catherine (Kay), *341*, 350,
355
discovers Betty's affair with
Brousse, 447–448
interned at Hotel Hershey,
441–443, 446
plans to travel to France with
"daughter" and Brousse,
432–436
Brousse, Charles Emmanuel, *4*, *341*,
344
Betty and Hyde and, 5, 21, 25,
27–28
Betty's relationship with her
father and, 57
death of, 465
engagement and marriage to
Betty, 6–8, 449–450, 464
in France with Betty after war,
3–8, *7*, 25–27, *26*, 451–456,
456, 463–465
intelligence about Japan and, 392
interned at Hotel Hershey,
441–443, 446
plans to travel to France with
wife and "step-daughter,"
432–437, 439–440
Brousse, Charles Emmanuel, and
Vichy embassy operations, 331
Betty meets, 342–344, 346
Betty recruits as agent, 346–351,
354–357
Betty's recruiting of Grandville
and, 376, 379, 380, 382–388
dangers of, 357–358

Brousse, Charles Emmanuel *(continued)*
  Henry-Haye's questions about
    Betty and, 387–388
  information about Vichy plans in
    US, 351–352
  navy cipher operation planning,
    362, 369–371, 394–399
  navy cipher theft attempts,
    400–412, 417–419, 422
  US concerns about
    trustworthiness of, 390–392
  work at Vichy embassy, 339,
    340–341

Campbell, Sam, 460
Campbell-Orde, Eleanor, 83
Cape Matapan, Battle of, 316–317
Carr, Wilbur, 219
Cassell, Dr. and Mrs., 81–82, 97–98,
    232, 453, 455
Castelnou, France, 3–8, *7*, *25*, 25–27,
    26, 451–456, *456*, 463–465
Castlerosse, Valentine, 106–108,
    107, 110
Chastellaine, Marion de, 292–293,
    299, 308
Chevalier, André
  Betty and Brousse befriend,
    396–399
  during naval cipher theft
    attempts, 400–403, 409,
    410–411, 418, 420–421
Chile
  Arthur posted to, 84–85,
    234–235, 242–243, *243*
  Betty and Arthur in, 91–96, 98–99
  Betty leaves, 249–250, 255,
    258–259
  Betty returns to, wants to divorce
    Arthur, 271–274, 276–277
  Betty's intelligence work in,
    247–248
Chilton, Harry, 96, *139*
  Spanish Civil War and, 123, 125,
    134, 135, 138, 148–149, 166,
    190

Churchill, Winston, 287, 292, 338
  Italian navy and, 317, 326
  Lend Lease and, 293–295
  North Africa invasion plans and,
    359–360, 399, 416, 425
  Stephenson and, 212, 262
Ciezki, Maksymilian, 206
Connally, Thomas, 296–297
Coolidge, Calvin, 43, 48
Coordinator of Information (COI),
    365–367
Cuba, 256, 286
  Thorpe family in, 44, 46, 92
Cunningham, Andrew, 316–317
Cynamont Corporation, 282, 460
Cynthia (Hyde), 465
"Cynthia." *See* Pack, Betty Thorpe,
    as spy

Dana Hall School, 61, 62
Darlan, Jean, 337, 351, 358
Donovan, William J.
  Betty's wish to be interned in
    Hershey and, 444
  known as Big Bill, 367
  plans to send Betty to France
    with Brousse, 430, 436–437
  US State Department and, 429
  Vichy embassy missions and,
    366–367, 391, 396, 407, 416
Doublet, Leslie, 242–243, *243*
Downes, Donald
  Brousse's internment and,
    441–442, 444
  plans to send Betty to France with
    Brousse, 432–433, 435, 440
  Vichy embassy missions and,
    367

Eisenhower, Dwight D., 217
Elliot, Maud Howe, 47
Ellis, Howard "Dick," 361, 460–461
Enigma device
  Betty and monitoring of Poland's
    Black Chamber teams,
    215–216, 217

Black Chamber's attempts to
decode, 206, 207, 209–211,
215–216
breaking of Italian naval codes
and, 318
described, 206–207
information about, sold to
French, 208–209
Stephenson and, 211, 212–214
value of decoding, 216–217
Eusabio (Spanish chauffeur), 125–
127, 130–131, 133–134
Excaliber (US merchant ship),
268–269, *270*, 271–272, 273

Fairly, Paul, 269, *270*, 353
Betty aborts child of, 291
Betty's early intelligence work
and, 273–275, 277, 284–285
Lais and plans to scuttle Italian
ships, 323, 325, 326
Vichy embassy missions and,
422–423
Federal Bureau of Investigation (FBI)
British intelligence service and,
261, 263–264, 289
interest in Betty, 321–325, 358,
365, 369, 370, 380, 427–428
Fioretta: A Tale of Italy (Thorpe),
53–59, *54*, 61
Forbes, Courteney, 251–255
France
Betty and Arthur in Biarritz at
start of Spanish Civil War,
120–121, 124, *139*
Betty and Brousse at Castelnou,
3–8, *7*, 25–27, *26*, 451–456,
456, 463–465
buys information about Enigma,
208–209
see also Vichy French embassy entries
Fuqua, Stephen, 177–180

"Georgia Cracker," 395–396
first naval cipher theft attempt,
400, 404–406

teaches Betty to crack safe, 413–415
third naval cipher theft attempt,
416, 420
Gestapo
Brousse's sister-in-law and, 451–452
fears about, 338, 431–432, 435, 442
Glasser, Joseph, 441
"Gordon, Catherine Waterbury," as
identity for Betty as Brousse's
step-daughter, 433–435
Grandville, Count Jean de la
Betty's attempts to recruit, 375–379
reports spying to Vichy
ambassador, 379–388
Gubbins, Colin, 213–214
Guilio (Italian cipher clerk), Betty
gets naval codes from, 312–
316, 318–320

Hawaii, 52–54, 58, 60
Henlein, Karl, 220–224, 225, 245
Henry-Haye, Gaston, *344*
Betty tries to recruit for missions,
339, 340, 344–346
Brousse and, 350, 354–355, 356,
358, 387–388, 436
interned at Hotel Hershey, 441,
442, 446, 447–448
Hershey, Milton, 440
Hoover, J. Edgar, 263–264, 321, 417,
428–429
Hotel Hershey, Vichy diplomats
interned in, 440–449
Hull, Cordell, 251–252, 327, 443
Henry-Haye and, 339, 345,
438–439
see also State Department
Huntington, Ellery C. ("Mr.
Hunter"), 57, 366, 433
Vichy embassy missions and, 365–
366, 368, 369, 375, 391–405,
407, 416–417, 421, 423, 426
Hyde, Harford Montgomery
Betty's death and, 465–467, *466*
Betty leaves Castelnou to meet,
3–11, 13–19, 55

Hyde, Harford Montgomery
(*continued*)
biography of Stephenson, 12, 13,
22–23, 27, 281, 319, 460
Cynthia published, 465
meets Betty as "Cynthia," 12–13,
17–18
on nature of spies, 240–241
plans to write about Betty's life,
20–27, *25*, 281–283
post-war professional and
personal life, 22–23, 42
thoughts on Lais and Italian naval
codes, 318–320
travels with and interviews Betty,
27–28, 31–32, 52, 89–90, *90*,
195–197, 239–240, 331–332,
455, 461–463
writes Betty's memoirs, 459–461,
464–465

Innes, Edgar, 445–446
Ireland, Betty and Hyde in, 27–28,
31–32, 52, 89–90, *90*, 195–
197, 239–240, 331–332
Italian naval codes
Allies' need for, 301, 308–309
Betty contacts Lais and asks
about, 301–311
Betty receives from Guilio,
312–316, 318–320
British navy's use of, 316–318
Italian navy, Lais reveals plans to
scuttle ships in US harbors,
321–328

Jacobsen, Fernanda, 162–163, *163*, 165
Japan, Brousse provides intelligence
about, 392
Joyce, James, 89–90

Kennard, Howard, 35, 229, 230
Kimbel, William, 444–445
Kreiser, Thomas, 246
Kulikowski, Edward, 37–41, 197, 198

Lais, Alberto, *302*
Betty asks for help getting naval
codes, 307–311
Betty contacts, 300–304
Betty convinces she dislikes
England, 305–307
leaves US, 327–328
reveals plans to scuttle Italian
ships in US harbors, 321–327
Lais, Leonora, 306
Laval, Pierre, 356, 358, 371, 378,
430, 438
Leche, John, *157*
Betty's appointment with Prieto
and, 179–180
as Betty's lover, 166–171,
181–182, 187–189, 191, 453
Betty's operation to free Aruezza
and, 171–175
Betty's search for Sartorius and,
155–159, 160, 163, 165–166,
180–182
Lee, Hugh, 316–317
Lend Lease program, 293–295
Betty and, 295–298
Lubienski, Michal, 214, 462
Beck demands end of relationship
with Betty, 227–229
Betty's departure from Poland
and, 233–234
Betty's honey trap and
information about Beck's
negotiation with Hitler,
199–205, 224–225, *226*
Betty's monitoring of Poland's
Black Chamber Enigma teams
through, 215–216, 217
rumors he was getting information
from Betty, 230–231
trip to Germany, 218–220
Lyons, Frederick B., 444

Martello Tower, Ireland, 89–90, *90*
Menzies, Stewart ("C"), 261–262,
360–361

Mercurio, El, 244
MICE acronym, 283
MI6, 22, 39–40, 110, 118, 137,
    191, 242, 256. *See also* Ellis,
    Howard "Dick"; Shelley, Jack
Morton, Desmond, 212, 213
Mountsey, George, 190–191

Nación, La, 244–245
Neutrality Act, of U.S., 262,
    286–287
New York Herald Tribune, 358
North Africa, Allies' planned
    invasion of (Operation Torch),
    359–362, 366–368, 390, 398–
    399, 424–426, 433, 438–439
Norton, Peta, 35, 229–230
Nourmahal (Astor's yacht), 265–266,
    266

Office of Strategic Services (OSS*).
    See* Downes, Donald;
    Huntington, Ellery C.;
    Stephenson, William; *Vichy
    French embassy entries*
Ogilvie-Forbes, George Arthur,
    112, 118–119, *119*, 256
O'Malley, Owen St. Clair, 234,
    239–240, 281
Orbita (ship), 251–257

Pack, Anthony George (son)
    Betty's pregnancy with, 67,
        77–81
    birth and adoption by Cassels,
        10–11, 81–83, 95, 453, 455
    death of, 10, 455
    visited by Betty, 97–98, 232
    visits Betty in Castlenou,
        454–455
Pack, Arthur, *139*
    Anthony Pack and, 10–11, 67,
        77–83
    awarded Order of the British
        Empire, 96

Betty's conversion to Catholicism
    and, 112
Betty's divorce plans and,
    276–277, 346
Betty's engagement and marriage
    to, 33, 68–71, *71*
Betty's relationship with her
    father and, 57, 71–72
Betty's work during Spanish
    Civil War and, 134–136, 143,
    146, 149, 153–154, 190–192
daughter's birth, 98, 99, 100
death of, 452–453
described, 33
disappears in Spain and Betty
    searches for, 125–134
flees Spain for Biarritz, 120–121,
    124
health concerns and return to
    England, 35–36, 199, 203, 232
military and diplomatic service
    of, 33–35, *34*, 72–74, *73*
posted to Chile, 234–235,
    242–243, *243*
posted to Poland as cover for
    Betty's spying, 190–192
social background of, 72
tracks down Betty after she leaves
    Chile, 249–250, 258–259
visits Betty in Washington, DC,
    353–354
Pack, Betty Thorpe, as adolescent
    and child, *51*
    birth and siblings of, 46
    as debutant, 64–66, *65*
    education of, 59, 61
    in Europe, 59, 61
    Fioretta: A Tale of Italy written by,
        53–59, *54*, 61
    first lover of, 63–64
    in Hawaii, 59, 61
    name at birth, 46
    rebellion and aloneness of, 49–51
    in Washington DC, 43, 46–49,
        59–60

Index

Pack, Betty Thorpe, as adult, *26*
  aborts Fairly's child, 291
  affair with and rescue of priest in
    Spain, 113–119
  Arthur's OBE and, 96, *97*
  Arthur's visit to, in Washington,
    353–354
  birth of daughter Denise, 98, 99,
    100
  cancer diagnosis and illness of,
    28, 42–43, 106
  converts to Roman Catholicism,
    111–112
  death of, 465, 466
  divorce from Arthur, plans for,
    276–277, 346
  engagement and marriage to
    Brousse, 6–8, 449–450, 464
  engagement and marriage Arthur
    Pack, 68–71, *71*, 74–76, *76*,
    83–84
  first love affair of married life,
    94–95
  flees Spain for Biarritz, 120–121,
    124
  in France with Brousse after war,
    451–455, *456*
  Hyde and plans to escape from
    life at Castelnou, 3–11, *4*,
    11–27, 55
  meets Sartorius again and begins
    affair with, 101–106
  miscarries Brousse's child, 443
  mother's death and, 8–10, 56, 455
  pregnancy with and birth of
    Anthony, 10–11, 67, 68,
    77–83, 95
  returns to Castelnou, 463–464
  travels with Hyde and evaluates
    her life, 27–28, 31–32, 52,
    89–90, *90*, 195–197, 239–240,
    331–332, 455, 461–463
  writes memoirs with Hyde,
    459–461, 464–465
Pack, Betty Thorpe, as spy

  affair with Brousse discovered
    and cover blown, 447–448
  asks to be interned with Brousse,
    442–446
  in Chile, 247–278
  cover as reporter developed
    (Betty Thomas), 242–246, 255
  during sail from Chile to New
    York, 251–257, 271–272
  in Germany with Lubienski,
    218–220
  Lend Lease and, 295–298
  meets Hyde in 1941, 12–13,
    17–18
  plans for living in France as
    Brousse's step-daughter,
    429–438
  quality of written reports of,
    248–249
  recognized as "symbolized
    agent," 138
  recruited in Poland, 33–42
  Roosevelt asks to meet, 450
  work name "Cynthia," 3, 289
  see also Poland; Spanish Civil
    War; Washington, DC; *Vichy
    French embassy entries*
Pack, Denise Beresford (daughter), *98*
  after Arthur's death, 453, 454, 455
  birth of, 99, 100
  in Chile, 273, 277, 353–354
  death of, 465
  parents' divorce and, 276, 277,
    306
  personality of, 454
  in Poland, 192, 249–250
  during Spanish Civil War, 46,
    120, 125, 134–135, 141, 143,
    154
  during World War II, 230, 243,
    249, 353–354
Paget, James, 268
Paradol (Peruvian diplomat), 254–255
Parry-Jones, Montagu, 247–248,
  257–259

Pepper, John Arthur Reed (J.
Howard)
asks Betty to move to
Washington, 277–278,
284–291
Betty's first mission for, 292, 293
Betty's intelligence from Lais,
300–311, 321–327
gives Betty work name
"Cynthia," 289
Vichy embassy missions and,
335–338, 339, 348, 350, 354,
355, 356–357, 361–362, 407,
413, 415, 416, 423
Pétain, Henri Philippe, 337, 356,
371, 430
Poland, Betty's intelligence work in
Arthur reassigned to as cover for,
190–192
Black Chamber's attempts to
decode Enigma, 206, 207,
209–211, 215–216
Black Chamber Enigma teams
monitoring, 215–216, 217
Henlein's office burgled, 220–
224, 226, 245
expulsion from country, 229–234
"honey trap" for Lubienski,
198–205, 224–225, *226*
Kulikowski's information, 33–41,
197, 198
reports on situation in, 244–246
Prendis, Carlos, 244–245
Prieto, Indalecio, 178–185, 191

Quiet Canadian, The (Hyde), 12, 13,
22–23, 27, 281, 319, 460

Rejewski, Marian, 210
Rivett, Rosie Pack, 83–84, 139, 453
Roman Catholic Church
Betty converts to, 111–112
Spanish Civil War and, 116
The Room, of Astor, 264–265,
268

Roosevelt, Franklin D.
aid to England and, 265–267,
266, 268, 293–295
asks to meet Betty, 450
North Africa invasion plans and,
359–360, 438
US-British intelligence
cooperation and, 254
Vichy embassy missions and, 357,
367

Sartorius, Carlos
disappears during Spanish Civil
War and Betty searches for,
142–143, 147–159, 160–165,
176–182
meets Betty as adult, 101–106,
120
meets Betty when she's 14, 61–63
released from prison, *188*, 192
visited in prison by Betty,
185–187
Sartorius, Carmencita, 103, 104,
105, 142
Schmidt, Hans Thilo, 207–209
Scottish Ambulance Unit, in Spain,
162–164, *163*
Shelley, John, 248, 284
Betty's work in Poland and, 198,
199, 205, 219, 220, 222, 230,
231, 234
Enigma and, 213–214
recruits Betty for intelligence
work, 39–41
"Ships Observers' Scheme," during
World War II, 267–269
Sims, Mitzi, 297
South Pacific Mail, 245
Spain
Betty and Arthur in, 99, 100–
106
Betty reports on Civil War,
134–136
conditions before Civil War,
115–119, *117*

Index

Spain *(continued)*
  conditions during Civil War,
    120–123, *126*, 139, 161–162,
    164
Spanish Civil War, Betty's
    intelligence work during
  frees Aruezza, 171–175
  obtains release of 17 prisoners,
    182–185, 192
  pleads for release of Sartorius,
    182–185
  searches for Arthur, 125–134
  searches for Sartorius, 142–143,
    147–159, 160–165, 176–182
  secures supplies for field hospitals,
    140–142, 143–147, 149–150
  transports Franco supporters to
    border, 134–135
  visits Sartorius in prison, 185–187
State Department, of US
  Betty and, 438–448
  dislike of British spies, 428–429
  Henry-Hyde's threats and,
    387–389
Steinmetz, Charles Proteus, 212
Stephenson, William, 57, *214*, 285,
    350, 460
  Astor and, 267–269
  background, 211–212
  builds British secret service in
    North America, 262–263
  codename Intrepid, 263
  Enigma and, 211, 212–214
  Hoover's dislike of, 428–429
  known as Little Bill, 368
  Lais and need for Italian naval
    codes, 300–301
  opinion of Betty, 216, 331, 449,
    463
  plans to send Betty to France
    with Brousse, 429–431,
    436–437
  recruited as intelligence asset,
    212
  Vichy embassy missions and, 357,
    361, 367, 391, 407

  visits Betty as "Mr. Williams,"
    333–336, 338
  see also *Quiet Canadian, The*
    (Hyde)
Sunday People, 459, 460

Taft, Robert, 295
Thompson, Iain, 23, 459–460
Thorpe, Cora (mother), *9*, 257,
    290–291, 298, 299, 342, 459
  background, 44–45
  Betty's debut and, 65–66
  Betty's marriage to Pack and,
    75–76, 272–273
  Betty's relationship with, 8–10
  death of, 56, 455
  Denise Pack goes to live with,
    454, 455
  marriage of, 46
  social ambitions of, 43–44,
    46–49, 275
  Stephenson and, 334–335
Thorpe, George (brother), 46, 51
Thorpe, George Cyrus (father)
  background, 44
  Betty's relationship with, 56–57,
    71–72
  death of, 136, 342
  marriage of, 46
  military service of, 44, *45*, 46,
    47–48, 53
  resigns commission and moves
    family to Washington, 59
Thorpe, Jane (sister), 46, 257, 290, 428
Thyssen, Fritz, 212
Turing, Alan, 217

Ulysses (Joyce), 89–90, *90*
United States
  Betty's first missions as
    "watcher," 292–293
  cooperation with British secret
    service in World War II,
    261–269
  Italian navy's plans to scuttle
    ships in harbors, 321–328

Lend Lease and, 295–298
see also Federal Bureau
of Investigation; State
Department; Vichy French
embassy entries; Washington DC
entries

Valero, Dr. Luis, 144, 146, 149, 150, 151
Vandenberg, Arthur, 296, 297–298
Vichy France
Americans rounded up and
interned in after North Africa
invasion, 439–440
history of, 336–337
Vichy French embassy, Betty's
intelligence work and, 343
dangers of, 357–358
initial approach to Brousse and
Henry-Hyde, 338–346
recruits Brousse as agent,
346–351, 354–357
Stephenson and Pepper contact
about, 333–338, 351–352
Vichy plans in US and, 351–352
Vichy French embassy, Betty's theft
of naval ciphers from
Allies' need for, 359–362,
366–368, 424–426
Allies' use of, 424–426

attempts to recruit Benoit,
371–375
attempts to recruit Grandville,
375–389
code names during, 393
failed attempts, 400–412
planning for, 362–364, 369–370,
390–399
successful theft, 413–424, 424
US involvement in, 365–368

Washington, DC
Arthur visits Betty in, 353–354
Thorpe family in, 43, 46–49,
59–60
Washington, DC, Betty's
intelligence work in
asked to move to, 277–278,
284–291, 289
Italian naval codes and, 299–320
Italian plans to scuttle ships in
US harbors and, 321–328
see also Vichy French embassy entries
Washington Evening Star, 443
Waterbury, Shaw, 432
Whitehouse, Norman, 271–273
Wilde, Oscar, 22, 42
Willingdon, Lord, 258, 276

Yeats, William Butler, 195, 195–196

About the Author

HOWARD BLUM is a contributing editor at *Vanity Fair* and the author of the *New York Times* bestseller *Dark Invasion* and the Edgar Award–winning *American Lightning*, as well as *Wanted!*, *The Gold Exodus*, *Gangland*, and *The Floor of Heaven*. While at the *New York Times*, Blum was twice nominated for a Pulitzer Prize for investigative reporting. He is the father of three children and lives in Connecticut.